'A rich, discursive thesaurus of a book . . . as entertaining as it is informative.'

'An intimate picture of the places, people and spirit of the essential Spain, and the photographs contribute much, seeking to capture the real character and daily concerns of Spaniards rather than presenting postcard views.'

'Splendid, wide-ranging photographs by Robert Vavra . . . a remarkable book: I can think of nothing anywhere near so thorough.'

'All of Michener's varied talents as reporter, researcher and story teller extraordinaire are brought to bear in this delightful Iberian odyssey.'

ALSO BY *James A. Michener*

and published by Corgi Books

IBERIA

VOLUME ONE

Spanish Travels and Reflections

JAMES A. MICHENER

PHOTOGRAPHS BY ROBERT VAVRA

CORGI

IBERIA

VOLUME ONE

SPANISH TRAVELS AND REFLECTIONS

IBERIA VOLUME ONE

A CORGI BOOK 0 552 98732 8

Originally published in Great Britain
by Secker & Warburg Ltd.

PRINTING HISTORY
Secker & Warburg edition published 1968
Secker & Warburg edition reprinted 1969
Corgi edition published 1971
Corgi edition reissued 1983

Corgi Books are published by
Transworld Publishers Ltd.,
Century House, 61–63 Uxbridge Road,
Ealing, London W5 5SA

Made and printed in Great Britain by
Thomson Litho Ltd., East Kilbride, Scotland

Acknowledgments

The balanced view which this book endeavors to maintain regarding the Muslim occupation of Spain was checked against the anti-Muslim point of view expressed in Louis Bertrand and Charles Petrie, *The History of Spain* (London, Eyre and Spottiswoode, New York, The Macmillan Company, rev. ed. 1952).

In my general attitude toward Fernando, Isabel, Carlos V and Felipe II, I was much influenced by R. Trevor Davies, *The Golden Century of Spain 1501–1621* (London, Macmillan, rev. ed. 1958).

All statements made about the Inquisition were weighed against Henry Kamen, *The Spanish Inquisition* (New York, New American Library, 1965).

Data relating to the siege of the Alcázar in Toledo during the Spanish Civil War were checked against Cecil D. Eby, *The Siege of the Alcázar* (New York, Random House, 1965).

All material relating to the Carlist pretenders was checked against Theo Aronson, *Royal Vendetta, The Crown of Spain 1829–1965* (Indianapolis, Bobbs-Merrill, 1966).

The quotation castigating bullfighting comes from Eléna de La Souchère, *An Explanation of Spain* (New York, Alfred A. Knopf, 1965), a powerful assault on many aspects of contemporary Spain.

The passage illustrating the interlocking relationships between Spain and England is quoted from H. V. Morton, *A Stranger in Spain* (New York, Dodd, Mead & Co., Copyright © 1955 by Dodd, Mead & Company. London, Methuen & Company Ltd.) and that regarding Carlos the Bewitched from John Langdon-Davies, *Carlos, The King Who Would Not Die* (New York, Prentice-Hall, 1963).

Data and opinions in the last chapter were constantly checked against those expressed so felicitously by Walter Starkie in his *The Road to Santiago, Pilgrims of St. James* (London, John Murray, 1957). I used principally the Spanish edition (Madrid, Aguilar, 1958).

For the enumeration of the attendants waiting upon Juana la Loca at Tordesillas I am indebted to Amarie Dennis, *Seek the Darkness* (Madrid, privately published, 1961). Mrs. Dennis also consented to talk with me about various aspects of the Isabel-Juana story, for which I am grateful.

To Mary Elizabeth Brooks I am indebted not only for her excellent study of King Sebastião of Portugal, *A King for Portugal* (Madison, University of Wisconsin, 1964) but also for the instructive dialogue we held in Madrid in which she explained sidelights of this bizarre episode. Where my account differs from hers I have so indicated in the text.

After my manuscript was completed I had the privilege of meeting in person that queen of American bullfight aficionados, Alice Hall of Georgia. Her preferences were

ACKNOWLEDGMENTS

so violent and so persuasive that I modified certain opinions I had previously expressed in the taurine material.

In the text I have expressed my appreciation of the help provided by Don Luis Morenés y Areces, Marqués de Bassecourt, who helped me on three different occasions: in Las Marismas, in Madrid, and on the pilgrimage to Santiago de Compostela. I have never known a better traveling companion nor a man more imbued with his subject, in this case a love of Spain.

During the two months that I concentrated on the question of bullfighting I had the pleasure of Matador John Fulton's company, and while I must not saddle him with any of the heterodox opinions I express about his profession I do wish to thank him for his expert guidance.

For permission to explore the Coto Doñana I am, like naturalists around the world, indebted to José Antonio Valverde, who serves as custodian for this rare corner of Europe. Many of the incidents I report as to the passing of the year in the Coto I owe to Dr. Valverde.

To Patter Winslow Ashcraft I am indebted for some of the finest picnics I have ever had. To wander across Spain without halting for varied picnics would be to miss the best the country has to offer and from this fate I was saved by Mrs. Ashcraft.

To my two old diplomatic friends from Afghanistan days, Steven Baldanza and Osborne Day, I am indebted for their help in guiding me around their new duty posts, Baldanza in Lisboa, Day in Madrid.

I cannot adequately express my dependence upon and appreciation of Professor Kenneth Vanderford, Ripon College, Ripon, Wisconsin. At my request he read the manuscript and checked it against his encyclopedic knowledge. Barely a page escaped his savage eye. On esoteric points he was a prince of debaters. He also assumed responsibility for all translations from Spanish into English, except where historical ones had to be followed.

My deepest gratitude must go to that extraordinary tertulia of the Café León. That a group of distinguished members of the Real Academia de Española should have welcomed me, a stranger, and should have given their time to my questions was a testimony to the warmth of hospitality which Spain extends to the visitor. I am especially indebted to José María de Cossío, whose robust humor and wide spread of interests impressed me, and to that delightful and irreverent scholar from the University of Texas, Ramón Martínez López.

To the scores of other advisors, like Juan Quintana and Virginia Smith on bullfighting, William Frauenfelder on Cataluña, Ignacio Herguete G. de Guadiana on Trujillo, Luis Ybarra González on Las Marismas, Luis Morondo on the music of Victoria, Father Jesús Precedo Lafuente on Santiago de Compostela, Alcalde José Filgueira on Pontevedra, Fernando Zóbel on contemporary Spanish painting, José María Lassaletta on wildlife, Tess LaTouche on daily gossip, Brewster Cross on flamenco, Dr. José María Muguruza on the Prado, David Peace on tourism, and Madelyn Mack on one woman's view of the romance of Spain, I owe a debt which can never be repaid.

January 15, 1968   J A M E S   A .   M I C H E N E R

Contents

IBERIA

Spanish Travels and Reflections

FOLLOWING PAGE: *Hard and dry like the bark of the cork tree is the land of Spain.*

INTRODUCTION

OCEANO
ATLANTICO

CABO FINISTERRE

Barcelona

Teruel
Castellón de la Plana
Burriana
Madrid
Valencia

Lisboa

Sevilla

MAR MEDITERRANEO

MILES
0   100

I have long believed that any man interested in either the mystic or the romantic aspects of life must sooner or later define his attitude concerning Spain. For just as this forbidding peninsula physically juts into the Atlantic and stands isolated, so philosophically the concept of Spain intrudes into the imagination, creating effects and raising questions unlike those evoked by other nations. During the four decades that I have traveled in Spain I have always wanted to describe the impact this vibrant land has had upon me, and now I have an opportunity to do so.

Did any traveler ever enter Spain in a more appropriate manner than I? While a student in Scotland, I had shipped as chart boy aboard a Clydeside freighter which lugged coal to Italy and brought back oranges from Spain to be used in the marmalade factories of Dundee. We sailed from Glasgow, buried in coal dust, as ugly a little tramp steamer as ever skirted the Bay of Biscay. Against headwinds we made only ninety-six miles a day, pitching and tossing the while, so that I was well fed up with the trip before we ever saw land. Then out of the Atlantic we spotted Cabo Finisterre off the port bow, and for much of one stormy day we kept it in view, a tantalizing taste of Spain, solid, dark, mysterious, looming out of the gray waves.

As our freighter rose and fell in the troughs this glimpse of land began to haunt me. More than anything else in the world I wanted to see the Spain of which Finisterre formed the western rampart. Past this point three and a half centuries ago Sir Francis Drake had come to harry Spanish shipping and to burn Spanish ports. Here the Armada had formed for its assault on England, and the headland as I saw it that stormy day was well suited to historic purposes. It was dark, heavy, unlike anything I had previously seen. It was in truth land's end, the western promontory of the European continent, and it challenged the mind.

Well, we left Finisterre and plowed our way monotonously south, and a long time later, when I had grown accustomed to the pitching of our uncomfortable freighter, we steamed into the Straits of Gibraltar and I saw, again to port, the sun-drenched uplands of Algeciras, and they were so different from what I had seen in the storm off Finisterre, so inviting and so startling in the vividness of their color, that I again felt the urge to flee that ship and go ashore, forgetting Italy, which had been the purpose for making this trip.

But we left Gibraltar behind us, then Mallorca, then Corsica, and finally we emptied our coal at ancient Civitavecchia, that dreariest of all Italian ports, where Michelangelo had once served as city architect in charge of fortifying the harbor and where Henri Beyle had spent long years as French consul, publishing his reflections under the name of Stendhal. He and Michelangelo distracted me for a while, but often as I traveled over Italy on leave from the coal barge I recalled those two fleeting glimpses of Spain and longed for the day when our empty ship would sail into some distinguished port like Valencia or Barcelona to pick up our oranges. I imagined myself striding ashore to inspect at first hand the greatness which I felt sure existed in that dour land. The captain of the freighter wasn't certain which of the ports we would head for, but trusted Glasgow to advise him by the time we reached Mallorca.

When we were abeam of that island the wireless finally spoke: 'Castellón de la Plana,' and the captain was pleased. 'Beautiful little city,' he said.

I ran to my charts and found that Castellón lay between Barcelona and Valencia, the actual city being some two miles or more inland from the harbor. It was a major port for the shipping of oranges and traditionally the scene of Spain's first fair of the year, at which the opening bullfights of the season were held. 'Castellón is one of the best places in Spain for beginning a visit,' the captain assured me.

During the passage from Mallorca to the mainland I memorized the shipping instructions contained in *Pilot for the East Coast of Spain* and prepared myself spiritually for my entrance to the country by rereading the best passages of *Don Quixote*. But on the last evening we received a wireless directing us to avoid Castellón de la Plana and to proceed instead to the tiny village of Burriana, where oranges were awaiting us.

'Burriana has no harbor!' I protested, for the *Pilot* said: 'Ships anchor in the roads and prudent ones keep a sharp watch on their lines.'

'They barge the oranges out to us,' the captain explained.

'Then we don't land?'

'No.'

My disappointment was so apparent that he added, 'But you can ride ashore on one of the barges and join us next week in Valencia.'

I had rarely heard finer words, and all that night I stayed on deck, waiting to catch my first glimpse of the point at which I would enter Spain, but no lights showed, and finally in the east, over Mallorca, which we had left astern, the sun began to rise and a soft Mediterranean beauty suffused the air.

My first view of Burriana? It wasn't a view. It was a smell, for the offshore breeze carried to our dirty little freighter the odor of orange blossoms, heavy and pungent and inescapably the odor of Spain. Then, in the direction from which this superb aroma came, I saw the low shore begin to rise from the waves and with incredible swiftness present itself. Our ship slowed. The anchor chains went out. Lines were thrown to men in rowboats, who attached them to buoys, and gradually we swung to in the current, ready to receive whatever cargo awaited us.

It was then that I saw the immemorial aspect of Spain, and my introduction in the minutes that followed was so perfect that it still stands for me as a permanent vision of Spain. Later I was to see the bullfights in Ronda and the cathedral at Santiago de Compostela and the roomful of Velázquez paintings at the Prado, and the pass at Roncesvalles where Roland perished and the great, bleak olive orchards of Badajoz and the Holy Week processions in Sevilla. I was to see the Spain that men have written about for two thousand years, but seldom would I see anything so representative of Spain.

Since the little farming village of Burriana had no harbor curving out to protect the shore, it could have no pier; storm waves driving in from the east would periodically destroy attempts to maintain a quay. So the huge barges which conveyed the oranges to the freighter had to be loaded ashore. Each barge was hauled onto dry land and crammed with barrels containing oranges until it must have weighed several tons.

'Why barrels?' I asked, watching the procedure with binoculars. 'They are barrels, aren't they?'

'Steel barrels.'

'Why?'

'You'll see.'

Obviously, when the barges were loaded they had to be dragged back into the water in order to be floated so that they could be rowed out to our ship. How to do it? In Roman times businessmen using this coast for the transfer of freight to Italy had solved the problem. They reared a breed of oxen that thrived in salt water, and now these huge beasts, working in the sea with often only their eyes and horns visible, backed close to a barge while workmen attached chains to their harness. Then with men who also lived mostly in the sea whipping at them and cursing, the great beasts strained while everyone ashore pushed on the barge. Slowly, slowly the near-swimming oxen and the men and the shouting got the barge moving. Slowly it left the shore. The massive oxen moved deeper and deeper into the sea, so that men directing them had to keep afloat by grasping the oxen's horns, and in this way the oranges in their steel barrels were ferried out to our ship.

The first Spaniard I ever met was a workman of Burriana, dressed only in a breechcloth, swimming to meet me with his left hand grasping the horn of an ox. He was a poor man and existed only by this brutal work, which kept him half submerged all day, but he had the face of a satyr rising from a swamp, and when I first saw him he was laughing. His skin was bronzed like leather and he had not shaved for some days. He had enormous arms and very quick eyes and saw at once that I was a stranger, perhaps an American, who might pay for a ride ashore in his barge. In a guttural voice, using a Valencian argot, he grunted at me. Of the first sentences spoken to me in Spain I understood not a single word.

I did understand, of course, that he was proposing to carry me ashore in his barge, for a fee. I agreed and started to climb into the barge, but our captain interrupted. 'There's no point in going ashore now. It's only five o'clock. No buses to Castellón yet.' He was right, so to the disappointment of the bargeman I said I'd wait.

'But only me,' he insisted in words I did understand. 'Not those other . . .' He indicated the next barge coming to our ship, and I wished I had enough command of the Valencian dialect to understand his profane description of his competitors. It must have been extreme, because when he repeated it for the benefit of the incoming crew they threatened him. But he laughed.

Till the sun was high I stayed on deck, watching the nautical oxen of Burriana haul loaded barges, then talking with the rugged men who brought the barges to our freighter, but each time my satyr returned he renewed his contract with me. 'When I go ashore I'll go with you,' I assured him. I would have been afraid to go with another.

I now discovered why the oranges were being delivered in steel drums, for the captain directed that a hose be thrust down into the Mediterranean where the water was clear, then ordered the deck hands, 'Knock out the bungs,' and presently all the drums were opened and I saw that the oranges inside had been cut in half. The resulting juice, of course, did not fill the barrel, and the empty space was now to be filled with sea water.

'What's the idea?' I asked.

'Everything sloshes back and forth, all the way home to Dundee,' the captain said.

'To accomplish what?'

'It prepares the rind for making marmalade.'

There were two schools of thought aboard our ship. The captain held that the action of salt water ate away the pulpy part of the rind and left the skin translucent, as required in the better brands of marmalade. The pulp and juice would be thrown away. 'Nonsense,' one of the deck hands argued. 'Everything in that barrel is mixed with sugar and then boiled down to make that bittersweet taste of a true Dundee marmalade. Without the salt water it wouldn't be worth a damn.'

A tugging at my sleeve reminded me that my laughing satyr was back, and this time I allowed him to lower me into his barge, now empty of drums. He had arms like some prehistoric man, and to him I was a child. His animals were unlike any I had ever seen before, and together we moved toward the shore of Spain. When I saw the process of launching the barges close up I was appalled at the energy required. It was medieval or worse. It was an expenditure that I could not comprehend and it continued all day and all year, men and animals working themselves to death.

But the men thus engaged were so handsome, their smiles so compelling that there was something different about them, something powerful and stoic. This was their lot and they would not complain. Ashore some were having breakfast and they invited me to join. I knew that I was taking someone's share, but I could not resist such an opening meal in my new country and I paid my bargeman for my share of food. I can taste it yet: anchovies, which have always been my delight, hard bread, harder cheese and red wine. How good it was, how honest in its Spanish quality.

I wondered if any previous traveler to Spain had entered through this nonexistent Burriana? Later I was to enter through many different ports, but none has ever compared with the beauty of that first morning, nor with its significance. Because in subsequent years, no matter how superficial my visits might be or my reactions to them, I could rely on the fact that at the beginning, if only for a moment, I had been allowed to see deep into the quality of Spain. I saw the toiling men, the congenial peasants, the straining beasts, the honest food. I smelled the salt of the shore, the oranges of the inland fields, the burning chicory that passed for coffee, the sourness of the red wine, the harsh seductiveness of cheap anchovies. It is this Spain that has been with me through the years, and whenever in subsequent visits I have again come close to that particular vision I have felt at home.

Thirty-five years ago the road from Burriana to Castellón de la Plana ran through orange groves, at the end of which stood the charming little city that was immersed in festival when I saw it for the first time. For two days I enjoyed about as fine an introduction to Spanish life as a young man could have, for it was the custom in Castellón in those years to conduct the traditional evening parade along unique lines. In the center of town, as in all Spanish localities, unattached men walked round and round the plaza in a counterclockwise direction while unmarried girls walked arm-in-arm in the opposite direction, so that in any one complete transit a man who kept to the outer circle was constantly staring into the faces of beautiful girls, each of whom he would encounter twice. I know it is difficult for people who have never courted in this way to believe how easy it is to conclude understandings in two hours of such parading, but when one has actually participated in the constant meeting and judging and winking and nodding that takes place, he knows how effectively the courtship is conducted.

Well, this evening paseo is the same in all Spanish small towns and in some large ones too, but Castellón added a feature which was most attractive. Only half the girls paraded in the square. The other half rested in balconies overlooking the promenade, from which they threw down onto the men passing below small darts trailing colored streamers. Since I had been easily recognized as an American, not many of whom got to a place like Castellón in those days, I found myself the target of many such darts and I brushed them away.

'Stupid!' a harsh laughing voice sounded, and I turned to see that the satyr bargeman who had ferried me ashore that morning was walking behind me and explaining in a proprietary manner who I was. 'Stupid!' he repeated, gathering up the darts which I had brushed from my clothing. He explained that it was not the darts but the colored streamers that were important and must be saved. 'Because,' he said in Spanish that I only half understood, 'at the end of the parade you are entitled to visit any balcony decorated in the colors matching the streamers you hold.'

We paraded as a team, and when I saw my bargeman in ordinary clothes and shaved I realized that he was not much older than I and already his thundering life in the surf hauling immense weights had made him an old man. We collected many darts that first night, and when the music stopped he led me to one balcony after another, and we danced and drank and ate anchovies and met the beautiful and shy girls who had pinned us with their streamers. Since I was a stranger, and what was worse, probably a Protestant, the older women of the houses kept severe watch on me, but the bargeman whispered that any girl of Castellón who had even a little intelligence would know how to slip down into the square, and he was right.

Later that night he led me to a corner where two girls waited, and the four of us went to a vaudeville show, where the bargeman insisted upon paying for the tickets. I tried to prevent this, knowing that I could afford the money better than he, but in true Spanish style, as if he were a nobleman of the grand school, he flashed the money I had paid him that morning for the ferry ride ashore and said loudly, if I understood his Spanish correctly, 'He paid this morning. Tonight I pay.'

I remember the entertainment for two reasons: there I saw my first zarzuela (brief light opera) and was captivated by it; and in the vaudeville portion I watched two robust comedians who, whenever they wanted an extra loud laugh, announced that they had come from Burriana. At each mention of my nonexistent seaport the crowd roared. It was like comedians in New York who coax cheap laughs by saying they're from Brooklyn or those in Chicago who achieve the same effect by being from Peoria. Apparently every community has a neighbor which it regards as ridiculous and I had chosen for my landing place in Spain a town that was the butt of the coast between Castellón and Valencia. My bargeman did not laugh at the jokes nor did I.

What a marvelous fiesta that was, my first in Spain, with a huge workman to guide me and orchestras and girls throwing streamers and comedians making jokes about Burriana, and the great warmth of Spanish hospitality as one knows it in a provincial city.

I cannot remember now how I discovered my technique for exploring a strange land, for I have followed this procedure for as long as I can recall. I enter the country unannounced and without a letter to anyone. I stand back and look at the scene before me, talk with anyone who cares to talk with me, then go to the bus station and buy a ticket for the end of any random line. This drops me in some village out in the country, and there I spend a couple of days just sitting and looking and talking. This produces some very dull days, but also some memorable ones.

At the end of World War II, I did this in Canton and saw enough of China to nourish my imagination for decades. I used the same system in Bali, and later in Japan I skipped out of Tokyo and wound up in Morioka, a small city to the north, where I had a series of experiences through which I gained an understanding of Japan that would have been denied me otherwise. I often forget Tokyo but never Morioka. With its lantern-lit little shops and its sprawling rock-strewn river, Morioka will be with me always. Anything good I have written about Japan stems from Morioka.

Now, in Castellón I went to the bus station and found that my plan wouldn't work. It seemed that the only buses then available ran to Burriana, but there was a railroad which wandered about the countryside, and on the advice of a straggler I purchased a ticket to Teruel, thus projecting myself into a corner of Spain not often visited by strangers.

The train that carried me there consisted only of third-class carriages, a euphemism for boxcars lined with rough-plank benches which were filled before the whistle tooted, so that more than half the passengers had to stand. When started, the train moved quite slowly and threw an unusual amount of cinders through the screenless windows. It was jerky in motion, creaky in sound, antique in appearance and utterly captivating.

For it was filled with human beings of a kind I had not met in my college textbooks on Spain. Here there were no grandees, no industrial giants. There were no caballeros in leather, no beautiful women in mantillas. There was only a jostling crowd of extremely poor people, dressed in the oldest of clothes, huddled together in a dirty boxcar. This was a Spain for which I was unprepared, yet as I settled down and began to make friends with these apparently suspicious and silent people, I found myself among some of the most congenial persons I had so far encountered in

Europe, and the interminable trip developed into exactly what I had hoped for.

For the first hour the train chugged south along the coast toward Valencia and the oppressive smell of the boxcar was offset by the sweet aroma of oranges, but then the line diverged abruptly to the west and we began to climb a steep valley marked by low mountains, a rushing stream and poor forests. Most of that day we climbed slowly upward, so that I became convinced that Teruel must be perched on a considerable mountain, an impression which has never left me. How dull, how tedious that long day's trip could have been, with cinders in my eye and hunger in my stomach. The land was bleak, with scarcely a town or any human element to relieve the monotony, and such stragglers as we did see appeared to be shepherds, incredibly poor. Even their dogs were scrawny and unlovable.

But the more forbidding the terrain the more delightful the peasants in my boxcar. These were tremendous men and women, hard as treated leather, determined as the mountains among which we were traveling. When at a junction I purchased a generous supply of bread and cheese to throw into the common pot, I gained admission to the group, as it were, and the wine bottles were passed to me and the tins of anchovies and the rock-hard ends of sausage. We were all so hungry by now that our odds and ends of food seemed a feast and it was natural that the men and women who sang best should offer us a series of quiet songs, nothing boisterous and nothing to tempt a man into unseemly bellowing, but rather a quiet, forceful series of statements about love and rural life and the fiestas that occur in small towns. I could understand few of the words.

But as the day wore on I talked much with these people of the boxcar. They were peasants, even those who lived in towns like Teruel and Castellón, and their life was indescribably hard; one of the strangest bits of information I gathered in my long conversations was that most of these people were wearing their best clothes. It was something important to be making so long a trip by train and they were wearing the best they had. How pitiful they seemed, with trousers mended four times at the same spot with four different swatches of cloth, with dresses in which whole panels had been replaced by cloth of a different color. Shoes were shabby beyond description and socks were filled with holes even in the nonessential parts that clung about the ankles. The men's caps were mostly torn and the women's shawls were ragged at the edges, and not because of fringes either. Such teeth as had been lost had not been replaced and many of these people showed need for a doctor, to whom apparently they had no access. Speaking only of outward appearances, these people were as poverty-stricken as any I had ever seen.

But about them, in all they did, there was a stolid dignity and a profound joy. When they sang it was as if they were in a cathedral, for they took each note seriously but not pompously, and their voices blended

Peasant.

for powerful effect. When they spoke it was only after weighing each word, not for its effect but for its appropriateness. The volubility which one thinks of in relation to Latin peoples was not evident here, but rather the taciturnity of New Englanders or Scots. But in both the singing and the conversations there was joy, and when a joke was told it brought forth the guffaws common to all rural people.

It was a remarkable day, one of the best I would ever spend in Spain, and at last our tired and cinder-throwing engine chugged up the final hill and brought us into the station at Teruel. 'Adiós, norteamericano!' the passengers said softly as I hauled down my small bag and asked directions for the heart of the city. These people had provided me with a solid introduction to Spain and I would be forever indebted to them. I was loath to separate from them, but the journey was ended and they were now headed for their separate homes. I visualized them going to English-type cottages with hollyhocks about the door, as if they were the ordinary rural people of Europe. Later I would see what kind of homes they actually lived in.

For me Teruel was the introduction into a new world, the hard, remorseless, poverty-stricken world of provincial Spain. The lives I saw in Teruel were terribly confined within some of the narrowest circles I have ever known. The streets were equally narrow, as if hewn out of solid rock. The architecture was not pleasing, like the panoramas shown in my textbooks on Spain. The restaurants were uncongenial, the theaters were ugly and the band in the central plaza played off-key. But there was a compelling durability about this town that one had to admire, and the longer I stayed there the better I liked it. I remember chiefly the acrid smell of roasting chicory or some similar coffee substitute, so that even today whenever I chance upon the smell of burning chicory I think of Teruel.

On my first morning in the city, according to habit, I wandered out past the edges of town to see in what respects it might be different from the Burriana region or from Castellón, and as I was walking along a country road I heard a voice calling, 'Eh, norteamericano!' I turned to find at the doorway to a house one of the men with whom I had shared my bread and cheese on the train the previous day, and he invited me into his home, something that I later wished he had not done, for I can still see it as it was that day, and having seen his home I could no longer preserve storybook myths about this powerful land of Spain.

The walls were of stone unchinked with cement or mortar. They had, however, been tightly packed with clay and were both water- and windproof, forming a solid and pleasing barrier against the elements. The floor was of packed earth, worn smooth by centuries of use, for I judged the house to have been built at least three hundred years earlier. No dust rose from the floor and it was surprisingly even, for through the centuries the earth had been leveled until it was now at least as flat as an average flagstone floor. The house had two rooms, the partition between them consisting of some of the poorest lumber I have ever seen, scarcely good enough for the making of a cheap industrial crate in a country like Germany. I could see through the wall at many spots where warping had occurred or the chipping off of fragments, for the boards were paper-thin, and this in an area where forests had once abounded and where to a lesser degree they still existed. If lumber was being harvested in the Teruel district, none of it was filtering down to homes like this.

The house contained one table, one chair, one bed, one cradle. That was about all. There were no cupboards, no shelves, no rocking chairs, no benches, no sideboards, no bathroom, no iron stove, nothing. A man some fifty years old and his wife of about the same age had each worked in Teruel for forty years, for they had begun at the age of ten, and frugally they had saved their money, and at the end of twoscore years of labor this was what they had accumulated.

I was a stranger and was not afraid of rebuffs, so I asked to see everything. What clothes did they have? What eating gear? What food supplies? What books? Books? Neither wife nor husband could read. Clothes? Mainly what they had worn on the train, plus older ones for working, and I have already described what the good ones looked like. Food? They had enough to live on for three days, for they had no refrigerator, and after three days they would go to the store and buy more food, if they had the money. I did not know the Spanish word for hope, but in a roundabout way I asked them what their plans were for the future. The future? What future?

And so I wandered back and forth across Teruel, that austere mountain city, and allowed the reality of Spain to beat in upon me. One evening I went to the cathedral, if I am using the proper word for so mean a church, and there I attended my first religious service in Spain. It was overwhelmingly impressive, with candles and choirs and priests who seemed to bear the weight of this poor settlement upon their necks. The people of Teruel that I saw worshiping that night were devout and to them religion was terribly important, but as I looked about the gloomy church I found in the congregation few of the peasants I had ridden with on the train. This praying group came from a different stratum and I was pleased to have a chance to see it. The church people were better dressed than my earlier acquaintances and better shaved too, but they were equally solid, and when I met them later in cafés or stores they were equally attractive.

I had an exciting time in Teruel, a moving time for a young man trying to discover for himself what Spain was like, and after I had seen several of the better-class houses in the city, finding them to have floors such as we had in Pennsylvania and bookcases and shelves for storing food and colorful patios, I began to wonder if I had been unlucky in first stumbling upon that earthen-floored hut containing almost nothing. Had I by chance been deceived? Was rural Spain better than I had judged?

So I went out into the country in the opposite direction and stopped at three different farmhouses selected at random, and at each I introduced myself and was generously received. The farmers and their wives offered me water and wine, if they had any, and seemed pleased to talk with a norteamericano who had taken the trouble to learn their language, however poorly. They showed me their homes: earthen floors, one table, not enough chairs to entertain formally even one guest, few clothes, no stores of food.

When I returned to Teruel, I was met at the edge of the city by two

From any train window there is the chance of seeing unexpected beauty.

armed men dressed in nineteenth-century uniforms featuring two-cornered patent-leather hats called tricorns after an older version which had three points. They were members of the Guardia Civil, whose job it was to keep watch on everything that happened in rural areas like Teruel, and they traveled in pairs, having learned that it was safer to do so. They did not stop me but fell in beside me as I walked. They were cordial and correct as they asked, 'Looking at the countryside?'

    'Yes.'

    'Visiting friends?'

    'Not friends.'

'And when are you leaving Teruel?'

'In the morning.'

When the train pulled out they were there, extremely pleasant and smiling, their highly polished hats gleaming in the morning sunlight as if they were part of the chorus for a New York production of *Carmen*. They were my last sight of Teruel.

I was to rejoin my ship at Valencia, that powerful and often rebellious capital of the eastern coast, and as my dirty little train chugged into the center of the city I was made aware that Valencia was to be something special. I didn't know it at the time, but I was arriving on the Saturday evening which marked the height of the fiesta that celebrates the end of winter, and as I left the station the sky above Valencia was filled with exploding fireworks and the air with shouts and music and screams of delight. Valencia is the fireworks capital of Europe and outdoes itself at the fallas (bonfires). In the public square enormous wooden structures are raised, representing horses or galleons or Mont Blanc in Switzerland or the leaders of the nation, and each foot of timber is wound with colorful explosives, while chains of smaller firecrackers hang in festoons in all possible directions. I mean that these structures are sometimes as high as three-story buildings and are very solidly constructed.

Well, when the maximum crowd has gathered and the wind is right, these mammoth things are set afire, and as the wood begins to burn and the explosives ignite and the lovely loops of firecrackers explode, it seems as if the whole city of Valencia is going up in flames. It is really something to see, one of the great spectacles of Europe.

And the cafés! They were filled with well-to-do people and the food was excellent, emphasizing fish provided by the Mediterranean. The theaters were crowded and the same comedians who had delighted me in Castellón had arrived to tell the same bawdy jokes about being forced to spend the night in the hotel at guess where . . . Burriana! And as the chambermaid was described and her sexual capacities suggested, the Valencian crowd roared approval. Each time the name Burriana was mentioned the people of Valencia howled. Here the paseo was a wild affair, with some of the best-dressed women I was to see in Spain going with the clock and hordes of young men in fine suits marching in the opposite direction to inspect them. Apparently, in Valencia the people of Spain lived well.

But what I can never forget was the next day, when a tall, heavy man stopping in my hotel said in fine Spanish, 'Sir, I trust you will be attending the bullfight.'

'Is there one?'

'At five,' he said graciously and offered to lead me to where I might buy a ticket. As we paraded through the streets I noticed that the men of Valencia paid deference to my companion and some spoke to him with a kind of reverence. At the ticket window, not at the bullring but at a downtown office, the same respect was paid, and I finally asked, 'Who are you?' and he explained that he was picador for one of the men fighting that afternoon. I was less impressed then than I was to be later.

The cartel that afternoon contained the names of three matadors who were to be remembered in the history of Spanish bullfighting: Marcial Lalanda, Domingo Ortega and El Estudiante. The first was one of the most poetic matadors ever to grace the rings of Spain, and passes which he invented are still being used by his successors. Ortega, an illiterate farmhand often referred to as el de Borox (he from the trivial village of Borox), was to become the cold classicist and the idol of those who love an icy, controlled excellence. On this day in 1932 he was just beginning his career at the advanced age of twenty-four. In the 1950s he was still fighting now and then, a man remarkably durable and never hurried or vulgar. El Estudiante was something special, a young student named Luis Gómez who had graduated from high school but who had given up his studies for glory in the bullring. He was to make a less lasting contribution to the history of bullfighting than either Lalanda or Ortega, but his arrival on the scene and under the conditions I have described was emotionally exciting, and he was to have a series of good years.

I could not have been introduced to bullfighting under more auspicious conditions: a professional picador to choose my seat, a poetic matador to open the fight and an austere classicist to compete with him, followed by the young student whom Spain was taking to her heart. I settled down in my front-row location and waited. The interior gates of the plaza swung open. The band burst into music. Bugles sounded and the opening parade was under way. I did not know enough to identify the matadors, nor the banderilleros, but behind them on horseback rode the man who had helped me buy my ticket, and in his leather pants, cockaded hat and articulated leg armor he looked enormous, as knights must have looked centuries ago when they ventured forth to battle. He nodded to me as he rode past and I felt that I was part of the fight.

Some years before, when still a student in a small Pennsylvania college, I had been cajoled into attending my first symphony concert, at which Arturo Toscanini was to conduct Beethoven's Fifth and Third in that order, and I can truthfully say that in the first minute of this music I understood as much about orchestral music as I was ever to know, even though I studied it avidly during subsequent years. So also, in that first minute in the bullring at Valencia, I understood bullfighting, even though I have been improving my knowledge at rather close range ever since. When Lalanda came out to unfurl his cape and with a series of breath-taking passes bring his bull under control, I understood that I was watching a theatrical display and not a sport. When the bull killed the first horse— because if I remember correctly either pads were not used that day in Valencia or only inadequate ones if they were—I understood that I was participating in a tribal tragedy dating back to prehistoric times and not in a game. At Valencia in those days they still used on cowardly bulls the black banderillas with firecracker heads that exploded harmlessly above the bull's neck muscles, frightening him into action, and when a pair of these went off not ten feet from where I sat, with the bull's face pointed at mine, I saw the effect on the animal, saw him stare at me in amazement, then leap sideways in the air and thunder off, and I was forever after a friend and a student of the fighting bull. And when on his first bull el de Borox took his truncated red cloth for the final act of his fight and dominated a towering bull as if the latter had been a tame puppy, I understood that this spectacle was intended to show puny man engaged in his war with the powerful forces of night. I was never to see Ortega better than he was that day, and I left the ring hopelessly addicted to this short, swarthy, cold perfectionist. I was curiously pleased to discover that my picador belonged to the cuadrilla of Ortega and not to one of the others. Later I was to travel briefly with this cuadrilla and to see Ortega in various plazas, and he was as great a matador as I thought him that first day. I concluded then, and have never changed my mind, that if I were to be a matador I would want to be like Domingo Ortega. Being far too chunky in the bottom to qualify as even a third-rate matador and not being hefty enough to be a picador aboard a horse, I never entertained any illusions in this direction even though at intervals I have spent a lot of time with the bulls and have even fought the smaller calves, but as a writer I have often remembered Ortega and have tried in words to attain some of the controlled effects he achieved with cloth and sword. To me, el de Borox would always be a Spanish archetype.

That Sunday night the picador and I went to a café near our hotel, where we were joined by a gang of Valencian bullfight fans who started to discuss the day's events in an animated dialect which I could little understand, and it was their opinion that Ortega had been exceptional. However, the purpose of the evening was not to rehash the bullfight but to enjoy a famous flamenco team of a woman dancer and a male guitarist. They had come from Madrid, I believe, or possibly Sevilla. At any rate, the smoky hall was crowded and waiters scurried about serving sweet wine and cakes or sour wine and anchovies, and our table chose the latter. Girls provided by the management wandered among the tables and three invited themselves to join us. The picador insisted that they provide one who could speak English, but none was available. They did, however, find one who spoke South American-style Spanish, and her I could understand.

What few lights the café had were dimmed. A single chair was placed on stage to be occupied by a round, fat, baldheaded man carrying a guitar. He was greeted with applause and launched directly into a composition which I would remember as one of the best I was to hear in Spain. I asked the girl beside me to explain the song, and she said that flamenco had more than a dozen standard types of song, like malagueños, fandangos and peteneras. This was a good example of the last. When I asked what words accompanied the music, she said, 'We have many versions. But the best tell the story of a beautiful Jewish girl named Petenera.'

> Where are you going, Petenera?
> Where are you going, Jewish maid?

I suppose that 'Petenera,' as this particular song was called, has become more a part of me than any other piece of folk music I have ever heard, the story of a Jewish girl and her tragic effect upon a small Spanish town. It must be very old, dating back at least to the 1400s, when Jews were common in Spain; the music is not exceptional and the words are arbitrary, but others have testified to the fact that the song as a whole has a powerful effect on them too, so I am not unusual in liking it.

It was obvious that this fat man on the chair was a notable guitarist, for he could make his instrument roar and whisper, laugh and sob. Both he and his music were very Spanish, and I relished each, but in due course he struck a series of commanding chords that sounded much like a machine gun, and onto the stage whirled my first flamenco dancer. She was a woman in her forties, not at all pretty and much fatter than I would have expected, but after that quick inventory I forgot her visible characteristics, for she could dance.

On Monday morning an event occurred that was to come back to me with terrible effect in the years that followed, although when it was happening I could not have anticipated its significance. I was in the central square, or at least one of the central squares, where the ashes of Saturday night's fire were being cleared, when from one of the government buildings I saw a procession crossing toward me. It was composed of many men in fine dark suits, including three or four in formal morning wear. In the center of the front rank was a most ordinary-looking man, apparently in his fifties, undistinguished in face, slightly dumpy in body and awkward in manner. I remember distinctly that even then I thought him to be a man of good though flabby will, and somebody beside me whispered that he was the President of Spain. It was Niceto Alcalá Zamora, the quiet man chosen to head Spain after the departure of King Alfonso XIII, who had slipped out of the country only the year before, thus avoiding the necessity of abdication. In this simple, fumbling man I saw the Republican alternative to the Bourbon dynasty (in Spanish, Borbón) and I was not impressed.

Then, to my astonishment, the cortege of black-suited men came straight at me, and a big crowd gathered behind me, so that I was wedged into position. President Alcalá Zamora—a fussy lawyer who was known, in a mixture of affection and contempt, as Botas (Old High Button Shoes) —spoke casually to several people in the crowd, then stopped and faced me.

'You are a stranger, I believe?'

'An American,' I said.

How long ago it seems
that I first saw Valencia.

'Ah, norteamericano. How do you like Spain?'

'The fireworks last night,' was all I could manage.

'What else have you seen?'

'Teruel.'

There was a long silence, and the president softly said, 'Teruel. Not many get to Teruel,' and he was gone.

When I returned to the hotel I found that the picador had departed with Ortega's cuadrilla for a fight in some other part of Spain but had left me an envelope containing a free ticket for the novillada (a bullfight in which novices rather than full matadors appear) scheduled for that afternoon. The young matadors put on a fight of some skill even though facing bulls somewhat smaller than the full matadors had fought. Having tasted the day before the essence of bullfighting in the work of Lalanda and Ortega, I was eager to apply what I had learned to a less professional performance. I saw much that day and have often wondered who the three aspirants were. Did they go on to glory? Were they men whose names I am now familiar with? Or were they merely three more among the hundreds who manage a fight or two in Valencia or Sevilla or Córdoba and then vanish? I suppose there must be some way I could track down their names, because for that one Monday in Valencia they were proficient.

When the time came for me to leave Valencia, I reflected: I've seen the best Spain has to offer. The well-dressed businessmen. The luxurious clubs, they're as good as any in Europe. The gaiety of a first-class fiesta. Good hotels, good restaurants, good entertainment. A substantial city that seems to be well run. I've even seen the president himself, moving unguarded among his people and willing to talk with a norteamericano. I have seen Spain.

But as I rode out to the port of Valencia to rejoin my ship for the long haul back to Scotland, I could not help recalling the peasants of Teruel and the abysmal and almost terrifying poverty that was their lot. Between these two Spains, and remember that I had not yet seen the superarrogant nobility of Sevilla, there existed such a gap that I simply could not bring it into focus. It was like the test the oculist gives you when you have weak eyes: 'You will see before you two halves of a picture. Use all your muscles to make them form one single picture. Try! Try!'

Now, if the two halves are things like a countryman in Scotland as opposed to a banker in Edinburgh, there is at first a discrepancy, but as one exercises his muscles he can bring them together into one fused portrait of Scotland that is not difficult to comprehend. The countryman remains a countryman and the banker a banker, and they can stand side by side with no embarrassment. In the same way you can fuse a coal miner in Johnstown, Pennsylvania, and a storekeeper in Pittsburgh. But to fuse the rural peasant of Teruel and the rich clubman of Valencia lolling in his leather chair after a gorging meal was for me impossible, and I began at that moment to formulate that series of speculations regarding Spain which were to exercise me for the next decades. Whenever I read about Spain it was to find answers to these questions, and remember that they were posed some years before the Civil War disfigured the country. These are the questions of peace, and whenever I traveled in Spain or talked with Spaniards in America or England, I continued to study only these permanent questions. Later, after the war had ended, I applied myself to these speculations and did not torment myself with questions as to who was right or wrong in the war, for I have always regarded Spain as my second home and I have wanted to know about its enduring quality, not its current preoccupations. These are the speculations which have concerned me.

Speculation One. Spain and Italy are both peninsulas that jut out from the mainland of Europe, and in the north each is marked by mountains which formerly cut the inhabitants off from the main intellectual and political movements of the continent, but Italy was able to adjust to those continental movements and even to mold and lead them whereas Spain was not. Why? It is true that for a relatively brief period during the reigns of Carlos V and Felipe II, Spain succeeded in reversing this tradition and in governing much of Europe, but in the long run of her history she was emotionally confined to her peninsula whereas Italy was not. Why?

Speculation Two. In the period of greatness referred to above, Spain faced east toward her possessions in Italy, north toward her important holdings in the Low Countries, west toward her vast empire in the Americas and south toward involvement in Africa, but she never seemed able to make up her mind as to where her basic interests lay and thus frittered them all away. Why this indecision?

Speculation Three. During a period of some four centuries prior to 1492, Spain had shown herself more hospitable to varied cultural, religious and ethnic groups than any other major power, including those in Asia and Africa, and this tolerance appeared to be an established way of life, yet with startling speed she reversed herself and extirpated from Spanish soil all Jews, Muslims, Protestants, Illuminati and Jesuits, transforming herself into one of the most homogeneous and frightened people in the world. What accounted for this dramatic reversal?

Speculation Four. With her drive toward uniformity and centralism, why has it been Spain who has preserved so strongly a regional pattern of life? With her devotion to a royalist theory of government, why has she so persistently produced strong democratic movements? With her love of personal freedom, why has she repeatedly sought her major solutions in dictatorial forms of government, and why do these work so well with the Spanish people?

Speculation Five. Why did Spain, when she was already one of the richest countries in Europe, spend so much energy gaining control of the riches of the New World, then allowing this influx of gold and silver to generate an inflation which converted her into the poorest country in Europe and one of the poorest in the world? This is a perplexing question, for it touches upon one of the real tragedies of history and has implications for present nations. I used to consider this self-impoverishment of Spain a tragedy that could not be explained and assumed that it had occurred without anyone's being aware of the problem; but that is not so. Recent studies have proved that certain Spanish theorists in the sixteenth century understood that a sudden importation of raw wealth which had not been created by productive work within the nation would create an inflation which would bankrupt Spain, and they warned against it. But they were not listened to. Why?

Speculation Six. Prior to the industrial revolution which re-formed the face of Europe, Spain was a leader in the manufacture of quality goods, a leader in world trade and a leader in agriculture. Had she merely projected this leadership at a normal rate of growth and had she been able to make the relatively simple adjustments that were afoot throughout the rest of Europe, she would probably have remained the leader in manufacturing, trade and agriculture and might even have improved her relative position. Instead, almost consciously and with calculated arrogance, she dedicated herself to an opposite course. She hamstrung her manufacturers, restricted her trade and crippled her agriculture. Within a few generations world leadership in these crucial fields had passed into the hands of France, Germany and England, and to a lesser degree, Italy. Who can explain this extraordinary series of wrong decisions?

Speculation Seven. For several centuries Spain was one of the exciting leaders in art, music, drama, poetry, the novel, philosophy—both as producer and consumer. Then abruptly the leadership was abandoned. The traveler to Spain can have no more perplexing an experience than to visit the Prado Museum and see there the paintings of Italians like Titian, of Flemings like Roger van der Weyden and of Germans like Dürer and to realize that during the lifetimes of those men Spain was the art capital of the world, and then to search in vain for a Spanish museum which contains comparable samples of the Frenchman Cézanne, the Italian Modigliani, the Russian Soutine, the Austrian Kokoschka or the German Klee. One fails to find the work of even Spanish-speaking artists like Picasso, Miró, Orozco and Rivera. What can explain this dramatic volte-face?

Speculation Eight. No aspect of Spain is more perplexing to the foreigner than her passionate devotion to the Catholic Church, which she has defended at heavy cost in wealth and manpower, while never being reluctant to oppose the Pope when she considered him in moral or political error. Several times Spanish kings mounted armies to attack the Vatican, and both Carlos V and Felipe II, who are described in Spanish history as the nonpareils of Catholic orthodoxy, were excommunicated because of their anti-Rome behavior. Papal decrees were often refused entrance into Spain; Spanish kings and cardinals simply refused to promulgate them, and ever today there is a tendency for the Spanish Church to consider one of its main tasks to 'save Rome from itself.' Such contradictory behavior is one of the continuing anomalies of Spanish history.

Speculation Nine. On my first day in Teruel I found that the contradictions I v as becoming aware of could be explained only by reference to what might be termed the central mystery of Spanish psychology. How can the Spaniard, who is so outgoing, so earthy, so in love with the trivia of daily existence, be at the same time so withdrawn and inwardly mystical? In this book the reader will not find an answer to this permanent enigma, but he will find, I hope, certain illustrations of it from which he can draw his own conclusions.

In other words, to travel in Spain is not like traveling elsewhere. The people are exciting, but so are they in Greece; the land is compelling, but so is it in Norway; art forms like flamenco, the bullfight and the decoration of the central plaza are unique, but so are the art forms of Italy; and if reflections on Spanish history drive the stranger to speculation, so do reflections on German history. What makes Spain different is that here these speculations are positively unavoidable. The people are so dramatic in their simplest existence that one must identify with them, and when one does he begins to think like a Spaniard; the art forms are so persuasive that the stranger is sucked into their vortices, even against his will; and the problems of history are so gigantic and of such continuing significance that one cannot escape an intellectual involvement in them. Some travelers, of whom I am one, find also an emotional involvement in Spanish history, and when this happens we are lost, for then Spain forever haunts us as it has haunted our predecessors, Georges Bizet, Henry de Montherlant, George Borrow and Ernest Hemingway.

What I am saying is that Spain is a very special country and one must approach it with respect and with his eyes open. He must be fully aware that once he has penetrated the borders he runs the risk of being made prisoner. I believe I sensed this danger on that silvery dawn many years ago when I stood off the shore of Burriana and watched the heaving men and the straining oxen, dimly aware that in nearby Castellón there was a fiesta which awaited me and in the hills cold Teruel, which would be forever one of the principal cities of my mind. I knew then that Spain was a special land, and I have spent many subsequent trips endeavoring to unravel its peculiarities. I have not succeeded, and in this failure I am not unhappy, for Spain is a mystery and I am not at all convinced that those who live within the peninsula and were born there understand it much better than I, but that we all love the wild, contradictory, passionately beautiful land there can be no doubt.

FOLLOWING PAGE:
Cork harvester.

BADAJOZ

OCEANO
ATLANTICO

MILES
0   100

Barcelona

Salamanca

Madrid

Trujillo
Alburquerque
Mérida
Lisboa   Medellín
Badajoz
EXTREMADURA
Jerez de los Caballeros

Sevilla
Jerez de la Frontera

MAR MEDITERRANEO

B adajoz still lay forty miles to the north. In a hot bus that talked back to itself I was plodding through the vast region called Extremadura, that empty, rocky section of Spain lying southwest from Madrid along the Portuguese border. It was a day of intense heat, with the thermometer well above a hundred and ten. For as far as I could see there were no towns, no villages, only the brassy, shimmering heat rising up from the plains and the implacable sky without even a wisp of cloud. When dust rose, it hung in the motionless air and required minutes to fall back to the caked and burning earth. I saw no animals, no birds, no men, for they refused to venture forth in this remorseless heat.

In fact, the only thing in nature that moved was the sun, terrible and metallic as it inched its way across that indifferent sky. I was relieved therefore when the bus descended a long hill and we came to a meadowland filled with trees, but such trees I had not seen before. They were not tall like elms, nor copious like maples. They were low, extremely sturdy, with dark gray trunks and gnarled branches that reached wide, so that each tree was given a considerable area to itself. The meadowland in between was filled with small yellow flowers, as if it were a carpet of gold, accented here and there with concentrations of white daisies and punctuated by the massive trees with their dark crowns.

I had barely inspected this pleasing landscape when the trees changed radically. Their trunks, up to a height of perhaps ten feet, turned suddenly bright orange, as if they had been painted that morning. And before I could adjust to orange-colored trees they were replaced by trunks of angry russet, then by trunks of a dark and heavy brown, and finally by trees whose trunks were the original gray I had seen at first; but all the trees, whether orange or gray, sent their limbs twisting and turning in the hot air as if they were gasping for breath.

'What is it?' I asked the driver.

'Cork forest. The bright orange means a tree that was stripped of its cork a few days ago. Enough time and the bark grows gray again.' We saw a low shed back among the spacious trees but no sign of life. 'The cork harvesters are taking a siesta,' the driver explained.

We next came to a grove with quite different trees; the trunks were badly shattered, as if the trees were dying; in some there were holes through which I could see; the branches were low and carried delicate leaves that were dark on top, silvery gray on bottom, with clusters of small black fruit. 'Olive grove,' the driver said. 'When the breeze comes through, the leaves flutter. Beautiful.' But this day there was no breeze.

Most of the land was barren, with no trees at all. The soil was rocky and red from decomposing ferrous elements. At times a stream-bed, empty of water for the past five months, crawled like a wounded snake across the plain, but often there was not even this to watch. I longed for at least a buzzard to mark that merciless sky, but none appeared. 'Sleeping,' the driver said. 'Everything is sleeping.'

We came to a village, a truly miserable collection of adobe huts clustered about an unpaved square. One bar was open, apparently, for its doors were not closed, but no men were visible behind the strands of beads that served as a curtain for keeping out the flies. Farther on there was a town, and since it was now nearly five in the afternoon people were beginning to move about, but the heat was so intense that no work was being done. It was a town that had little to commend it except its longevity; Roman legions had known this town, and when their expeditions had ended in the years before the birth of Christ, Caesar Augustus had allowed the oldest veterans to take up land here. Over the ravine at the edge of town ran a stone bridge that had been used in its present form for more than two thousand years.

'You want to stop for a drink?' the driver asked.

'Not in this town,' and we pushed on.

We came now to fields that looked as if they might have been cultivated and to a series of oak and olive forests that were well tended. 'We're getting close to Badajoz,' he said, pronouncing the word with respect. As evening approached, the heat grew more bearable and in one river valley we actually felt a breeze. We climbed a hill, turned west and saw below us the Río Guadiana, which farther on would form the border between Portugal and Spain, and in its valley stood a city without a single distinction: no towers, no ancient walls, no exciting prospects. The eastern half looked old and unrepaired; the western half, new and unrelated to the rest; and there was no apparent reason why a man in good sense would descend the hill to enter that particular city, for this was Badajoz, the nothing-city of the west. 'Precisely what I wanted,' I said.

In America when I had explained to my friends that I was heading for

Badajoz, they had shrugged their shoulders because they had never heard of it, and when I told my Spanish friends they grimaced because they had. 'For the love of Jesus, why Badajoz? It has absolutely nothing.' In Spanish this last phrase sounds quite final: 'Absolutamente nada,' with the six syllables of the first word strung out in emphasis. They tried to dissuade me from going, explaining that Badajoz was a mere depot town along the border, that it was lost in the emptiness of Extremadura, and that if I was determined to visit a remote town, why not a beauty like Murcia near the Mediterranean, or Jaén in the mountains, or Oviedo, where the relics of Christ were kept? 'Why Badajoz?'

Why indeed? I had not tried to explain, but there was an explanation and a good one. When I heard the word Spain, I visualized not kings and priests, nor painters and hidalgos, nor Madrid and Sevilla, but the vast reaches of emptiness, lonely uplands occupied by the solitary shepherd, the hard land of Spain stretching off to interminable distances and populated by tough, weatherbeaten men with never a ruffle at their throats nor a caparisoned horse beneath them. In short, when I thought of Spain, I thought primarily of Extremadura, the brutal region in the west, of which Badajoz was the principal city.

There was a reason. Apart from my first brief visit to Castellón de la Plana and Teruel as a student, my introduction to Spain had come in the American southwest, in the empty areas of New Mexico, Arizona, Texas and California, where the Spanish impact had been great. To me, a Spaniard was a man like Coronado, who had ventured into Kansas in 1541. Hernando de Soto and Cabeza de Vaca were my Spaniards and the unknown men who settled Santa Fe and Taos. The Spain I had known in western United States was a heroic Spain, the Spanish landscape with which I was familiar reached at least four hundred miles in any given direction over largely empty land. To have been a Spaniard in those early days in New Mexico and Arizona signified, and the closest approach to that Spain in the home country was Extremadura.

My second contact with Spain was different. I had spent considerable time in Mexico and at one period or another had lived in all but two of its states, always seeing Mexico as a land that had been discovered, occupied, developed and ruined by Spaniards. I knew well the routes traveled by Hernán Cortés in his conquest of the Aztecs, and I had studied those haunting plateresque churches built by his followers in towns where silver was mined. There were few Spanish buildings in Mexico that I had not explored, and some of the happiest days of my youth were those spent in drifting across the plateaus of Chihuahua or exploring the jungles west of Vera Cruz. But whenever I looked at Mexico, I saw Spain. Mexican culture was meaningful only as an extension of Spanish culture, and the cyclones of Mexican political history were merely a reflection of the home country.

Early in my study I discovered that most of the Spanish heroes who had operated in the Americas had come from Extremadura. The New World was won for Spain not by gentlemen from Toledo and Sevilla but by a group of uneducated village louts who, realizing that they had no future in their hard homeland, had volunteered for service overseas, where their Extremaduran courage proved the most valuable commodity carried westward by the Spanish galleons.

Extremadura was my Spain, and no one who had missed my experiences in New Mexico and Old could appreciate what Badajoz meant to me, but when I saw this unlovely, battered town, called Pax Augusta by the Romans, and when I saw about me the suspicious, dour Extremadurans, whose ancestors had conquered not cities but whole nations and continents, I felt that I had come back to my own land.

My first experience in the city proved that I was in Extremadura. The hotel to which I had been sent was dark and mean and tucked away on a side street. The clerk growled, 'We can let you have a small room for tonight. Fifty pesetas.' This was eighty-three cents and I judged I could go a little higher, so I said, 'I'll be here for a month, so if you have a larger room . . .'

'A month! In that case the room will be sixty pesetas.'

This confused me, and I started to explain that elsewhere if a man stayed for a month the price went down, not up, but he stopped me. 'We don't want people coming here. We have too many already.' I looked about the dark lobby and saw no one. I was about to point this out when he snapped, 'You can't have a room for a month. Nobody can have a room for a whole month.' He looked at me suspiciously, as if to ask, 'Why would a foreigner want to stay in Badajoz for a month?'

My second experience was one that I look back upon with affection. Through the warm night I walked to the main square and asked a policeman where a hungry man could get a decent meal, and he took me by the arm and said, 'There's only one place—Restaurante Colón. And you'll thank me later.' He led me to an old narrow building whose face had recently been lifted with purple plastic, chrome and neon. I hesitated but he pushed me in, and I found a menu which offered a bewildering selection: green plate, gray plate, black plate, ivory plate and white plate, each for about a dollar twenty. When the waiter came, a very tall, thin Extremaduran, he grabbed the menu away and whispered, 'If you want the best, take the zarzuela.' I was pretty sure I knew what a zarzuela was, so I asked, 'How's that again?' And he growled, 'Take the zarzuela.'

A zarzuela, unless I was out of my mind, was what I had seen in Castellón de la Plana, a short Spanish-type musical comedy in which the songs are closer to opera than those of an American musical. I had seen some good zarzuelas and had enjoyed them, but now I was being asked to eat one.

I must have shown my apprehension, because the waiter said an extraordinary thing: 'My friend, if you trust in the goodness of God, take the zarzuela.' Such advice I could not ignore, so I nodded, fearing the worst.

Instead I got the best: a ramekin containing olive oil, a judicious amount of garlic, some baked potatoes, chopped onions, pimientos, tomatoes and a heavenly assortment of shrimp, crayfish, squid, octopus, hake and filet of sole, all done to a golden brown and served with croutons and an effervescent white wine. It was a savory introduction to Badajoz and I had to agree with the waiter that sometimes the goodness of God must be trusted.

When I finished, it was still light and I had no intention of going back to my gloomy hotel. I decided instead to stroll through the streets of Badajoz and to see with a fresh eye how a Spanish city looked. I wanted, as it were, to build a base of understanding to which I could add as I visited the nine other cities of my projected tour, and in retrospect I am glad that I did this, because if one understands Badajoz he will understand Spain.

The Restaurante Colón stood on the main plaza, and as I left it I faced the cathedral, a low, squat ugly building built many centuries ago and one of the least attractive in Spain. It carried a square tower of no distinction, decorated by nine urns on each side, looking like the battlements of a fortress and not a cathedral. Eight bells hung in the tower, but during my stay I did not hear them ring. The massive walls had no Gothic windows, nor did they carry any ornamentation to relieve their drabness. The building was entered by a sadly inappropriate door flanked by four Ionic columns which some architect had added in the eighteenth century in an attempt to dress up the façade, and on the great slab-sided front facing the plaza appeared the two words which I would see carved into the walls of churches all across Spain: JOSE ANTONIO. The letters were accompanied by seventeen laurel wreaths cast in rusting iron.

Although the cathedral was unusually ugly it conveyed a sense of dignity, for it was a frontier church-fortress, and only the security which it provided had allowed Badajoz to survive its sieges and attacks. It was then and remained now the center of Badajoz life, and the society which it supervised was much like it: ancient, unornamented, solid and well able to protect itself.

The plaza which the cathedral dominated was small and awkward and as undistinguished a main square as I would see in Spain. There were old buildings of no quality and others like the Restaurante Colón whose face-lifted façades gleamed garishly in plastic and neon. The Banco Mercantil had recently been redone in ultramodern style and looked rather handsome. Its windows were low, and to keep idlers from sitting on the sills, the latter were decorated with sharp, tall spikes. The six white columns of the Palacio Municipal supported a balcony ready for an orator who never came.

What was the chief characteristic of the plaza? That it was jammed with automobiles and had the same parking problem as Rome, London or New York. The parking of cars was supervised by a corps of crippled war veterans who collected their fee whenever a car drew up to the curb. Traffic through the very narrow streets leading into the plaza was constant and was guided by policemen with a good sense of humor. Every four or five minutes large buses passed through the square on various routes which took them to all parts of the suburbs. The buses hauled large numbers of passengers, as they did throughout Spain.

Having completed a rapid survey of the plaza, I closed my eyes and asked, 'Is there anything here that would prove I am in Spain?' I looked again, and apart from the obvious signs in Spanish, saw nothing that would betray the origin of this city. It could have been Italy, or southern France, or even rural Texas. I want to make this point secure because travelers often expect strange cities to look a certain way, but with modern technology, architecture and traffic most of them look alike. If I had tried this test of 'Where am I?' in the plazas of the villages and towns of southern Extremadura the answer would have been, 'This can only be Spain,' but in the cities, no. They are international.

Yet even as I said this I saw two minor things that would have betrayed a Spanish origin. At the far end of the plaza stood a statue to the painter Luis Morales (1509–1586) and in the next small square another statue to another painter, Francisco Zurbarán (1598–1664). Spain is inordinately proud of its painters and writers. The Spanish jet which had brought me from New York bore the name *El Greco* and I tried to imagine an American plane, patronized by our businessmen, bearing the name *Jackson Pollock*. And on one of the plaza walls stood the type of marble plaque common in Spain. This one recalled the salient event of recent Spanish history, the Civil War:

SPAIN

CONQUEROR OF COMMUNISM

IN THE CRUSADE WHICH BEGAN THIS DAY

TO ENSURE PEACE FOR THE EMPIRE.

FOR UNITY, FOR GREATNESS, FOR LIBERTY

IN THE SIGN OF FRANCO, THE CAUDILLO.

¡ARRIBA ESPAÑA!

17–18–19 JULY 1936

When I left the plaza I entered the old part of Badajoz, and was delighted with the narrow streets and the memories of Spain as it used to be. This was a pleasing part of town and here I was not in Rome or Texas. This was authentic Spain, but when I moved to the west and to the area of big new buildings, sprawling schools and hospitals, I might once more have been in any modern European city. Taken building by building, Badajoz was a respectable-looking city, clean, well organized and modern. Homes, stores, theaters, the lesser churches and the public offices were about what one would expect in a city of similar size in Italy or France. Beauty there was not, but solidity there was. There was also evidence that the citizens had money, for whenever in my tour I reached a high point of ground, I saw numerous television aerials; sets in the city could bring in both Portuguese and Spanish programs.

What kind of people lived in Badajoz? I returned to the main plaza and found an outdoor table, where I sat for some hours simply looking at the passers-by, and as the cooler temperatures of evening arrived a good many people appeared for their nightly stroll. As to the girls, they looked exactly like girls of similar age in New York or London. They wore the same amount of make-up, the same length of dress, the same hairdos. They giggled in the same way at private jokes, and when they walked with young men they held hands and sometimes kissed in public. If the young women gave no signs of being Spanish, certain of the older women did, but only because they wore much more black than I would have found in England or America.

Young men looked exactly like their cousins around the western world. In dress they were wholly indistinguishable from boys their age in Chicago or Mexico City, except that not many wore their hair long. They did, however, carry transistor radios, which they used as abusively as young people elsewhere. Spaniards are conservative in dress and this became especially noticeable when I studied the older men, for of all groups they alone did betray the fact that they were Spanish, but only because they wore extremely somber clothes. I saw not a single sport shirt, nor a blazer, nor even a light-colored suit of any kind.

In facial appearance I could not detect among the young any characteristics that would brand them as Spanish, but as both the girls and boys grew older a certain Spanish look did seem to appear; I mentioned this to an Englishman whom I met later, and he said, 'You're wrong. If you put a hundred of the older people in various European cities, you'd not be able to identify them. France, Italy, Greece, Turkey would absorb them without your knowing. Sweden and Finland? No. The Spaniards are a little darker than the European average and against the blonds of those two countries they'd be conspicuous.'

One point I must make clear. You could sit in the plaza at Badajoz for three months and see no women trailing by in mantillas. You'd see no castanets, no high ivory combs, no colorful shawls tied about the waist. Nor would you see any men dressed like Don Quixote or conquistadors. No bands of guitarists gather at midnight, wrapped in cloaks, to serenade women behind iron grilles, and the Spanish types one sees in *Carmen* are visible only in the bullring, where in the infrequent fights matadors dress as they did a century ago.

Yet certain trivial customs create a Spanish atmosphere. There being little public assistance as we know it in America, it is traditional for blind people to roam the streets selling lottery tickets; cripples park cars or peddle things, and consequently one sees more deformity in Spain than he would elsewhere. There is, however, no begging. Shoeshine boys are also more numerous, but usually they are grown men who move endlessly from one café table to the next, calling '¿Limpia?' (Shall I clean?), so that in the course of two hours one could have his shoes shined by ten or fifteen different men.

One of the sure signs that this is Spain is the number of young married women who have allowed themselves to get fat. On my first night in Badajoz, I estimated that Spanish women of thirty years and older weighed about twenty pounds more than American or French women of comparable age and social background. I commented on this to a Spaniard, and he said approvingly, 'It's one of the most beautiful sights in Spain. To sit in the plaza at dusk and watch the fat married women roll by with their husbands and children. It's beautiful because in Spain, once a woman is married, she never again has to fight the dinner table. She has her man and nothing on earth can take him away from her, so she doesn't give a damn how fat she gets. In Spain there's no divorce and her children cannot be taken away nor her home either. She's safe. Of course, her husband will probably take a mistress. Three-fourths of the fine Spanish gentlemen you've been meeting and enjoying so much have mistresses. But they'd have them whether their wives were slim or fat. So our women eat and love their children and go to the movies and gossip and put their faith in the Church, and to hell with dieting, and you won't find a more contented group of women in the world.'

The newspapers for sale in the plaza were a strange lot. Generalísimo Franco, the country's dictator, was an old man and his successor had not been determined, and this was a matter which might decide the fate of Spain, but public discussion of this vital problem was forbidden, and to read the papers in Badajoz one would have felt that the general was going to live forever. I am speaking here of 1961, shortly after the inauguration of President Kennedy, when American newspapers were already speculating on what might happen in the 1964 election, and especially the 1968, but of Spain's greater problem there was no discussion. In place of political news the papers offered reams of fine writing on sports, many columns on the Church, emphasizing the activities of the Pope, and because the men who owned the newspapers were monarchists, a constant stream of stories about how European countries that lived under kings were better off than those that didn't.

The marriage of Prince Carlos of Bourbon to Princess Ana, daughter of the Count of Paris, was characterized by its simplicity.

Will Princess Benedicta of Denmark never find a husband? There is still hope, but available men are few and for the present she loves only horses.

Queen Isabel of England, on her forthcoming visit to Germany, will decide what shall be served at state banquets. Even though Prince Felipe of Edinburgh loves lobsters, none will be served because Isabel prefers little German sausages.

One got the feeling that the Spaniards would have enjoyed arguing politics in their papers, but it was forbidden, so they satisfied themselves with sports and religion and the doings of distant royalty.

And so it went. Badajoz was Spain, and no place else. It was sharply different from Portugal, which lay only four miles away, but it was not an exaggerated Spain, not a musical-comedy land at all.

In the morning I set out to visit random stores to see for myself what it would cost a Spaniard to live in Badajoz as compared with what I paid at home. I started by listing the dinner I'd had at the Colón:

Item	*Badajoz*	*U.S.A.*
First-class dinner	$ 1.20	$ 4.50
Hotel room	.83	14.00
Man's shoes	8.00	10.00
Child's schoolbag	.50	1.50
Woman's slip	1.60	4.00
Two-piece woman's suit	30.00	75.00
Kelvinator refrigerator	235.00	160.00
Woman's blouse	6.50	8.00
Man's suit	37.00	75.00
Wash-and-dry shirt	8.00	6.00
Slide rule	11.50	22.50
Fine girl's sweater	5.00	12.00
Man's haircut	.25	2.50
Calico dress	7.50	10.00
Girl's cosmetic kit	1.30	1.50
Cheap ball-point pen	.07	.29

When one considers that the average wage in Spain is sharply lower than that in the United States, these prices are on the high side, but remember that recurring costs like food and lodging are much cheaper in Spain. Also, practically anything available anywhere in the world is available in Spain. I saw Norwegian sweaters, Italian shoes, Argentinian wool, German scissors and French encyclopedias—all within a few minutes.

Consider the case of the fish market where I spent a morning talking with the proprietor and his stream of customers. It was run by Armando

37

Olivera and stood at the busy corner of Sepúlveda and López Prudencio. At first sight it looked as if it would offer three or four kinds of inexpensive fish; in fact, it had more than thirty. Señora Gutiérrez wanted some hake, brought that morning by truck from Huelva on the Atlantic. Señora Meléndez plumped her shopping bag on the marble counter and said she wanted a bagful of backbone joints from the huge swordfish that had come from Portugal. She was making a fish stew and the joints contained much meat, but when the package was weighed and paid for, sixteen cents, Olivera chucked in an extra slice of pure meat, for which he was thanked.

At least half the fish available in this shop was frozen, much of it coming from Norway and Germany. I was surprised to see in the freezer a large selection of whole frozen chickens from Denmark, butter from Ireland and frozen meat pies from England, all at prices sharply lower than they would have been in America.

Spain makes it easy for the foreigner to convert his dollars into pesetas. In even the smallest town, if it has a bank, one can cash his traveler's checks with ease. In Badajoz there were, I judged, about fifteen banks or offices which performed this service. I used the Banco Mercantil, the exterior of whose building had impressed me during my survey of the plaza. Inside, it was as brisk and bright as a new branch bank in Omaha and much more so than one in Glasgow. I presented my check and passport to a young man, who greeted me in English. In less than a minute he typed out slip #453, handed half to me and passed the other half along to three different officials, who initialed it and handed it to the teller, a very busy man. I waited in a long line while the teller dealt with slips #440 to 452. Finally he called, 'Cuatro cientos cincuenta y tres.' I presented my matching half of the slip and he counted out the money. 'We are pleased to have you in Spain,' he said in Spanish.

I was eager to find out what an average day for a Spanish business-man consisted of, and on one of my walks I came upon the Casino de Badajoz, a distinguished men's club whose broad plate-glass windows, fronting on the main street, were always occupied by gentlemen who seemed to do nothing but ogle the passing girls. Without any kind of introduction I entered the club and explained my problem to the major-domo, who grasped the situation at once, offered me a beer and summoned a club official, a delightful talker whose monologue I shall repeat as he gave it:

'This club is the heart of Badajoz. Very old, very honorable. It costs thirty dollars to join and twenty dollars a year dues, but the waiting list is so long you'd not have a chance right now. As a foreign visitor, however, you would be most welcome on a temporary basis. On the second floor, the big television room. Next to it our enormous ballroom. These red and white

This fat pig, fed on acorns from the forests of Extremadura,
has been dead for two years and may hang proudly
in the butcher's window for another two before it is eaten.
Price in Spain, twenty-three cents a pound.

furnishings, the mirrors, the red plush boxes, the stucco figures on the ceiling . . . we think these lend a touch of elegance. I don't know who carved that "Venus Holding a Mirror" or the huge "Judgment of Paris," but they're old and familiar and lend a sense of permanence. We have four floors here, all marble, a barbershop, billiards. At the green tables in this game room a lot of money has been won and lost. The bar, the library. We get papers from all over Spain and Paris too. Our restaurant used to do a large trade, now the snack room does more. We offer much to attract children and in the evening women are welcomed too. But, as you can guess, it's this big front room that establishes the quality of the club. In the course of a week you'll see in this room all the men who run Badajoz. You might almost say Extremadura. Even the soldiers and the priests you'll see here. It is marble, has those five impressive front windows, the big comfortable leather chairs. The large painting shows a country wooing. I think the man is playing an oboe. But this is the heart of the club. This is the room that means more than home to the men of Badajoz.

'No, the man you ask about is not from Badajoz. You see, each city in Spain has one top club like this, and if you belong to it in your home town, you automatically have privileges in all the others. The man you're looking at is from Sevilla.

'You want to know what the average day of a club member is? You must remember that these are well-to-do men, the leaders of Badajoz, and this is an agricultural region. So your average man would have to be a farmer. Let's take that one in the big chair, staring out the window. His name is . . . we'll call him Señor Don Pedro Pérez Montilla. He lives about twenty miles south of here. Has one large plantation of cork trees, another where he grows wheat, some pigs and sheep. About two thousand acres altogether. Has three cars. An English Land Rover to get about the plantation, a Spanish SEAT 1500 for his own driving and a SEAT 600 for the rest of his family. Of course, he never drives himself. Has a driver who does that. He must rise rather early, for in the morning, after breakfast of a roll, some coffee and a glass of anís (anisette), he supervises his farms. But every day he reaches this club not later than twelve-thirty. Plays dominoes in the back room. Talks with his friends. About two-thirty in the afternoon he drives back to his farm, makes his lunch on soup, eggs and potatoes, meat and fruit and takes his siesta. He's back at the club by six-thirty and always sits in the chair you see him in now.

'At that time he's joined by three other men, whom he's known for forty years. They form what we call a tertulia. That's an informal club that meets every day to gossip. What about? Don Pedro's tertulia are all farmers, so they talk about cork and olives and sheep and whether a Land Rover is better than a Jeep. Yes, every day for forty years that's what they've talked about. Politics not very often. Religion never, because all four men in the tertulia know what the others think on those subjects.

Sometimes no one speaks for forty minutes. When that happens they all look out the window at the pretty girls in the paseo. The tertulia meets in those four chairs till about ten at night, when Don Pedro drives back to the farm for his dinner of consommé and tortilla [in Mexico, a flat unleavened bread of maize; in Spain, a potato omelet]. A man like Don Pedro would never eat in a restaurant, but one night four years ago he did invite a guest to the farm for dinner.

'Don Pedro reads the *ABC* each morning, but nothing else. He goes to the movies only when they show Gary Cooper or John Wayne. He has two fine daughters who went for a while to the convent school, but now they're waiting for someone to marry them. Don Pedro would probably not allow them to marry a man whose family did not belong to our club. Otherwise where would the new family fit in?'

A word about Spanish names. To explain the tradition fully would require many pages, for it is unbelievably complicated, but ideally every Spaniard, male or female, has two surnames, the first and more important being the father's and the second the mother's. Thus Pedro Pérez Montilla can properly be referred to as Señor Pérez Montilla or simply as Señor Pérez, but to refer to him as Señor Montilla would be a real gaffe. Spanish also has the handy little words Don and Doña, which have no equivalent in English and cannot be translated; they are used only preceding a given name, allowing one to refer to a man or woman by the given name with no presumption of intimacy. Thus our friend can be called Don Pedro or Señor Don Pedro Pérez Montilla. When he married, let us say to Leocadia Blanco Alvarez, his wife did not surrender her surnames but merely added his, preceded by the preposition de (of), so that her name became Señora Leocadia Blanco Alvarez de Pérez Montilla, and she may properly be addressed as Doña Leocadia, or as Señora Blanco, or as Señora Blanco Alvarez, or as Señora Blanco Alvarez de Pérez Montilla, or as Señora de Pérez Montilla. Frequently the paternal and maternal surnames are joined by either a hyphen or an y (and), which means that Don Pedro's son could be named Antonio Pérez Blanco, or Antonio Pérez-Blanco, or Antonio Pérez y Blanco, although in recent years the last has become less frequent. Many Spaniards today, in common usage, simply omit the maternal surname entirely or abbreviate it to a single letter. On the other hand, if Don Pedro and Doña Leocadia belong to the nobility or the aristocracy (or if they want to put on airs) the son will adopt the name Señor Don Antonio Pérez Montilla y Blanco Alvarez.

The problem is further complicated when a man has a family name which is unusually common and a maternal name which is less so, for then he becomes known by the more distinctive of his two names, which is only sensible. The five most common Spanish surnames, in order of frequency, are García, Fernández, López, González and Rodríguez, and just as the Englishman named Smith or Jones is accustomed to adding a hyphenated second name, such as Smith-Robertson, so the Spaniard becomes García Montilla, sometimes with the hyphen. It is in conformity with this custom that the great Spanish poet Federico García Lorca is so often referred to simply by his maternal name. Anglo-Saxon readers encounter difficulties with the names of such historical figures as Spain's two cardinals who exercised political leadership, Mendoza and Cisneros; in history books you will find many pages about them, and they were at least as famous as Richelieu in France and Wolsey in England, yet if you try to look them up in a Spanish encyclopedia you will find nothing unless you happen to know that the former was born Pedro González de Mendoza and the latter Gonzalo Jiménez de Cisneros. In each of these instances, however, the distinctive name is not maternal but merely a place name added in hopes of making a common name distinctive. So far I have discussed only the simple cases; the complicated ones I had better skip.

In a small Spanish city to which a friend had sent me a postal money order I had a rueful introduction to this problem of names. My friend had assured me by phone that the money had been sent, and the post office had advised me that it had arrived and that upon presentation of my passport it would be paid. Accordingly, I went to the post office, but before telling the clerk my name, handed him my passport. He studied it, consulted his file of incoming money orders and said, 'Nothing here.' I explained that I knew it was in hand, so with much politeness he searched his papers again and said, 'Nothing here.' This time I noticed that he was looking in the *A* file, so I suggested, 'Perhaps if you look in the . . .'

'Please, Señor Albert,' he said. 'I know my business.'

In my passport he had seen that my name was James Albert Michener and he was smart enough to know from that who I was, and he had no cash for any Señor Albert. When I tried to explain what my name really was he became angry, and I was not able to get my money until Spanish friends came from the hotel to the post office and explained who I was. When the money was paid, the clerk took my passport again, studied my name and shook his head. When he handed back my papers he said, 'I am sorry for your inconvenience, Señor Albert.'

The nightly paseo which Don Pedro watches from his window is common to most Spanish cities, but in Badajoz it has special features because the city has not one main plaza but two. Plaza San Juan, which faces the cathedral, we've seen, but Plaza Generalísimo Franco, the larger of the two, we have not. They are connected by the street that runs past the big windows of Don Pedro's Casino de Badajoz, so that what in other cities is called 'a turn about the plaza' becomes in Badajoz a substantial march: back and forth along Plaza San Juan, down the long street past the Casino, then around the Plaza Franco, where band concerts are held from eight to ten.

Badajoz, as seen from this latter plaza at night, is a delightful city.

'These gardens are for all and are to be cared for by all,' states a large sign beneath which iron tables are set out for groups of eight or ten teen-agers. Nursemaids in starched uniforms parade up and down with infants in carriages, and a host of children under six play among the trees till midnight. 'They've been taking a siesta all afternoon,' a mother explains. At the corners of the park semicircular benches made of bright tile are occupied by soldiers and their dates, while at the tables along the outer edges men sit in groups talking about the same topics that are being discussed in the Casino. At ten-thirty or eleven the older people wander home for dinner, and the long day ends.

In all but one of the cities discussed in this book I will be drawing upon recollections of more than one visit. I have been to Badajoz four different times, to Madrid about twenty, to Sevilla a dozen, to Teruel two; it was not until my last visit to Spain that I saw Barcelona for the first time. Of the various things I was to see in Badajoz, I think the most meaningful occurred during my first visit when I was standing idly in Plaza Franco toward midnight as the stragglers were heading home. A married couple named Serrano were seated at the table next to mine, and as I rose to go back to my hotel the man said, 'You're not going to miss the cathedral?' I asked why not, and he said, 'Because it's May 13.' I asked what was special about that date, and he said, 'Come and see.'

We walked back to the cathedral, where families were entering the ugly main portal accompanied by more than a hundred young people. I entered the dark interior; little boys in robes were handing out lighted candles that produced marvelous shadows across the low-vaulted ceiling. The interior of the cathedral was even more depressing visually than the exterior, for late in the life of the church some enthusiastic canon had built a choir and plastered its walls with a cheap stucco that was supposed to look like cut stone. The four bottom rows were painted a dirty beige, the nine top, a sickly puce. But spiritually the interior had the same bold force that I had observed in the cathedral as a whole; I was inside a great fortress which contained no nonsense or embellishment. In time of peace worshipers came here to pray; in time of war to defend themselves.

At midnight bells tolled and five dignitaries of the church in full regalia conducted a service which I could not understand. 'It's not a mass,' the Serranos told me. 'It's an invocation to the Virgin.' There was a moment of silence as the hundreds of candles flickered, and then Señor Serrano whispered, 'It's May 13. The Virgin of Fátima. We're very close to Portugal, you know.'

When the praying stopped I assumed that the services were over, but they were just beginning, for now a procession formed at the altar and left the cathedral, entering the dark city, and all who bore candles fell in line and began a solemn march down Calle del Obispo San Juan de Ribera, through the silent Plaza Franco and out into the suburbs lying to the northwest. The procession consisted of some four or five hundred worshipers, perhaps as many as a thousand, for it stretched a long distance. At the head marched a priest with an electronic bullhorn, through which he sang endlessly in a husky voice,

'Ave, Ave, Ave Maria,
Ave, Ave, Ave Maria . . .'

until all marchers took up the chant and Badajoz echoed with praises of the Virgin.

Through the darkness we approached a tall building some seven or eight stories high which was used as a girls' school; it was dark and silent, but as the priests at the head of our column reached its doors, suddenly from the roof several hundred girls in white lit their candles and began chanting, 'Ave, Ave, Ave Maria.' The effect was stunning. The marchers stopped. The priest with the bullhorn sang no more, but the girls' voices, drifting through the night, lent the procession a religious quality that was profoundly moving. Quietly word passed along the column, 'Proceed,' and in silence we left the school, from which the echoes of chanting could long be heard.

Now we were in the country, toward two o'clock in the morning, and a three-quarter moon lit our way, so that we could see the trees and the towers of some building about a mile distant. The priest with the bullhorn resumed his chant and finally we came to a halt before a building, which I never did identify. Its front contained many balconies which were jammed with monks and nuns, and everyone bared his head as the priests who had led us from the cathedral began a service in praise of Our Lady of Fátima. It was a solemn, deeply moving moment, and many kneeled.

In the days that followed I was reminded again of the first essential for anyone who wishes to understand Spain: in every manifestation of life Spain is a Catholic country, and if citizens are willing to march several miles at midnight to honor the Virgin, they are equally willing to abide her surveillance in daily life. Down the street from the Casino de Badajoz stands an old palace at present converted into the offices of the diocese, from which the schools of Badajoz are supervised. The walls contain graduation pictures from the College of Our Lady of Carmen, in which, by Spanish tradition, the boys are dressed as admirals of the fleet and the girls as queens with tiaras, except that the boy who gained top grades is dressed as a fifteenth-century grandee with lace ruffs. There is no education not under the control of the Church and its orientation is to the past.

On the door of the parish church nearby hangs a poster classifying the motion pictures to be shown in Badajoz this week:

The National Catholic Confederation of Heads of Families.
Remember these classifications:
Class 1.   For everyone, including children
Class 2.   For those fourteen and above

Class 3. For those eighteen and above
Class 3-R. For those eighteen and above, but watch out
Class 4. Gravely perilous to morals

These restrictions apply in all dioceses and cannot be changed by any officials in those dioceses.

Of the forthcoming pictures only one was in Class 1, *The Sound of Music*, called in Spanish *Smiles and Tears. Return from the Ashes*, with Samantha Eggar and Maximilian Schell, was condemned for stressing 'lust, adultery, illicit relations, crime and sadism. On one church door I saw this condemnation of an especially bad show: 'This should be seen only by those ninety-four and above.'

One experience especially demonstrated the force of Catholicism in Spain. I had taken a long walk out into the country on a narrow road that led to Olivenza, and on the way back I stopped to inspect a group of clean, good-looking buildings called the Maternity Hospital of the Virgin of Solitude, and as I stood at the gate a man came out whose wife had just been admitted and we spoke of the good work such hospitals did.

'Who runs them?' I asked.

'The Church. Who else?'

'Are there any public hospitals?'

'I don't know what you mean. The Church gives us our hospitals and schools. Don't they give you hospitals and schools in your country?'

'We provide such things with taxation.'

He pondered this for some moments, then asked, 'You mean the government taxes you for what the Church gives us? You have to pay for them out of your own pocket?'

I tried to explain that in many countries, England and Germany for instance, taxes provided schools, but he interrupted, grabbing me by the arm. 'Tell me, would sensible men trust politicians to run a hospital? The Church you can trust.' He was unable to imagine a society which operated on a system of taxation, and his final question was, 'You mean to say you allow politicians to teach your children? The Church you can trust, but not those others.'

In Badajoz I also learned something about the government of Spain. At the post office I purchased ten air-letter forms and paid six pesetas (ten cents) each for them. I went back to the cathedral plaza and spent most of one morning writing ten letters, a job I find difficult, for words do not come easily to me. The next day I took the ten letters to the post office to mail, but a clerk refused them, saying, 'The price of air-letter forms went up this morning from six pesetas to ten.'

'All right. Give me ten four-peseta stamps and I'll stick them on the letters.'

'We can't do that, sir, because it states very clearly on the form that if anything whatever is enclosed in the form or added to it, it will be sent by regular post.'

45

'Then let me give you the difference, and you stamp them as having ten pesetas.'

'There's no provision for that, sir.'

'Then what can I do? Mail them as they are and let them go regular mail?'

'No, because they're no longer legal. They've been declassified.'

'It took me a long time to write these letters. How can I mail them?'

'Take each one. Place it inside an airmail envelope. Readdress the envelope and place twelve pesetas' worth of stamps in the corner and mail it as a regular air-mail letter.'

This I did, and the letters were delivered in various countries, but I was so astounded by the procedure that I called upon a high government official to ask how such things could happen. His answer was revealing. 'The clerk did right. The forms you bought were valid yesterday. Today they're not. Each form states clearly that nothing may be added, so there was no way to mail the old forms.'

I pointed out that in half a dozen different countries, including my own, I'd faced this problem and it had always been a simple matter to paste on the additional postage, at which he said, 'In other countries, yes. But no nation in the world is so difficult to govern as Spain. No people are so fundamentally anarchistic as the Spanish. Therefore, when we say that nothing may be stuck on the envelope we have got to mean it. If we fluctuated on this point, we might be driven to fluctuate on others. The Spaniard understands when the clerk stands fast. If the clerk once wavered, he might be dead the next day.'

'But it's so unfair! You sell the forms one day and cancel them the next, with no redress.'

'My friend. The whole affair cost you what? Ten times six pesetas. About one dollar American. That's money lost, and it's too bad. But you will talk about this everywhere in Spain and word will filter out to many people. And they'll say, "See! Our government means just what it says, even with foreigners." Your loss will do much good, by friend. Because we Spaniards are devils to govern.'

That is why, throughout Spain, one sees so many members of the Guardia Civil, always in pairs, as I had seen them in Teruel. No truth in Spain is more difficult for the traveler to ascertain than that regarding these men, who are in effect the masters of rural Spain and men of tremendous power in all society. I shall recite seven stories for which I can personally vouch, having either witnessed the incident or known the persons involved.

An American couple working at a United States Navy base could not find quarters on the base but did find a comfortable house in a nearby town. They had a thirteen-year-old daughter who went to the local school. One Thursday the parents arranged for her to be picked up by friends at the base and to stay with them overnight. At five o'clock that afternoon two officers of the Guardia Civil appeared, saying, 'Señora, your daughter has not passed our headquarters this day. Is there trouble?' It is said that every human being who lives in the Spanish countryside must be personally known to the guardia, who are able to report on that person's movements, ideas and behavior.

An Englishman driving a small car of British make had a breakdown on a lonely road out of Salamanca. A pair of guardia walked by, ascertained his trouble, walked on to a telephone, called their headquarters twenty miles away, directed the guardia there to find at some garage a part for the British car, then walked back to the Englishman and stayed with him until a passing truck driver dropped off the part.

An Englishwoman staggered into an Extremaduran town with a terrifying tale. She had been in a little village where a gang of gypsies had molested her, trying to steal her purse. Two officers came on the scene and began to rough the gypsies up, whereupon the latter, fed up with previous pressure from the Guardia Civil, cut their throats to the neckbone. Someone from the village ran to report the murders to a neighboring Guardia station, whereupon four pairs of guardia climbed into a truck, drove to the scene of the murder, threw a cordon around the gypsy encampment and proceeded to machine-gun every human being therein.

The weekly bullfight at Sevilla was going badly and a riot started. The local police who attend all bullfights tried to control things, but the crowd laughed at them. The riot looked as if it were going to get out of hand, so the squad of guardia who are kept in reserve at all such functions started quietly down from their seats high in the rafters. As they descended men began to whisper, 'The Guardia Civil.' Slowly the guardia moved into the arena, taking up positions facing the unruly mob. They drew their revolvers and quietly looked at the rioters. There was not a man in the mob who doubted that within the next minute the guardia would begin to fire, and the riot collapsed.

An American working in a bar along the Mediterranean coast got drunk and slugged a guardia. He was hauled off to a military jail, where he was held incommunicado for six weeks, for the guardia are under military rule and offenses against them are judged by court-martial. Efforts of a most extraordinary kind were made to gain the young man's release, but to no avail. 'We can't allow anyone to strike a member of the Guardia Civil,' his friends were told. 'No one.' Finally he was brought to secret trial and sentenced to seven years in military prison. That was four years ago. The night before I wrote this paragraph I was advised by an American who knew the young man that word had been quietly passed that he could have his freedom if he could scrape together a fine of $7,000. Word of this affair traveled widely among the hordes of young Europeans and Americans barging into Spain in the summer: 'No matter what you do, no matter what happens, never touch a guardia.'

A New York woman, lost in the outskirts of Madrid at midnight, was escorted to her hotel by two members of the Guardia. When we asked her why she was in the Madrid countryside at midnight, she explained, 'In New York or Chicago or San Francisco, I would be mortally afraid to go out alone after dark. A woman simply isn't safe in the United States after dark. But in Spain, with the Guardia Civil on the job, I am safe to go anywhere. No one is going to abuse me. So when I come to Spain the thing I like to do most is to walk at night. Tonight I got lost.'

An intelligence officer of the United States Navy told me, 'We had this incident in which one of our kids in uniform committed a major crime. No question about it. But we didn't know whether he'd had accomplices or not, so we put our best brains on the job, and when we were through we checked with the Guardia Civil and they'd done the same thing we were doing, but they had a dossier on this kid that was unbelievable. They knew everything he'd done for months past, who all his gang were, who was involved. In the States I've cooperated with our F.B.I. on similar cases, but in thoroughness they don't compare with the Guardia.'

About such an organization opinions can vary. Conservatives believe the Guardia to be the agency which permits Spain to exist and that without these pairs of police Spain would fall apart in anarchy. Liberals recall García Lorca's harsh phrase, 'those patent-leather men with their patent-leather souls.' At the outbreak of Civil War in 1936 one of the first things that happened in small villages across Spain was the slaughter of the Guardia Civil, so in the ensuing war they fought on the side of General Franco, revenging themselves for the outrages committed against their brothers. I have heard many foreign travelers arguing that the Guardia Civil was an invention of the Franco regime; actually they are well over a century old, having been created in 1844 to replace the militia, which had proved to be politically unreliable, and since then, no matter what form of government has ruled Spain, the guardia have been needed to keep order. In recent years the Franco government, in an effort to popularize the Guardia, has encouraged the press always to refer to them as La Benemérita (the well-deserving) in much the same way that Manhattan police are called 'New York's finest,' and it is common to see stories in which the brave Benemérita captured a bandit or the compassionate Benemérita helped a widow. A Spaniard told me, 'We Spaniards are really bastards to govern. If we didn't have the Guardia we'd have no country. And remember this. If the Communists had won in 1939, every guardia you see today would still be a guardia. Only he'd be a Communist guardia. For to rule Spain without them would be impossible.' He then used a phrase I had not heard before: 'We have the old spirit of Viva yo. In Spain you must always take into account Viva yo.'

I must explain Viva yo because the phrase is essential, but before I get

Afoot, on bicycle or on horseback,
officers of the Guardia Civil in pairs move
back and forth across Spain.

to it I would like to introduce a few other words which I shall be using frequently. When I was in college I mowed the lawn of Professor J. Russell Smith, a Quaker geographer who wrote a series of books about foreign lands. During the academic year Professor Smith was usually absent, for he taught at Columbia University, but in the summers he often spoke to me, and one evening he mentioned some of the principles which governed his work. I forget all of them but one: 'James, if thee ever has cause to write about a foreign land, remember this. Don't pepper the page with foreign words printed in italic. That's pedantry and accomplishes little. But when thee has compiled a list of foreign words which thee thinks necessary, identify those which thee will be using at least three times in the chapter at hand or a dozen times in the book as a whole. These are the words thee really needs. Use them. But define them very carefully when thee first introduces them. Then define them by allusion on second use.' The significance of this advice was somewhat lost on me at the moment because of the extraordinary thing he said next: 'I discovered this principle by necessity. I was trying to teach graduate students about strange lands and I could see they were being drowned in words. So I asked myself, "What is the most successful expository material available today?" And I read the Bible to see how St. Paul expounded his ideas and I read the Tarzan books to find out why people who knew nothing of Africa were finding them so easy. I studied other works as well, but those were the two that taught me how to write.'

In dealing with Spain one is especially tempted to scatter italics. Spanish words are easy to pronounce, are often self-explanatory and do have an attractive power of suggesting to the reader that he is listening to castanets. I have never considered this an honorable way of writing and have followed Dr. Smith's advice, but in writing of Spain certain words are inescapable. Without them I do not see how one can come even close to explaining this country or his reactions to it. Herewith, then, the words which I intend to use throughout this book, for they relate to the soul of Spain and are indeed of its essence.

Duende. In my recent visits to Spain I have heard no other word so frequently used to express important ideas, whereas years ago I did not hear it at all. In fact, my rather large Spanish-English dictionary, compiled originally in 1852, does not even contain the word, and one issued as late as 1959 offers several irrelevant meanings like *elf, ghost, hobgoblin, hypochondriac, the restless one, glazed silk, small copper coin,* but no connotation resembling the one which now dominates Spanish conversation. I find myself unable to define duende, yet it seems to have become the sine qua non of Spanish existence. Without duende one might as well quit the game, and I mean this seriously. To say that a friend or performer has duende is the highest praise one can bestow, and an experience which I prized came one night in Badajoz when we had been drinking late in the public square before the ugly cathedral and I made a painstaking observation in garbled English-Spanish, at the conclusion of which a student said solemnly, 'Sir, you may be a norteamericano but you have duende.' What was it I had? Let me refer to Japan in an attempt to explain. The Japanese have a word which summarizes all the best in Japanese life, yet it has no explanation and cannot be translated. It is the word *shibui*, and the best approximation to its meaning is 'acerb good taste.' For example, a bright yellow could never be shibui but a dusty purple might be. A kimono decorated with golden dragons would not have the slightest chance of being shibui, but a gray-black one with a single silver crest the size of a half-dollar might have. Architecture, landscaping, theater, art forms, total personal appearance, conduct—all can be shibui if they are properly acerbic, restrained and in the great tradition of Japan, but what the word finally means no one can say, for it relates to the soul of Japan, which is itself undefinable. Duende is a word like that, but since Spain is not a country given to acerb restraint, the connotation is different. The dictionary of the Real Academia de la Lengua (language) defines it as 'mysterious and ineffable charm.' A night club has duende if all things are in proportion, all properly Spanish, and if a sense of lovely, swinging motion pervades. A singer possesses duende if suddenly she can tilt her voice in such a way that everyone automatically cries '¡Ole!' (Bravo!). A bullfighter has duende when he displays not bravery but unmistakable class. The essence of the word lies in its peculiar usage, as in the sentence I heard not long ago describing a dancer, 'My God! He has duende upon him.' I judge from this that duende is something that no man can will upon himself, but occasionally, when he is one with the spirit of a place or with the inherent quality of Spain, it rises from some deep reserve within him. I am aware of its presence when I see it, and I would suppose that the indulgent scholar at Badajoz was wrong when he conferred duende upon me. I know of no foreigner in Spain who has ever shown me duende except that extraordinary American John Fulton Short, whom we shall meet later. In areas where he yearned for duende, I suspect he did not achieve it, but one night during the fair in Sevilla, in a high attic where some dancers, guitarists and singers had gathered, Short danced in such a way that duende shone upon him. It was something to see. I'm sure that when Hemingway was young and in the first blush of his exploration of Pamplona he had duende. In his last crumbling years when he was trying to retrace his steps he wasn't even close. García Lorca compiled a considerable essay on duende in which he suggested that the best definition was one given accidentally by Goethe when speaking of other matters: 'Paganini had that mysterious power which all sense but no one can explain.' Lorca cites other quotations which indicate an understanding of the word. Of Manuel de Falla's music: 'Whenever it is composed of black sounds it has duende.' And of a flamenco singer: 'You have the voice, you have the style, but you will never triumph because you have no duende.' Duende, then, is the essence that makes something Spanish.

Gracia. This is a lovely word, which my Spanish friends use a good deal and which for a long time I was unable to understand. 'Does it mean grace?' I asked. That and much more. 'Is it a sense of humor?' Without one you could not have gracia, but it would have to be a very gentle sense of humor, one that smiled quietly at the inanities of the world. 'Sometimes you use the word as if it meant good judgment or breeding.' It includes all of that and much more. Spaniards are fond of saying, 'Our coins state that Franco is caudillo by the grace of God. Fact is, Franco is caudillo because God has a sense of gracia.' I didn't catch the implication, and then one day while I was wasting time in the plaza at Pamplona, waiting for the bullfight to begin, I saw a fat girl with almost no neck and strangely cocked eyes, a girl one would not normally bother with, except that she had some peculiar charm that was immediately apparent to all who saw her, and the young man who sat with her knew this, for obviously he loved her. She radiated a warmth that made itself felt across the plaza, and I was so captivated that I had to raise my glass to her and nod. She must have thought that I was making fun of her, although that was not my intention, for she looked at me with a frank and melting charm that many beautiful women never attain, and smiled at me and raised her glass with an awkward gesture, making fun of me in her way. To my friends who had been trying to explain words, I said, 'That girl has gracia,' but they corrected me. 'That one is gracia.' We saw her often during the fair and noticed that she was never without male companions who seemed to find her fascinating. When the feria ended and was gone, my friends and I never referred to the beautiful Swedish girls we'd seen nor the German blondes who had decorated the city, but we often recalled the fat girl with no neck, for she had gracia, and when a girl has this she illuminates a plaza and gives it character. There is much in Spain that has a gracia which cannot be found elsewhere.

Ambiente. I once hired a car and took a Badajoz family for a picnic. I provided the wine, the cheese and the anchovies. They brought the bread, the meat, the cake, the utensils and the blankets. We were in high spirits and the countryside was beautiful. This was bound to be a great picnic in a land where picnics are a way of life. We drove first toward the Portuguese border and I saw several spots that were, to my thinking, ideal for an outing, but the wife, who was by no means the head of this family and who usually kept silent, said firmly each time, 'No hay ambiente,' which meant that the spot I was suggesting had no ambiance. Well, with the aid of the driver I uncovered some half-dozen other spots, but in the opinion of the woman none had ambiente, so we turned around, retraced our route and headed south, where a series of equally desirable spots unfolded, each to be dismissed with that scornful 'No hay ambiente.' Finally we came to

As a beautiful young girl this woman was, of course, kept behind iron bars to protect her from young men.

an old farm beside a stream, with large olive trees, a grassy meadow, ducks on the water and cattle in the opposite field. Immediately we saw this spot, so gracious in the midday sun, with shade for all and room to move about in, we realized that our critical woman had been right. The other spots had not had the proper ambiente for a picnic. This one did. It longed for people to enter into it and spread their blankets beside its stream and upon its flowers. A Spaniard would willingly travel an extra fifty miles to find a spot with ambiente. Let word get around that a restaurant has ambiente and it is filled. If a vacation spot has ambiente its registration is crowded. The antique bullring at Ronda has ambiente, so that even though it lies perched in almost inaccessible mountains, people from all over Spain willingly travel long distances to see a fight there. The entire city of Sevilla has ambiente and is loved therefor. Madrid is too young to have achieved ambiente yet, but since it has power it is respected. What bestows ambiente upon a place? I don't know. But I have often been with Spaniards who have walked into what outwardly appeared to be a rather ordinary place and have been struck instantly by its charm. 'This place has ambiente!' they have cried, and in that split second I have known that it did. How did they know? How did I know? No one can explain, but without ambiente a thing can scarcely be Spanish. With ambiente it needs little else.

Pundonor. Many languages have cultivated special meanings for the word honor, and nations using those languages have developed particular connotations for this word. I think one would agree that in France, with its tradition of dueling, the concept of honor has had a rather more delicate definition than in America. In imperial Germany, where the dishonored infantry officer was left with a revolver as the only solution for having transgressed the code, the definition was also specialized, and no other nation has been able to enforce the strict interpretations that England observes regarding a businessman's word of honor. In Japan a whole culture, the samurai's, grew up around this word. However, in other countries in which I have lived but had better not name, none of the above concepts has any currency, and in the United States we have been rather more lax in our application than Germany and France and markedly more lax than England and Japan. But it has been left to Spain to cultivate not only the world's most austere definition of honor but also to invent a special word to cover that definition. Of course, Spanish has the word honor, which means roughly what it does in French, but also the word pundonor, which is a contraction of punta de honor (point of honor). At any rate, it is not sufficient for a meticulous Spaniard to worry about his honor. Many things that an American man can in all decency forgive, the Spaniard cannot. If he is a man of pundonor, he must take action against insult. A young man with four unmarried sisters had better cultivate a nice sense of pundonor. A politician, a businessman engaged in intricate dealings, a stage idol and above all a bullfighter must be studious of their pundonor, and in this book, where I deal with several men noted for their pundonor, I shall make use of this uniquely Spanish word, for I have found that whenever I am perplexed about what a Spaniard might do under certain circumstances, or the nation as a whole for that matter, it is instructive to ask, 'Under these circumstances what would a man do who subscribed to an acute or even a preposterous sense of honor?' And from endeavoring to answer this question I often find clues as to what the Spaniard will do. After all, *Don Quixote* is an engaging study of Spanish traits not only because it lampoons the concept of pundonor but also because it demonstrates that no man ever possessed pundonor to a greater degree than the doleful knight.

Sinvergüenza. Sin = without. Vergüenza = shame. A sinvergüenza is a man the precise opposite of one with pundonor. In no country of the world except Japan is it so damaging to a man to charge him with being a sinvergüenza, and when one throws this accusation against another he must be prepared to defend his judgment.

Estupendo, including other such extravagant words as *maravilloso, fantástico* and *magnífico*. Few Americans and no Englishmen have ever mastered these peculiarly Spanish expressions, for we have reserved them for things like Cecil B. De Mille movies and the circus. But observe my experience in Madrid. I had rented a car and like others found much difficulty in parking it, but at a restaurant nearby I became acquainted with a doorman who seemed to have psychic powers in determining where empty parking spaces would be. For this service I tipped him rather gener- ously, I thought, about a quarter in American money, which he accepted grudgingly. Against my better judgment I raised the tip to thirty-five cents, with no appreciable modification of his manners, and then to forty cents, which brought only the same surly acknowledgment. However, one day I went to this restaurant with Víctor Olmos, the ebullient *Reader's Digest* editor for Spain, who wheeled into the parking area, slammed on his brakes, leaped from the car and left it. When we returned, the attendant hurried for the car (he dawdled disgracefully when getting mine) and cried, 'Señor, I found you a place.' 'Estupendo!' Olmos said as he gave the man a six-cent tip. The attendant's face was wreathed in smiles. 'Fantás- tico!' Olmos added. 'Simply maravilloso.' The attendant nodded and I could see that he felt good all over. When I next parked there I gave him a twenty- cent tip and cried 'Estupendo!' and he beamed. Later on it was fantástico and extraordinario, and I had built myself a secure place in his attentions. My car came promptly now, for like a good Spaniard he needed words as much as he needed money, and the words he wanted had to be the most expansive and inflated available. In Spain words form a kind of currency which must be spent freely, and to do this is not easy for an American, yet not to do it in Spain is to miss the spirit of human relationships. For this purpose I prefer estupendo. Its four syllables, properly pronounced, ripple off the tongue, and if one drags out the *pen* for four or five seconds, the effect can be seductive. For the American it can also be corrupting. For example, when I showed Robert Vavra, whose photographs illustrate this book, the first completed chapter, he cried, 'Don Jaime! Estupendo!' For a moment I was delighted that my work had found favor in his expert eye, but before I had a chance to make an ass of myself I realized that he had been living in Spain for a long time. What he meant was that the material was not wholly offensive. Estupendo, properly used, means 'It might get by.'

Viva yo. This phrase will not be found in dictionaries. Some time ago there was a competition for the cartoon which best expressed the Spanish character, and the winner, without a close second, was one showing an arrogant little boy urinating in the middle of the street and spelling out the words 'Viva yo,' which could be translated as 'Hurray for me,' except that the guts of the phrase is the implied second half, 'and to hell with everyone else.' A comprehension of the Spaniard's addiction to Viva yo will help anyone trying to make his way in Spain. When the little car barrels right down the middle of the highway, forcing everyone else into the ditch, you don't swear at the driver. You say 'Viva yo' and you understand what happened and why. When you pay seven dollars for a seat at the bullfight and find it occupied by a man who will not move, you don't punch him. You say 'Viva yo' and steal someone else's seat. The spirit of Viva yo animates groups as well as individuals and sometimes the entire nation. It crops up in unexpected places and accounts for some very funny news-paper stories: 'Last night the music lovers of San Francisco, California, stormed the box office and paid up to fifty dollars for seats to hear the great Spanish tenor Alfredo Kraus make his debut in that city. Also in the cast was the Australian soprano Joan Sutherland.' When a group of Span-iards who had emigrated to Australia changed their minds after a year and came scuttling back to Spain, an editorial announced: 'They said that they had returned because they loved Spain better than any other country on earth, they wanted to live within the embrace of the Catholic Church, which was their spiritual home, and they had learned that if they didn't leave right away they would be drafted into the Australian army for service in Viet Nam.' The little boy spelling out his philosophy on the street grows up to be a man determined to live by that philosophy, and at times he can be aggravating. Even the poorest Spaniard subscribes to the spirit of Viva yo and is prepared to act upon it. This makes for some trying times, but with gracia they can be weathered. If, however, one finds that the constant exhibition of Viva yo irritates him, he should stay out of Spain and probably Texas too.

As for the other Spanish words that one would naturally want to use, most of them have found their way into the English language and can be adopted without definition. Some of the more common are: agua, alcalde, blanco, caballero, conquistador, flamenco, fiesta, mantilla, paseo, patio, plaza, rojo, sierra, siesta, tortilla and such bullfight terms as banderilla, banderillero, cartel, cuadrilla, matador, picador, toro and torero. The word toreador is also in the English dictionary but no one in Spain uses it any longer, for it is held to be archaic.

While assembling the above list I discovered to my surprise that pundonor has also become a good English word, although in our language it identifies a specific point of honor rather than a general attribute. And of course it does not carry the philosophical connotations which it has in Spanish.

It was my intention when visiting the major cities of my itinerary to make certain side trips to smaller towns and villages which held points of unusual interest, and Badajoz presented an opportunity for four such expeditions, all within Extremadura. One of the side trips was not an opportunity; it was an obligation, but of it I shall speak later.

The first trip took me into Roman Spain. How had Rome gained control of the peninsula? By 15,000 B.C. indigenous Iberians were well established along the coasts and had probably wandered inland, following rivers like the Guadiana. By 1300 B.C. Celtic invaders from the north had begun to displace them and had pretty surely reached Extremadura. By 1120 B.C. Phoenicians were building lighthouses on prominent peninsulas and founding the city of Gades (Cádiz), making it the oldest continuously occupied city in Europe. By 630 B.C. Greeks had arrived, and two centuries later the Carthaginians had taken charge of much of the peninsula. Historic names such as Hamilcar and Hannibal then appeared in Spanish history, the latter taking a Spanish wife and commanding territory as far inland as the site of Mérida, but the Second Punic War, 218–201 B.C., determined that Spain would pass under the control of Rome. This control was easier to establish along the coasts than it was inland, so what Rome could not gain in battle she tried to win by guile, and it was in 147 B.C. that the part of Extremadura surrounding the future site of Mérida became important.

Then Viriathus, a brilliant uneducated shepherd of the region, decided that the continued pressures and treacheries of Rome could no longer be tolerated. He led an uprising of Extremadurans that was subdued only because the Romans invented some new treachery which cost 9,000 Extremaduran dead and 20,000 men sold into slavery, among them Viriathus. As a Roman slave he learned much, and when through heroism he escaped, it was to raise fresh troops and to lead a major war against the Romans. At one point he controlled most of central Spain and even laid siege to Cádiz. He inflicted heavy defeats on Rome, and an army of magnitude was sent from Italy to subdue him once and for all, but he outmaneuvered it and killed many. He became the first hero of Spanish history, a native-born Extremaduran who had repulsed Roman armies.

But then Scipio Aemilianus, adoptive son of the house that had defeated Carthage, was dispatched with a major expedition to put an end to the business. Refusing to fall into the kind of military trap that Viriathus had sprung against previous Roman armies, Scipio baited a trap of his own. He entertained three of Viriathus' envoys and discussed peace with them, but while doing so he suborned them with wine and gold and sent them back to their leader, bedazzled by promises. The three ambassadors did not report to Viriathus but lingered outside the camp until he was asleep, then slipped into his tent and murdered him. Thus died Spain's first hero, a self-taught general of marked courage and considerable skill; after his death Scipio pacified the peninsula, and Spain became as much a part of the Roman Empire as Italy was. In fact, the first two Roman settlements established outside Italy and conferring citizenship were located in Spain.

The importance of Spain is illustrated by that unbroken chain of Spaniards, that is to say, men born in Spain or of Spanish parents, who made significant contributions to the Roman Empire. Three emperors who

FOLLOWING FACING PAGES:
Roman bridge, Romany folk.

well exemplified the glory of Rome—Trajan, Hadrian and Theodosius—
were Spaniards. So were the two Senecas (in Spanish, Séneca), the second
of whom we shall meet in more detail at Córdoba. Lucan the historian,
Quintilian the master of rhetoric, Martial of the epigrams, men of foremost rank in Roman literature, were also Spaniards. There were others
who served Rome well, the latest family being one that came long after the
empire, the Borjas (Borgias) from Valencia, who supplied two popes,
Calixtus III and the infamous Alexander VI, father of Lucrezia and Cesare,
and one saint, Francis Borgia, third general of the Jesuits.

To see Roman Spain at its best, one must visit Mérida, thirty-six miles
up the Río Guadiana from Badajoz. Its history began only in 25 B.C., when
the Emperor Augustus authorized the veterans of his Fifth and Tenth
Legions to retire from active service and take farms in the area, to be
known henceforth as Augusta Emerita (Augustus' Veteran Colony), whence
Mérida. A long bridge was then built over the Guadiana, and Mérida
became a chief link in communication between Hispalis (Sevilla) in the
south and Salmantica (Salamanca) to the north.

Rome built greater cities in Spain than Mérida, but it was the one
whose monuments have been best preserved, and a visit to its museum and
excavations is like a trip to ancient Rome. It has a wealth of important
structures: an immense circus seating 30,000, where chariot races were
held and where flooding enabled boats to engage in naval battles; a
well-preserved amphitheater of 14,000 seats, where slaves were fed to wild
beasts; an aqueduct of giant proportions; and numerous arches and memo-
rials. Three sites, however, are of special attraction. The theater, which we
know to have been built during the second year of the city's existence,
must have been a thing of marked beauty; it was a perfect semicircle with
four separate flights of seats reaching high in the air. The proscenium
utilized the full diameter of the circle and was backed by five double-tiered
pulpits, or forums, supported by innumerable white marble columns. For
about sixteen hundred years the theater lay forgotten beneath rubble,
which preserved it, so that when serious excavations started in this century most of the stones and pillars still existed and had only to be raised to
their original positions. Today the theater is a masterpiece of imperial
architecture, and one can sit in its lovely semicircle and imagine how it
must have looked when Plautus or Terence was being presented. Or he
can climb onto the central forum, where statues of gods once more deco-
rate the rostrum, and imagine what it was to have been a Roman actor
touring the provinces. This theater is a national treasure of Spain and is
again being used for dramatic presentations.

The museum housed in an old church in the center of the city is more
informative in that it contains a fine cross section of the art uncovered in
Mérida in the last two hundred years. Its massive heads and clean-limbed
statues are some of the best that have reached us from Roman times,
including an especially provocative head of Augustus as a god, wearing a

mysterious cowl over his marble locks, but I preferred two smaller heads which legend claims are his adoptive son and grandson, Tiberius and Claudius. The statue of the former shows a fleshy young man with heavy jowls, thick neck and flat-topped imperial hair. The face is handsome but the mouth is thin and cruel, and if this is indeed a portrait of Tiberius, it catches the spirit of that difficult man. Claudius, on the other hand, shows a frail and narrow face, slight neck and small ears. The hair is done in a more poetic manner and is less flat. The marble face has a thoughtful look that could be taken perhaps as vacant, and the mouth is weak like that of a stammerer. Again, the essential personality of Claudius has been captured.

But the glory of Mérida lies in the Roman bridge, a half-mile long, composed of eighty-one huge arches. It crosses the two arms of the Guadiana and today carries autobuses on its ample roadway where two thousand years ago it carried marching legions and their carts. It is a splendid construction, and those solid pillars that bear the brunt of any flood are pierced by a small narrow arch to permit the passage of excess waters. It was built of granite, perhaps before the birth of Christ, and has this curiosity: the arches are numbered beginning at the Mérida end and records have been kept as to what happened to which. Thus we know that Arches 11–16 were rebuilt by a Visigothic king in 686. Arches 21–22 were blown up by Spanish-English forces in 1811 to prevent Napoleon from using the bridge during the siege of Badajoz. Arches 29–31 were washed away during the flood of 1860, and 32–33 were lost in 1877. The Roman bridge was so important to this part of Spain that in Extremaduran documents it was referred to simply as 'the bridge.' It remains a majestic structure.

The arches have long served a double purpose, for they not only support the bridge but also offer protected camping sites for gypsy caravans that travel this road. I used to walk out across the bridge and descend to the meadows on the far side, and there under the arches I would see gypsy families, their beds spread out beneath the arches, their tables set with spiced food, their women in bright costumes, their men in more somber dress but each with a rattan cane which was his badge as a horse trader. Beyond the arch I would see groups of cattle, and I suppose that these camping sites have been used in this way for the five hundred years the gypsies have been in Spain. They are an undigested element in Spanish life, beyond control of state and Church alike. Up to a few years ago they were not even allowed in the armed forces, and when Spaniards argued with me about discrimination in the United States, I used to ask them about gypsies in Spain. Their answer was, 'Gypsies! They're different.'

During my wanderings in Mérida I stayed at the Parador Nacional, and because I shall be tempted to describe so many of these paradors scattered about Spain, I had better describe this one fully and have done with it. The noun parador is derived from the verb parar (to stop). A parador is therefore a stopping place, an inn, and these have been established by the government in recent years to help meet the sudden and enormous influx of tourists. They stand in spots which tourists would like to visit but where private capital either could not or would not build adequate accommodations, and in the opinion of travelers they are the best system of inns in the world. Their charges are unusually low, about a half or two-thirds of what one would normally pay for a good hotel in Spain, and the plan seems to be for the government to operate them only as long as necessary and when they have proved their feasibility to sell them to private operators.

Where practical, the paradors are housed in ancient buildings, such as old convents, monasteries, castles no longer in use, hospitals dating back to the age of the Catholic Kings or inns in which Columbus may have slept. One characteristic distinguishes them all. In Spain interior decoration is apt to be pretty bad, favoring dark massive objects unfitted to the human eye or fundament, but the paradors have been decorated by some of the most skilled art connoisseurs in Spain so that each is an experience in good design; each contains handsome old furniture and is embellished with paintings and brocades centuries old. The food is exceptionally good; the personnel is trained centrally and then sent out to the remote areas where the paradors are located. To travel across Spain by halting each night at a parador is to know travel at its best and most reasonable.

At Mérida the parador is housed in the Convento de los Frailes de Jesús, which stands in the heart of town and dates back to sometime around the year 1500. The numerous air-conditioned rooms stand on several different levels, which indicate how the old convent was added to as the number of friars increased, and as one climbs extremely old stone stairs to his room, with its floor of hand-hewn planks eighteen inches wide, it takes no imagination to picture oneself in Spain four centuries ago. But the chief beauty of this parador is the cloister of the convent, now used as a kind of salon. It exists unchanged from its original days, a quiet, beautiful square outlined by columns and arches. The former are very old, but the capitals which top them are something you may not see again in your travels, for they go back to Visigothic days, that period during which raiders from the north of Europe swept over Spain, drove out the Romans and established Christianity as the state religion. The central part of the cloister is now a garden filled with flowers and fine shrubs and with a well so old no one knows its date.

During the year of which I shall be speaking I should be visualized as living in such surroundings. Many of the paradors I stayed in were more beautiful than the one in Mérida; some were larger; others were in older buildings; and in still others the food was so good as to qualify as some of the best in Spain. Of course, large cities like Madrid, Sevilla and Barcelona

Gypsies.

have no paradors, for there they are not needed, but in most areas of the country they are within striking distance and represent the best value in Spain.

I especially enjoyed the parador at Mérida because from it I could walk to the Basílica de Santa Eulalia, and I want to spend a few moments discussing this stalwart old medieval church, since it establishes certain themes which will recur in this book. In either A.D. 303 or 304, when Christianity was fighting for a foothold in Spain, a group of children in Mérida became infected with the new religion, held to be both infamous and treasonous by the priests of Rome's official paganism, and much effort was spent in trying to win the children away from Jesus, but they were truly inspired with the new religion and refused to apostatize. One day when a high official pleaded with special force, the girl Eulalia, then twelve or thirteen years old, reared back and spit in his eye. To teach the others a lesson she was burned at the stake. Her tomb is reputed to be somewhere within the area covered by the present basilica; however, when we get to Barcelona we will find that certain partisans of that region are convinced that her remains were translated there, where she is also the patron saint, but serious students believe that two different saints are involved, the Barcelona one being a literary version of the Mérida. At any rate, their saint's days are different, December 10 in Mérida and February 12 in Barcelona. Much bitterness has been spent on this issue, complicated by the fact that the city of Oviedo claims that Eulalia's tomb was moved there in 783.

On the ancient wall of the church appears in huge letters the name JOSE ANTONIO, and beside the main entrance stands a very old Roman temple. As I entered the basilica I had the good fortune to meet a priest whose life had centered upon Mérida, Father Juan Fernández López. From a very small village he had come here to school at the age of six, had gone to Badajoz for his seminary training and then returned to Mérida to work. He looked as if he were still in his twenties, with a squarish face, dark complexion and bubbling enthusiasm. He was an exciting guide and I mention him in such detail because wherever I went in Spain I was to meet either by accident or plan such men. They are scholars in a quiet way, enthusiasts for their city or their church, willing sharers of what they know. I shall not list them all as I go along; let Father Fernández of the Basílica de Santa Eulalia represent them, for they are one of the chief adornments of Spain, a country where education is not widespread and where the truly educated man is a kind of monument to himself.

Father Fernández was especially eager that I see two things: the pair of old and friendly chapels flanking the main altar, for they showed all the ancient grace of line and structure that I had missed in the cathedral at Badajoz, and the pulpit. At the latter Father Fernández wanted me to note particularly the bas-relief scenes depicting the saints

Servandus and Germanus, because he had a tale to relate about how these boys who he claimed were from a nearby village, but who were actually from Sevilla and Cádiz respectively, had attained sainthood. I did not hear what he said because I was attracted by a quite different saint carved on the pulpit, and since he is to form the leitmotif of this book and the subject of the last chapter, I had better introduce him properly at this first appearance.

He was Santiago (St. James), the patron of Spain. He was presented as a squat, sturdy man holding a staff, and a big-bellied gourd and wearing a large-brimmed hat decorated with cockleshells. He was a pilgrim, and judging from this first statue of many that we shall see, a doughty traveler prepared for whatever he met on the way. This was the famous Santiago. My heart warmed to meet him, for he had played an intimate role in the building of Spain.

Before I left Mérida I went to the two final buildings that help summarize its history. The first was a gangling, ugly fortress at the end of the Roman bridge. It was a square structure, much longer than a football field on each side, and had been built originally in 835 by Moors who had by then thrown out the Visigoths and established Islam as Spain's religion. In 1230 Christians again occupied the city, and the fortress passed into the hands of that para-military organization, the Knights of Santiago, who ruled it as their personal domain, a misrule which lasted to 1500.

The final building was something quite different. Atop a small hill at the south end of town stood a modern bullring, where bullfights were held occasionally in the summer, and normally I would not have bothered with what appeared to be an ordinary modern edifice that could be duplicated in any of a dozen small cities. The unique thing about the bullring in Mérida was that by accident it stood precisely upon the spot where in Roman times a great Mithraeum had stood, that mysterious and dark temple to the rock-born Persian god Mithras, who had killed the divine bull from whose body sprang all plants and animals on which man exists. In any Roman garrison town, and at its height Mérida housed 90,000 legionnaires, the Mithraeum was the most important temple, because in its subterranean caverns occurred the taurobolium, the ritual in which soldiers banded together to purchase a pristine bull, then huddled beneath a grating on which the bull was ceremoniously slaughtered so that the hot blood of the animal could run down over them, conferring invincibility in battle. How many bulls must have been slain in the Mithraeum of Mérida in those years when Spain was the manpower reservoir for the empire!

Today, on the spot where these sacrifices occurred, other bulls of that same breed are sacrificed for somewhat similar emotional reasons: their mysterious power confers immortality on those who fight them and on those who participate in the spectacle. I did not see any bullfights in Mérida because prior to my departure from home, Conrad Janis, son of the well-known New York art dealer, had taken me aside and said, 'The one thing you must see when you get to Spain is this new matador Curro Romero. Hottest thing to come along in many years. The greatest.' He spoke with a certain intensity. 'Curro cites the bull from a distance, seems to mesmerize him. Brings him forward very slowly, as if he were a lap dog, then wraps the bull around him to form a magnificent piece of sculpture. He's enchanting—and remember his name. Curro Romero. No matter how far you have to travel to see him, take my word. He'll be worth it.'

Young Janis was a hard-headed witness, not given to hyperbole, and if he spoke so highly of a new matador, the man merited attention, so I studied the posters that appeared in Mérida, but unfortunately Romero was not scheduled to fight and I did not see him performing at the Mithraeum, where bulls had been worshiped two thousand years ago.

I was now ready for my second expedition. East of Mérida, in a bleak landscape commanded by a low hill on which cowers a crumbling castle, stands the miserable village of Medellín, a collection of low houses strung along unpaved streets. In midsummer the heat is unbearable and the dust as copious as the flies. The church, whose thick old walls seem to be falling down, is closed most of the time, and the main plaza is as empty and unrewarding as any in Spain. Here is Extremadura at its most unforgiving, yet this little town is a shrine to which a few devoted travelers come each year from overseas to pay homage to one of the molders of history: Hernán Cortés, conqueror of Mexico and archetype of the conquistador. Born of poor parents and foreseeing no opportunity in a village like Medellín, where life was dominated by whatever family happened to occupy the castle on the hill, Cortés struck out for the New World, where his harsh Extremaduran training enabled him, with a bare handful of men like himself, to conquer the Aztec empire and deliver it to Spain. His achievement was heroic, for he brought not only the gold and silver mines to the king but also a new race of people to the Church.

In the weed-grown plaza of Medellín, above the spare white houses with their tiny windows and red-tiled roofs, stands one of Spain's uglier statues. Cortés in bronze looks over the land he deserted and he is brutal in his arrogance. His right leg is rigid and pushed back, so that his hip is high, while his left leg is cocked and resting on some vanquished object. His right arm, holding the baton of authority, is drawn back, while the left holds the unfurled flag of conquest. He wears an ornate helmet and his heavily bearded face is grim with determination. Behind his legs dangles the scabbard of a huge sword, and he might well be called 'The Spirit of Extremadura.'

The heavy base is adorned by shields bearing the local spellings of the names of those strange places where the emigrants from this town gave their lives: 'Méjico, Tebasco, Otumba, Tlascala.' At the site of the cottage from which he left for conquest stands the plaque: 'Here stood the house where Hernán Cortés was born in 1484.' (Most scholars say 1485.) But one looks in vain for the school established with the wealth he won, or the library, or the hospital, or the university, or even the factory set up for personal gain. The richness of Medellín, her men, was exported and nothing came back. No nation in history ever won so much wealth for itself in so short a time as did Spain in that half-century from 1520–1570, nor did any other nation ever retain so little for itself. Gold came by the shipload from Mexico and Peru, paused briefly in Spain and, having accomplished nothing, sped on to Italy and the Low Countries. Again and again in mournful repetition this will be the story of Extremadura, and when I see a defrauded village like Medellín, I am appalled at the bad deal Spain accepted in that crucial era. In fact, she ended up worse off than she had been when it began, for all the bright young men who might have developed Spain were gone. One might argue, I suppose, that the social system in Spain was such that if an energetic man like Cortés had stayed in Medellín he would have been submerged by the reactionary force of the castle on the hill, and that in escaping to Mexico he at least accomplished something. But whether that argument is valid or not, the fact is that when he succeeded in Mexico some of the fruits of his conquest should have filtered back to his homeland, but that did not happen and today Medellín stands as one of the most mournful places in Europe.

A brief explanation regarding historical and geographical names in this book. It is not just to refer to Spaniards by their English names. The Catholic Kings, whom we shall meet later, were not Ferdinand and Isabella; the great emperor who will dominate the next chapter was not Charles the Fifth; and the mighty and complex man who married Queen Mary of England was not Philip the Second. They were, respectively, Fernando and Isabel, Carlos V and Felipe II. I once put this problem to a tertulia of savants, whom we shall meet later in Madrid, and they, having faced the problem in their own writings, proposed a sensible rule: 'What name would you have used when speaking to the man face to face?' The conquistador we know as Cortez was surely Cortés. Therefore I shall use Spanish names, except in the case of Cristóbal Colón; after all, he was an Italian who did not get to Spain until 1484, when he was in his late thirties, so that Colón is as much a perversion of his name as is Columbus. The same rule will govern geographical names, which means Extremadura not Estremadura; Sevilla not Seville; Zaragoza not Saragossa; and La Coruña not Corunna; also, in Portugal, Lisboa and Porto. However, in the case of adjectives derived from place names, special problems arise. Strictly speaking, a man from Extremadura is an extremeño, a man from Madrid a madrileño, a man from Andalucía an andaluz, and one from the Basque Provinces a vascongado, all, you will notice, without capital letters. Some of these forms are so difficult to identify that I have preferred to use standard English forms, which in the cases cited above are Extremaduran,

Andalusian and Basque; but in Spanish cultural life the word madrileño carries with it such specific meanings that I shall keep it, with a capital letter.

At Trujillo, farther north, I had the good luck to know Don Ignacio Herguete García de Guadiana, grandson of a famous doctor who had served the last two kings of Spain. Himself a businessman in Madrid, his aunt lived in Trujillo, where she occupied one of the noble houses fronting the main plaza. Don Ignacio was a short man, handsome in appearance, and the most rapid speaker I have ever known; he seemed a volcano of ideas and I could understand why he had prospered in Madrid. He had a countryman's sense of humor and a deep appreciation of Spanish history. He also had three beautiful daughters, each destined to be taller than himself and representative of the young people of Spain.

'It's the plaza that counts,' he said as he finished showing me his aunt's house, with its tall ceilings and fifteenth-century adornment. 'Come out on the balcony and see the best small plaza in Spain.' We stood there for a long time as he pointed out the features of this architectural gem, so beautiful and compact that it ought to be preserved as a kind of museum. 'Up there, as a solid backdrop, the old castle. Marvelously preserved. You must imagine it in 1470, when a famous gentleman of these parts, Colonel Gonzalo Pizarro, used to prowl the streets of this town on romantic forays. He sired a chain of illegitimate sons, the most famous of which was Francisco, who left here to conquer Peru. In the background you see a chain of fortress churches, each a rough jewel rich in memories. Now look at how that side of the plaza is composed entirely of flights of stairs interlocking at different levels and at different angles. It's like music in brick. We used to block off the plaza and hold great bullfights, with people sitting on the flights of stairs. The pillared arcades which line the plaza are necessary in a place like Trujillo, because our noonday heat can be pretty strong. I know other towns have arcades too, but have you ever seen any that were more exactly suited to their setting than ours? That large house over there with the huge iron chain across the front? It dates back to the twelfth century and belonged to a noble family who befriended the Emperor Carlos Quinto, who stopped here on his way to marry Isabel of Portugal in 1526. The chain indicates that Carlos granted immunity from taxes to the owner. It belonged to the Orellana family, one of whom discovered the Amazon. My cousin owns it now, but this one over here is more famous. The big shield shows that it belonged to the Pizarro family. Long after the conquest of Peru, Pizarro's descendants took the title Marqués de la Conquista and that building was where they lived.

'The statue on horseback? You'll be interested in that. It's Pizarro in the uniform of a conquistador. It was sculpted by either the wife or the daughter, I've never known which, of the famous Spanish expert from New York, Archer M. Huntington.'

For some time Don Ignacio continued to point out the marvels of this little plaza; there were seven or eight old homes with Ionic pillars and severe ornament which were works of art, but I lost my heart to a small building tucked away in a corner beyond the Pizarro palace and now serving as the town hall. Its façade consisted of three tiers of arches, each of the same width but diminishing in height, so that the top ones were very wide and flat, the middle wide and fairly flat and the bottom wide and properly tall. The combination was unique and vivacious, and during all the time I was in Trujillo I kept looking back to that delightful building, one of the most charming things I saw in Spain.

The castle of Trujillo consists of great cubes of masonry formed into towers and long, blank walls. It is magnificently preserved and bleakly empty. Throughout Spain we shall see many castles; in fact, the nation has adopted as its tourist symbol the legendary 'Castle in Spain,' and there are many fine examples, but nowhere one properly fitted out as it was in the fifteenth century. They are always either empty, or being used for grain storage, or redecorated into hotels, or perverted altogether, but nowhere can one see a castle as a castle, and I think this regrettable. At Medina del Campo, where Isabel the Catholic died, there is one which could easily be restored, and at Almodóvar del Río, west of Córdoba, one of the finest castles in the world, but it will be no use to visit either. If I suffered any major disappointment in Spain, it was that a country which had such great treasure in castles did so little with them, for I believe that if one were properly restored, travelers would come great distances to see it, as a reminder of an age that has gone.

While sitting in the plaza one day I had an unexpected glimpse of rural life. Earlier I had noticed a truck fitted out with seats which seemed to contain an unusual number of passengers, but I had thought no more about it. Now this same truck drew up to the plaza and disgorged fourteen primly dressed rural people, including a bride and groom. There was no jollity in the group, although a wedding had apparently taken place and I supposed that the celebrants were headed for some kind of banquet, but they were very poor people, very poor indeed, and as they passed I saw that the groom was a sunburned, stolid, square-faced peasant of about forty and his bride a particularly ungainly spinster about five years older. I cannot recall ever having seen a woman so unlike a bride, so ill at ease in chiffon. As she passed my table I smiled, and she returned the stare of one who had worked very hard and had come not to a celebration but to a one-day respite, after which the work would resume. They were not headed for a banquet but to an ice cream stand, where the groom stood beside the clerk dispensing the cream and counted out his guests, one at a time, and each received a small ice cream sandwich costing four cents. That was fourteen times four or fifty-six cents for his wedding feast. The country people stood in the sunlight eating their sandwiches, then climbed back into the truck. 'Where are you from?' I asked one of the men. 'Medellín,' he said, 'we've come here to celebrate.' He then added gratuitously a statement the significance of which I would understand later: 'He came home from Germany to marry her.'

The most domineering building on the plaza was the Pizarro palace, an uninspired baroque construction whose baronial shield was unlike any I'd so far seen. Counting its pedestal, it was three stories high, covered the corner of its building and wrapped around a considerable expanse of each wall. 'I'm glad at least one of the conquistadors returned home to grandeur,' I said, but Don Ignacio corrected me. 'That wasn't the home of the Pizarro you know. It was the palace of Hernando, and his story is perhaps even more interesting.'

As I sat in the plaza talking with Don Ignacio and his friends I learned much about the Pizarros of Trujillo. Fiery old Gonzalo Pizarro, who lived to be ninety-eight according to legend, seventy-seven according to history, had been a hero at the conquest of Granada and had also served with that master Spanish soldier known simply as el Gran Capitán, who had disciplined Italy in the age of Columbus. Some claim that the old colonel lived in the castle that dominates Trujillo, others give him a smaller castle in the neighborhood, but the likelihood is that he lived in a house that formerly stood on the site of the present Pizarro mansion. Of one thing we are sure. Between wars he had a penchant for visiting his elderly Aunt Beatriz, who had taken orders in a convent, and after paying his respects to the old lady he liked to climb into bed with one or another of her maids. In this manner he had one son, Francisco, another Juan, and a third Gonzalo, each by a different mother, plus a daughter María, a second daughter Francisca, a third Graciana and a fourth Catalina, all by the mother of his third son. He also had two legitimate daughters and a son, Hernando Pizarro, a clever and prudent lad who wound up with the big house.

There being no future in the Pizarro family for seven bastards, the first two girls became nuns, the last two married men from the region and the three boys became soldiers. When Francisco led his pitiful little army to the conquest of Peru, the first thirty-seven positions were occupied by men from Trujillo, and the five top positions were held by himself, his legitimate brother, his two bastard brothers and a half brother who was the son of his mother but not of the old colonel. The remainder of his army of 167 were from other parts of Extremadura. The manner in which Pizarro led his clan to victory is a saga of heroism and brutality, for it seems inconceivable that so few Spaniards could conquer a land so vast and a civilization so advanced; perhaps only men trained in the hardness of Extremadura could have done it.

In the fighting, Pizarro and his illegitimate brothers were usually in the forefront, with legitimate Hernando in the rear looking after business

affairs, and in victory the same division of labor was observed. The Pizarro men were well advanced in years for such adventures, Francisco being in his fifties, but their sagacity offset their age and they became rulers of a vast part of South America. Then one by one the bastard brothers fell on evil times; there were betrayals and assassinations, so that it was only the canny bookkeeper Hernando who survived. His brother Francisco had married an Inca princess, Inés Yupanqui, and they had had a lovely daughter Francisca, who was Hernando's niece and whom he married. In 1629 the grandson of Hernando (and also the great-grandson of Francisco) applied for the right to inherit the title originally granted to the conquistador, and this was approved, so that the house on the square became the seat of the Marqués de la Conquista. To look at its massive shield is to recall the history of both Spain and Peru, for the statues which grace it represent Francisco, his wife Inés, their daughter Francisca and her husband, canny Hernando, who was also her uncle.

Judged from today's perspective, the conquistadors of Extremadura seem monstrous men devoid of pity, cruel destroyers of civilizations as splendid as their own, and as hard as the barren land from which they sprang. Their crimes against Aztec and Inca can be understood, for the conquistadors were few and the enemy were many; but the callous manner in which they betrayed their fellow Spaniards was appalling. Typical is the history of Pizarro: he did not try to defend his protector Balboa when the latter was hounded to execution by the venality of his friends, but later he found himself accused the way Balboa had been and was assassinated by his friends. To us he seems to have been false to every promise he made, and his offenses against common decency comprise a catalogue; but from Spanish historians the judgment is otherwise, largely because Pizarro did bring into the Christian Church thousands of pagan Indians. As Presbítero Clodoaldo Naranjo wrote in 1929:

> Pizarro was the genius brooding over a vast empire, subduing enemy pueblos, founding cities, organizing institutions, sacrificing his own interests, loving his soldiers as if they were his sons, exact in discipline, faithful to his king, yielding to no man in pundonor, to no man in just administration of the public welfare, to no man in the high religious propriety of his actions. With the Cross raised high he commenced his enterprise, with the Cross aloft he founded his cities, and with the Cross sealed with his own blood he gave up his life.

Louis Bertrand, leading French expert on Spain, in the fine historical summary he wrote with the Englishman Charles Petrie, supports the Spanish judgment:

> These conquerors have also been accused of destroying, through ignorance and barbarism, precious civilisations like those of the Aztecs and the Incas. This is making civilisation a laughing-stock. Let me repeat once more: those rudimentary civilisations have been overestimated in the most ridiculous

way, with the object of lowering and defaming the Spaniards and Catholicism, held as responsible for this alleged destruction. Can one regard as civilised the Peruvians, who did not know how to write, and who reckoned years and centuries by knots tied in cords; or the Mexicans, who used infantile hieroglyphics for history and chronology; peoples who had neither draught beasts nor beasts of burden, neither cows, cereals, nor vines; peoples who were not acquainted with the wheel, and had not reached the Iron Age; peoples among whom man was reduced to the role of a quadruped, whose bloody religion admitted human sacrifices, and who had markets for human flesh? If the conquistadors destroyed much and practised needless cruelties—destruction and cruelties which are as nothing beside those of modern war—they blazed the trail for the missionaries who saved for history everything that was essential in those embryonic civilisations, and but for whom we should know absolutely nothing about pre-Columbian America.

The final judgment, however, is the pragmatic one made by Mexico, whose citizens, remembering the brutalities of Cortés, still refuse to permit statues of the conquistador within their country.

My reflections were broken by Don Ignacio, who ran off to intercept a friend, whom he brought to our table. 'Dr. Ezequiel Pablos Gutiérrez,' he said, introducing a lively red-headed man in his early fifties. 'Medical graduate of Salamanca and alcalde [mayor] of Trujillo.'

'How do you like our city?' the alcalde asked, after introducing his wife and daughter.

'I've fallen in love with that little building over there.'

'The one with the three tiers of arches? That's my office.'

'You're lucky,' I said.

'We're thinking of converting it into a parador.'

'When it opens, reserve me a room for a month.' I could imagine nothing better than to have a room in such a parador and from it to survey the pageant that unfolded in the plaza.

'Right now we have other plans,' the alcalde said, 'so jump in the car.' He drove rather spiritedly along a country road leading east of Trujillo and soon we were in the heart of Extremadura, the low hills, the flat burning land and here and there the olive groves.

'I like this land very much,' I said. 'I think I must be an Extremaduran.'

'If a man is tough enough to love this land, he will never forget it,' the alcalde said. 'Never. I see men who go away. Big jobs in Madrid. Buenos Aires. But always they come back to the barren soil of Extremadura.'

We drove for a dozen miles, it seemed, and Señor Pablos turned down a lane and headed for what looked like an Arizona ranch house. 'This is my ranch,' he said. 'I raise fighting bulls here. Look!' On the horizon I saw a herd of perhaps thirty sleek black bulls. In the setting sun they were handsome beasts, watching us with disdain as they continued their feeding. Between us and them there appeared to be no fences, but they were so far away that they presented no danger. 'They never attack if they're kept in a group,' the mayor explained. 'Only when they're alone and insecure.'

Don Ignacio's car pulled up beside ours and we descended to enjoy a long, easy evening in the country. I noticed that Señora Pablos disappeared rather quickly, but her lively daughter and a young man who obviously hoped to marry her took charge of bringing horses for those who wanted to ride. Workmen from the ranch came with reports of what had been happening, and there seemed to be a good deal of muffled talking and arranging going on, centering upon a tall, very graceful young man who had joined the party, but I failed to detect what was under way.

After the sun had set, leaving a fine reddish haze over the ranch, the alcalde said, 'We're going to ride back up in the hills. Horses or automobiles.' At the head of our column rode six horsemen from the ranch, but before long they left us and cut across country toward the bulls we had seen earlier. Without disturbing the bulls they rode on to a fenced ravine where young heifers were grazing, and in a neat concentration of effort they cut out eight or ten and began herding them toward us. I still didn't understand what was happening, but at the top of the hill we came upon a clean, pure little building, totally whitewashed and built in the form of a circle. It was a private bullring maintained by the alcalde for testing his animals. The tall young man was a matador, and the herdsmen were in the process of driving three heifers into the corrals for testing with the cape.

It was almost dark when we finally took our places atop the wall of the ring, and the red of sunset had been replaced by a purple that already obscured the hills. Birds who normally nested in the ring flew gracefully back and forth as if trying to drive us away. The voices of the herdsmen were guttural as they reassured the heifers moving into the corrals, and the alcalde was excited as he directed the opening and closing of gates that shut each heifer off into its own small pen from which it would later catapult into the ring. It was so dark that I wondered if it would be possible to fight the heifers or even to see them.

A moment of silence, then the alcalde's reassuring voice, 'Open that one!' and as the gate to the ring swung open a heifer, from whom fighting bulls are reputed to inherit their bravery, erupted into the ring, raised a cloud of golden dust and began charging at anything that moved. Three workmen without capes provoked her by jumping out from behind barrier·, then ducking back in as she charged headlong at them. Finally the matador stepped out with his magenta-and-yellow cape, at which the heifer dashed as if it were a lifelong enemy. Three times, four times, five, she doubled back on herself and slashed at the offending cape. In the darkness she seemed like a mysterious thunderbolt hurtling across space, and I could understand why it was popularly said that 'the cow determines the bull.' Such fury, if applied to a full-grown bull of a thousand pounds, with widespread horns and powerful neck, could make a formidable enemy.

The darkness deepened rapidly, so that the moving figures on the sand, bound together by a swirling cape, became ghostlike and the shadowy matador as strange a creature as the animal he was fighting. Birds, startled by the unfamiliar scene, now began to cry, and from behind the barrier the foreman of the work crew called out, 'That's enough.' The matador withdrew; a gate was opened; the heifer leaped at something that moved beyond the gate; the gate closed and the arena was still.

'Shall we let in another?' the alcalde called down.

'We can't see to cape it,' the matador called back.

'We'll let her run through anyway,' the alcalde shouted, and the ropes were pulled to make the various doors swing open. A heifer, larger than the first, ripped into the arena; obviously she could see in darkness better than the men opposing her, for within a few seconds she had bowled over three men, one after the other, and had ripped the cape out of the matador's hand. He prudently fled behind the barrier and called, 'Get her out of here. She has radar.' The gates swung open and the little cyclone swept majestically from sight, having defended her terrain against all comers. The ring was closed down and the birds settled into the nests of which we had deprived them.

When the matador joined us he said, 'I'd like to have seen that last one in daylight. She charged like a thunderbolt.'

'She comes from a good strain,' the alcalde said proudly, and we trailed back from the testing plaza to the ranch house, where Señora Pablos had laid out a vast country-style supper lit with torches, and under the starry Extremaduran sky we began to eat the crisp salad, the rugged potato omelette and something I was not often to taste in Spain, a good cheese. It was tangy and of excellent texture, and the men asked for seconds and I for thirds. 'Where did you find such a good cheese?' I asked, and the alcalde's wife replied, 'I make it. I came from a farm family and we always had good cheese.' The night grew cooler, so the workmen started a fire and we finished our supper with sparks flying into the air and transforming themselves into stars. I took this opportunity to get an expert opinion from the matador. 'In New York a young man told me there was a new star in bullfighting, Curro Romero. Is he any good?'

Matadors are notoriously envious, but this one said, 'You should go to much pains to see Romero, for he is special. He is very slow with the cape, like a guitarist who is sure of himself and doesn't have to stamp and whistle. At the end of the fight he is a genius, wrapping the bull around him as if it was a blanket. Never have you seen anything so slow. If you're going toward Sevilla, watch out for him. He's worth seeing.'

We then spoke of Trujillo during the various wars of succession and of how it so often backed the wrong contender, and of the conquistadors wandering across the Americas, and the alcalde repeated a prediction from Clodoaldo Naranjo's local history. 'I am not afraid to assert, almost prophetically, that the day is not far distant when the greater part of America will feel for Trujillo the same veneration that in its religious life it feels for those spots which were the birthplaces of messiahs and prophets.'

Thus ended my three casual expeditions out of Badajoz: to Mérida and its Romans, to Medellín and Cortés, and to Trujillo and its Pizarros. Now the obligatory trip was to begin and I headed south to the little town with the lovely name, Jerez de los Caballeros. In Spain, as in the United States, where we have several Portlands and many Springfields, names of towns are apt to be repeated in the various provinces, so some kind of distinguishing phrase is frequently added. Thus there is the great Jerez of the wine industry; it lies south of Sevilla on the old Christian-Muslim frontier and is called Jerez de la Frontera; and there is Jerez de los Caballeros on a hill commanding a large section of the Extremaduran plains. Who were the knights of the name? Originally they were a band of murderously tough Knights Templars who owned the city and were responsible for guarding the town against Islam; in the last chapter of this book, when visiting a similar city in the north, we shall learn what happened to these unfortunate Templars. When they vanished the rugged little city passed into the ownership of the Knights of Santiago, who used it as an anchor in their assaults on the infidel. Jerez de los Caballeros was an embattled city, and when I first saw its towers from a creaking autobus bouncing over dusty, unpaved roads, it seemed like a haven whose protection I would enjoy, but as the bus crawled closer I began to have doubts, yet it was imperative that I visit Jerez, for I was drawn there by a kind of pilgrimage.

The only thing I knew about Jerez came from a travel book written by an Englishwoman. She had had a miserable time, finding nothing to commend, but even her savage condemnation of the place—poor food, inhospitable people, bad beds, foul climate—had contained a whisper of attraction, as if to say, 'If you want to see Spain at its worst, test yourself on Jerez de los Caballeros.' English writers have a particular knack for describing a strange place in terms that are both repellent and attractive, especially when they write about Spain.

It is difficult to explain why the best writing on Spain has usually been done by Englishmen, but that seems to be the case. I have sometimes thought that it was because the sherry trade required Englishmen to live in Spain, but I could find no one directly connected with that trade who had written with any charm of the peninsula. I've also suspected that it might be the Englishman's intuitive yearning for the sun which accounted for his preoccupation with Spain, but that doesn't seem to stand inspection either. Whatever the reason, if you want good reading on Spain, read the English.

Richard Ford's classic account remains unsurpassed. It came into being because Ford, son of the man who created London's mounted police, married the daughter of the Earl of Essex and gained thereby a yearly income and a sickly wife whose doctor ordered her to travel in a warmer climate. In 1830 Ford took her to Spain, where they lived for three years and where she regained her health.

As a result of this stay, Ford acquired an immense library on Spain, and in 1839 when the London publisher John Murray happened to remark that he was looking for a guidebook on Spain, Ford volunteered. Five years later he delivered the manuscript for his famous *Handbook for Travellers in Spain,* but after it was printed in 1845 Murray grew apprehensive that it was too outspoken and suppressed it. Later an expurgated version was published and it became a classic. Finally, in 1846, a supplementary volume titled *Gatherings from Spain* was issued, and the two taken together are the foundation of Ford's reputation.

I prefer George Borrow's strange narrative *The Bible in Spain,* in which he recounts his experiences in 1836–1840 as an itinerant peddler of Bibles. As the book's editor said: 'It was in an atmosphere of hatred, intrigue and adventure that Borrow lived, striving manfully to print and propagate an alien gospel among the fanatical Spaniards.' It is a robust book, opinionated, specialized and often infuriating. It is written in an apocalyptic style which recalls Doughty's similar writing on Arabia and remains indispensable for anyone wanting to dig below the surface into Spanish matters, but I would think that Catholics might find it irritating. Two facts about the book interest me. Borrow too saw Spain first at Finisterre: 'On the morning of the 10th of November, 1835, I found myself off the coast of Galicia, whose lofty mountains, gilded by the rising sun, presented a magnificent appearance.' And he too started his journey at Badajoz, on January 5, 1836: 'In a moment I was on Spanish soil, and having flung the beggar a small piece of silver, I cried in ecstasy, "Santiago y cierra España!"' (This is the traditional battle cry of the nation. Its literal translation is 'St. James and close Spain.' Its meaning is 'Help us, Santiago, and let's go, Spaniards, in closed ranks.') Then Borrow adds: 'I was now at Badajoz in Spain, a country which for the next four years was destined to be the scene of my labors. The neighborhood of Badajoz did not prepossess me much in favor of the country which I had just entered.'

Ford and Borrow are classics, but they are garrulous. For a highly condensed view of Spain one can do no better than V. S. Pritchett *The Spanish Temper* (1954). It requires only a few hours to read but such high specific gravity as to provide enough hard material to keep mind working for weeks. Constantly Pritchett throws out challenging observations: 'The very day when Fernando VII closed the university Sevilla, he opened a school for bullfighters there.' 'Spaniards are disciples of Seneca, natural stoics who bear and forbear.' 'If El Greco painted out of the day and the land, Goya paints out of the night.' 'It was a Spaniard who founded the first order of Commissars in Europe, the Society of Jesus (Jesuits).'

For the essential romanticism of Spain, I suppose one should rely upon Somerset Maugham's sardonic *Don Fernando* (1935), for although the great storyteller never wrote a novel about Spain, it haunted his life, and it was to this country that his alter ego Philip Carey in *Of Human Bondage* dreamed of escaping, a dream which was truncated by his involvement with Mildred. The essays in *Don Fernando* are exasperating, and some of them seem unduly precious, but they are fun and throw such an oblique light on Spain that the reader will often find himself discovering a new set of meaningful shadows.

A good analysis of Spanish character is Havelock Ellis' *The Soul of Spain* (1908). Neither systematic nor complete, the little book contains so much wry comment and so many particular judgments that it constitutes one of the best approaches to matters Spanish. On a recent rereading of this pivotal work I was impressed by something that had escaped me the first two times around. Ellis, like me, had made his basic acquaintance with Spain not through the mother country but through the colonies, in his case Peru. He thus saw the peninsula reflected, as it were, in the shield of Theseus, and apparently this is a good way to approach Spain, for then certain fundamental characteristics stand forth which might otherwise be missed. At any rate, Ellis loved Spain and wrote of it with deep affection, whereas many who approach it more directly fail to do either.

If the reader finds my account too favorable to Spain, I direct him to *Silk Hats and No Breakfast* (1957) by Honor Tracy, in which this witty Irish woman presents a bittersweet account of her travels in 1955. She saw little that was not contemptible and expressed her contempt by citing one pejorative incident after another. No aspect of Spanish life was sacred and none was accorded charity. It is an old-fashioned book in that everything foreign is held up to ridicule, and I would suppose that Spaniards despise it.

Finally, since the Spanish Civil War of 1936–1939 was a major historical event of the first half of the twentieth century and since I am not going to belabor it, I recommend two books: for the background, Gerald Brenan's *The Spanish Labyrinth* (1943), and for the war itself, Hugh Thomas' *The Spanish Civil War* (1961). With typical British impersonality and with a high regard for truth, Thomas picks his way magisterially through the debris of this anguished period to produce what will long be the classic account of the war. It seems to me that he writes the general truth concerning these sad events, and the fact that his book has been unofficially adopted by the Spanish people as the legitimate narrative of the war signifies that the winners at least do not consider it offensively wrong.

For light reading, and as an antidote to the acerb quality of Honor Tracy's work, one could profitably look into H. V. Morton's *A Stranger in*

Spain (1955), in which this professional traveler relates Spanish history to events occurring simultaneously in England. This presupposes the hypothesis that real history was occurring in England, but that interesting by-plays were occurring at the same time in Spain. This makes England the universal measuring stick, but since Americans tend to know English history better than they do American, and certainly better than Spanish, there is an advantage to Morton's system:

> I never really grasped what a good claim Philip II had to the English throne. I suppose a Catholic genealogist at the time of the Armada would have infinitely preferred his blood-relationship with the House of Lancaster to Elizabeth's tenuous Tudor connexion with the House of York; and perhaps had the Armada been invincible we might have heard a great deal about this. . . .
>
> John of Gaunt's adventures in Spain are an odd and fascinating little chapter in Anglo-Spanish history. . . . John of Gaunt, whose first wife was dead, married Constance of Castile, while his brother, Edmund of Langley, married her sister Isabel. In twelve years' time John of Gaunt and Constance took an English army to Spain to claim the throne of Castile, though the expedition ended not in war but in wedding bells. They gave up all claim to the throne upon the marriage of their daughter Catherine to Henry III of Castile. This is the Catherine who is buried in Toledo, a woman who, as a little girl, lived in the Savoy and saw the Strand in those days when London was
>
> > . . . *small and white and clean,*
> > *The clear Thames bordered by its gardens green.*
>
> She knew Geoffrey Chaucer, who must have taken her on his knee many a time, and she probably had as governess that much-maligned woman, Catherine Swynford, Chaucer's sister-in-law and her father's mistress. She would have remembered the turmoil of Wat Tyler's rebellion and the sacking of her father's place in the Strand. . . .
>
> Catherine could not have had a happy life in Spain. Her husband was an invalid, and like so many queens of Spain she was left with an infant heir and lived in terror that he might be taken away from her. But he was not. He became John II of Castile and the father of Spain's greatest queen, Isabel the Catholic. It is interesting to think that Isabel's grandmother was the daughter of John of Gaunt. . . .
>
> Important as this marriage was, it is surpassed in interest by that of Catherine's younger sister, the flighty Isabel, with John of Gaunt's younger brother, Edmund of Langley. They became the ancestors of Edward IV, Edward V, Richard III and Elizabeth of York, who was eagerly married by Henry VII to bolster up his weak claim to the throne by linking himself with the House of York. So Spanish blood, fairly thin by this time no doubt, passed to Henry VIII and Elizabeth.

Not widely known is the fact that one of the first English writers to deal with Spain was Samuel Pepys, who made an official navy trip to Tangier in 1683–1684 and wrote a secret report of the matter when he got home. His *Tangier Report* was not distributed generally until 1935, when it appeared in the official papers of the Navy Records Society, and the following excerpts will explain why:

A Spaniard says, 'Go with God' and not 'God go with you.'

Rather a hole in a suit than a patch.

Won't piss in the streets, but will against your door.

They shit in pots and wipe their arses with linen cloths.

The laboring Spaniard eats five meals a day. And the greater part of Spain eat nothing but what they make of water, oil, salt, vinegar, garlic and bread, which last is the foundation of all.

Wear spectacles abroad, and some only to seem readers.

You may starve and tax them as you please so you do not beat them, but give them good words; while we English fill our bellies and you can do or say what you will to us.

The bus dropped me at the edge of Jerez de los Caballeros and I walked up Avenida José Antonio toward the central plaza, which was as ugly as the one in Badajoz. There I made inquiries, and at first no one knew what I was talking about and I was afraid that my long pilgrimage was to be fruitless, but finally a bartender understood and said, 'Cross the plaza, pass the bank and look for Calle Capitán Cortés.'

'It isn't Cortés I'm looking for,' I explained.

'You go to house Number 10. That's it.'

I followed his directions and found the Calle Cortés to be narrow, attractive and clean, but there was no indication that what I was seeking might lie in such a street. I wandered along, looking at the houses, which seemed like a row of individual forts, until I came to Number 10. It was low, smaller than its neighbors, and bore no sign or distinguishing marks except that it was immaculately clean, having been freshly whitewashed. I doubted that this could be the house I sought, so I asked a woman who was passing by. She was most charming, and with a reassuring smile said, 'This is it. You norteamericanos never believe it, but this is it. You must be the fiftieth I've told this year.' She banged on the red door, pushed it open and called, 'Señora Ordóñez. Visitor from América del Norte.'

A very old woman, with gray hair and all her teeth, came to the door, saying softly, 'Come in. It is my pleasure.'

She led me into a small entranceway decorated with colored photographs of Egypt taken from an air-line calendar, and stopped before a dark alcove the size of a closet. 'He was born in that corner, the great Vasco Núñez, who discovered your Pacific Ocean.'

'You mean Balboa?'

'If you want to call him that.'

I wished to stay in the alcove to pay my respects to the first European to find the ocean which had meant so much to me, but she insisted that I see her kitchen, a delightful room with open beams, rickety doors, windows that didn't quite fit, stairways built of uneven stones and a characteristic that I had read about but had never seen: the whole had been whitewashed so many times—say twice a year for five hundred years—the limestone had built up to such thickness that all corners were conquered by a softly undulating cocoon of white stone. The doorjambs were rounded; the crevices where upper walls met the floors had become delicate quarter-circles, and nowhere in this room could I see a harsh edge or a straight line, as if much living had smoothed out the roughness. At three spots in the white room flowers stood, more brilliant than French wallpaper, and outside in a very small garden I could see where the old lady kept two fig trees, an arbor of grapes and six or seven hens.

The house looked as if it had been built to illustrate a child's fairy tale, but Ana Ordóñez assured me it had long served as an ordinary home. 'My husband and I worked on a farm, but about forty years ago we decided to move into town and bought this place. At the time we didn't know it was the house in which Núñez was born.' I was to find that in Jerez there was no Balboa, the name we know him by, but there was a Núñez, which was his official name. 'After we had been here a while . . . remember this was forty years ago when there weren't so many travelers. Well, people began to stop by to see where Núñez was born. People on this street remembered the family, and this tiny alcove is where the birth took place. No, I charge nothing to see it. I've had a good life and my children watch out for me. I am honored to mind the house where Núñez lived.'

I looked again at the alcove, thinking of my debt to this poverty-stricken man of Jerez who had left Extremadura, tried to make a go of it in the islands of the New World, but found himself so deeply in debt that he had to smuggle himself to the mainland at Panama in a cask of provisions. There his fortunes improved, for his quick ear caught two bits of rumor: beyond the mountains swept a vast ocean not yet seen by white men, and far to the south along the shores of that ocean lay a land called Peru, heavy with gold. Due solely to the determination and courage of Balboa, an expedition forced its way through the jungle to the crest of the mountains and from there looked down on the Pacific. Among the soldiers was Francisco Pizarro, who first heard of Peru from Balboa.

On his return to the Atlantic side Balboa dispatched enthusiastic reports back to Spain, plus samples of his booty. His promise of much gold excited the home government and he was made admiral of the South Sea, but he was a driving man who aroused the envy of others, and before long his superiors grew bitter over his grandiose plans for conquering Peru. The governor of Panama waited and watched and one day trapped him. A drumhead court-martial convicted him of treason, not against Spain but against the local governor. With no show of justice, Balboa was sentenced to death. Like a common criminal he was publicly beheaded in 1517, but his enthusiasm for Peru found refuge in the mind of Pizarro.

In spite of this mournful history, Balboa's birthplace caused me to chuckle over a bit of delightful nonsense that occurred years ago when I was a student in Scotland. One of the first newspaper columnists, an Englishman with an irreverent sense of humor, announced a poetry contest for schoolboys. He said that he had heard so much adverse comment on boys of the current generation, he wanted to show the people of Britain that some at least were interested in things of the mind. For weeks he reported the contest daily, with clergymen praising his effort and judges saying that this was the sort of thing Britain needed. Finally the winner was announced, somebody like Malcolm McGrory from a rural school, and his poem was printed with pride:

> Much have I travelled in the realms of gold,
> And many goodly states and kingdoms seen;
> Round many western islands have I been
> Which bards in fealty to Apollo hold.
> Oft of one wide expanse had I been told
> That deep-browed Homer ruled as his demesne;
> Yet did I never breathe its pure serene
> Till I heard Chapman speak out loud and bold:
>
> Then felt I like some watcher of the skies
> When a new planet swims into his ken;
> Or like stout Cortez when with eagle eyes
> He stared at the Pacific—and all his men
> Looked at each other with a wild surmise—
> Silent, upon a peak in Darien.

The columnist ended with a condescending paragraph in which he said that this poem, uneven though it was, showed promise for a boy of fourteen and that if young McGrory applied himself he might one day be entitled to call himself poet.

Well, the roof fell in. From all over the British Isles people wrote in, pointing out that Malcolm McGrory had filched his prize-winning sonnet right out of the collected works of John Keats. The columnist, as I remember, played it straight and tried to place the blame for this fiasco on the judges, who should have known better than to be hoodwinked in this way. He was then off for another dozen columns bewailing the lack of honor in the younger generation, and especially in Malcolm McGrory, who would try to fob off onto the British public, many of whom read books, a cheap theft of this sort. He predicted a very bad end for Malcolm.

It is strange that Keats should have immortalized the wrong man, so

With inherent grace this Spanish family poses naturally
before their cracked and ancient oven.
The boys will probably go to Germany.

that even in death Vasco Núñez was cheated. In Jerez de los Caballeros, I could find no statue to him, nor to the town's other outstanding conquistador, Hernando de Soto. (The nearby town of Barcarrota claims De Soto, but this is an error.) There was, however, a Plaza Vasco Núñez, an odd-shaped square at the end of Avenida José Antonio, marked only by a watering trough for horses and a large metallic sign: Coca-Cola.

Friends came to Jerez to drive me back to Badajoz, and as we were passing through a cork forest, whose silence was broken only when a herd of pigs, grubbing for acorns, grunted at us, we came to a clearing which housed a small village, from which two members of the Guardia Civil ran out to halt us. Wondering what law we had broken, we pulled to the side of the road.

'What's wrong?' the driver asked.

The Benemérita pointed to where four villagers were bearing the inert body of a man. 'He fell from the church steeple,' a guardia said. 'He was cleaning it. May God have mercy on him.'

'What do you wish of us?'

'Turn the car around. We've got to take him to Jerez.' To me, the man seemed quite dead, but the second guardia put his hand over the man's heart and said, 'He's still alive.'

Since the two guardia would not split up, it was arranged that they would occupy the back of the car with the unconscious body and that the man's wife would ride in front. That meant that I would have to wait in the village until the car returned, and this I volunteered to do, so the car sped back down the road to Jerez and I was left alone with a group of disturbed villagers.

A tall, very thin man in his late forties and his almost equally tall wife, also thin, suggested that I come to their house in the village and wait there. They led me about a quarter of a mile from the road, accompanied by eight or ten villagers, and took me to an immaculate cottage with a dirt floor, one table, a rope bed and one chair. Although I offered the wife the chair, I was forced to take it, and while I waited there for a couple of hours the villagers sat on the floor about me and we talked of many things.

'Is América del Norte really as rich as they say?'

'We have many poor people. And even those who are not poor have to work hard.'

'As poor as Spain?'

'Our worst, yes. Farmers like you, it's better in America.'

'Can black men live in América del Norte wherever they want?'

'No, but things are getting better.'

'Are there also Catholics in América del Norte?'

'Many. In the little town where I live there are many.'

They sent for a neighbor who had some cigarettes and he arrived to offer me one, very formally, and when I said I didn't smoke, he carefully folded back the top of his pack and returned it to his pocket. Another neighbor brought a bottle of wine and two badly chipped glasses and he and I had a drink.

'How much a day do you make in the fields?' I asked, because it was obvious that these people wanted to talk about important things.

'Forty pesetas a day.' (Sixty-seven cents)

'For grown men?'

'Yes.' They told me that they stripped cork for the man I had watched in the Casino de Badajoz, Don Pedro Pérez Montilla, and they spoke well of him. 'He has three automobiles,' they said, forming their hands into fists, about a foot apart, and moving their elbows sharply up and down to simulate a chauffeur driving a car.

'How do you feed yourselves? Clothe yourselves?'

'The credit goes to our wives.' The man who said this nodded slightly, not to his own wife but toward the mistress of this house, and when I looked at her grave, dark face I could better understand that wedding feast at Trujillo, when the rural bridegroom had spent fifty-six cents, most of a day's income, to honor his stalwart bride with ice cream sandwiches.

The men and women who sat with me in the bare kitchen were a handsome lot, rich in gracia. Their faces were strong and deeply lined, but their eyes shone with humor. Their rough corduroy clothes were cleaner than one would have thought possible under the circumstances. I recalled the list of prices I had collected at the stores in Badajoz, and now, against a wage of sixty-seven cents a day for the head of a family, they seemed appallingly high. A man's suit of clothes for thirty-seven dollars. That would be two months' wages, and no wonder the men about me wore homespun.

Then as I looked into the sober faces of the men who worried about their friend who had fallen from the steeple, I had the sensation that I was back in that farmhouse which I had visited in Teruel, more than thirty years before, and it was apparent that no matter how much urban Spain had prospered in the intervening decades, little wealth had filtered down to the farms. I could not recall any land other than India where the discrepancy between the rich and the poor was so great. Don Pedro, who owned the cork forest in which these men worked, drove three cars but his workmen earned sixty-seven cents a day. In Badajoz, during the nightly paseo, I had seen hundreds of people dressed as well as my neighbors dressed in Pennsylvania, but in no part of America could I find farmers living at the miserable level that these Spanish farmers lived. It was a miracle, I thought, that Spain maintained its tranquillity when such conditions prevailed, and I could understand why the Guardia Civil patrolled the villages.

'Is it true,' one of the villagers asked, 'that in América del Norte you eat corn?'

I nodded, and they burst into laughter. 'We grow corn . . . for pigs.' They laughed again and asked if it were the same kind of corn. I nodded, for in the fields of Extremadura I'd seen some corn which if eaten young would have been as good as what we ate at home. 'Corn is for pigs and Mexicans,' they said, and I wondered if that was why Spain refused this food. When the conquistadors invaded Mexico they found the Indians eating tortillas, and in their pride, turned their backs on this major source of food. Viva yo.

'How many people live in your village?' I asked.

This was the question that unlocked the floodgates of communication, for there was much they wanted to tell me. Forty years ago, when the speakers were young . . . 'we had more than two hundred people here. You can see the church, it's rather fine. But in recent years it's been impossible to live in Extremadura. The wages are just too low. So, many of our young men go to Germany and work there for six or seven years.'

'How many from this village?'

The doleful litany began. 'My two sons, and the son of Gómez, and her two cousins, and the priest's nephew.'

I judged there must have been about fifty men of the village absent. 'How many would you say?' I asked again.

'Well, maybe sixty.'

A woman interrupted. 'But you understand, they're not all in Germany. A good many have gone to Barcelona.'

At this name the group grew silent, as if it were a worse fate to go to the Spanish city of Barcelona than to the German city of Düsseldorf. A woman explained why. 'When our men go to Germany we know they'll come back. In Germany they find no Catholics, no girls to marry. So as they work they remember life back home, some girl in this village. And they come home.'

'Barcelona?'

'It's Spain,' a man said. 'My younger brother went to Barcelona. He found a girl there. Life in Barcelona . . .'

He spoke of the city as if it held the Holy Grail. 'I tell you,' another villager said, 'in Barcelona it's as good as it is in New York. He was there one week and found a job at a hotel on the Costa Brava. Tourists. Now he speaks French . . . my brother.'

'It would be a lot better,' his wife said, reflecting a family argument, 'if we could all go to Barcelona.'

'Do your men like Germany?' I asked.

The villagers pointed to a man who had spent five years there, and he did not speak, but he did make three most informative gestures which I was to see often. With his right hand he fed himself, signifying, 'In Germany you eat well.' With the thumb and forefinger of his right hand he felt the cloth of his shirt, meaning, 'In Germany you can dress decently.'

And with two hands he made the sign of a man driving an automobile. These were the universal comments on Germany.

'You mean to say you had an automobile in Germany?' The man nodded. 'Then why did you come back to Extremadura?' The man blushed and pointed with his head toward his wife.

'Aren't your women allowed to go to Germany, too?'

I didn't understand the answer to this question and my Spanish was not good enough to pursue the nuances. Either the Spanish government would not allow women to go or the pressure of Spanish rural society was so great that any female who dared to leave was considered as good as dead. From what happened next I suppose it was the latter, for the villagers, seeing that it was going to be some time before my car returned, took me on a tour of their village, and I heard a lament that I was to hear often in rural Spain. 'This house is closed. They went to Barcelona.' Or, 'This house is closed. The sons went to Germany.' One man said, 'I used to work in Jerez de los Caballeros. There were twenty thousand people there then. Now there's only fourteen thousand. You must have seen the shuttered houses.'

They were taking me to the church from whose steeple the injured man had fallen, and on the rude oaken door of the church I read a poster in which some bishop of the diocese had long ago laid down the rules which were to govern local life:

1. Women shall not appear on the streets of this village with dresses that are too tight in those places which provoke the evil passions of men.
2. They must never wear dresses that are too short.
3. They must be particularly careful not to wear dresses that are low-cut in front.
4. It is shameful for women to walk in the streets with short sleeves.
5. Every woman who appears on the streets must wear stockings.
6. Women must not wear transparent or network cloth over those parts which decency requires to be covered.
7. At the age of twelve girls must begin to wear dresses that reach to the knee, and stockings at all times.
8. Little boys must not appear in the streets with their upper legs bare.
9. Girls must never walk in out-of-the-way places because to do so is both immoral and dangerous.
10. No decent woman or girl is ever seen on a bicycle.
11. No decent woman is ever seen wearing trousers.
12. What they call in the cities 'modern dancing' is strictly forbidden.

July 11, 1943

The church was not open because with the sharp decline in population it was no longer possible to provide a full-time priest. In fact, I judged from what I was told here and elsewhere that priests were in rather short

supply. On one side of the church, carved deeply into the stones of the wall and whitewashed, was the name JOSE ANTONIO.

Wherever we went in that village the story was the same: 'He went to Germany,' and I reflected that in the Golden Age of Spain the men of Extremadura had gone out to Mexico and Peru to build civilizations there, and none of their work had profited Spain; now their descendants were leaving to build up Germany, not Spain, and the creative energy of the land was once more being perverted.

'No,' a woman reproved me when I raised this question, 'the men do send home money. There are many of us who would die if it were not for the money from Germany. It's not all loss.'

As she said this I came upon that sign which had blossomed across Spain in recent months. The Franco government, always alert to remind Spaniards of their blessings, had pasted on fifty thousand vacant walls posters reading: 'Twenty-five years of peace.' I pointed to the sign, and a man said, 'He's the only leader in the world who can say that to his people. He did bring us a quarter of a century of peace.'

Back in Badajoz, I sought out the structure which for a few weeks in 1936 focused the eyes of the world upon this city. I was told that plans were under way to tear it down and I trust this will be done, for while it stands it is a monument to evil. If you go to the cathedral and stand at the main entrance, you will see off to one side the narrow and lovely Calle de Ramón Albarrán. 'Who was he?' I asked half a dozen men from Badajoz. No one knew, but several said, 'Oh, that was a family well known in these parts.' If you follow this street, looking at the fine doorways on either side with their marble stoops which women wash each morning, you will pass a neat barbershop and then the impressive entrance to the College of Pharmacy, and at the far end, where the street terminates before a massive red building, you will find yourself facing the bullring. It is this building that is the terror and shame of Badajoz.

Today it is simply another plaza de toros, round in shape and with a billboard from which hangs a tattered poster announcing the latest motion picture to be shown inside: Gregory Peck, Ann Blyth and Anthony Quinn in *El mundo en sus manos*. Spanish is defective in that in such a construction you don't know in whose hands the world is, because *su* stands for his, her, its, your, their or one's, and you must guess which. The interior is rather attractive, in a nineteenth-century sort of way, for the tiers of seats are made of rough stone and the slender columns supporting the partial roof are of a handsome ironwork, with intricate grillwork serving as capitals. On the grayish yellow sand, where the bull would normally be fought, stands a forest of folding metal chairs facing a very large improvised screen for outdoor movies. A rusty yellow band of paint runs around the wooden barrier that encloses the fighting area, while off in the distance to the left rises a tall new office building of many floors.

Bullring at Badajoz.

America started here.

On the morning of August 15, 1936, this bullring served as the setting for one of the early climaxes of the Spanish Civil War. At the outbreak of the rebellion of General Franco's rightist army forces against the legally constituted Republic, Badajoz like most of Extremadura had come out in defense of the Republic, but General Franco's disciplined army units, beefed up with crack Moorish troops from Africa, swept northward along the Portuguese border, ducking into sanctuary in Portugal when necessary, and by a flanking movement isolated Badajoz and defeated the Republicans. The Spanish war now faced its first public test: How would the Franco forces, when the world was watching, deal with the citizens of a city that had surrendered after fighting in defense of the government?

On that morning of August 15 Moorish troops swept through the city, arresting any men suspected of having aided the government, and many old grudges were paid off. Estimates vary as to the number of prisoners thus collected, but Jay Allen, of the Chicago *Tribune,* who reached the city some days later, says that after interrogating as many witnesses as possible he reached the conclusion that there must have been about eighteen hundred, including a fair number of women. They were herded into the ugly plaza, marched past the cathedral doors and chased down the Calle de Ramón Albarrán, where spectators on balconies jeered at them as they scurried by. Into the bullring they were herded while the seats in the stands filled with citizens eager to see what was going to happen to their neighbors. Then soldiers of the rebellion, infuriated by reports of atrocities which government troops were supposed to have committed against captured rebels, turned their machine guns on the mass of prisoners and shot them down as they huddled against the yellow striped fence. Those who tried to escape by running were shot in the way partridge and deer are potted in the field. Of the massacre Allen said, 'There is more blood than you would think in eighteen hundred bodies.'

Later researchers, working upon a matter which has always been shrouded in mystery and shame, concluded that the figure given by Allen was too high. They pointed out that he did not reach Badajoz until August 23, eight days after the massacre, and that he relied only on the reports of excited and confused witnesses, whose estimates would have to be guesswork. It is now believed that the number who so died may not have been above four hundred, and some question the event altogether. I have never spoken to a man who would admit that he had been in the bullring that day, but once at a café in Sevilla I was shown a man who admitted to having been there. I asked if I could speak with him, and friends approached him, but he stared at me across the tables and shook his head no. Men in the bar said, 'He told us it was the worst thing a man could see on earth.'

I cannot permit the bullring at Badajoz to be my last memory of Extremadura. I left the city one morning for a trip to Alburquerque, with the blazing sun overhead in an unmarked sky. There seemed no living thing abroad, neither insects nor birds nor lizards, and when I was thinking that this was a man's land and that if a young Norwegian or Englishman or American really wanted to test himself he should leave Cádiz in July and proceed slowly up through Extremadura to Salamanca, and then he would know whether he was man enough to challenge Spain, I saw across the drought-stricken field an old man riding on a two-wheeled cart behind a slow-moving horse. I hailed him and asked how things were, and he said, 'I'm getting by. My two sons are in Germany. But they'll come back. Men always come back to Extremadura.'

FOLLOWING PAGE:
The passion of Spain.

III

TOLEDO

OCEANO
ATLANTICO

MILES
0   100

Barcelona

Madrid

SIERRA DE GREDOS
Yuste   Talavera de la Reina
             Toledo
Río Tajo   Orgaz

Guadalupe

Lisboa

Sevilla

Ceuta   MAR MEDITERRANEO

The city of Toledo, a bejeweled museum set within walls, is a glorious monument and the spiritual capital of Spain; but it is also Spanish tourism at its worst. Anyone who remains in this city overnight is out of his mind, and I was scheduled to stay four weeks.

I was checked into a ratty hotel whose desk crew must have been trained in the gorilla cage of a second-rate zoo, except that if they had treated animals as they did humans, some society would have prosecuted them. Throwing a key at me they snarled, 'Room 210.' They should have said, 'Cell 210.'

It was cramped, poorly designed and hot. These inconveniences I could have adjusted to, but in addition it was noisy. In fact, it was so noisy that the clang of ordinary traffic, such as I had heard at Badajoz, was like the muted dress rehearsal of an orchestra lacking drums, cymbals or trumpets.

The lone window of my narrow room looked out upon a cramped courtyard occupied by a garage specializing in the repair of motorcycles, none of which had mufflers, and there must have been an epidemic of faulty ignition systems in Toledo, for never had I heard such coughing, choking and spitting as came up from that nest of cycles. The noise was magnified, of course, by the restricted area in which it took place and by the reflecting walls which hemmed in the court.

Some twenty children played about the doors of the garage, engaged in a game requiring three boys to hold hands while making a dash through the opposition in an effort to touch a truck whose motor was being disassembled by means of hammer blows which struck resisting metal and echoed through the court. The game had three parts: Those holding hands screamed as they ran. The defense screamed encouragement to one another. And the workmen hammering the truck hurled curses at both.

From a nearby doorway a mother, determined that her son not become a delinquent, screamed an unceasing series of cautions: 'Diego, stay away from the truck!' 'Diego, stay away from the motorcycle!' 'Diego, stay away from the big boys!' Diego, whoever he was, paid no attention.

Just when I concluded that I had come upon a kind of absolute noise, two additional motorcycles roared into the compound with exploding motors, whereupon the children left their game and screamed approval of the new machines while the workmen banging at the truck bellowed warnings to stay clear of the machines and Diego's mother issued, at the top of her voice, a new volley of instructions.

Under these circumstances a siesta was impossible and even resting with my eyes open was forestalled, so I left the clamorous room and decided to explore the city, but when I reached the elevator it was ominously dark. It was out of order, so I walked downstairs and searched for the Zocodover, the lively central plaza which I had enjoyed in years past, and there in relative peace I watched as long-distance motorbuses from Milan, Amsterdam and Stockholm poured tourists into the city. In addition, scores of local buses brought Spaniards to Toledo, so that on this day Toledo must have been one of the busiest tourist cities in Europe. Foreigners came to see the cathedral and the El Grecos; Spaniards came to pay silent homage at their national shrine, the Alcázar, and there were so many people in town it was difficult to find a seat at any of the attractive cafés, and I began to comprehend what a tourist crush had enveloped Spain in recent years.

If I left the Zocodover, I was confronted, wherever I went, by rows of little shops selling acres of the cheapest tourist junk: damascened ash trays, inlaid penknives, letter openers that tried to make you believe they were ancient Moorish daggers, florid ceramics showing a wan knight tilting at a windmill, and gaudy banners woven with iridescent colors. These graceless shops numbered not in the dozens but in the hundreds, and it was depressing to think that the once-great crafts of Toledo, which had supplied the medieval world with splendid wares, had so degenerated.

In the early evening I returned to the hotel to try a tardy siesta, but the elevator wasn't working and when I reached my room the noise from the courtyard was simply unbelievable. New children had joined the games; new motorcycles were being tested; and Diego's mother had returned to her monitory job with new energy. It was difficult to believe that the taciturn Spaniard of history could make so much noise, but apparently his repression of centuries found voice whenever he came into contact with an internal-combustion engine. No man, I was to discover, derives so much pleasure from racing an engine with the exhaust open as a Spaniard; it is a national characteristic.

In a kind of numb despair I walked back downstairs, the elevator still being inoperative, and sought a restaurant for dinner. By bad luck I fell into the hands of a restaurant dedicated to the business of gypping foreigners, most of whom appeared in the city for only one day and were gone, so that they could be outraged with impunity. I was about to witness an example of this policy.

The Spanish government, aware that the golden rewards of tourism could evaporate as quickly as they appeared, has taken sensible steps to protect the tourist; the chain of paradors is proof of this. Restaurants are required to offer, in addition to their à la carte menus, a special tourist menu from which one can get a good meal and a bottle of wine at a fixed price. By ordering from this menu one can eat really well in Spain and at about half the price he would expect to pay in either France or Italy.

But. I sat down, looked at the menu and said, 'I'll take fish soup, Spanish omelet and flan.'

'And what wine?'

'Whatever comes with the meal.'

'Nothing comes with the meal.'

'But it says right here . . .'

'You have to order that. Then it's extra.'

'But the menu says . . .'

'You're pointing at the tourist menu.'

'That's what I ordered.'

'Oh, no! You didn't mention the tourist menu.'

'I'm mentioning it now.'

'You can't mention it now. You've got to mention it when you sit down.'

'But you haven't even given the order to the kitchen.'

'True. But I've written it in my book. And it's the writing that counts.'

'You mean that if I'd said "tourist menu" at the start, my meal would have cost me a dollar and sixty cents?'

'Clearly.'

'But since I delayed three minutes the same meal is going to cost me two-sixty?'

'Plus sixty cents for the wine.'

I tried to point out how ridiculous such a situation was, but the waiter was adamant, and soon the manager came up, looked at his waiter's book and shrugged his shoulders. 'If you wanted the tourist menu you should have said so,' he grumbled.

'I'm saying so now.'

'Too late.'

I rose and left the restaurant, with the waiter abusing me and the manager claiming loudly that I owed him for having soiled a napkin, which I admit I had unfolded.

I escaped but projected myself into an even worse mess, for I chose what seemed to be the best restaurant in Toledo, where I announced quickly and in a clear voice that I wanted the tourist menu.

'What a pity! With the tourist menu you can't have partridge.'

'I don't believe I'd care for partridge.' I had had it on a previous visit and was not too taken with it. 'Just the tourist menu.'

'But on the tourist menu you get only three dishes.'

'That's exactly what I want.'

'But on that menu you don't get special wine, and I know you Americans prefer a special wine.'

'I'll drink whatever you Spaniards drink.'

'We drink the special wine.'

I insisted that I be served from the tourist menu, and grudgingly the waiter handed me a menu which offered an enticing choice of five soups, eleven egg or fish dishes, seven meat courses and six promising desserts, but of the twenty-nine dishes thus available, twenty-six carried a surcharge if ordered on the tourist menu. Technically, one could order a dinner that would cost the price advertised by the government, but if he did so he would have two soups, one cheap fish and no dessert. Madrid had laid down the law, but Toledo was interpreting it.

As a traveler I work on the principle which I commend to others: No man should ever protest two abuses in a row. Few men can be right twice running, and never three times straight, so I ordered three dishes, each of which carried a surcharge: soup, roasted chicken, flan. The soup was delicious and the ordinary wine was palatable and I sat back to enjoy the meal which had started off so badly.

Unfortunately, I had chosen a table that put me next to a good-looking, ruddy-faced Englishman whose tweed suit gave the impression that he must at home have been a hunting man. As he finished his soup he said to his wife, 'First class, absolutely first class.' He had, as I suspected he might, ordered the partridge, but when the waiter deposited the steaming casserole before him, the Englishman looked at it suspiciously, waited till the waiter had gone, then asked his wife quietly, 'Do you smell something?'

'I think I do,' she replied.

'And do you know what it is?'

Without speaking she pointed her fork at the partridge, whereupon her husband nodded silently and brought his nose closer to the casserole. 'My goodness,' he said in a whisper, 'this is fairly raunchy.' In gingerly manner he tasted the bird, folded his hands in his lap and said, 'My goodness.'

His wife got a piece of the bird onto her fork and tasted it, looked gravely at her husband and nodded.

'What to do?' he asked.

'You obviously can't eat it.'

'I wonder should I call the waiter.'

'I think you'd better.'

I was now in a relaxed mood and had no desire to see the Englishman make a fool of himself, because obviously he wanted to avoid a scene. 'With your permission, sir,' I said, waiting for him to acknowledge me.

'Of course.'

'I'm afraid there's nothing wrong with your partridge, sir. It's how they serve it in Spain. A delicacy. Well hung.'

With admirable restraint the Englishman looked at me, then at the offending bird and said, 'My good man, I've been accustomed to well-hung fowl all my life. Gamy. But this bird is rotten.'

'May I, sir?' I tasted the partridge and it was exactly the way it should have been by Toledo standards. Gamy. Tasty. A little like a very strong cheese. Special taste produced by hanging the bird without refrigeration and much admired by Spanish hunters and countrymen. 'It's as it should be,' I concluded.

The Englishman, not one to make a scene, tasted the bird again but found it more objectionable than before. 'I've shot a good many birds in my lifetime,' he said, 'but if I ever got one that smelled like this I'd shoot it again.' He picked at the casserole for a moment and added, 'This poor bird was hung so long it required no cooking. It had begun to fall apart of its own weight.'

Once more I tried to console him: 'I've had Toledo partridge twice before, and I promise you, it tasted just like yours.'

'And you lived?' He pushed his plate away but refrained from complaining to the waiter. He did, however, look rather unpleasantly at me, as if to reprimand me for trying to convince him that he should eat such a bird.

At this point the waiter brought my chicken, and I am embarrassed to report that it smelled just like the partridge. It was one of the worst-cooked, poorly presented and evilest-smelling chickens I had ever been served and was obviously inedible. I tried cutting off a small piece, but blood ran out the end and the smell increased. I followed through and tasted it, but it was truly awful and I must have made a face, for the Englishman reached over, cut himself a helping, cut it into pieces and tried one while giving the other to his wife. Neither could eat the sample, whereupon the Englishman smiled indulgently and said very softly, 'See what I mean?'

When I tried to erase the taste of that dreadful chicken with a drink in the Zocodover, the effect of the lively square was killed by a couple at the next table who had with them that curse of the modern world, a very loud-playing transistor radio which ground out exactly the kind of cheap jazz I could have heard if I had traveled not to Spain but to Waco, Texas. And when I got back to my hotel the elevator still wasn't working but the mechanics below me were. Diego and his mother had gone to bed, thank God, but an older set of delinquents were now playing with motorcycle throttles and I was still not asleep.

I was kept awake not by the motorcycles, which did shut down before midnight, but by television, which from five or six nearby sets, all emptying into my enclosed courtyard, offered the Spanish-language version of *Bonanza,* one of the reigning favorites on Spanish television. I doubt if there is any country in Europe which has the unremitting noise quotient of Spain, and on this night I was to understand why. Anyone who has a television set must play it at top volume to let his neighbors know he has it. Anyone who has a motorcycle must run it open-throttle to impress those who aren't so lucky. And now a family down the alley, who had neither TV nor motorcycle, showed the world what they did have by playing their radio full-blast, with Mahalia Jackson, to whom I am normally partial, bellowing 'He's Got the Whole World in His Hands.' How I got to sleep I don't know, but early in the morning I was awakened by a dishwasher serenading me with 'Cielito lindo' while he dropped cups and saucers.

And yet it was Toledo that would reveal the essence of Spanish history. It was a city crammed with meaning, and in exploring it I experienced a kind of schizophrenia: my routine living was as unpleasant as I would know in Spain, for the noise grew as the service declined, but the significance of Toledo increased until I felt it to be a spiritual home in which I was a privileged guest. It remains the city which I recall with greatest frequency if not the most affection.

To appreciate Toledo one must see it from afar, for it is a mighty fortress on a rock. It is practically unassailable and its history has been a succession of sieges, some of which the insolent city withstood for years. From the east the Río Tajo (Tagus) comes wandering out of the plain and bumps into the rock of Toledo. Rebuffed, it turns south, runs almost completely around the rock, then meanders off toward Portugal to enter the Atlantic at Lisboa. It thus protects Toledo on three sides, and to think of the city without the river would be meaningless.

The northern flank of the city has no river, but an escarpment provides a natural bulwark which armies could not overcome. Within these defenses a considerable settlement grew up in ancient times to serve as the capital of Spain throughout the greater part of its history. The general pattern of the city today is roughly what it was two thousand years ago, for as an official told me, 'Forty years ago we had a population of about forty thousand. Today we have the same. And forty years from now it will still be the same, unless we build skyscrapers. For we have used up our rock.'

To remind myself of Toledo's unique posture, I walked one day out of the city, across the bridge over the Tajo and up onto that road that swings to the south, and when I had climbed to a high point I stopped to look back. How magnificent Toledo was, with its two salient bulwarks: to the right, the blunt, four-square Alcázar, a gigantic fortress with no artistic grace whatever, and in the center the glory of Toledo, the Gothic cathedral, whose spire and extended walls can best be appreciated from where I stood.

On the city side of the river, dwellings and monuments crowded together like animals in a storm, but on the country side the land stood practically empty. The Tajo was a line demarcating civilization from nothingness, and until Toledo was captured no invading general could claim that he had subdued Spain. This was the sequence of occupation with the approximate dates when Toledo fell into new hands:

Prehistoric	Iberians
Early Historic	Celtiberians
192 B.C.	Romans
A.D. 411	Wandering Germanic Tribes
A.D. 453	Visigoths
A.D. 712	Muslims
A.D. 1085	Spaniards

At Mérida we have witnessed the impact of Roman rule; in the next chapter we shall see the Muslims at Córdoba; and in all parts we can observe Spaniards, but it is only in Toledo that we can glimpse that nebulous period of three centuries when tribes from northern Europe dominated the peninsula.

The first Germanic tribes that spilled over into Spain after the debacle of the Roman Empire were mere adventurers and brought little except fire and disruption. Vandals, Alans, Suevi, they left no mark on either the culture or the population of Spain and were so disorganized that it was relatively easy for the superior Visigoths (the name means Noble Goths and refers to the West Goths) to supersede them. The Visigoths played an important role in the civilization of Spain. They brought a vigorous if heretical Christianity, and when on May 8, 589, King Reccared finally abjured his heresy and pledged allegiance to the Catholic Church of Rome, he installed Spain's most prized possession.

The Visigoths also introduced a codified law, a sensible tax system, a centralized government and an element of strength in the Spanish character. Since these Goths ruled Spain for nearly three hundred years and stayed on after their final defeat, they must also have made a strong contribution to Spanish blood, and it is they who account for the large number of blue-eyed Spaniards. On the other hand, they left almost no literature, little art and no substantial architecture. I recall few mass movements of people that left behind so little visual proof that they had occupied a country.

Toledo was probably an imposing city when it served as their capital, but the only echo of its grandeur is found in the Santa Cruz Museum, a few steps east of the Zocodover, where a few Visigothic remains are on display. In a corner room downstairs stands a typical example, a tombstone from the sixth century, carved in a soft limestone which should have been easy to work; but its letters are so puerile, its design so trivial and its effect so unsatisfying that one can see that it was carved by a man who had no sense of proportion or art. It is one of the few ancient stones I know that must be called ugly; yet in the next room stand beautifully carved Roman stones of about the same period, and these were surely available to the Visigoths as examples.

As one moves from room to room the conviction grows that the Visigoths were ungracious men; the capitals they used to top their columns are crude and the columns are poorly carved, as if a shaggy bear had done the job with his claws.

And yet, in the far room on the second floor, when I had about given up on the Visigoths, I came upon a piece of stone, number 196, which was positively superb, and having seen it, I had a new appreciation of the Visigoths. I commend it as one of the best things in Spain.

It is about eight inches high and was once square, about thirty inches on the side, but now one of the corners has been damaged, which does little harm; indeed, it lends a feeling of history. The four sides of the stone, a rather soft, whitish limestone, are sloped inward and decorated with rude square crosses of the kind known as formée. Broad at the ends and tapering to a point where the vertical and the lateral bars meet, the four triangular parts give the impression of a huge stone Iron Cross, as if this early work of the Goths had served as the pattern for present-day Germans, which it probably did. The crosses are accompanied by rows of massive and ungainly fleurs-de-lis plus other odds and ends, the whole decoration producing a feeling of combined awkwardness and signifi-cance. The stone is not inspired, but it is devout; it is not beautiful, but it does evoke a sense of primitive worship.

On top it has been hollowed to form a basin, and through one side, the cutting having been performed crudely, a drainpipe issues, for this is a baptismal font, and here the Goths committed themselves and Spain to the Christian religion. I never tired of looking at this stone; it seemed to me to have the rude force attained by our best modern sculpture, and I suppose if Henry Moore or Richard Stankiewicz were called upon to produce a baptis-mal font for a contemporary church it would look something like this. Of all the Visigothic stones I have seen in Spain, this one speaks most clearly and purely of that shadowy age when these northern barbarians fumbled and grumbled their way to victory and defeat.

Legend says that the Visigoths lost Spain because a voyeur king spied on a naked princess. Roderick, fated to be the last king of Toledo, had assumed the throne in 709. A married man, he conceived a great passion for the daughter of his friend and counselor, Count Julian, who governed Ceuta in Africa. King Roderick used to secrete himself in the bushes near a cave, still shown to tourists, on the other side of the Tajo near where I had stopped to see the city, and from this hidden spot he watched Florinda bathe. One day, while doing so, his passion overcame him and he leaped from his hiding place and raped the girl. Count Julian, seeking a revenge which would repair his daughter's honor, was ridiculed by the king much as Rigoletto, the father of Gilda, was ridiculed by his count. Rigoletto missed his revenge; Count Julian did not. He fled Toledo, went south to Gibraltar, crossed over to Ceuta, and there invited the Muslims to help him teach Roderick a lesson. He led the Moors into Spain, where they defeated Roderick, and then he brought them to Toledo and showed them how to cross the Tajo and penetrate the defenses. Of Roderick, when the battle ended, there remained only a kingly scarf and a glove; his fate was never known, but the rule of the Goths was ended and they left behind only that litany of strange and un-Spanish names used by their kings: Reccared, Witeric, Wamba, Witiza, Quindasvinto. The long dominance of the Muslims had begun.

The heart of Toledo is the Gothic cathedral, begun in 1227 and finished more than two hundred and fifty years later. It is so beautiful that one could never exhaust its variety, so evocative of the religious and civil history of Spain that it can never be fully understood. It is a masterpiece of concept and execution.

I care little for the exterior, what I have been able to see of it, for the façade is so uneven it looks as if Visigoths had planned it. The left spire is marred by three curious circles of projecting flanges such as boats use on their pier lines to prevent wharf rats from climbing aboard; it therefore looks as if it were prepared to repulse an assault of angels. The right spire was never finished, and what exists of its base was severely mutilated by a late addition. The various doors leading into the cathedral have been admired by some, but they are poor things compared to what we shall see in the north. But even if the exterior were a masterpiece it wouldn't matter, because you can't really see it. Houses and shops are jammed against it, and only from across the river can one see the part that soars above the surrounding roofs and gain an idea of what the building must have been before it was so sadly encroached upon.

But inside, it is quite a different matter. One does not enter through the main façade but through a cloister that stands off to one side. Whenever I step into the cathedral itself, I go to the first closed door on my right, lean back against it and allow my eye to wander the full length of the left aisle to remind myself of how enormous this church is. One morning I stepped it off, about a yard to a step, and it measured 136 paces, well beyond the length of a football field.

From my vantage point at the door I can see three things: the immense sweep of the aisle; the massive structure in the center of the cathedral, which houses the choir and the altar; and at the far end the Capilla de Santiago, which terminates the aisle. This chapel is something very special.

Seen from where I stand, the ground-level part of the chapel is

*The joy of first communion, at which time
the young Spaniard joins her ancient Church,
is a memory that abides
through a lifetime.*

composed of an iron grille which provides a lovely tracery and a subtle movement which invites the eye to look past the great bulk of the altar and around into the ambulatory. Above the grille, stained-glass windows lend color and variation to the scene. Aloft, the vaulting crisscrosses in various angles and planes, creating a polyphonic counterpoint whose intricacies never end. This distant conjunction of elements is like a perpetuum mobile placed at the end of a long line of stone trees whose trunks are the majestic pillars of the cathedral, and although there will be much for me to see in this subtle building, nothing will excel this simple yet complicated view down the aisle to the distant chapel. With this view one gains an insight into what a cathedral is supposed to be.

Let us walk from my door down the length of the church to the Capilla de Santiago. A quarter of the way down on the left stands a small golden chapel, put there to break the long sweep; it is placed exactly right, for it lends a touch of color without creating confusion: this cathedral is surprisingly free of clutter or the kind of garbage that often mars the minor churches of Spain. Now on the right we see the heavy walls of the choir and altar. Light strikes us as we cross the transept, a small cathedral in itself, and at the end we face the chapel whose components I have described.

It contains two works of note. High on the wall Santiago rides a brightly colored merry-go-round horse caparisoned in gold and shells. This is the same Santiago we saw as a pilgrim in Mérida, but in this evocation he is Santiago Matamoros (Moor-slayer), brandishing the enormous sword with which he slays Muslims, one of whom we see beneath the horse's hooves getting his head slashed off. We will meet this ferocious Matamoros riding over much of Spain but never in a more stylish presentation.

On the pavement of the chapel stand a pair of splendid marble tombs, each supported by four kneeling knights of the Order of Santiago, and from looking at them one can appreciate how grand and powerful that order was. The tombs form the end of a story both tragic and amusing, for they contain the bodies of the Conde Alvaro de Luna and his wife. The conde was born in 1388 as the illegitimate son of a rural family. Having no family prospects, he maneuvered himself into position as the confidant of Isabel the Catholic's father King Juan II, whom we have already met as the grandson of John of Gaunt, and so charmed him that he, Alvaro, became the effective ruler of Spain and the most notorious legal thief in history. His appetite for land and money was so voracious that after a few years he had amassed a million and a half coins of Spanish gold, eighty million lesser coins of Castilla and Aragón and seven trunks of Italian gold coins. He was Master of Santiago, which made him one of the most powerful lay forces in religion, and Condestable de Castilla, which empowered him to control the countryside. By one clever trick or another he acquired outright ownership of one hundred and twenty different towns. In the days when Colonel Pizarro was a boy in Trujillo, for example, Don Álvaro owned the city. His end was sardonic. Always loyal to the king, he engineered for Juan a most favorable second marriage to Isabel of Portugal (who would become the mother of Isabel the Catholic), but no sooner had she become Queen of Spain than she decided that the Conde de Luna must go. 'He is stealing the nation,' she told her husband as she organized a cabal of nobles who arrested the conde on some irrelevant charge, gave him a drumhead court-martial and sped him to the execution block. He was buried in the Capilla de Santiago, and that is where the humor comes in, for his family erected over his grave a life-sized portrait statue so articulated that when Mass was being said at the main altar some twenty yards away, a servant who followed the motions of the priest could manipulate a series of underground chains which made the statue stand, sit or genuflect at the proper points of the service, creaking loudly as it did so. So far as we know, this was the world's first mechanical man and it became so notorious that more people watched it than the priest. This continued for some thirty years until one day Queen Isabel said sternly, 'Get that thing out of here!' What became of the praying statue no one remembers.

Toledo's cathedral has a score of similar focal points, each laden with historical and spiritual significance; I wonder if there is another church in the world whose interior is so rich and at the same time so beautiful. I propose to speak of only four of the treasures: the choir, the main altar, a preposterous thing called the Transparente and the sacristy, which may be the most rewarding of all because of two paintings it contains.

In the center of the cathedral, facing the main altar, has been set down a very large masonry cube whose outer walls of stone are tastefully carved. It is the inside which is noteworthy, a symphony of dark beige alabaster and oil-stained wood, accented here and there by fine statues in marble, bronze and a lighter alabaster. To appreciate the quality of this noble structure, large enough to hold a chorus of up to eighty priests who chant during celebration of Mass, you must visualize the five layers of art which fit together, one on top of the other, to form the stalls in which the singing priests sit. At the lowest level, of course, are the carved misericords, those half-seats which can be quietly propped up when the service is long and leaned against so that the singer seems to be standing up while he is actually sitting down. 'Cheater-seaters,' I heard an American girl explain to a friend. Since misericords were used by the human fundament, custom allowed them to be carved to represent devils, fiends, vices and other low forms of life, so that in some cathedrals the misericords present scenes of sexual malpractice and abomination. The second layer is formed by the backs of the choir stalls, where a series of fifty-four carved wooden panels depict scenes from the Conquest of Granada. The third tier consists of misericords for an upper row of choir stalls and above them the great treasure of the choir, a series of wooden panels depicting standing figures from the Bible, and these are magnificently carved. And at the top, above the two ranks of choir stalls, runs a fine series of standing figures carved in pale alabaster that shines so as to make the faces of these noble figures seem alive. Any one of these five components would have made this choir notable; taken together they form one of the chief treasures of Spanish art.

I should like to comment briefly on only three of the components. The battle scenes by Rodrigo the German are an extraordinary production insofar as magnitude is concerned, for each of the panels is large and contains dozens and sometimes scores of separate figures. Since they were carved shortly after the Conquest of Granada the observation of armies and weaponry is of historic value. I am not so sure about the art. There is a decided monotony of design; in panel after panel a set of identical towers appears off-center left or right, against which an army moves with a confrontation of sorts between heroic Christians and abject Moors, all the warriors presenting a sameness of figure and face. This is one war in which the Muslims, who had defeated the Spaniards for some seven hundred years, fail to win a battle. On the other hand, these repetitious panels do contain much delightful observation on the wildlife of the countryside, and some of this work is of merit. Taken as a whole, the panels are delightful, and what they lack in art they compensate for in their ability to convince the viewer that he is seeing the Conquest of Granada, not as it happened, but as Fernando and Isabel desired it to be remembered.

The topmost parade of alabaster warriors used to please me very much, for it presented the heroic figures of Bible story in the dress of German knights of the fifteenth century, and I especially liked old Roboam (where does he appear in the Bible and under what name, I used to wonder; later I found that he was a link in the genealogy of Christ as given in Matthew), who stands tenth in on the right-hand side, next to King Solomon. He strides ingratiatingly, with a military sash pulled about his body, reminding me of Lohengrin. But in later years as I have grown to know the figures better I have concluded that they are fairly ordinary, possibly because the wooden figures below them now seem so wonderful.

This endless line of Biblical figures, carved in the darkest wood, is probably the most important Renaissance work in Spain, and was completed between 1539 and 1543 by two men with contrasting styles, the figures on the right as you enter the choir being by the Frenchman Felipe Vigarní de Borgoña and those on the left by the Spaniard Alonso de Berruguete. At first acquaintance the work of the former is easier to appreciate, especially panels like the one near the middle showing Jacob wrestling with the angel, in which the intertwining of figures is done with invention and grace. Vigarní's share of the work contains another half-dozen panels of high merit, particularly the one in the corner showing a man with an ox.

But as I grew to know the panels my taste inclined more and more to the remarkable portraits carved by Berruguete. They are sometimes heavy but always inspired; they are decidedly awkward but always moving; they are particularly tortured, like the late work of El Greco, but never tedious. A good panel with which to start an appreciation of Berruguete is the one to the left of the alabaster relief in the central wall, for this shows St. Peter and is not successful: the chair is grotesquely done, the keys and book are out of balance and the savage distortion of the figure produces no artistic gain. In fact, the whole idea misses. The four evangelists who appear next to Peter are ordinary, for they seem not to know what to do with the books they carry, and even John the Baptist, who comes next, emphasizes a tortured distortion rather than an artistic form.

So far Berruguete shows less talent than Vigarní, but on the left-hand wall he offers a series of figures that are explosive in their excellence. Jerome and his lion are magnificent; I have never seen a better Abraham preparing to sacrifice Isaac; Eve, as she stands nude plucking the apple, is wonderfully seductive, her eyes closed in rapture, her face wreathed in an enigmatic smile; a blindfolded old Sibyl with her prophetic tablets seems to have been carved by Michelangelo, so reminiscent is the weather-beaten face. The panels are not well designed and display a clutter that a purist would not have indulged in, but they are powerful and speak with the clear, strong voice of the Renaissance.

Before leaving the choir you should look at the rare marble statue of the standing Virgin and Child which graces the altar. She wears a white robe and is known as the White Virgin. (Legend says she was the gift of St. Louis, King of France, some time in the thirteenth century, but most art historians are satisfied that she was carved no earlier than the fourteenth, which knocks that legend in the head.) Her title is curious in that both she and Jesus have very dark faces; indeed, He looks like an adorable little Negro baby. I mentioned this once to a Spanish friend, who was outraged, so I asked him how otherwise he explained the darkness of the pair, and he replied, 'It's difficult but they're not Negroes.' Later when we meet the Virgin of Montserrat and the Virgin of Guadalupe we will find that they too are dark, as is San Fermín, the saint after whom the yearly feria at Pamplona is named. There I was warned, 'We will forever damn you if you say Fermín was a Negro. Dark, yes. Moorish, yes. Negro, never.'

Facing the choir, but separated from it by the full width of the transept, is a second structure containing the high altar, and this area is so lavish that books have been written about it alone, but I shall refer only to the reredos because the rest of the place overwhelms me and I doubt that I could do it justice. To approach the reredos you must pass through the wrought-iron screen which cuts it off from the main body of the church. It is an exquisite piece of work, so classically proportioned and so intricately executed that it allows the worshipers outside the altar area to participate as if they were inside, yet it marks them off as not being priests. This is one of the most delicate screens ever forged of iron and is ideally suited for this cathedral. It was authorized at the late date of 1548 and was wrought by Francisco de Villalpando, who took ten years for the job. Today the hinges of its great gates swing as easily as they did when installed, and Americans who are not familiar with screens ought to see this masterpiece.

The gold-leafed reredos which soars above the tabernacle is so intricate and ornate as to be more like a fantasy than reality. Immensely high, its upper figures seem to be trying to escape through the roof of the cathedral. It is composed of tier upon tier of religious tableaux carved in high relief on larch wood, then covered with gold leaf. One panel, for example, might contain as many as five life-sized figures set off from nearby panels by yards of intricate filigree work, but the construction is so gigantic that one has no sense of clutter but rather of a heavenly pageant which one is permitted to glimpse through a golden frieze. There are fourteen such scenes, any one large enough for an average church, plus ten huge figures of patriarchs and prophets, all topped by an enormous

Crucifixion featuring a mammoth Jesus surrounded by the two thieves on their crosses and the two Marys in red. A predella offers a series of smaller panels, also crowded with gold figures, and a fine Virgin and Child. In the center of the reredos stands an enormous tabernacle used in the Mass; each inch is ornamented in gold and encrusted in jewels.

What I have failed to convey is the effect of this intricate flowering of Late Gothic: it is so resplendent and dazzling that in a lesser building it would be overpowering if not preposterous, but in the far reaches of this cathedral it seems necessary. It was put together—that is the only phrase to describe its construction—within the brief period of two and a half years by a team of craftsmen whose names indicate how artisans moved about in Europe at the beginning of the sixteenth century: Rodrigo the German, Petijean of France, Diego Copín of Holland, Juan and Felipe de Borgoña, Francis of Antwerp, and two Spaniards who designed the whole, Enrique de Egas and Pedro Gumiel. When I was younger I did not care much for the confection this team threw together, and I amused myself by imagining Egas shouting one afternoon, 'Petijean, we need six more statues just like the last ones.' But when I saw it recently I was awed by the sheer bravado of the thing; its mass is overpowering; its intricacy is as well planned as a Bach fugue. If Egas did indeed call for carved saints by dozen lots, he knew where to put them when he got them.

The reredos is so placed that the tabernacle, which is the raison d'être for the whole, is in shadow, and in the early days of the eighteenth century it was decided that a shaft of light should be brought through the rear wall of the cathedral and then through the back of the reredos so as to illuminate the tabernacle. This might also solve another problem; just as Queen Isabel had objected to people's staring at the articulated statue of the Conde de Luna during Mass, so two centuries later devout Catholics were objecting to the fact that others less devout were wandering about the ambulatory during service, and it was thought that if they could see the tabernacle from the rear they would respect it and be silent when Mass was being read. The result of these two needs was the Transparente, so named because light would pass through solid walls. It is one of architecture's cleverest juggling feats, if not one of art's successes.

Into the back of the high altar a circle was cut so that persons in the ambulatory could see through to the tabernacle and know when it was being used. At the same time, high on the opposite wall of the cathedral, a very large hole was cut, perhaps twenty to thirty feet across, to admit a shaft of light that would fall upon the tabernacle thus exposed. It was a bold solution, made possible only because the outside walls of the cathedral, erected about 1227, were strong and could withstand being pierced, and because the altar had been so solidly built that it did not collapse when a fairly large hole was driven through. Thus, in the mornings when Mass was being said and when the sun stood in the eastern heavens, shafts of sunlight came unimpeded to illuminate the filigreed tabernacle when seen from either front or back.

Of course, two gaping holes resulted and it was the steps taken to mask them that constituted the marvel of the Transparente, known in Spain as 'the eighth wonder of the world.' Tastes of the time were on the florid side, and the Transparente became the most florid baroque accomplishment of its period. It is a fantastic thing. The clue to its bewildering opulence comes with the identification of the team who built it: the Spanish architect Narciso Tomé assisted by his four sons, two of whom were architects, one a sculptor and the last a painter. Tomé put his whole family to work, and when the holes were completed, the sculptor and the painter, aided by teams of assistants, began producing a whole company of saints, angels, prophets and cardinals. Some were painted flat on the walls of the openings but in wonderful perspective, so that from the great distance at which they were seen, and from below, they appeared to be sculptures. Most were sculpted in marble or bronze and some of these were polychromed. Intricate abstract designs suggesting flowing robes and foliage were created to hang over corners so that the architectural details of the piercing could be masked. And splendid groups of figures, so intricate that the eye could hardly unravel them, were put together so that the opening leading to the tabernacle could be hidden and yet permit light to pass through unimpeded. As a jigsaw puzzle, the Transparente of Toledo is without peer, and the pieces are full-sized human beings.

Now to fit the puzzle together. It is apparent, I hope, that we are speaking about two rather large holes separated by a considerable distance, the first low down at the back of the main altar, the second across the ambulatory very high up and on the outside wall. Well, Narciso Tomé and his four sons solved this by posting along the edges of the outside cut a stunning array of Biblical figures who seem to pour into the cathedral from the heavens. They twist and tumble, clutch at one another and raise their hands in prayer, fall and slide, gesticulate and grimace, forming a veritable cascade of heavenly figures from which we slowly pick out the significant fact: at the outer edge of the opening sits Jesus Himself, on a bank of clouds and surrounded by the angels of paradise.

This upper half of the Transparente is the lesser of the two parts and the more restrained, for the whole back of the reredos has been converted to a tower of marble which reaches from floor to ceiling. When it was finished a problem arose: 'How to join the two halves?' and here Tomé and his sons showed ingenuity. The painter provided a mural which crosses the top of the cathedral and ties the two halves together. It is a daring and successful device, in which painted and sculptured forms unite to make one vast procession, but to try to pick out the various parts from below makes one dizzy. We can, however, enjoy the massive structure that backs the high altar, for it is composed of four identifiable parts: at the bottom a

FOLLOWING FACING PAGES: *Left, the Transparente: upper hole.*
Right, the wedding of sculpture and fresco.

beautiful enthroned Mother and Child; quite high up so that most visitors miss it, a Last Supper with thirteen full-sized polychromed marble celebrants; at the very top, so that her head almost touches the muraled ceiling, the Virgin Mary ascending into heaven; and in the center, masking the opening to the tabernacle, a whirlwind of angels and clouds, one of the most successful depictions of wild movement ever to have been achieved in marble.

That's the Transparente, save for some score of separate standing figures and a forest of highly ornamented pillars that lend a pattern to the whole. It is blatantly a work of the early eighteenth century and could have been created, I suppose, only by a man who had four sons who could paint, carve, cast bronze and work upside down while suspended from ropes which passed through the ceiling.

Art of a different quality is to be found at our last stop, the sacristy, a long hall which one enters through an avenue of sixteen El Grecos, depicting the twelve disciples, Jesus, Mary, Santo Domingo and an extra portrait of St. Peter. Any one of these, appearing by itself in a foreign museum, would become a famous work; it is interesting to study the second portrait of Peter, one of the finest of its size El Greco ever did, for it shows Peter weeping and reminds one that the artist must have had a special fondness for him. He always painted him with such love.

Our purpose in visiting the sacristy, however, is to see two paintings more important than the portraits. They are among the finest examples of Spanish art, and with their help we shall discover something about the soul of Spain.

The first is the more conspicuous and more easily grasped. At the far end of the long hall, framed as an altarpiece, stands the 'Spoliation of Christ' by El Greco, depicting the mysterious figure of Jesus draped in flaming red as he is taunted by the rabble while in the foreground a carpenter in a yellow smock prepares the cross. Gaunt, ethereal faces stare out from the crowd; a woman in ochre robe and purple dress, her back to the viewer, raises her hand dramatically as a Roman guard, posed by some man brought in from the streets of Toledo, stands in polished armor. Flags and spears and plumed helmets fill the top of the picture. One sees the passion and terror of sixteenth-century Spain. It is a stunning picture and El Greco must have liked it, for a nearby museum has a smaller copy, but it lacks the vitality of this great presentation.

A few yards away, set so far back in a niche that the unobservant might miss it, is a slightly smaller picture by Goya, 'The Arresting of Jesus on the Mount of Olives,' a vigorous night scene, earthy and with no sense of mystery. Christ is shown as a faltering man robed in a curious pinkish white, while the soldiers who surround him are counterparts of those depicted in Goya's series of etchings 'The Disasters of War.' They are not Romans, but rather peasants from the central plateau of Iberia, and their leering faces can be seen even today in the villages outside Madrid. The picture is a haunting thing, a country scene of torment in which Jesus appears to be actually suffering the indignities being thrown at him by the mob, and those hurried visitors who miss this fine work miss something very good and very Spanish.

In neither of these powerful pictures do I find anything of Jesus the religious figure nor of the Holy Land as I knew it in Israel and Jordan; I doubt that in the strictest sense they ought to be called religious pictures. But in each I find an infinite amount of Spain in its basic manifestations, the mystical of El Greco and the practical of Goya. The former, with its tortured figures and demonic faces, recalls the agonies which Spain has always inflicted upon itself, the self-condemnation, the religious fervor, the leaping of inspired minds directly to the throne of heaven, the impassioned singing and violence. These things I can see in the El Greco, where flaming red dominates and leads the eye to colors no other artist would dare place in juxtaposition, just as no sensible man laying out the history of a nation would dare give one country the contradictory experiences that Spain has known. In the Goya, on the other hand, I see the earthiness of Spain, the robust animal-like characteristic of the soil and the men who work it. These ugly, extremely human and likable faces remind me of the Spaniards who cursed as they pulled the oars at the Battle of Lepanto, who cursed as they mounted a guerrilla resistance against Napoleon, who suffered through the sad mismanagement of their country and who have survived whatever defeats and humiliations have been visited upon them. It is not by accident that in this canvas, which shows one of the most solemn moments of Biblical history, when the first physical step toward the Crucifixion was being taken, a goodly number of the participants are laughing. As one reads this book he must not forget that at the most solemn moments of Spanish history someone is laughing, sardonically perhaps, but laughing.

I never leave the cathedral at Toledo without paying my respects to two contrasting figures, now shadowy but once of earth-moving power, who ruled from this building and whose confrontation continues throughout Spanish history, for they are so dramatic that they seem to have been created by a playwright rather than by the chances of history. They are the two fiery cardinals, Mendoza and Cisneros, who had large roles in governing Spain, Mendoza from 1482 till 1495, Cisneros from 1495 till 1517. Pedro González de Mendoza (1428–1495) was the fourth (some say fifth) son of a noble family and his presence in the church was an accident: he was really a confirmed layman pushed by his relatives into a position from which he could exercise power. In clerical robes he led the armies of Fernando and Isabel and helped them gain the crown. He was first into Granada at the end of the conquest, served as civil governor of Castilla in the footsteps of Don Alvaro de Luna, and was one of the few at

court who understood what Columbus was talking about. Taking his religious vows lightly, he sought Rome's forgiveness for having sired illegitimate children, but being prudent as well as lecherous he made his appeals in group lots. He was cast in heroic mold and maintained his own court and armed guard, and he left behind him in Toledo so many monuments that he seems as alive today as he did in that period when he was helping usher Spain into its period of maximum greatness. His tomb stands at the left of the main altar and is a fantastically pompous affair of pillars, arches, statues, niches plus a gaudy marble casket in which he lies in regal splendor befitting his nickname, 'third King of Spain.' When I studied Mendoza in books I never cared much for him, but it was not until I saw his tomb that I understood why.

To me the best thing he did was to sponsor as his successor Gonzalo Jiménez de Cisneros (1436–1517), who had begun his life as a poor boy in a town near Madrid and who when entering orders changed his name to Francisco in honor of his patron. Of a shy retiring nature, he hid himself in a convent, where his piety commended itself to Queen Isabel, who made him her confessor. The better she knew him the more she respected him, and one day she handed him a letter from the Pope appointing him Archbishop of Toledo, but he refused the honor, an impasse which she solved by appointing him anyway. Soon Fernando, desiring some strong administrators at the head of the Spanish Church, connived to have him made cardinal, and one of the first things this quiet, bookish man did was to conscript an army of twenty thousand soldiers to invade Oran and Tripoli to teach the Muslims a lesson. There is a touching account of how, on the eve of a great battle in which he would lead the troops, he reflected upon the irony of a fate which had made him, a seeker after retreat and silence, the general of an invading army.

Much more was in store for him. When Fernando died in 1516, Cisneros found that he had been appointed in the king's will to serve as regent of Castilla until Fernando's grandson, Carlos I of Spain and V of the Holy Roman Empire, should reach Spain, which he had not yet seen. That year Cisneros was eighty, and without hesitation he launched upon one of the miraculous years of Spanish history. He challenged the power of Adrian of Utrecht, the tutor of young Carlos, and frustrated his plans to make Spain an appendage of Austria. He battled the nobles and recovered from them powers which he felt Carlos ought to exercise when he became king. He put down the intrigues of the courtiers who wanted to pass the throne of Aragón along to Carlos' younger brother, Fernando of Austria, who had been brought up in Spain. Under his own supervision he built several buildings that are notable still. He strengthened farming and initiated steps which would have ensured Spain great agricultural wealth

xcept for the worm holes through his forehead,
is saint seems as alive today as he did
ree hundred years ago. He is for sale
the streets of Toledo.

had they been pursued. He armed the nation's ships against the pirates of the Mediterranean and the freebooters of the Atlantic, thus establishing himself as the father of the navy which seventy-two years later culminated in the Armada. He spent much time furthering the development of the new university which he had founded at Alcalá de Henares. He watched over the publication of one of the world's premier examples of scholarship, the *Biblia Poliglota Complutense* (the Polyglot Bible of Alcalá de Henares, completed in 1514–1517 but not set into type until 1522), which he had fathered and in which, for the Old Testament, the Hebrew, Greek and Latin texts were printed side by side, 'with the Latin in middle,' as the preface pointed out, 'like Jesus between the two thieves at the Crucifixion.' For the Pentateuch, that is, the first five books, a fourth column was provided, giving the Aramaic text of the Targum of Onkelos; for the New Testament, of course, only two columns were needed, Greek and Latin. All subsequent Biblical scholarship would be dependent upon this great work. And most important of all, Cisneros quietly rebuffed every attempt to put on the throne of Spain the rightful heir, Juana la Loca (Mad Joanna), daughter of Fernando and Isabel and mother of Carlos I. He argued that even though Juana had divine right to the throne—which fact none denied—she was so incompetent that she could rule only through a regency, and this he feared would be so prolonged that only evil could result. (He was right; in her virtual prison Juana lived for another thirty-nine years.) Quiet, relentless in pursuit of all he believed in and champion of the rights of the boy king whom he had never seen, Cisneros by force of character held Spain together on the eve of its greatness.

His last act as regent was to leave Toledo and move in wearying stages to one monastery after another so as to be ready to consult with Carlos as the youth entered Spain for the first time, but the trip was so arduous that Cisneros fell ill. Fable claims that he died from anguish after reading a letter, which Carlos had sent ahead, rebuking him for assumption of powers and dismissing him from all offices. But historians believe that Cisneros had died before the letter arrived.

The cathedral at Toledo contains a strange memorial to Cisneros, and it contrasts favorably, I think, with the flamboyant tomb of Mendoza. At the southwest corner of the cathedral stands the Capilla Mozárabe. When the Moors overran Toledo they offered the conquered two alternatives: convert to Islam or remain Christians and pay certain special taxes. The Mozárabes (would-be Arabs) were those who followed the second course. They remained Christians and through the centuries developed their own peculiar style of celebrating the Mass. In 1085, when Alfonso VI conquered the city, his wife and his religious advisor, both of them French, prevailed upon him to enforce throughout his realm the newly proposed Cluniac reforms, which required the adoption of the Roman type of Mass. The Mozárabe was thus frowned upon, which was right because it was through the various consolidations of power and uniformity proposed by the Cluniac reforms that the Catholic Church attained the cohesion it needed for the tasks ahead, and a single form of the Mass, understandable in all lands, was one of the greatest unifying forces. On the other hand, it was sardonic that the Mozárabes, having been allowed to practice their form of Mass by the Arabs, should now be in danger of losing it to Catholics. Stubbornly they held onto their version for four hundred years, from 1085 to 1485 and beyond, in spite of real pressure from Rome; finally Cardinal Cisneros decreed that if any people were so devoted to their form of worship their wishes should be respected, and at the southwest corner of the cathedral he authorized a chapel to be built for perpetual observance of the Mozárabe rite. It is this chapel, ugly on the outside, lovely inside, that disfigures the right side of the façade, but the spirit that animated Cisneros to this generous act is considered his finest memorial. Today only one hundred and fifty families still follow the Mozárabe rite, and they remember Cisneros with affection.

Obviously Cisneros is a hero of mine, for wherever one meets his trail one finds greatness. It is my duty, therefore, to report that he undertook two additional responsibilities: he served as head of the Holy Inquisition for all Spain and many of its worst excesses were committed under his leadership. When Carlos, writing from Flanders prior to his arrival in Spain, suggested to Cisneros that reforms in the inquisitorial process might be advisable, the cardinal wrote back: 'The Inquisition is so perfect that there will never be any need for reform and it would be sinful to introduce changes.' It was also Cisneros who supported Isabel's expulsion of the Jews from Spain, but later, when planning his Poliglota, he searched Europe for Jewish scholars expert in Hebrew and brought them to Alcalá de Henares, where he protected them as they taught.

While renewing my acquaintance with the cathedral I continued to experience Toledo tourism, and I began to appreciate why personal services were so bad. Each morning as I walked downstairs, for the hotel elevator still didn't work, I found fifty or sixty suitcases stacked in the lobby and buses waiting at the door. Foreigners streamed down the stairs, checked their luggage with bleary eyes and crawled into the buses, not to return. It reminded me of herding Texas cattle, and there was no reason why the overworked men behind the desk should bother to identify as individuals the animals moving in and out. In fact, I was surprised that the service was as good as it was, except that I was somewhat irritated one morning when the desk man looked up with surprise and said, 'Dios mío, are you still here?' Finally, one afternoon as I returned weary from a long walk through the city, the elevator was working. It lifted me to floor two-and-a-half and there conked out altogether, leaving me suspended for thirty minutes.

On the other hand, I had found a good restaurant and a waiter who actually laughed. Once when I tipped him rather more than usual, he confided, 'I'm saving this to get to Madrid.'

'You taking a job there?'

'No. I love bullfights and Curro Romero is fighting on Sunday. He's the best. Care to come along?'

I was much tempted, because I had not yet seen Romero, but I had reached the point where my extended walks into out-of-the-way places were beginning to produce an affection for Toledo which I did not want to imperil. 'You go,' I said. 'I'll see Romero later.'

'Don't delay,' the waiter warned me, 'because he does such things with the bull that any day he might get hurt.'

My walks took me into many corners of Toledo, one of the most interesting being the south side of the city, where the poor lived. I had not intended going there, but a donkey came by hauling a milk cart and I followed it for some time and found myself in a warren of medieval streets that led down the cliffs to the banks of the Tajo. In a few instances I saw the kind of poverty I had seen in the farm villages in Extremadura, but most of the houses I stopped at were those of what one might call the respectable poor, with adequate clothing and good food but not quite enough of either; and no matter how poor the house it usually was next to one with a television aerial. I spent some time with a pauper who made his living by walking into the country and collecting reeds which he bound into whisk brooms, tying their ends together with a rope he made from vines. He worked at the base of a tree near the river. 'This is my factory,' he said. It consisted of one very old knife for cutting his materials and a stick on which he wound his rope, with room at each end for him to stand on, so that when the time came to bind his reeds he could pull very hard against the stick held down by his toes; old beggars must have used this system in Egypt two thousand years before the birth of Christ. 'I make enough to live on,' he said. When I asked him how much, he said, 'I can make three of these brooms a day, when the weather's good, and I sell them for eight cents apiece.' I asked if he could live on twenty-four cents a day, and he said, 'I beg too.' When his whisk was finished he showed me how to bang it against the tree. 'Women appreciate it when you've knocked out the seeds.'

I now came upon a courtyard which explained much about Toledo's noise, for a group of six or seven young men were preening their motorcycles as carefully as men in London preen their Jaguars. The motorcycles were of a kind new to me, for although each had one front wheel, it had two rear wheels on which was slung a trucklike body capable of carrying, I should judge, about a quarter-ton. It was these motorcycles which made the noise and moved the cargoes of modern Spain. The rich in Spain have

In Spain one has a constant image
of suspicious people peering out
from half-opened doors to check upon
who or what is passing

always loved automobiles; recently the middle class have been able to afford them too; but the poor can afford only their motorcycle trucks, and the government would face revolution if it passed laws forbidding them. If I were dictator of Spain, I would certainly not restrict the motorcycles, but I would earmark a large budget for the development of a muffler system.

I was often stopped by Spaniards who wanted to talk about foreign countries or their own, and if the newspapers were afraid to talk politics, the people were not. Jokes were common. Generalísimo Franco was traveling through the countryside when his coach broke down. Desiring to know what his people thought, he walked alone to a farmer and said, 'How're things?' and the farmer said, 'Lousy. The government doesn't know its ass from its elbow.' Franco became angry and said, 'Don't you know who I am?' and the farmer said, 'I've seen your face somewhere before,' and Franco said, 'You'll find my name on all the principal streets, everywhere.' The farmer dropped his hoe, looked up with delight and cried, 'Oh! Señor Coca-Cola!'

When I say that 'I talked with this man or that,' I am using the verb in a restricted sense. I read Spanish fluently, understand it partially and speak it poorly, but I have memorized some twoscore old-style phrases of considerable gentility and these I can rattle off, so my speaking consists of something like this: 'My esteemed señor, would you do me the favor of seeing . . .' I begin rapidly, thus creating the impression that I know what I'm talking about, but I end like this: 'if . . . you have . . . one . . . beer . . . cold . . . very?' Encouraged by the speed of my opening, my listener responds at a natural rate, and when he does I understand about two-thirds of what he says, especially if it concerns a subject on which I know the basic vocabulary. Of course, in philosophical discussions I am often at a loss in critical moments because I fail to catch whether Miguel de Unamuno said that Spain was lost or that Spain was inspired. But I do not hold back because of my ineptness, and I have talked for many hours with many different kinds of Spaniards.

I had now descended to the Tajo at the spot where a dam constructed centuries ago created a waterfall, and here I stayed through twilight; always before, I had seen the fall from the top of a cliff, distant and silent and lovely, and I was now surprised at how much noise it made. An old man came to sit with me and we looked for some minutes in silence at the ruins of the mill that jutted into the river. 'You from América del Norte? Must be a great place.' I asked him why he thought so, and he said, 'Our newspapers say so many bad things about it.' I asked him if he'd want to go to America, and he said, 'For the money, yes. Here it's hard for a man to earn enough. But for the life over there . . . the speed . . . the noise . . . no, thank you.' I asked him if Spain were easier now. 'Much better. At last they're getting some sense into their crazy heads in Madrid.' Something moved close to me in the darkness and I jumped. 'What's that?' 'My cows,' he said. And there, on an edge of Toledo I'd not seen before, a farmer was herding five black-and-white cows who apparently found a good living among the thickets that grew along the riverbanks.

Whenever I wandered back toward the center of town I found myself engulfed in the deluge of tourists and I resolved to find out how Toledo copes with this industry. Leaving the cathedral one morning and keeping the cardinal's palace on my right and the city hall on my left, I followed a narrow path to the beautiful Plaza del Consistorio, from which ran the Pasadizo del Ayuntamiento, a covered footway running through the heart of a store specializing in stones from early Christian times. Leaving this I walked along a chain of pleasant streets that brought me to Santo Tomé, the church which holds El Greco's 'The Burial of Count Orgaz,' and a little farther on I stopped at San Juan de Dios, 20, at the damascene shop of Luis Simón, a handsome, fleshy man in his forties, with prematurely gray hair. He said business was slow at the moment and he'd be glad to show me around his factory, and from what I saw I judged that he specialized in good workmanship applied to the kinds of things that were bound to sell: penknives, ash trays, brooches, decorative swords. Taking a piece of steel and a blowtorch, he softened a mixture of wax, resin, red earth and olive oil and set the steel into it. As soon as the flame was withdrawn the mixture hardened and Simón was ready to work. 'I employ fourteen people throughout the year. It took me five years to learn the trade, another five to become good, but now in Toledo we have a school of applied arts, and young men can speed the process. If they have skill they earn a good living. You'll notice my men are all young. During the Crusade of 1936 we lost a whole generation of artists. Older men were killed off. Younger men were not trained. The steel I'm using, as you can see, is very soft. They make it for us specially in the mills at Bilbao.'

As he spoke he was scoring the steel with a sharp-pointed knife, laying down a series of fine lines with burred edges about 1/120th of an inch apart. When he had completed a section running in one direction he turned the steel and worked across the lines, so that in the end he had an area completely covered by crisscross lines of the finest delicacy. Luis Simón was obviously a master workman, but in answer to my question he said, 'Of course, I could make any object you see in the shop. But today I'm too busy selling. The manufacturing I must leave to my men. This gold I'm using comes to us from Madrid but I believe they buy it from Germany.' Across the burred edges of the steel he was running a strand of very thin gold wire of great brilliance, and when he had laid out an ancient Arabic design consisting of triangles and solid spaces, he gently tapped each wire into position, and as he did so the roughened edges of the lines caught at the gold and held it fast. He then picked up a small mallet and a blunt-headed instrument and with some force hammered the gold wires into permanent position, closing the edges of the lines about them. 'That gold

FOLLOWING FACING PAGES:
Waiting for the bus.

can never be pulled out now. Try it,' and when I had unsuccessfully tried, he said, 'We now bake the steel so that the gold forms a permanent bond and the empty spaces of steel become jet black. That's what damascene work is.' He showed me his salesroom, where an ash tray seven inches across, decorated in a gold-and-silver Moorish design of considerable intricacy, sold for twenty-seven dollars. 'Twenty-four karat gold and pure silver,' he explained, 'but we have others of less complicated design, same size, for as low as sixteen dollars.'

He was proud of the swords made in his shop, immense things with braided-steel handles. 'We have our own forge, and water-temper the steel just the way they did in this street when a Toledo blade was famous throughout the world. The sword you're holding is five feet long with a woven handle and we can sell it for nine dollars. But this one, smaller size, gold inlaid, is an exact copy of a sword used ceremonially by Queen Isabel . . . Try it, it's completely flexible. Costs three hundred dollars. We also make fencing swords. This one for beginners, only four-sixty and completely flexible. Best fencing sword with inlaid handle, sixteen dollars. This one, of course, we're proud of. The bullfighter's sword. Heavy. Very strong. For beginners this one for six dollars. For the real thing, maybe fifty dollars. When my father worked here, all matadors' swords came from Toledo, because we were the world's finest sword makers, but starting about 1910 a firm named Luna in Valencia took away the business, and they did make good swords. Today most matadors get theirs from Bermeja in Madrid, and so it goes.'

As to tourists, Señor Simón was in favor of them. 'They are our existence. We can survive if we get twenty good customers a day. I try to meet each one because I have a funny sense about what people want and what they'll be willing to pay. More than half our customers are French, but the norteamericanos come second and they tend to buy more when they do come. I speak French, English, Italian and a little German. My two daughters work with me. One speaks French and English; the other, French and German. I learned my languages by listening, when I was a boy working at the benches, while others did the selling. I'd repeat each word over and over. I used to work in a pretty big factory. Forty people. We had a deal with travel agencies. They'd steer their tourists to us and we'd sell a two-dollar bracelet for three dollars and give the agency a split. They watched us like hawks to see how much we were selling, and we'd try to work it so that the tourists wouldn't buy then but would come back later on. I got tired of such business and started my own. No guides, no agencies, no runners. We pay commissions to no one. I emphasize this because Toledo has been badly hurt by the last printing of Mr. Fielding's book on travel in Europe. He warns the norteamericanos, "Don't buy anything in Toledo. You can get it cheaper in Madrid." One norteamericano after another tells me, "Mr. Fielding told me to buy in Madrid, so I'm going to wait." I say, "Can't you make up your own mind?" but they say, "Sure, but who wants to be robbed?" Fact is, Mr. Fielding was right. The shops to which the guides take you do rob you, and you can buy the same thing cheaper in Madrid. But the truth is that if you come to shops like mine, and there are dozens like me in Toledo, even near the Zocodover, you get bargains that no one in Madrid can match. Look at my prices and compare. The guides know this and they have to protect themselves, so now they tell the norteamericanos, "Sure, Señor Simón's price is a little lower. Why shouldn't it be? Everything he sells is machine-made." This is a tough business but we make our way.'

As he spoke, an American woman came into the store to conclude a bargaining session that had extended over three days. 'In spite of what Fielding says, I'm going to buy from you.' She was satisfied that Señor Simón's prices were about as good as she was going to find and she was prepared to place her order: 'Six of the larger ash trays, four pairs of scissors, four penknives, six water jugs, six small swords for letter openers, one large plate, one larger sword . . .' I understood what Simón meant when he said that with twenty customers a day he could get by. This woman's bill was going to be close to two hundred dollars and she was delighted with the things she was getting. 'This store is so clean and well lighted it's a pleasure to do business here,' she said. When she was gone, Simón said, 'It ought to be clean. The municipal government sends an inspector here once a month to be sure the shop looks appealing. In Toledo, tourism is a big business . . . the biggest we have, and we've got to do everything we can to offset the bad blow Mr. Fielding gave us.'

On my way to inspect the damascene factory I had noticed, at Calle de Santo Tomé, 6, an attractive restaurant whose main dining room was the patio of an old convent. It was run by a vigorous young man named Mariano Díaz and his robust, handsome wife Sagrario. 'And seven others, all members of the family,' Don Mariano explained. He was proud of his restaurant and wanted to talk about it. 'I'm from Toledo. My father has a restaurant of his own on the other side of town and I've always wanted to be in the business. It was Sagrario's father who started this one, and I took over when I married Sagrario. Her father came from Valencia, during the Crusade. He couldn't stand the Communists who were in control of the city, so he fled. Started a bar on this corner, but the big growth came when Sagrario and I took over. We have 225 seats now and during most of the summer they're filled every noon. We pay commission to no one . . . no guides, no tourist agencies, no runners. We don't want that kind of business. You look at us and if you like the way we look . . . We spend a lot of time keeping this place clean and attractive, and all of our business comes from walking tourists who say, "That old convent looks interesting. Let's eat there." It used to be a Franciscan convent. We rent it.'

Señor Díaz was the kind of man I enjoy meeting in any field of

endeavor, because he loved his work and took pride in explaining its tricks and triumphs. He was a big, tall man with an expressive face, a young man, too, barely in his thirties, filled with plans for a better Toledo. 'Some of us younger people wanted to put up a hotel, a real fine place where you wouldn't be ashamed to stay. We figured about sixteen thousand dollars a room and we could have financed it, but then we asked ourselves, "what will we do about the winter?" And the more we studied, the more we realized that any money we made in summer would be lost in winter, when nobody comes here. Maybe we'll work out something else. I'm not worrying. I have enough to keep me busy trying to make this a fine restaurant. Did you see where the French guide gave us a two-fork rating? You can get a fine meal with us and not spend too much money. We offer three different menus. A la carte, and you can get a good meal from it for a dollar eighty-five. Special lunch of the house, a dollar thirty. And of course, the tourist menu at one fifty-five. How do the customers choose? A la carte forty percent, house special thirty percent, tourist thirty percent. Our very best meal, I would say, was partridge Toledo-style. Estupendo! There's a farm not far from here that kills two or three thousand partridges a day in season. The French, who know good cooking, always go for partridge because at two-twenty it's a sensational bargain. The norteamericanos? Well, they don't understand that game has to be hung. Sometimes they say it smells, so we take it back and serve them boiled chicken. They say it doesn't smell.'

I spent a long time with the Díaz family, nine of them including the wife's sister, who must be the most beautiful waitress in Spain. Kitchen, washrooms, tables and crockery were all immaculate. 'The government's smart,' Díaz said. 'They have one corps of restaurant inspectors who live in Toledo, another in Madrid. They send the Toledo men to inspect Madrid and the Madrid men out here to inspect us. You could be one of the Madrid men, for all I know. They pull tricks like that on us, but they have no problem with me because we police ourselves. We try to do everything possible to make tourists happy, and the disgraceful business you had when you ordered from the tourist menu too late would never happen here. The girls speak a lot of languages. French is most important, especially in a restaurant, because a norteamericano sits down and says, "Bring me that," but the Frenchman wants to know does it have a sauce, are the vegetables fresh, is the cream chilled. Frankly, the French are more fun, but we do everything we can to make the norteamericanos feel at home. They will spend money if they're encouraged.'

As to the food in El Plácido, as the quiet place was appropriately named, it was among the best I had in Spain. Don Mariano and his wife tried to push the stewed partridge, but when I resisted, they shrugged their shoulders and he said, 'It's the French who know how to eat. I suppose you want boiled chicken?' I took the mixed salad, which was crisp and delicious.

Right across the street, at Calle de Santo Tomé, 5, stood an element of the tourist industry which had always fascinated me, the marzipan factory of Rodrigo Martínez, who ran the big retail shop on the Zocodover where trays of marzipan in various shapes have seduced generations of travelers. In Spain this delicacy is called mazapán and has many distinctive qualities which differentiate it from brands sold elsewhere in the world. Señor Martínez was a small, conservative man in his fifties, cautious in all he did and said, and quite unable to understand why a stranger would be interested in anything so Spanish as a mazapán factory. Gingerly, as if I were a commercial spy, he released one bit of classified information after another in what was one of the most painstaking interviews I have ever conducted.

'If it weren't for the oil contained in the seed kernel of the almonds,' he began in the middle, 'mazapán would last indefinitely, like the dried meat they chop up in northern countries.' I must have shown my bewilderment at such a beginning, for he added slowly, 'You're probably like all other strangers and think that we get our almonds from Andalucía in the south. But we don't. The almonds that do grow down there aren't very good. We get ours from orchards along the Mediterranean coast. South of Valencia. Some of the best almonds in the world and to my taste much better than those grown in Arab countries. More consistent. Almonds and oranges grow in the same kind of soil and the same climate, so they compete.'

He must have concluded that that was all I needed to know about mazapán because he stopped. After some moments of silence he added cautiously, 'If you did want to make mazapán you'd get the best almonds you could find and dip them in boiling water, then run them through this friction machine, which scrapes off the skin. Look at that pile of skins. It has no commercial use whatever, doesn't even burn well. When the almonds are clean and shining white you move them over to this machine, but be careful to set the grinding wheels fairly far apart. Into the hopper you put one part almonds, one part cane sugar, and this machine breaks the almonds into pieces and mixes the sugar with them. Almonds cost about eighty-five cents a pound and sugar about ten cents a pound, so you can see that there's a great temptation to put in a lot of sugar and a little almond, but that makes wretched mazapán. Watch out for the man who puts in less than half almonds. You now throw the whole mass back into the grinder, but this time you set the wheels very close together, so that the almonds are pulverized. Then you press the paste into forms and bake it in a moderate oven for about fifteen minutes, take it out, paint it with a glaze of water and sugar and finish it off for another ten minutes to give that lovely brownish crust. That's the best mazapán you can get in the world.'

Señor Martínez was still suspicious, but he asked softly, 'Would you care to see what we do for Christmas?' I tried to show the enthusiasm I was feeling, and he brought down from a high shelf a set of empty circular boxes covered with bright decorations. 'Into these round boxes we coil long lengths of mazapán made in the shape of eels. They have scales of sugar, eyes of candy, and are filled with crystallized cherries, candied sweet potato, apricot jam and sweetened egg yolks. This big box sells for about four dollars, and lots of children think the thing inside is a real serpent, but of course it's only mazapán. I supply stores all over Spain and some in América del Norte, too.'

I said that I was especially fond of marzipan and frequently bought small samples in America, at which his face took on the glazed look that overtakes a Frenchman when you praise California wine. 'I'm afraid that in América del Norte you've never tasted real mazapán. Friends have sent me samples and it's mostly sugar. Very bad. But wait a minute. In Mexico City there's a man who learned how to make mazapán here in Toledo. During the Crusade he was on the other side, and when peace came he didn't want to live in Spain any longer, so he went to Mexico.' He paused, evidently remembering his long-absent friend, exiled from Toledo by the Civil War. 'I've heard some very good things about the quality of mazapán he's making in Mexico, but I'm sure you don't get any of it in New York.'

The interview had ended, and I was about to leave when I saw a sign which read: 'Exquisite paste for making the classic almond soup, in packages of any weight, eighty-seven cents a pound.' 'Is that how you make almond soup?' I asked with some excitement. 'Do you know our great almond soup?' he asked, his face brightening. 'I was introduced to it the other day. Best soup I ever tasted. Like angels' wings.' He became positively animated and said, 'Even better. We make a paste . . .' as if he could not believe my sincerity, he asked, 'Do you really like almond soup? Norteamericanos don't usually like it. It's the French who know something good when they taste it.' I assured Señor Martínez that from the first moment I had tasted this delicious soup, fragrant and heavy with flavor, I had delighted in it. 'The first bowlful they gave me had a rose petal floating in it. One rose petal, deep red against snowy white.' He realized that I knew what I was talking about and said, 'We don't use rose petals much any more. But we make this paste. You take two hundred grams of the paste and one liter of very cold, rich milk. You add a little handful of sweet biscuits well flavored and a small touch of carnela.' I asked him what carnela was, thinking that he must mean caramelo. No, he meant carnela. Everybody knew what carnela was, but my dictionary didn't give the word, so I didn't find out. 'You put these together and beat them thoroughly. Then serve ice-cold . . . or if it's Christmas, when we use almond soup a lot, you can heat it. Like our sign says, it's classic.'

As we talked we were surrounded by trays full of marzipan, some plain, some shaped in little cups and filled with apricot jam, and now Don Rodrigo offered me samples, delighted to have found someone who appreciated his art. As I ate, he said, 'After the battle of Navas de Tolosa in the year 1212 there was famine in many parts of Spain, so the monks of San Clemente convent, here in Toledo, developed the secret upon which our industry is founded. How to crush almonds so they will stay good to eat after four or five months. We sent our paste throughout Spain and that's how Toledo became famous for this delicacy. The secret? Well, when I was telling you how to make mazapán . . . the wheels and the sugar and the hot water . . . well, I didn't tell you everything.'

Much later, when I happened to have a bowl of almond soup in Madrid, the host sprinkled it with cinnamon. 'Canela,' he said. 'The final touch.'

When I left the marzipan factory I wandered to the west and came to a promenade that ran along the top of a cliff, from which I could look down into the river below. As I strolled along I came to a notable old building which stood hidden behind a high brick wall, as if it were a jewel under protection. A creaking gate let me into a Moorish garden which could have existed in that spot a thousand years ago when the Moors still occupied Toledo. Palm trees and lemon and orange grew in lovely patterns. In one corner a fountain bubbled, sending echoes across the graveled walks, and there were benches from which I could study at leisure the low and unimpressive building. I could not identify it: possibly it had been a mosque, or a synagogue or a church, for it seemed to partake of many characteristics. At the bottom it was built of unfinished brick; at the top, of a muddy stucco, which had begun to peel. The windows were off-center and the entrance was notable principally for a very old wooden door decorated in Moorish design.

I pressed against the door and it opened slowly to reveal a most beautiful building which looked like a mosque. The interior was filled by twenty-four octagonal columns, each topped by a capital of Arabic design supporting Moorish arches, but when I looked for the Muslim mihrab which would show worshipers the direction of Mecca, I found instead a Christian altar, for this was the famous Santa María la Blanca church and its origin was one of the compelling stories of Toledo.

To understand it we must leave Santa María and go to another part of Toledo, where in the Plaza Santo Domingo el Real we find imbedded in a wall a plaque which reads: 'Memorial to the fiestas which the Valencian colony of Toledo held in honor of San Vicente Ferrer solemnizing the Fifth Centennial of his glorious death, May 1919.' Vicente Ferrer was an inspired Dominican orator who operated around Valencia at the end of the fourteenth century. His preaching was so persuasive that he was credited with the conversion of thousands in lands as remote as Ireland and Italy. He was especially famed for his ability to convince Jews of their error and was responsible for converting many. In 1405 he came to Toledo to deliver a series of sermons against the Jews, which caused one historian to describe him as 'the bloodthirsty enemy of the Jews, intolerant and vehement, with an oratorical style both vibrant and tempestuous and a destructive eloquence without par.'

Following one inflamed sermon, his audience became so infuriated with the obstinacy of Toledo's Jews who refused to heed the words of Ferrer that they swarmed out of church, ran through the streets gathering a mob and burst into the Moorish building which I have been describing. It was then operating as a synagogue, from which the mob hauled all Jews they could find, dragged them to the promenade overlooking the river, cut their throats and threw them onto the rocks below. In one tremendous spasm the Jews of Toledo were practically eliminated, and no sooner were they gone than their synagogue was consecrated a church, and so it remains to this day.

One would suppose that after such tragedy the Jews would have had enough of Toledo, but a few years later the quota was again about normal. Jewish traders flourished, and although their original synagogue had been lost to them, since a building once consecrated could not revert to a prior use, they were encouraged to worship in another building nearby, which still stands as Spain's finest example of a synagogue. Thus matters stood until 1492, when Queen Isabel, acting under guidance and pressure from Cardinal Cisneros, decreed that all Jews in her kingdom must either convert to Christianity or go into exile. It is strange, in this day, to read on the interior wall of the cathedral a huge sign which commemorates the expulsion:

> In the year 1492, on the second day of the month of January, Granada with all its kingdom was captured by the monarchs Don Fernando and Doña Isabel, the Most Reverend Don Pedro González de Mendoza, Cardinal of Spain, being archbishop. This same year, at the end of the month of July, all the Jews were expelled from all the kingdoms of Castilla, of Aragón and of Sicily. The following year 93 at the end of the month of January, this holy church was completed, Don Francisco Fernández de Cuenca, archdeacon of Calatrava, being in charge of the decoration, painting and tracery of the vaults.

I had not intended saying anything about 'The Burial of Count Orgaz,' the chief work of El Greco, for this has been so well and so repeatedly described that there seemed little I might add, but I passed the church of Santo Tomé so often on my way to the synagogue of Santa María la Blanca or to the damasquinado shop of Señor Simón that I thought it silly not to revisit the magisterial painting; however, I did not do so until one afternoon when a party of English tourists asked me the way to St. Ptomaine's and I accompanied them to the church, where I took a seat with them and decided simply to look at the painting as if I had never seen it before. Santo Tomé's makes it easy to see its stupendous El Greco: a section of the church is set aside for this purpose, with eight comfortable Renaissance armchairs facing the picture, plus benches for ten and folding chairs for an additional thirty-five. It was late afternoon and we were the only group in the church; soon the English travelers left and I was alone in my Renaissance chair with the marvelously fresh and well-lighted canvas before me.

Like most universal masterpieces, this one has many fine passages and others that are frankly bad. There are three glaring defects: the picture breaks into two unrelated halves, an upper and a lower; the yellow-robed angel that is supposed to unite them is one of the sorriest figures El Greco ever drew and fails completely in his mission (in Spain all angels must be male); and the clouds of little bodiless angels consisting only of head and wings are ridiculous and, unlike the similar putti of Raphael and the other Italians who used the convention with charm, accomplish nothing. The unresolved breaking into two halves is caused by that much-vaunted line of heads which is one of the glories of the work but which in its excellence creates a problem that El Greco could not surmount. The faulty angel is poorly designed, poorly placed and poorly executed, which is curious, since El Greco used the same device with success in other paintings. As for the clouds of bodiless angels, I am not one to discuss El Greco's success or failure with this device because to me the convention has always seemed stupid, but I do know that in this great work it clutters up the heavens with ugly or even repulsive forms, whereas in certain Italian works it seems to add a sense of mysterious unearthliness. What I object to most, however, is that the putti are badly painted, and as one looks at the canvas with a fresh eye unimpeded by what others have seen, they merely add to the general clutter of a work that was poorly organized to begin with.

On the other hand, as I slowly studied the canvas I found hidden beauties which had escaped me on previous visits. In the lower left-hand corner of the painting, the right-hand panel of St. Stephen's cloak contains a small inserted depiction of the stoning of St. Stephen, which would have constituted one of the world's principal art treasures had it been painted as a full-scale canvas of its own. The naked figures throwing rocks would have anticipated Cézanne's 'Bathers' by three hundred years. In fact, this little excerpt is so good that it alone would establish El Greco as a major painter. I was similarly struck by the group of three heavenly musicians in the cloud to the Virgin's right, that is, at the extreme left-hand margin of the painting. These three in their powerfully sculpted robes are drawn and painted about as well as figures could be when seen from below, and I wondered that I had not noticed them before. Again, if they had formed the subject matter for a full-sized canvas they would now be famous. The marvelous figure of St. Peter, robed in saffron, with two giant keys dangling from his limp right hand, proves once more the affinity El Greco felt

Sunlight through the window of the synagogue
where the friends of El Greco once worshiped.

for this particular saint; he never painted Peter better than here, and in doing so, achieved one of his most successful religious portraits. But when one looks at the painting for a long time, three or four hours perhaps, one is struck mostly, I think, by that host of paradise that fills the upper right-hand corner. Here are the tormented figures from the streets of Toledo, the half-idiots that El Greco loved to paint, the aimless ones, the God-driven. They crowd in upon the scene, beseeching the Virgin to receive the soul of the Conde de Orgaz and present it to Christ, robed in white, who waits above. They are a remarkable assembly, more compelling and more Spanish, I think, than the notables lined up below, even though El Greco himself stands among the latter. For me the painting repeats the dichotomy of Spain that we saw earlier in the two paintings by El Greco and Goya: the sober, secure and well-groomed nobles who now keep and have always kept Spain under rigid control, and the wonderfully human peasant types whose fiery passions have provided the torment and vision of the land, but as I look at the latter crowding heaven I ask, 'If this is paradise, what must hell be like?'

The Conde de Orgaz, a citizen of Toledo and lord of the town of Orgaz, some twenty miles south of the city, died in 1323, and El Greco painted the legendary miracle of his burial in 1586. The conde had assumed responsibility for enlarging and rebuilding this church of St. Thomas the Apostle at the turn of the century, thus assuring his ultimate burial in the church. In 1312 the conde increased his fund of heavenly gratitude by obtaining from the queen a grant of property in Toledo so that a community of Augustinian friars, formerly located in unhealthful surroundings on the banks of the Tajo, could move within the walls, and by insisting that the new church should be dedicated to St. Stephen, the same as the old one had been. 'When the priests were preparing to bury him,' as the tablet below the picture explains, 'an admirable and unusual thing, St. Stephen and St. Augustine came down from heaven and buried him here with their own hands. Since it would take long to explain what might have motivated these saints, ask about it of the Augustinian friars, who are not far from here, if you have the time. The way is short.' The plaque then continues with a fascinating bit of local history: 'You have heard the gratitude of heavenly beings; hear now the inconstancy of mortal men. The same Orgaz bequeathed to the curate and ministers of this church, as well as to the poor of the parish, two sheep, sixteen hens, two wineskins full of wine, two loads of firewood and eight hundred of the coins that we call maravedis, which they were to receive annually from the residents of Orgaz. Since these people refused for two years to pay the pious tribute, in the belief that with the passage of time the matter would be forgotten, they have been forced to pay it by order of the Chancery of Valladolid in the year 1570, the case having been prosecuted energetically by Andrés Núñez de Madrid, curate of this church, and Pedro Ruiz Durón, the administrator.' It was undoubtedly this successful lawsuit that led to the commission-ing a few years later of the painting. I should add that the above inscription is in Latin.

Two of the finest portraits in the standing file belong to this curate Núñez (the golden-robed, iron-faced prelate holding a book at extreme right) and to the administrator Ruiz (the ecstatic figure clothed in white surplice standing nearest the spectator). Among the worthies one finds the grave and bitter-faced old Covarrubias brothers, El Greco's son and others who may have been well known in Toledo when the painting was done.

The line of standing figures has always bothered me, so I was pleased to come upon the facts relating to its inception, because I believe the sequence of events helps explain how great works of art are sometimes evolved. There had been talk in Toledo of applying to Rome for the sanctification of the Conde de Orgaz, seeing that heaven itself had sent messengers to supervise his burial, but the movement had got nowhere, so Father Núñez proposed that at least the body of the conde be moved to a finer tomb, but his archbishop said, 'No, it is not proper that sinful hands should move the body that saints themselves have buried.' Father Núñez thereupon came up with a third proposal: 'Mark Orgaz's humble grave with a painting which will retell the glories of the conde,' and to this the authorities agreed. So a contract, which still exists, was drawn up between Father Núñez and El Greco, perhaps with Administrator Ruiz looking on, in which the artist outlines his understanding of what he is being required to do:

> On the canvas will be painted a procession, showing how the curate and other clergymen were performing the offices for the burial of Don Gonzalo Ruiz de Toledo, lord of the town of Orgaz, and St. Augustine and St. Stephen descended to bury the body of this caballero, one holding him by the head and the other by the feet, depositing him in the sepulcher, and present-ing round about many people looking on, and above all this will be depicted a sky filled with a heavenly scene.

As in many cases of Renaissance masterpieces, it was the client who determined much of the basic design, and El Greco saw to it that the two men who were footing the bill, Núñez and Ruiz, occupied prominent positions when the job was done.

Two sayings sum up all we require to know about this monumental work. One of the Spanish critics responsible for generating world interest in El Greco said of him and of this painting in particular, 'When he's good there's none better and when he's bad there's none worse.' One Englishman, as his group left that day, said of the painting, 'This is the best thing in Spain and the cheapest.' To spend an hour or two before this superbly presented picture, lounging in a Renaissance chair, costs eight cents.

On one of my casual wanderings through Toledo, I came to the quiet Plaza de Carmelites, on whose wall appeared this notice:

GLORY TO THE CARMELITE MARTYRS

FOR GOD AND FOR SPAIN

THERE WERE ASSASSINATED IN THIS STREET

IN JULY 1936 BY THE MARXISTS

THE FOLLOWING RELIGIOUS

The names of seventeen friars were listed, and I was once more brought face to face with the Civil War; no city knew worse atrocities than Toledo. In the beginning days it looked as if the Republic were going to win, and since Toledo had always been conservative and the seat of Catholic power—for the Bishop of Toledo is the primate of Spain—men who felt they had old scores to settle with the Church killed wantonly, as this sign testified. Later, when the war in Toledo had settled into a siege-type operation, Republican hotheads imported from Madrid coursed through the streets rounding up all conservatives, whom they herded in large groups to that very precipice from which the Jews had been flung in 1405, and there they slaughtered the prisoners in obscene brutality, sometimes throwing their bodies over the cliff as had been done 531 years before; history in Spain has an ominous way of repeating itself. As might be expected, when the Franco forces triumphed a savage retaliation was launched by the victors, who applied one simple rule: if the man has fought on the Republican side, kill him. And how was the best way to tell if he had fought? Look at the right shoulder of his coat. If it is worn it means that he has been using a gun, so shoot him.

How many conservatives the Republicans killed in Toledo cannot be calculated, but it was in the thousands; how many liberals the Franco forces slaughtered is not known, but the number was at least as large.

In this vengeful killing and counter-killing occurred one act of incandescent heroism which has come to summarize the Civil War as seen from the Franco side, and the visitor to Toledo can explore the history of this event. On a hill overlooking the Río Tajo stands an old square fortress on a site originally selected for this purpose by the Romans and used by the Moors when they held Toledo as their northern capital. Rebuilt many times, destroyed repeatedly by mines and fire, it could never have been beautiful, but after the defeat of Napoleon, who burned it, an attempt was made to bring the various parts of its façade into some kind of harmony, and the result, while far from artistic, did have a certain heavy balance. It was a four-story building, very large, with four squat and brutal towers topped by dark metal spires of no quality whatever. It was called the Alcázar (Ahl-kah-thar, with a heavy accent on the second syllable) and

This massive door knocker reminds one that the Spanish home has usually been a fortress.

more prominently even than the cathedral it dominated the skyline of this old fortress city.

In the summer of 1936 its barracks were practically empty, because a short time before, the cadets living in the Alcázar had been involved in a fracas in the Zocodover, and so Republican leaders of the government, eager to find an excuse for disciplining the army, which they did not trust, had banished the young army men to another barracks some distance from Toledo. This meant that the senior official remaining in the military area was a fifty-eight-year-old colonel of infantry, José Moscardó e Iriarte, heavy of face and heavier of bottom. He then held a job he loved, director of the army's physical education program, for his passion was sports, especially soccer, and he was about to leave Spain to serve as national representative at the Berlin Olympic games.

When his superiors launched their rebellion in Africa against the Republicans, Colonel Moscardó summoned all military personnel in the Toledo district, plus elements of the Guardia Civil, into the Alcázar, and there, on July 21, assembled 1205 fighting men plus 555 noncombatants, among whom were 211 children. They had ammunition but little food; they did have some horses, and when night fell on that first day they must have felt that they would be in the Alcázar for a week at most. They were to stay, at the point of starvation, for ten weeks.

Outnumbered, outgunned and under constant attack, with only the determination of Colonel Moscardó to provide any kind of military leadership, the defenders of the Alcázar hung on. The Republicans made many sorties against the stout walls but quickly learned that they would not be able to take the fortress by direct assault. However, they had other devices and these were potent.

On July 23, the third day of the siege, according to the modern Spanish legend, a Republican leader called Colonel Moscardó on the telephone and told him he held his sixteen-year-old son prisoner. He threatened to have him shot if Moscardó did not surrender the Alcázar immediately.

Republican: Do you perhaps think my statement is untrue? You are now going to speak with your son.

Luis: Papa!

Moscardó: What's happening, son?

Luis: They say they're going to shoot me if you don't surrender.

Moscardó: Then commend your soul to God, shout ¡Viva España! and ¡Viva Cristo Rey!, and die like a hero.

Luis: A very strong kiss, Papa.

Moscardó: Goodbye, my son, a very strong kiss.

The Alcázar was not surrendered and later the boy was shot. One who underwent the siege reported that it was this event that steeled them to an acceptance of starvation and death, 'Because who could go to the colonel and complain about what the siege was costing him when the colonel had given his son?' Today on the wall of the room where Moscardó held this phone conversation hang translations of it in all important languages; the English is a botch job and very un-Spanish, because someone felt that Anglo-Saxons would not understand a father's sending his sixteen-year-old son a kiss. The English comes out like this:

Moscardó: Then turn your thoughts to God, cry out, 'Long Live Spain,' and die as a patriot.

Luis: All my fondest love, father.

Moscardó: All of mine to you.

(Facts concerning the Alcázar are so confused and open to challenge that I have relied upon one principal source, *The Siege of the Alcázar* by Cecil D. Eby [1965], which is in the main pro-Franco. Many important data used by Eby have been controverted by anti-Franco sources, often with good reason, as in Herbert Rutledge Southworth's *The Myth of the Crusade of Franco* [1964], which cites many sources to prove that the famous telephone conversation was either apocryphal or—if it did happen—without the inflated significance it has been accorded. The Moscardó son, who was sixteen at the time, is now living happily in Madrid at Calle Castelló, 48. There was an older son who was shot, but under much different circumstances.)

When the Republicans could not take the Alcázar either by frontal assault or by pressure on Moscardó, they wheeled up heavy artillery which fired point-blank into the fort, and when this failed they summoned airplanes which dumped tons of bombs to knock the old walls apart. The walls did collapse, but the men inside did not, so the attackers resorted to a sensible device: they brought miners down from the Asturias coal fields to dig a tunnel under one of the towers. There they piled a vast charge of high explosive and warned Moscardó that they were going to blow the Alcázar to bits. They even summoned newsmen from Madrid to watch the end of the siege. The explosion came at 0631 in the morning of September 18, the sixtieth day, and true to prediction, it annihilated the southwest tower in a blast that could be heard forty miles away in Madrid. The Alcázar had fallen, and the news was sent around the world.

But inside the building the stubborn old colonel recoiled from the shock, assembled his assistants and through the smoke inspected the damage. The tower was gone, the wall was breached, but for the Republicans to take advantage of the blast they would still have to climb the hill, cross the rubble and take the building at bayonet point. Moscardó doubted that they were willing to pay the price.

He was right. In the days that followed, the siege degenerated into a bloody, ruthless struggle of many Republicans trying to overcome a few Franco men holed up in the ruins. Day by day artillery shells and airplane bombs proceeded with the destruction of the walls until the Alcázar seemed a good two-thirds gone. The patio was filled with rubble and the upper rooms were no more. How the ruins, which appeared to offer no hiding places, could hold out was a mystery.

Many of the defenders were killed in the fighting; others died of causes relating to starvation. Among the greatest heroes were the women, who not only helped the men but looked after the children as well. And day after day Colonel Moscardó sent out the radio report which would become the catchword of the siege, 'Sin novedad en el Alcázar' (Nothing new in the Alcázar, or, as some translate it: All quiet in the Alcázar).

When it seemed that one more push from the Republicans must wipe out the defenders, word came that a column of General Franco's troops had reached Talavera de la Reina and would shortly arrive to lift the siege. A race between Franco's oncoming troops and the Republican besiegers then developed, with odds in favor of the latter, but the iron-willed men in the Alcázar held out against all pressures, and on September 28, the seventieth day of the siege, when the defenders had become matchsticks through hunger, General Franco's troops arrived. The first contingent to enter the Alcázar was a unit of black Moors from Africa. Their ancestors had been thrown out of this city in 1085. Now, 851 years later, they were returning. It was then that the dreadful reprisals began.

The newsmen who accompanied Franco's forces into the city were eager to make of Colonel Moscardó, now a general, the hero of new Spain, but they found him a stolid, unimaginative old man whose main concern was still soccer. The awful realization dawned on them that when Moscardó had said, 'nothing new in the Alcázar,' he had not been uttering a heroic statement but the simple truth as he saw it. His job, as senior officer present, had been to hold the command he found himself with, and he had done so.

The somewhat doddering old fellow was a source of embarrassment to the Franco government, for he was unquestionably the salient hero of the war, but when he was assigned to a military command commensurate with his fame, he fumbled it and continued to send in reports: 'Nothing new at the front.' Finally, with the coming of world peace, the perfect job was found for him: he put on his general's uniform and as Conde del Alcázar de Toledo, represented Spain at the London Olympic Games of 1948 and the Helsinki ones of 1952. That he enjoyed.

I wanted to see what the Alcázar was like, so on a warm September day I left the Zocodover and walked down into the valley where the Republicans had had the command post for shelling the fort. Above me loomed the Alcázar, newly rebuilt but as brutal and ugly as ever, and I shuddered at the thought of being a soldier required to scramble up that hill and assault that fort. Later, when I had climbed to the plaza at the east end of the building, I saw the grandiloquent monument erected to the men of the Alcázar, and for a strange moment I thought I was in another century. Victory, whose garments flowed behind her wings, held aloft a golden sword while two women knelt in grieving position. Behind Victory stood two well-carved friezes in white marble featuring workers and women mourners. On the front of the monument was carved the word Faith, represented by a man with shield and sword; on the right Valor, a blindfolded woman holding a cross; and on the left Sacrifice, a man offering a lamb. On the back I saw a good pietà in which a shrouded woman bent over a fallen man, while far away on either end rose three tall metal shafts topped by the fasces, the eagle and a third symbol I could not decipher: it looked like a large cross with studded edges.

Leading up to the monument were flights of stairs, balustrades, promenades and landscaped areas much like Hadrian's villa at Tivoli, but juvenile delinquents or cryptic Republicans, as the case might be, had gone about toppling the ornaments which graced the approach, so that the whole had a sense of a crumbling Roman forum. All was noble; all was very nineteenth century; all yearned for the past.

*Statue of the Commander Villamartín
machine-gunned daily by the Reds during
their siege of the Alcázar*

Inside the Alcázar, I caught many glimpses of the Spanish army at work, for set into the walls were tablets whose words evoked past glories:

THE XXI GRADUATING CLASS OF INFANTRY

1914–1917

ON ITS GOLDEN ANNIVERSARY

TO THE DEFENDERS OF THE ALCAZAR

1964

In one corner a white plaque read: 'Here on September 11, 1936, was celebrated the only Holy Mass of the Siege. Catholics! This corner is land sanctified by the visit of the Divine King. To our heroes.' Another shield read: 'To those who endured the siege by the Communist hordes and converted this Alcázar into a symbol of the unity and independence of the nation.' But the most telling item was something I had seen on my earliest visit, when the gaunt old fortress was still in ruins. It was a magazine and a most unlikely one, *The Illustrated London News* for January 24, 1914. Colonel Moscardó had found it in the Alcázar library and had used it to help barricade his windows from Republican bullets. It was opened to a complicated story: 'Sold by Rumour. A Fine and Famous Holbein Portrait.' The painting was shown in a small photograph, 'Thomas Cromwell, Earl of Essex,' owned by the Earl of Caledon and rumored to have been sold by him for $150,000, a charge which he denied. A bullet had passed through the earl's head and nine others had splattered the page.

The best thing about the Alcázar has always been the cloistered central courtyard, not because the cloisters are attractive, for they are heavy and lack gracia, but because the area was spacious and did contain a famous statue of Carlos V in military uniform. The base carried two quotations uttered by the emperor on the eve of a crucial invasion of Africa, and these had become the slogans of the Franco forces who defended the building: 'I shall enter Tunis as conqueror or remain dead in Africa.' And: 'If in the battle you see me and my flag go down, rescue first the flag.'

As I stood in the Alcázar with this statue of Carlos, I reflected upon the years I have spent studying this emperor and his works. For me he has always been a central fact of Spain and one of the figures of world history who best repay study. When I was a young professor I used to daydream about what I would do if placed in charge of a college whose only responsibility was to provide a selected group of students the best possible education without regard to outside pressures from alumni, large contributors, the sports editors of the nearby metropolis or the general damn-foolishness of American life. Like any sensible man I would naturally sponsor only a general humanities program, reserving training courses like law, medicine, engineering or business for university specialization which would come later. My students would direct themselves to language, literature, science, philosophy, the fine arts and history, secure in the knowledge that if they mastered those subjects they would later be in a position to control such social functions as medicine, manufacturing, constructing, teaching and governing. In other words, I would stress with my students the widest possible exploration plus the most intensive analysis of two or three specific unities.

The latter, which would be the heart of my system, would be attacked in a radical way. Twice in the student's four years—once at the beginning and once at the end, so that he could see in himself his deepening capacity—I would ask him to spend the year or most of the year in studying one brief segment of history. During that time he would take no traditional courses whatever, no mathematics, no chemistry, no Literature IV. Instead he would immerse himself in the world culture operating at that period in time, and to do so he would study the art forms, the music, the contemporary understanding of geography, the philosophy, the religious convictions, the economics, the travel, the architecture, the writing and the daily life of the peasant. And he would be obliged to explore in depth the half-dozen nations or principalities which best illustrated the significant meanings of the age being studied.

I have often speculated on what periods would be most fruitful for such an approach and have felt inclined toward A.D. 70 and the fall of Jerusalem, and 1832 and the passage of reform in Great Britain, plus some one date to be agreed upon when Greece and Rome were in confrontation and another in the Middle Ages before dissolution of old patterns had begun. Any two of these, properly investigated, would provide a young man with enough insights to illuminate the rest of his life, but there has always been one period which has stood preeminent. If I were now forced to educate myself anew, it would be to this period that I would direct myself, the period when more notable men were in power and more ideas in conflict than at any other in world history.

It would be sometime in the 1530s, when Catholic Spain and France, Protestant England and Muslim Turkey were contesting the leadership of Europe and when Hindu India was preparing itself for the advent of Akbar the Great, and Orthodox Russia was beginning its consolidation under Ivan the Terrible. To understand this period would be to understand the movements that formed modern history. Observe the dates, the right-hand one representing more or less when the man in question came into power:

Francis I of France	(1494–1547)	1515
Henry VIII of England	(1491–1547)	1509
Carlos I and V of Spain	(1500–1558)	1519
Suleiman I of Turkey	(1495?–1566)	1520
Martin Luther	(1483–1546)	1519
Ivan IV of Russia	(1530–1584)	1547
Akbar of India	(1542–1605)	1556

These men were titans and they tore the preconceptions of their narrow worlds to shreds. They were builders, and when they died they left their nations a legacy of accomplishment. They were warriors who defended their realms and extended them. They were patrons of the arts and left their cities richer and their universities improved. Some were good administrators and set patterns which determined the future conduct of their lands, and all were men who wrestled with great forces.

Of the seven Luther was the most intelligent, Suleiman the most glorious, Akbar the finest human being, Francis the most cunning, Henry the most determined, and Ivan the most violent. Carlos V excelled in nothing, but it was he who commanded most of the world and who left the most lasting impression.

Americans are apt to ignore the tremendous power of Carlos and Spain in these critical years toward the middle of the sixteenth century. There was no nation which came close to rivaling Spain. Because of its ownership of the Low Countries and certain provinces which are now part of France, it exercised a pincers movement on that country and kept it frustrated. England, not yet a major power, was neutralized by marriage compacts. In the Mediterranean, Spain held control of the north coast of Africa and kept the Muslim power of Turkey at least at arm's length. Through its ownership of Sardinia, Sicily, Naples and some of the smaller Italian states, Spain exerted great pressure on the Papacy and exacted favorable decisions when it was not engaged in outright war against the Pope. And in Mexico and Peru it owned mines from which floods of wealth reached Spain, rarely to stay there.

The Spanish fleet, brought into being by Cisneros, was the best operating. The Spanish army was the terror of Europe. Spanish universities were without superiors. To Spain were attracted the foremost painters of Europe, and the merit of Spanish letters was acknowledged. It was truly an age of gold, when all nations lay in fee, as it were, to Spanish leadership and power.

All that was required, in those crucial years when the future of the world was being determined, was that Spain evolve some kind of government and economic system which would enable her to retain what she had and to build on it at a rate of growth comparable to that at which England, France and Germany would build. If Spain had maintained only that normal rate of progress, she would have remained the world's dominant power for two or three more centuries and we might now be speaking Spanish. The central problem of Spanish history is why Carlos V and Felipe II failed to discover the system of government and the patterns of growth required to sustain their nation.

At the foot of the hill on which the Alcázar stands is a fine museum which not many Toledo visitors see, and that is a pity, because it is a memorial to the greatness of Carlos V. It is housed in the old hospital of

Santa Cruz, built from funds left by Cardinal Mendoza, and the doorway is another flamboyant memorial showing Mendoza assisting the Empress Helena, mother of Constantine the Great, as she finds the true cross. The interior of the museum is of a type which I do not usually like, a conglomeration of tapestry, furniture, etching, carpeting, sculpture, bric-a-brac and mementos, with here and there a notable painting. But this museum is different, because it has been assembled with excellent taste. I have introduced half a dozen connoisseurs to it—ordinary travel literature does not stress it, perhaps because the custodians don't want too many visitors—and they have been enchanted.

I shall not speak of the paintings; the museum has only twenty-three El Grecos, including the 'Assumption of the Virgin,' one of his latest and greatest works. But I should like to comment briefly on the many objects relating to Carlos V. Here is the well-known bronze statue of Carlos, with jutting jaw, suspicious little eyes and hair coming down to a sharp V above his eyes. He seems a compact, determined man, visibly apprehensive about the tasks confronting him, for he was called to transform a peninsular mentality into one with a world outlook; he tried to avoid but could not the religious challenges thrown at him by that damned monk, Martin Luther; professors at the University of Salamanca were warning him that if a nation brought in so much gold from Mexico and Peru it might go bankrupt because of the ensuing rise in the cost of living, but that made no sense at all; and the various popes in Rome kept passing edicts which caused confusion.

Along this wall, strung out for some forty-five feet, is the printed scroll depicting his coronation as Holy Roman Emperor. In the procession we see hundreds of figures—kings, scribes, musicians, heralds, cardinals, along with Pope Clement VII and a display of war machines. Oxen are being roasted and stewards are throwing out free bread to the peasants.

In this corner is a handsome little carving showing Carlos and his younger and more gifted brother Fernando, who excelled him in so many ways. Fernando looks larger, seems intelligent, is better-looking, but Carlos by holding on far outdistanced Fernando. It was he, not Fernando, who was elected Holy Roman Emperor, although at the end of his life he passed the job on to his brother.

At the far end of the museum, in a gallery two stories high, hang the blue battle pennants flown by Carlos' illegitimate son, Don Juan de Austria, at the Battle of Lepanto, where the Turks were contained in 1571. The largest of the flags is about sixty feet long, emblazoned not with nationalistic slogans but with I.N.R.I. and Jesus on the cross. Spanish galleons really did go into battle with the goal of saving Christianity.

Below the blue pennants rests a portrait of Don Juan, the preserver of Spain, for had he lost at Lepanto, Islam would have controlled the Mediterranean and Spain might once more have become Moorish. Don Juan is shown as a young man in ruffs and battle armor, with a bright-red scarf over his right shoulder; he was a man of such charismatic power that when he died in the Low Countries his body was cut into four parts, pickled in brine and smuggled home so that the French might not know so great an adversary was dead. Of course, as soon as the barrels had crossed the Pyrenees the body was sewn together again.

In another room I see the tall, brooding figure of Carlos' legitimate son Felipe II, husband of Mary Tudor and Spain's most typical king, and off to one side, in a place of honor, I see again that marvelous bronze statue of Isabel, the Portuguese princess whom Carlos married. Look at her, standing in a stiffly brocaded dress, bejeweled, confident, half smiling. She is regal and self-assured, and her statue is one of the most pleasing in Spain. Carlos loved her and was a good husband. If she was as charming as her statue, one can understand why.

On the walls of the upper cloister appear two gold-encrusted maps which summarize Carlos. The first depicts his numerous battle campaigns: 'Tunis 1535; Algiers 1529; Zaragoza 1518; Naples 1528; Brussels 1521; and chief of all, Mühlberg 1547.' The second map shows his travels and is a jungle of crossing lines which wander off to strange locations. It carries the well-known passage from his abdication speech: 'I have been nine times in Germany, six in Spain, seven in Italy, ten in Flanders. In peace and war I have been four times in France, two in England and two in Africa for a total of forty expeditions, without counting the voyages to my kingdoms. Eight times I have crossed the Mediterranean and three times the Ocean [to England]. I am at peace with all and from all ask pardon if I have offended anyone.'

These maps help explain a cardinal fact about Carlos: although King of Spain he was rarely in the country. His preoccupation was always with the other parts of his empire and he allowed the internal government of Spain to drift. At the beginning of his reign he set the pattern for much that was to follow. Faced by civil war throughout Spain, he summoned his nobles to distant Santiago de Compostela and told them, 'This nation is faced by a crisis which could destroy it. Do something. I'll be back in three years.' At a later period he was absent for fourteen years.

Carlos was never a congenial man, but in the last two years of his life he performed an unexpected act which captivated the imagination of his people and continues to do so today. While still possessed of full powers, he voluntarily resigned as emperor and turned his scepter over to his son Felipe. To appreciate fully what he did next I had to take a long expedition westward into the mountains of the Sierra de Gredos.

I drove north out of Toledo to the Madrid–Badajoz road, which carries traffic heading for Portugal. There I turned left for Talavera de la Reina, the ugly commercial town, center of Spain's ceramic industry and forever remembered as the place where Joselito, prince of bullfighters, was gored to death on May 16, 1920. West of Talavera, I headed north toward the

Gredos mountains, but before entering them turned west and drove along the foothills for about fifty miles through bleak and desolate scenery. How empty most of Spain is.

At last I came to a sign which indicated that a short distance off the road to the north lay the monastery of Yuste. I followed the dusty road which seemed to lead nowhere, when suddenly I turned a corner and saw a low, mean building of no attractiveness whatever but the goal of all travelers who want to pay their respects to Carlos V, for it was to this remote monastery, isolated, forlorn and with nothing to commend it, that the great emperor retired.

I had the good fortune to reach Yuste at the same time that two French priests drove up in their Renault. 'What a road,' they said, eager to compare experiences. The driver was tall and taciturn, but he had the facts. His passenger was on the chubby side and he had the enthusiasm.

'You must imagine Carlos in Brussels at the height of his powers,' the round priest said. 'Sixty years old, maybe sixty-five, and the most powerful man in the world.'

'Fifty-five,' the thin one said. 'Born 1500. Abdicated the Netherlands throne 1555. Abdicated the Spanish throne 1556. You can figure it out for yourself.'

'It was to this spot he came. Look. Not a house. Not even a church. Think how lonely it must have been for him, the great man, to end his days in such surroundings.' He shook his head sadly, then turning to his comrade, asked, 'How many years was he here?'

'Came in early 1557. Died in late 1558.'

'Two years of this desolate hell. Why?'

'Because he wanted to make his peace with God, that's why.'

We walked through the cold, dark monastery and imagined Carlos alone here and praying. 'He brought only one friend with him,' the fat priest said. 'What was his name?'

'An Italian engineer, Juanelo of Cremona. Remember, Carlos was emperor of much of Italy too.'

'It was what's-his-name from Cremona who invented a special pump for lifting water from the Río Tajo into Toledo. Carlos loved him and the two spent what amounted to an exile here.'

We left the forbidding monastery and walked through the unkempt grounds. To the north were the Gredos mountains, in all other directions the lonely emptiness of Extremadura. 'What a place for a great man to die,' the fat priest lamented. Apparently he was imagining how many of the good things he appreciated would not have been available had he accompanied the emperor.

'I believe he really came here to get closer to God,' the tall priest said. 'He prayed a good deal. He used to write to his son. "Above everything else hold fast to the Catholic Church. Support the Inquisition. Stamp out heresy." He really believed in God.'

The chubby priest, who was the more sentimental of the two, insisted that we go back into the monastery, although his friend and I were ready to push on. He led us to a bare room, of which he said, 'Here Carlos died. What age did you say?'

'Fifty-eight.'

'His body was kept here in this chapel for . . . How many years did you say?'

'Many years.'

'It was then translated to El Escorial and buried beneath that pile of granite.' He fell silent for a moment, then added, 'But here is where his soul will always rest.'

We three paid our respects to Carlos, ruler of much of the known world, determiner of Spain's history, defender of the faith. The two priests prayed and we shook hands. The fat one said, 'Amusing. An American who had no contacts with him. Two Frenchmen who fought him all his life. We meet here to pay him homage. What a miserable place.'

It was not till four years later that I came upon a modern biography of Carlos V which took the edge off our prayers and philosophizing at Yuste. Researchers have found documents that spell out what happened at Yuste and it was somewhat different from what the French priests and I had imagined. When Carlos sat in cold Brussels, contemplating retirement, his thoughts kept going back to a monastery he had once seen in the blazing summer heat of Extremadura and it was this that encouraged him to give up the crown and have some relaxation and pleasure in his last years. He drew up a list of those who were to share his lonely exile at Yuste and it totaled seven hundred and sixty-two people, but when it was suggested that so many might crowd the place he trimmed it down to a hundred and fifty, of whom two-thirds actually accompanied him to the monastery, where he was visited by a constant stream of nobles and members of the royal family. At first he calculated that he could get by on a yearly allowance of sixteen thousand ducats but soon found that he would need at least twenty, with another thirty thousand to serve as a contingency fund.

Inventories have come down to us of what Carlos lugged out to Yuste: magnificent tapestries, choice furnishings, paintings by Titian and jeweled bric-a-brac. The cells of the monastery were for his entourage; for him a special house was built with a man-made lake under his window so that he could fish for trout from his living room. His kitchens were supervised by a Portuguese who had been with him for years, a cook much addicted to heavy German sauces which, when accompanied by gigantic quantities of alcohol, inflamed his gout. When an attack came, Carlos retreated for a few days to a salubrious diet, then gorged himself on slabs of red beef and fish, both bad for gout. He insisted upon hors d'oeuvres of jellied eel and stewed partridge and loved desserts of the richest and heaviest sort. Such a diet alone would have insured the return of his gout, but he was also insanely fond of anchovies; his staff saw to it that little kegs of them were sent ahead whenever he took a trip. Naturally, when he had eaten his quota of salted anchovies he generated a huge thirst, which he slaked with large bottles of beer kept in buckets of snow brought down from the mountains.

When I read these new researches on Carlos the ascetic recluse of Yuste, I felt very close to him, for I too suffer from gout and I too crave anchovies above any other food; in this matter Spain has been a temptation to me, a kind of self-inflicted purgatory in which those marvelous little fish stare at me from every bar, in every salad, and I had real tears in my eyes when I read of how one day Carlos, after a long trip across the countryside, came to an inn where his keg of anchovies waited, only to find that they had been so jostled by horses coming across the mountains, they were reduced to a formless pulp. Today, thank heaven, Swedish research men have developed a simple pill which controls gout, and when I read the letters of Carlos and Felipe, for the latter inherited the disease in even more virulent form, and see how they hobbled about much of their time and developed the evil tempers which they vented on their underlings, I reflect that the history of Spain might have been much modified had the two kings been given not buckets of anchovies but a supply of Swedish pills.

The strangest fact about Carlos was not his retirement, nor his lust for anchovies, nor his extended absence from Spain, but that he ruled the country from 1517 to 1555 without being legally king, for during these years his mother, Juana la Loca, lived hidden away in a filthy room that we shall visit later. She was unquestionably Queen of Spain, and legal documents during the period bear her name first, followed by that of Carlos as her executor. She died on April 11, 1555, and Carlos abdicated the Spanish part of his holdings on January 16, 1556, so that he did finally acquire the kingship—but for only nine months. Scholars in increasing numbers are turning up evidence which suggests that Juana was not really mad but that it was to her son's advantage to keep her penned up, which he did.

Carlos V, this little man called upon to wage vast struggles, this least of the quadrumvirate—Henry of England, Francis of France, Suleiman of Turkey, Carlos of Spain—seemed at the time to be victor by virtue of his obstinacy and his dedication to one religious principle. It required the passage of two centuries to prove how wrong his decisions had been, how hollow his victories. The ideas of Francis and Henry blossomed into great kingdoms and empires, whereas those of Carlos withered into national disaster. It is such thoughts that torment one at the monastery of Yuste.

FOLLOWING PAGE: *Mosque.*

IV

CORDOBA

OCEANO
ATLANTICO

MAR MEDITERRANE

Barcelona

Madrid

Lisboa

San Calixto
Hornachuelos
Córdoba
Sevilla
Guadix
Granada

0   MILES   100

The traveler wishing to observe Islamic Spain has his choice of two cities, Granada with its Alhambra or Córdoba with its Great Mosque (in Spanish, Mezquita). Of the two the former is by a considerable degree the more exciting and also the easier to absorb, for its buildings, gardens and geographic setting are immediately recognizable as significant. It would take a dull man to miss the point of Granada, for its Alhambra is a museum of Islamic memories.

But for three personal reasons I chose Córdoba. It was more prosaic and therefore showed its Islamic heritage with less hyperbole. It had been the intellectual center of Islam, so that its influence lasted long after the expulsion of the last Moors from Granada. And in Córdoba had lived four of the Spaniards who were most important to me and I wanted to see where these excellent men had lived and why they had been born here and not in some more congenial place. It is interesting but accidental that each gained his greatest fame after he had left Spain.

Córdoba is a fine city laid out along the right bank of a bend in the Río Guadalquivir, and to reach the site of my first pilgrimage I had to walk down a pleasant avenue named after Generalísimo Franco and through a shady park, at the end of which I came to the limits of the old Jewish quarter, evacuated in 1492 but since occupied by working-class families. I followed an ancient Roman wall which had outlined the Jewish quarter and came to a Roman gate where a plaza had been built, providing a rustic vista marked by three reflecting pools lined with roses, cypresses and willows. At the end nearest the gate a series of low stone walls, handsomely proportioned, created a small plateau, in the middle of which rose a column of cream-colored granite on which stood the statue of a shortish, baldheaded man in a toga, bearing in his right hand a manuscript scroll of some sort, perhaps a tragedy in verse. His face was what I would have expected, that of a grave gentleman utterly unafraid of adversity or death or the persecution that might be visited upon him by the tyrant Nero. He stood looking away from the wall, away from Rome, and over the distant hills of Andalucía, his homeland.

He was Lucius Annaeus Seneca (c. 4 B.C.–A.D. 65), whom many consider to have been the foremost Spaniard who ever lived; more consider him the representative Spaniard. Philosopher, orator, essayist, playwright and poet, he not only had a distinguished literary career that marked him as the leading intelligence of his time, but he also became a political leader, serving as consul of Rome. He had been appointed tutor to the boy Nero, whose counselor he later became and whose excesses he modified. He was a Stoic by nature, a city man by preference and a manipulator of political forces by design. In all that he tried he succeeded and he was both a perfect Roman and the ideal Spaniard. In the end his flexible principles proved not elastic enough to keep up with Nero, and the emperor commanded him to commit suicide, which he performed with the noble stoicism he had recommended to others.

Most Spanish intellectuals, especially those with a mordant cast of mind, consider themselves the children of Seneca; his ideas are as vital today as they were when he first propounded them, and I have known one politician, one novelist and one bullfighter who have assured me that the principles by which they live and practice their art derive from Seneca. His capacity to see the world cynically but with wit endears him to the Spaniard; his exaggerated sense of pundonor was one of the foundations of that philosophy; and his skillful use of words served as a prototype for Spanish verbosity. I suppose that the best single thing I did to prepare myself for intercourse with Spaniards was to read Seneca again; he seemed as contemporary as a man lounging in a café, as thoroughly Spanish as anyone I was to meet. The more I reread his prosaic and often pedantic works, the more Spanish they have seemed, and I imagine that the two pole stars of Spanish thought are Seneca and Cervantes; at least they are the Spaniards who speak most directly to me.

To catch the flavor of Seneca's message it is necessary to hear him speaking at some banquet in Rome, where he was often in the company of the empire leaders. One recurring principle was stoicism and to this he constantly returned:

> Anyone may take life from man, but no one death: a thousand gates stand open to it.

> Behold a spectacle to which God may worthily turn his attention; behold a match worthy of God, a brave man hand-in-hand with adverse fortune.

> Fire tries gold; misery tries brave men.

It is not because things are difficult that we do not dare to attempt them, but they are difficult because we do not dare to do so.

The fear of war is worse than war itself.

Life, if you know how to use it, is long enough.

Seneca was constantly concerned with the application of philosophy to daily life, and some of his best writings are his sententious prose essays on the virtues and limitations of moral judgment. His plays, which deal with the same problem, are apt to be pompous if not ridiculous, for in them he sounds as if he were orating old-fashioned opinions to which he himself did not subscribe (a common fault of Spanish writing), but elsewhere some of his conclusions carry a striking sense of modernity:

> As wool imbibes at once certain colors and others it does not, unless it has been frequently soaked and doubly-dyed: so there are certain kinds of learning which, on being acquired, are thoroughly mastered; but philosophy, unless she sinks deeply into the soul and has long dwelt there, and has not given a mere coloring but a deep dye, performs none of the things which she had promised.

> Human affairs are not so happily arranged that the best things please the most men. It is the proof of a bad cause when it is applauded by the mob.

> A large library is apt to distract rather than to instruct the learner; it is much better to confine yourself to a few authors than to wander at random over many.

> Truth will never be tedious to him that travels through the nature of things; it is falsehood that gluts us.

> From the time that money began to be regarded with honor, the real value of things was forgotten.

A recurring theme of Spanish history is the failure of Spaniards, no matter in what part of the world they find themselves, to develop a workable system of self-government. It is strange, therefore, that the first great Spanish thinker directed himself repeatedly to this problem. I suppose Seneca said more on this topic than on any other, and to call him primarily a Stoic is misleading; primarily he was a speculator on what the role and forms of government should be:

> He who dreads hatred too much, knows not how to reign. Terror is the proper guard of a kingdom.

> That government is ill conducted, when the mob rules its leaders.

> Life is like a school of gladiators, where men live and fight with each other.

> He who has committed a fault is to be corrected both by advice and by force, kindly and harshly, and to be made better for himself as well as for another, not without chastisement, but without passion.

Man is a social animal, and born to live together so as to regard the world as one house.

The society of man is like a vault of stones, which would fall if the stones did not rest on one another; in this way it is sustained.

In view of the fact that Spain was to become the champion of religion and today considers herself the nation most deeply committed to the defense of Catholicism, it was appropriate that her premier philosopher should have concerned himself with this matter. Spaniards are proud of the fact that certain of Seneca's writings are sufficiently ambiguous to permit him to be called the first important classical figure to have embraced Christianity, but whether he did so remains a subject of controversy. The following quotations echo with curious overtones:

Live with men as if God saw you; converse with God as if men heard you.

God is nigh to you, he is with you, he is in you: I tell you, Lucilius, a holy spirit resides within us, an observer and guardian of our good and our bad doings, who, as he has been dealt with by us, so he deals with us; no man is good without God.

A great sacred spirit talks indeed within us, but cleaves to its divine original.

God is not to be worshiped with sacrifices and blood: for what pleasure can He have in the slaughter of the innocent? But with a pure mind, a good and honest purpose. Temples are not to be built for Him with stones piled on high: God is to be consecrated in the breast of each.

The same being whom we call Jupiter, the wisest men regard as the keeper and protector of the universe, a spirit and a mind, the Lord and Maker of this lower world, to whom all names are suitable. Will you call him Destiny? You will not err. On him depend all things, and all the causes of causes are from him. Will you call him Providence? You will say well. For it is his wisdom that provides for this world that it be without confusion and proceed on its course without change. Will you call him Nature? You will not commit a mistake. For all things have had their beginning from him, in whom we live and move and have our being. Will you call him the World? You will not be deceived. For he is all that you see wholly infused into his parts and sustaining himself by his own power.

As in many Spanish cities the central plaza, serving as a kind of huge open-air bus terminal, is named after José Antonio, and not far away is the statue of my second favorite Córdoban, Bishop Hosius (in Spanish Osio, c. 255–c. 358), whom I first met in Nicaea in Asia Minor when I was studying the Church council at which the Nicene Creed was promulgated as the normative theological guide for all Christians. Hosius was a man of enormous conviction who battled to establish the trinitarian definition of God under which Christianity would prosper; his archenemy was Arius of Constantinople, father of the Arian heresy subscribed to by the German tribes, including the Visigoths who ruled Spain, which taught that Jesus could not logically be coexistent with God but must be of lesser nature. Even before I knew that Hosius was a Spaniard, I was much attracted to him; he was a furious man, a terrible warrior for his interpretation of God and a fearsome enemy of those who did not agree with him. He ranged from Córdoba to Rome to Asia Minor to Constantinople, and wherever he went he brought reason and devotion. Repeatedly he was anathematized, abused, arrested and persecuted, but he continued to wage his war against Arianism, even offering his life to prove the rightness of his beliefs. He was a very human prelate, for when nearly a century old he lost his old fire and succumbed to pressures, publicly turning his back on all he had previously believed, accepting Arianism and paving the way for a conciliation that helped make Spain temporarily Arian. At a hundred and two the old renegade died—and I find something quite Spanish in his behavior, both his stern advocacy of an idea and his ultimate betrayal of it when conditions changed. Hosius is a complex and fascinating figure, one of the greatest churchmen and probably Spain's principal contribution to Church history.

Today in the quiet square facing the church of the Capuchins in Córdoba the old bishop stands tall and baldheaded in marble toga and sandals. In his left hand he carries a staff ending in a gilded bronze eagle perched on a cross which rises from a globe. Not even in death is he serene, for he seems eager to leap forward to the next brawl. At the base appear three good bas-reliefs showing the old man bared to the waist being flogged by Roman soldiers; defending the Trinity before one of the Holy Roman emperors; supported by three other churchmen wearing crosses as he expels a figure who must be Arius, author of the heresy. On the back stands the plaque: 'To Hosius, Bishop Confessor of Christ in Torment. Counselor of Constantine the Great. On the sixteenth centennial of the Council of Nicaea over which he presided, the citizens of Córdoba dedicated this monument, under the initiative of their prelate. December 31, 1925.'

In a corner of the Jewish section, opposite to the one where Seneca presides, appears one of the gentlest and most attractive statues in Europe. The courtyard which it dominates is paved in small pebbles set in cement; the walls are whitewashed and plain; brick archways form beautiful short vistas, and flowers bloom about the base of the statue and in the nearby windowboxes. The base consists of a series of random-sized brown rocks fitted into an attractive cube on which rests a plain marble bench containing the sitting figure of a man wearing the robes and twisted turban of the desert. In his lap he holds a book kept open by his right thumb; his face and bearing are those of a philosopher who is resting here in the quiet prior to meeting with his students.

It is Córdoba's memorial to a brilliant man whom the city treated shabbily, the Jew Moses Maimonides (in Spanish Moisés de Maimón, 1135–1204), a worthy partner to Seneca and Hosius. I suppose that intellectually he is the most brilliant man that Spain produced, a medical doctor of wide reputation who wrote basic treatises on such subjects as asthma, living healthily without medicine, and the principles of sexual intercourse. In fact, his medical knowledge was so comprehensive and his skill so highly regarded that he spent the last years of his life as personal doctor to Saladin in Cairo.

His chief fame, however, was as a religious philosopher, in which capacity he helped establish the norms of Judaism. He wrote brilliantly, argued persuasively, and laid down a body of principles which had much effect on non-Jews like Thomas Aquinas, Herbert Spencer and Gottfried von Leibniz. If one wants to savor medieval thought at its best, I recommend Maimonides' *Guide to the Perplexed,* in which he takes a bewildered applicant step by step through the religious process, providing rational explanations for the existence of God and for lesser theological problems. It is a beautifully composed work and explains why Jews consider him the foremost Jewish intelligence since the time of Moses: 'Between Moses and Moses, there was no one like unto Moses.'

Maimonides was born in Córdoba and lived not far from where his statue now stands, but shortly after his bar mitzvah the Muslims controlling the city launched a series of persecutions from which he fled. It was while wandering from one inhospitable city along the Mediterranean littoral to another that he became a notable scholar. We catch glimpses of him in Algeria, in Tunis, in Turkey perhaps, in Palestine definitely and finally in Egypt, where his medical proficiency earned him a livelihood. He was a prodigious worker, and one of the most attractive letters surviving from this age was written by him, explaining how he spent his days; he found time in his schedule for medical duties, contemplation, meeting with Jews seeking religious opinion, leadership of the synagogue and service as advisor to the sultan. His hours fitted together like the pieces of a mosaic and he reported that he had no time for even one additional obligation. His collected works, which are voluminous, are currently being edited and published uniformly by Yale University, which is appropriate, for he is one of the fathers of modern intelligence.

It was surprising for me to learn that Córdoba, so long the center of Islamic culture in Spain, contained no statue of the principal adornment of that culture, the philosopher Averroës (1126–1198), who played a major role in codifying Islamic thought and in bringing Aristotle to the attention of the west. It is quite possible that he knew Maimonides, whose life his own parallels, for he too was a medical doctor of note, and he too was expelled from Córdoba by the reactionary fanaticism of Moors, who despised books. He too ended his life as doctor-in-residence to a ruler in North Africa, in this case Morocco, and he was, in his field, at least as

Seneca.

brilliant as Seneca, Hosius and Maimonides in theirs. It is extraordinary that Córdoba contains no memorial to so famous a son, but if there was one I failed to find it. It would be pleasant, on my next trip, to discover that the city had remembered Averroës, for then I could make an intellectual pilgrimage to the four statues and thus pay homage in turn to the finest pagan of Spanish history, the finest churchman, the outstanding Jew and the most brilliant Muslim. No one can explain why it was Córdoba that produced these four excellent men from four different religions.

Today the city betrays few signs that it was for so long the center of Islamic rule in Spain. The Moors crossed over from Africa on April 27, 711, and before the end of that year had captured Córdoba, where they remained till June 29, 1236. They thus occupied the city for half a millennium, making it their resplendent capital, but except for the Great Mosque and a fortress called the Alcázar, it is easier to find Roman ruins than Islamic, and this is true throughout Spain; Moors were in the peninsula from 711 to 1492, but in city after city, like Toledo and Salamanca, one finds little to remind him that these centers were once Islamic; and when a building has been preserved, it has usually been so well masked by later architects that it goes undetected.

A word as to nomenclature. The warrior tribes that invaded Spain from North Africa were united in only one thing: they were followers of Muhammad and his religion Islam. Insofar as their beliefs were concerned, it is proper to describe these men as Islamic. Unfortunately, the adjective derived from Islam has never come into popular use for identifying an individual follower; we rarely say, 'He is an Islamite.' Instead we use the word Muslim, philologically derived from the same root as Islam (one who submits), so that the adjective Muslim is identical with Islamic. The noun Muslim identifies a follower of Islam, and it is proper to describe the invaders as Muslims. Tribally, they were composed from such varied sources as Berbers of the Atlas Mountains, who comprised the vast majority of the early invaders, and men from former Roman colonies reaching from Morocco to Egypt. They were a mixed lot. The designation Moor is an imprecise word of no scientific meaning; its derivation is not religious, nor geographic, nor ethnic. Some experts claim that it comes from the Greek word for black or dark; others say it is derived from some African word meaning black, but few of the original Moors were Negroes. Historically it has come to mean 'any member of the North African groups who invaded Spain, including the Arabs.' I shall be using the word in that sense.

Who were the Arabs? Technically they were members of that incandescent and superior group which spread out from the Arabian desert and with matchless speed overran surrounding cultures. Muhammad's Hegira took place in 622; he died in 632; the flood tide of the faithful did not reach Spain till 711, a delay of nearly eighty years. In that time the Arab leadership had been thinly dispersed, and it is unlikely that many pure Arabs crossed over into Spain, although it has always been popular to assume that they did. Spaniards prefer to speak of this experience as 'the Arab occupation,' as if the Muslims who surged across the Straits of Gibraltar had been mainly Arabs, but we know that in the first foraging party, which captured most of southern Spain within a few weeks and got all the way to Toledo, there were no Arabs at all. There were, however, small Arab cadres in most of the succeeding armies and Arab leadership in the government, but to extend this to 'the triumph of Arab culture' is meaningless, for there were few Arabs and less culture; the salient innovations in architecture, art, literature and philosophy were imported mainly from long-established cultural centers to the north of Arabia. It is, however, accurate to speak of an Islamic culture and to speak of it with a certain amount of awe, for at its heyday in Spain it must have been impressive. It reached Spain in later waves, after the Berbers and the other mountain folk had conquered the peninsula.

Finally, we know that when the fanatical fundamentalists of Islam, the Almoravids, conquered southern Spain in 1086, only to be supplanted in 1146 by the even more fanatical Almohads, there were no Arabs whatever in their ranks. Both groups were composed principally of mountain wild men recently converted to Islam and of the opinion that Arab leadership, what there was of it, had gone soft and was ignoring the true teaching of Muhammad. Of any thousand Islamic invaders chosen at random through the centuries, I suppose not more than three or four could have been Arabs, but Spanish writers have felt that in surrendering to Arab superiority there was honor, but in losing to Berber inferiority there was ignominy.

To be accurate we should content ourselves with saying, 'The Muslims brought Islam to Spain,' but that begs the question of who the Muslims were and where they came from. It has therefore become the custom to say, 'The Moors occupied Spain,' and this locution applies to everyone, whether from Morocco on the west or the Balkans on the east, and includes people from three continents, Africa, Asia, Europe, and all complexions of skin. The word blackamoor was invented to describe Negroes; the great bulk of the Moors must have been white men tanned by the sun, like Arabs.

The impact of Islamic culture on Spain is well exemplified by Córdoba, for during several centuries this city was among the most scintillating of the world and comparable to Damascus as a center of Islamic culture. It was rich in palaces, gardens, libraries and university buildings. Its ordinary homes were probably the finest in Europe; for their amenities they could draw not only from goods produced in the east but also those brought down from Germany and the north. Muslim chroniclers claim, no doubt with eastern exaggeration, that in those days Córdoba had a population of about one million (today 190,000) and more than three thousand mosques, public baths and palaces. It was supposed to have had 260,000 buildings in all, including 80,000 shops. Its principal library had 400,000 volumes, and its poets and philosophers made it the peer of Baghdad or Cairo.

It is important to realize that Córdoba was self-contained. Under a series of cruel but capable military leaders it served as capital for most of

FOLLOWING FACING PAGES: *Film makers from all parts of the world shoot motion pictures with Muslim backgrounds in Spain because the inhabitants recall the Moorish occupation.*

Spain and no longer felt itself subservient in any way to Damascus. It conducted its own affairs and enjoyed a reputation throughout the Muslim world as a center of learning and medicine. Córdoba had its own publishing houses in which scores of women were employed to make copies of the Koran for distribution to mosques throughout Spain, and love poems written in this city were circulated to all parts of the Muslim world. In the eyes of Córdobans, the North African tribes from which they had originally sprung were little more than savages to be imported now and then for military service. Córdoba was a mighty metropolis when Granada was a provincial headquarters, and it was not until Spanish Christians captured the city and ended the empire that Granada, protected by a rim of mountains, came into its own as the last great Muslim city in Spain. Córdoba was lost to Islam as early as 1236; Granada hung on till 1492, and that accounts for the predominance of the latter during the concluding centuries of Muslim rule.

To appreciate what Córdoba must have been like in its days of grandeur, you must make an expedition out into the country west of the city to the ruins of Medînat az-Zahrâ, but do it only if you are possessed of a vivid imagination, for otherwise the trip will be disappointing and even misleading. You depart from the park at whose edge I found the statue of Seneca, cross the railroad tracks and follow an interesting country road till a branch cuts off to the right and twists up a steep hill. At the top you find yourself facing an old fence and a barred door. Here there is certainly no grandeur of Islam, and when the door is opened by a woman in bedroom slippers you find nothing startling: the merest outlines of walls that once ran down the slope up which you have just driven, a few stones here and there indicating where important buildings might have stood, and well down the side of the mountain the only ruin that still has a roof. You would be justified in asking, 'Is this the glory of Islam? This barren hillside with its unimpressive ruins?'

Then the guide begins to speak, and if you are able to credit the greatness that once characterized Córdoba, you begin to visualize what Medînat az-Zahrâ must have been like in the year 960. 'We are five miles from Córdoba,' the guide says, 'and one day when a foreign ambassador came to see the caliph who was residing here, he found that a matting had been laid for him all the way from Córdoba. It was lined by soldiers and eunuchs and musicians who played music for him as he walked the five miles. Along the whole route umbrellas kept him protected from the sun and dancing girls accompanied him. When he reached this place he found a palace that covered the entire hillside. The sultan's rooms alone numbered four hundred. The roof was supported by 4,313 marble columns. The fountains were without number, for merely to feed the fish required eight hundred loaves to be baked each day. It wasn't a palace, really, but a sultan's city, all under one roof. More than twenty-five thousand people worked here. Slavonian eunuchs, three thousand seven hundred. Other male servants, ten thousand. Female servants, six thousand. Pages, at least a thousand. Musicians, many score. To feed only the people living under this roof required seven tons of meat each day, not to count the chickens, partridges and fish. It was the most luxurious palace that Spain has ever seen, or the world either, perhaps.'

To perceive in these desolate ruins the wizardry that was once Medînat az-Zahrâ requires faith, and certain critics have recently begun to question whether it was ever much more than the normal-type summer retreat favored by all Moors. They point out that such floor plans as can be extrapolated from the ruins do not begin to provide space for twenty-five thousand people, nor for a caliph's quarters of four hundred rooms. And if anyone did feed eight hundred loaves of bread daily to the fish, they must have thrown it in the Guadalquivir, because there was no space here for ponds of that magnitude. I found myself unable to accept the grandeur that my guide reported, yet I was aware that she had not invented these figures; they came from well-documented contemporary sources, so that if what has come down to us is mere invention, it was contemporary invention and not afterthought. It is possible that those marble waiting rooms in which ambassadors prepared themselves to face the caliph once existed, but they have vanished as if made of paper. In doing so they anticipated the disappearance of all Muslim culture from Spain. On this hillside men may have governed for a while and kept their thousand concubines, but their reality has evaporated and even the buildings in which they luxuriated are known no more.

Although I could not accept the figures given for Medînat az-Zahrâ, I was hesitant to dismiss the legend because only a few miles to the east stood the very real Great Mosque, and if a gigantic thing like that was possible, Medînat az-Zahrâ was not impossible. I first saw the mosque from the tower at the southern end of the Roman bridge which crosses the Guadalquivir, and from there it looked like an ordinary Christian church, ugly rather than otherwise, set behind old brown walls, some of which were crumbling, others of which bore false arches that led to nowhere and pillars which should have supported huge gateways but whose openings were bricked up. I spent a long time walking completely around the mosque and failed to detect any façade, or any part of a façade, which impressed me as worthy of what I had been told lay inside. In fact, the outer walls were grubby and what entrances there were consisted of uninspired square pillars between which had been set short and stubby doorways capped by Moorish half-moon arches whose tiles had fallen away in various spots. Few of the world's great buildings can be so disappointing from the outside.

Loath to believe that this was the building I sought, I withdrew some distance to study it afresh, and it appeared as before: a dumpy Christian church hidden by a wholly undistinguished wall, except that now I could see the bell tower, and a sorrier bit of architecture I had rarely come upon. It looked as if a tower twice as high had been built, with no style whatever, and then squashed down to half its height, so that all parts became sort of ridiculous. They were too fat, too compressed, too formless. Horizontal lines dominated the vertical, resulting in something that was neither a satisfactory Gothic tower to accompany a church nor a poetic minaret to grace a mosque, and I was ready to dismiss the Great Mosque as a fraud.

When I passed through the dingy walls to enter the Patio de los Naranjos (Courtyard of the Oranges) my disappointment was increased, for here I saw a rather large area of no distinction in which trees grew at random and around which walls ran, all in bad need of a washing. Especially drab were the walls of the mosque itself, a compromise between Moorish arches and Christian brick but having the dignity of neither. I was really perplexed as to why this building was so highly regarded, because so far I had seen nothing.

I then entered the mosque by an unprepossessing door and decided to look with unprejudiced eye at this so-called miracle; and as I stood in the darkness and began slowly to adjust to the shadows, I found myself in an architectural fairy tale, surrounded by so many pillars and arches that I could not believe they were real. I suppose that from where I stood I was seeing something like four hundred separate marble columns, each handsomely polished and with its own capital of Corinthian foliage. The arches that rose above these columns formed a maze which attracted the eye this way and that, for they were striped with alternate bands of yellow and red, and they were extra impressive in that in certain parts of the mosque they were double, that is, from the top of a capital one arch was slung across to the facing capital, and then three feet above that a second arch was thrown across in the same plane, producing a wild confusion of line and weight.

My first impression was of this wilderness of columns and arches; my second was expressed in an involuntary cry: 'It's so big!' I think no words could prepare one for the magnitude of this immense building. Its columns stretch away to darkness in all directions, so vast are the distances, and the fact that light enters at unexpected places adds to the bewilderment. Also, those vibrating bands of yellow and red increase the confusion, so that one cannot focus on a specific spot in the distance, for his eye is constantly drawn to another. The men who built this mosque, over the remains of a Visigothic church, had a vision of permanence and magnitude that still stuns the imagination.

My eyes never became adjusted to it, but when they had ceased darting this way and that, I started a slow circuit and after some minutes came to a section where the columns were of special beauty, a kind of creamy white and dark brown, and where the sets of double arches drew

Islamic tracery.

the eye to a focus on the far wall, where carving of the most exquisite sort graced a series of intricate arches. A group of French tourists went past, and I heard the guide saying, 'Now we approach the mihrab.' This is the niche set into the wall of every mosque, indicating the kiblah, that point which one faces when praying if he wishes to kneel in the direction of Mecca. The mihrab in Córdoba was the finest I had ever seen, and I am familiar with all the great mosques of the east except those in Mecca and Medina. It was a niche large enough to stand in, covered with delicate tracery in blue and bronze, with passages from the Koran written in gold against a blue ground. It was ornate beyond description, yet it hung together to create a sensation of Asiatic splendor as alien to the continent of Europe as the cry of the muezzin. I was overcome by the beauty of this spot, by the tragedy of its vanished significance. The psychological distance between this alcove and the cathedral in Toledo is at least as great as the distance between the moon and the earth. Perhaps it is greater, for one day, apparently, the moon and earth will be united by human contact but it seems unlikely that the mihrab and the cathedral ever will be.

Christian and Muslim were further alienated by a relic preserved in the Great Mosque, the verified arm of Muhammad. It was the holiest item in Muslim Spain and was invoked by generals when going into battle against the Christians. It seems to have had magical properties capable of inspiring Muslim armies and terrifying their opponents, and for the better part of a century this arm had a clear field in Spain, without losing one battle; then in desperation the Christians came up with a surprising countermeasure which bestowed invincibility on them, but we shall not meet this new force until the last chapter.

I had been wandering about the mosque for the better part of an hour, keeping to the outer walls because I wanted to savor the immensity of the place, when I became aware that a structure of some size rose in the middle of the eight hundred and fifty pillars, and I walked casually in that direction to find that my earliest impression of the mosque, the one I had gained from the tower at the Roman bridge, was correct. Here, lost in this wilderness of columns, hid a full-sized Catholic cathedral, and one of colossal ugliness. When the Christians captured Córdoba in 1236 and expelled the Moors, it was understandable that they should wish to convert the now useless mosque into a cathedral, for the Moors had done the converse in 711 when they captured the city. I think no one can complain of such conversion; it is one of the logical consequences of war, and if the truth were known, Sancta Sophia in Constantinople, which started life as a cathedral, did not suffer much by being sanctified as a mosque. In Córdoba, the Christians did little to damage the mosque; they merely ripped out a few rows of pillars so that the interior would look like a church with a central nave plus two aisles on each side, and thus it stood from 1236 to about 1520; I suppose the untrained eye entering the building in those centuries could not have detected that changes had been made, because the visual difference between a thousand columns and eight hundred and fifty cannot be significant.

However, when Carlos ascended the throne, the Christian hierarchy of Córdoba saw a chance to do something they had long wanted to do but which Fernando and Isabel, sensitive to the Moorish architecture of the south, would never have permitted. They wanted to erect across the inconspicuous nave a transept, which when properly covered and cut off from the rest of the mosque, would constitute a proper cathedral. They therefore petitioned Carlos for permission to do this, and he, knowing nothing of the problem, for he did not appreciate the south, carelessly granted it. Speedily Christian stonemasons went to work and built, right in the heart of the mosque, their monstrous structure. When Carlos finally visited Córdoba in 1526 and saw what had been done under his aegis he was ashamed, saying, 'If I had known what you were up to, you would not have done it. For what you have made here may be found in many other places, but what you have destroyed is to be found nowhere else in the world.'

I do not share the emperor's lament. As my own experience proved, one can visit the mosque without at first being aware that the gigantic church is there. It certainly did not spoil my visits, and while I know that without the cathedral I would have seen vistas that must have been profound, I could still see so far along the outer walls that my eye got lost in the arches. That the Christians had a right to use the mosque as a cathedral, there can be no question; that they found it necessary to build a transept, and such a gross one, is regrettable.

I spent many hours inside the church, for I found the choir a comfortable place to rest. I grew to like the intricate vaulting, and particularly the pink marble ox that held up the black pulpit; his carved entrails had burst loose in conformity to the local legend, which said that the Córdoban ox which bore the pillars for constructing the cathedral burst his insides with joy to think that the building was once more to be a church. The white eagle that served as a lectern also attracted my attention and I did much of my reading in its shadow. I rather liked the idea that what had once been a pagan temple of the Romans, then a Christian church of the Visigoths, next a mosque of the Muslims, was now a church for Catholics; it was proper and in the order of things, but in spite of the hours I spent there reading and thinking, I never felt it to be a consecrated place. It was more like an ornate museum, as if the contamination of having been a mosque had not been properly cleansed. This feeling did not arise from the fact that the cathedral was an ugly building, for in a sense that was appropriate; much of what Christians introduced when they expelled the Muslims was uglier than what it replaced, but on balance the change was inescapable; it was necessary for the development of Spain.

I was less generous in my judgment of that endless chain of second-rate chapels that usurp the outer walls of the mosque; once these walls had stood open so that worshipers might enter the mosque from any direction, and then when one was inside he looked through this maze of columns out to the free sky of Andalucía, and the impact must have been tremendous; but since the building was now a cathedral it required chapels, so the once-open walls were bricked shut, and as mournful a bunch of cubicles as I have ever seen was strung along them. How many are there, unused, undusted and unsung? One morning I walked past the locked gates of each one, not slowly, but pausing now and then to look at the moldering statues and the bad painting, and it took me twenty-nine minutes to make the circuit, for there must have been more than fifty. A few had touches of real charm, and I could see that others had historic validity in that they related to important figures in Córdoba's history, but for the main part they were a dismal, unattended group of structures which came off poorly when compared with the mosque they had helped deface.

One must be careful not to generalize about this matter, for a distinguished French critic whom we shall meet later in another context points out that it would be fallacious to condemn the Christians for defacing a Muslim masterwork, because Muslims had very little to do with the building of this mosque! The design came from the Christian basilica around which the original mosque was built. Most of the marble columns and their capitals were appropriated from existing Christian monuments in Spain or Africa. The workmen who built the mosque were Christians; even the glorious mihrab which I had liked so much was built by Christian workmen loaned to Córdoba by the Christian emperor at Constantinople, who also sent as a gift three hundred and twenty quintals of glass pieces for the mosaics (about thirty-five tons). 'Accordingly, in this great sanctuary of Islam, the first after that of Mecca, everything, or nearly everything, is Christian: the plan of the edifice, the material employed, and even the workmanship.'

Much confused, I left the Great Mosque. In many respects it was unsatisfying; its Christian and Muslim halves were uneasy with each other and failed to attain that harmony one finds in Sancta Sophia. There is here a sense of imbalance and restlessness, as if the Muslim component of Spanish life had accepted its role of submission and were trying to escape; or as if the Christian component were not content with its conquest and were endeavoring to suppress even further the Moorish. In such circumstances the Muslim explodes to the surface through weakened fissures. There is in much of Spain this contradiction: it is a Christian country but one with suppressed Muslim influences that crop out at unforeseen points; it is a victorious country that expelled the defeated Muslims from all places except the human heart; it is a land which tried to extirpate all memory of the Muslims but which lived on to mourn their passing; and it is a civilization which believed that it triumphed when it won the last battle but which knows that it lost in fields like poetry, dancing, philosophy, architecture and agriculture. To me Córdoba's mosque was the most mournful building in Spain, and on the evening after my first visit I went into the old Jewish quarter, where memories of the Moors still linger, to see if I could banish my unease.

If I had been disappointed by the mosque, I was enchanted by the little courtyards of the Jewish quarter, for I suppose they represent one of the perfect sights that a stranger can come upon in Europe, like the Spanish Steps in Rome or the island museums of Oslo. They are a series of small, informal patios strung out by accident along unimportant back streets, and they number perhaps a hundred. You see them casually through doorways as you walk along, and occasionally one acquires a greater importance than the others because it stands behind formal arches and has had professional attention. Mostly, however, they are family gardens, but unlike any you have seen before.

By luck, the first one I happened upon as I was looking for the restaurant to which I had been directed by a friend, was one of the best. I saw it through an open doorway, an ordinary patio surrounded on three sides by a low two-story house whose walls were whitewashed. The floor of the patio was paved with pebbles set on end, so that it had a pleasing design. A flight of stairs led to a second-floor balcony, over whose edge hung nineteen potted flowers with tendrils covering the wall of the balcony. The top of the balcony was lined with twenty-seven flowerpots which also dropped flowers in abundance, while the six posts supporting the roof each held three beautiful flowering plants. The two side walls could scarcely be seen. In one corner of the patio stood a well with a masonry rim, whitewashed and containing a dozen larger pots of roses and dahlias, while around the line where the walls met the patio floor scores of pots were ranged, each with some flowering plant. To the right of the entrance a low wall had been erected in previous centuries, perhaps when Jews still occupied the house, and it must originally have been intended for visitors to sit on like a bench, but now it too was crowded with flowerpots, all of whose plants were in bloom. The little patio was thus a theater offering a ballet of color against the stark whiteness of the walls. The flowers danced up and down the stairway, pirouetted across the balcony, around the well, up and down the posts, and in a kind of majestic march moved about the lower walls. How many separate plants were there? Well over a hundred, I suppose. How many colors? More than I could count. How many different kind of flowers? I'm not good at identifying them, but there were at least a dozen.

There was one patio which quite captivated me, for I had not heard of such a way of using flowers. In a whitewashed area of rough walls and arcades, some sixty flowerpots were hung from wire loops, and all were painted Muslim blue. This is a dark blue often seen in the Middle East, where it is

popular as a charm guaranteed to keep away evil spirits; on the road from Tel Aviv to Haifa, in the heart of Israel, there is an Arab village named Faradis (Paradise) that used to be painted blue. In Córdoba the concentration of blue pots against white walls was most charming, and when varied flowers crept down from the pots to hang in a hundred festoons, the effect was unlike anything I had seen before.

These two patios were in no way exceptional; I must have seen about sixty that evening as I wandered down the street of the Good Shepherd in the general direction of the Maimonides statue, but finally I found my restaurant and much to my satisfaction saw that a flamenco concert was scheduled for that night. I had dinner in a delightful room which duplicated something of the charm of the patios, and while waiting for the program to begin I wondered whether the spectacular display of flowers I had seen was an inheritance from the Moors, who were reported to have been excellent gardeners. I suppose I could have found comparable gardens elsewhere in Spain, but as a matter of record I didn't, so I concluded that these Córdoban patios were a Moorish carry-over.

About flamenco there is much debate. The easy explanation of this unique art form, which combines guitar playing, singing, chanting, dancing and staccato handclapping, is that it is a very old inheritance from Moorish days, in which the distinctive wail is an echo of the muezzin's cry with Jewish overtones; but if, as some think, it was derived from gypsy patterns imported from Asia rather than from Africa, it must be a fairly recent importation, for the gypsies did not reach Spain till 1435. We know that the name dates only from 1520, when the Flemish courtiers of Carlos V burst on the drab Spanish scene with slashed doublets showing flashes of brilliant color and gave their name to anything conspicuous or garish, like the flamingo bird and the flamenco dance.

I had been introduced to flamenco under appropriate conditions in that café in Valencia, because there I heard some first-class guitar playing and that important flamenco song 'Petenera.' In intervening years I had bought most of the good flamenco records reaching America, but they were not many, for much junk was then purveyed as flamenco, a custom which has not been broken. In Mexico I attended several flamenco parties, and they were awful, though the versions offered in New York were worse. The fact was that after that first superb evening I had heard no acceptable flamenco and it was gratifying to find myself now in the heart of the flamenco country, where I could catch up.

The room in which the dance was to be held could hardly have been more suitable, a cellar-type place with old iron-studded doors, a beamed ceiling, intricate trellises up which vines crept, and what looked like authentic Roman pillars except that they were topped by rude, country-

In the blazing heat of Andalucía how pleasant it is
to be inside a darkened room protected from the sun
by thick walls and growing plants.

Although to the practiced Spanish eye this gesticulating flamenco dancer would be spotted as an amateur, because his fingers are distorted in grotesque rather than poetic fashion, he is properly caught up in the spirit of the dance and is experiencing catharsis in the Aristotelian sense of the word.

style capitals that seemed just right for this room. The furniture was rough, and as the people near me talked I was pleased to find that the room had a fine resonance, for the brick walls absorbed sound. It promised to be an exciting evening.

Then the troupe appeared, five people dressed a little too finely for the work at hand. The three men (guitarist, singer, dancer) wore suits that were too professional in their tightness and cut. The two girl dancers wore dresses strongly modified by French ideas and their heels were of an exaggerated height. What was most disturbing, the girls were too young and too beautiful; when this is the case the dancer is tempted to say, 'Look at me, how lovely I am,' and not to do much honest dancing. The sleazy guitarist struck a few dramatic chords, ran a series of notes and went into the kind of sequence burlesque orchestras use to announce the impending appearance of their chief stripper. One of the girls rushed forth, assumed a fatalistic pose, stamped her feet a couple of times and grunted, '¡Ole!' I thought, Oh boy! All the duende of a boiler factory.

What a horrible evening it was. I had been trapped in a tourist show of the worst sort: the dancing was strictly Hollywood, with much heel banging and head gesture; the guitarist was nimble rather than profound and his playing tended toward the staccato chord; the singing done by the pomaded man in the tight suit was closer to the Beatles than to either Moors or gypsies. All this I could have borne, but the girls were arch and danced so as to display their legs up to their navels and one even wore a rose between her teeth; when I thought I had seen the worst, and that can be pretty bad, for in this country when taste abdicates, the results are unpredictable, the girls called onto the stage two German sailors, wrapped mantones (shawls) about the bottoms of the two men and proceeded to burlesque one of the few authentic entertainments Spain has to offer its guests. It was shocking, as vulgar as the scenes in Hawaiian night clubs when hula girls lure men onstage to make asses of themselves. The two Germans were good sports and one had a bawdy sense of humor: he grabbed at the skirts of the flamenco girls; they stumbled and he fell on his face. The audience roared approval and the guitarist played a version of 'Anchors Aweigh.'

The performance was so dismal that all I could do was sit there and recall the jokes I'd seen on television about flamenco. A dancer does the foot-stamping bit and the comedian says, 'He's mad at the floor.' The dancer looks back over his shoulder: 'He's very proud of his bottom. Wants to be sure it's still there.' The dancer looks under his left shoulder: 'He wants to see if he needs a deodorant.' The dancer stamps again: 'He wants the janitor to send up more heat.' It was on that level.

When the miserable night was over I walked back to the Maimonides statue and in that peaceful place contemplated the mockery that Spain was making of certain of its treasures, simply to collect a few tourist kroner or francs. I was in a rather bitter mood, when the musicians from the show came out and one asked me, 'How did you like it?' I did not know enough Spanish to tell him, so I said, 'I had rather hoped to hear something like a petenera.' The men stopped, for it was obvious that the name of that song was a rebuke. The guitar which they had abused grew heavy and the pomaded heads became ridiculous. 'Qué lástima! (What a pity!)' the guitarist said. 'Here we get few people who know peteneras.'

Spain runs a considerable risk of cheapening the very things that have made her attractive to tourists. She has enjoyed an enviable reputation in reports of men like Mérimée, Havelock Ellis, Somerset Maugham, Henry de Montherlant and the others who have been captivated by an authentic Spanish culture displayed with fierce honesty. If this culture is to be made a mockery of, and by Spain itself, then there will be little reason for anyone of good taste to bother with it. I cannot believe that the notable visitors of the past, men like George Borrow, Richard Ford, Sacheverell Sitwell and especially the keen French and German travelers, would have tolerated a scene like the one that was forced on me in the Córdoba restaurant; and had they been required, as I was, to sit through it they could have described it later only in words of scorn. It was cheap, and vulgar, and an insult to the visitor; but even worse, it was an abuse of the cultural heritage and it was this more than my own deprivation which infuriated me.

I am not going to bore the reader, city by city, with an account of my attempts to see in Spain a good flamenco; in each place I was abused about as badly as I was in Córdoba. It was all junk, save for a few nights when I happened upon a near-blind old man whose voice was gone but who had the pundonor of his trade and the gracia to communicate it to others. If on some subsequent trip to Spain I were to be told of a bar where one could occasionally hear real flamenco, I would travel a considerable distance to hear it; but if, as I suppose, it has all been corrupted by the quick tourist dollar, and if enough of the rest of Spanish culture goes the same way, I would be better off turning flamenco and Spain over to others, for it would no longer have much to say to me.

As for Córdoba the city, my days there were delightful. I had nothing much to do and spent long hours lounging in the sun at one outdoor bar or another in the Plaza José Antonio. Occasionally I would wander over to talk with old Bishop Hosius, but for the most part I rested and caught up with a lot of reading I wanted to do in the field of the Spanish novel.

My stay was made extra pleasant by the fact that I had a room in the local parador, which stands some miles out in the country on a fine hillside from which I could overlook the Guadalquivir as if I were a caliph at Medînat az-Zahrâ, which lay not far away on roughly the same spur of hills. For some reason which no one explained in advance, this parador has developed the best restaurant in Spain, better, I thought, than even the ultra-posh ones in Madrid because its cuisine was more honest, and people traveled long distances to dine here. The menu was not exceptional in its variety, but each dish was properly prepared. For example, I would not have expected to find in Córdoba the best sole à la Colbert I have ever tasted, but there it was, delicately flavored with butter and crisp along the edges.

Each day for a week my waitress warned me, 'You're missing the best thing we do if you don't take the rabo de toro.' Now those words had to mean *tail of bull* and I have never been a big partisan of braised oxtail, which is what I supposed it was. 'No, thank you,' I said.

Her other suggestions had worked out so satisfactorily that I was not easy in rejecting this one. For example, one day she said, 'No matter what you think you want, take the stewed partridge.' I recalled my unpleasant

Like flamenco dancers they stomp the stage on which they perform. They spread their fans, they move in graceful rhythms and cry out in rasping voices.

experiences with this delicacy in Toledo and started to say no, but she whisked under my nose a serving which she was delivering to a nearby table, and it was so enticing that I allowed her to bring me a portion, and thereafter whenever it appeared on the menu I took it, a truly fine dish. But the tail of bull I avoided.

One day I had as my guests a pair of archaeologists who had been digging in the Old Testament copper mines at Río Tinto, northwest of Sevilla (they said there was a wealth of digging to be done there in a civilization three thousand years old), and they were delighted when they saw rabo de toro on the menu. 'Famous throughout southern Spain,' they said, so I went along with them and tried it. By itself it would have made the parador famous, so after the archaeologists had left I went into the kitchen to ask the chef how he made this dish, and even a quick glance at the place told me all I needed to know about why this parador was so well regarded for its food. The kitchen was both old-fashioned with handsome clay pots and modern with stainless steel; immaculately clean, it was also properly cluttered with vegetables and shellfish, and the people working in it were a robust crew who had fun in handling food and dishes. My waitress whispered that the excellence of the place could be traced to the unmarried daughter of a leading Andalusian family who had surprised her friends by volunteering to work in the parador and who had ended by being its chatelaine.

Her chief cook was hardly what I had expected, a bull-like man who spoke in a confused rush with few verbs, but since he was using Andalusian, a much truncated dialect, I may have missed the verbs. He avoided all *s* sounds and most *d*'s and invariably used *er* for *el*.

Castilian	Andalusian
mismo	meemo
madre	mare
bueno	wayno
Jaime Ostos	Aim O-o
el matador	er matao
los amigos	lo jarmigo
cuidado	cuiao

The last word, pronounced in drawling whine *kwee-ow,* in which the last syllable rhymes with *now,* means "take care" and is much used in the region; it is practically the shibboleth of the true Andalusian.

The chunky cook was pleased that someone wanted to know how he made his rabo de toro: 'So it's a good bull's tail, fat, much gristle in the joints. Taste from the gristle. Cut, cut, pieces not too big. Roll in flour, much salt, braise in fat. Cuiao! Don't burn, but cook well. Must have juice left for sauce. Everything is the sauce. Cuiao! No spices. No pepper. Onions well fried for flavor. Olive oil, but cuiao! Not too much. Garlic, celery, carrots, mushrooms, but not one water. Cuiao! No water, or you make soup. Bake one hour and half in hot oven. To serve put three joints bull's tail in ramekin, sauce, vegetables, two fresh onions, bake few minutes to turn brown. Cuiao! No water, no wine.'

As I sat on my hillside looking down on Córdoba, I became so preoccupied with Muslim Spain that I decided to take the journey over the mountain to Granada, where my driving companion had an excellent idea. He wanted me to approach Granada by a special route, so short of the city he turned to the south and took me a good twenty miles away. He turned into a narrow twisting side road that led into the mountains of the Sierra Nevada, where we came upon a remote village perched on the edge of a cliff, a most frightening but beautiful spot. 'Here we'll have our picnic!' he said, and as we unpacked the car and sat beside a stream which tumbled into a valley far below, he pointed to the encircling mountains and said, 'Tourists spend a lot of time oohing and aahing over the Alhambra, but it teaches them nothing about Islam. It's this that explains why Granada was able to hold on for so long. The Christians couldn't root the Muslims out of fastnesses like this. For more than three centuries they tried, but with no luck. This is Granada. Not the city back there.'

It was an ideal spot in which to contemplate the fortunes of Islam; the combination of mountain and valley refreshed the eye and the sight of people moving about the landlocked village at the edge of the cliff gave one a sense of historical continuity. Under Muslim rule their ancestors had lived in those homes and after the collapse of the Muslim kingdom they had probably reverted to Christianity. Royal lines had come and gone but these farmers and smugglers had bothered little, and now, when their country perched on the edge of a precipice of uncertainty as to what might happen when Generalísimo Franco left, they were as unconcerned as ever. This was really timeless Spain, even more remote than the parched villages of Extremadura, for here movement in or out was much more difficult.

'The wonder of the Christian Conquest of Granada,' my friend said, 'was not that it came when it did but that it came so very late. For nearly eight hundred years the Christians of Spain conducted what they describe as a permanent crusade. That's why no Spanish knights appear in what we call the Crusades. They were occupied at home. But they rarely fought all-out battles. It was mostly a "you let me hold Toledo and I'll let you hold Córdoba" business. Muslim armies served Christian kings and Christian knights worked for Muslim caliphs, and a kind of happy-go-lucky truce operated most of the time. By 1242 the Christians had maneuvered themselves into such a favorable position that one final push would have kicked the Moors out, but they dawdled for another two and a half centuries. I suppose when Spanish generals pictured themselves leading their armies over terrain like this they lost heart.'

On the rocky earth by our picnic ground I traced out a series of maps showing Spain in various periods, insofar as I could remember them, and my friend was right. In 711 the Muslims had conquered a defunct Spain with indecent ease. Had there ever before been a nation so large that had collapsed so swiftly to an invader with so few men? In one battle, the chroniclers tell us, more than one hundred thousand well-armed Christians evaporated before twelve thousand partially armed Berbers, and the conquest of most cities was more like a procession than an invasion; even Toledo fell with shocking speed. In contrast, when the time came for the

Christians to reconquer Spain, their advance was slow. The final stage began in 1482, when Fernando and Isabel, with a more or less united Spain behind them, were at last able to bring the weight of the nation to bear on Granada.

On our way back to inspect the city we reached the mournful point on the road known as El Ultimo Suspiro del Moro (The Last Sigh of the

This Spanish horse, so thick-necked and muscular that it seems to have been sculptured from bronze, exhibits its Arab ancestry.

Moor), where Boabdil is supposed to have paused, as he abandoned Granada to the Christians, for one last look at his noble city. Here he lamented his loss, whereupon his mother remarked, 'You do well, my son, to weep as a woman for the loss of what you could not defend as a man.' From this spot the towers of Granada, set down among mountains, were exciting enough to evoke a sigh.

We did not stop there, however, nor in the city itself, but went to that hill east of the city on the road to Guadix where one can look down upon Granada and perceive its structure. Two rivers join, and instead of plunging through the mountains eastward to the Mediterranean, start west across Andalucía to enter the Guadalquivir near Córdoba. At their confluence a town grew up prior to the Romans, under whom it flourished. It provided a starting point for the Muslims when they sought a mountain capital safe from Mediterranean pirates and Christian land armies. The main body of the city crouched in valleys but the gypsy quarter perched on a hill. 'It's the other hill you should study,' my guide said, and it was from this favorable position that I looked down onto the most famous hill in Spain. Its crest consisted of a long, narrow wooded area completely enclosed by a turreted wall inside which were many gardens, pools and rambling buildings, the whole creating a sense of beauty and repose.

'Which building is the Alhambra?' I asked.

'Everything within the walls. The whole complex of woodland, water, gardens and buildings. It all goes together to make the Alhambra.' Seeing it thus from a mountainside, I was able to appreciate the inventiveness of the Muslim architects in converting a considerable hilltop into a natural palace in which gardens and fountains were as important as buildings.

I can still recall my first experience within the walls of the Alhambra. My friend had gone to confirm our reservations at the parador, which stands within the Alhambra and is a part of it, and I went off into one of the gardens, and there an old man, clad much as he would have been five hundred years ago, was gathering figs, pulling the branches down with a crook and examining each fruit to see if it was ripe. He gave me one, black as night and filled with seeds. From all parts of the garden I smelled the heavy scent of boxwood, and in the valley below, where the city stood, I could see mists covering the roofs. In the trees at the edge of the garden, birds sang and beyond them rose the somber wall and the turrets that protected it. This was the Alhambra; the buildings would come later.

If I had been disappointed in Córdoba's Great Mosque, the contrary was true in Granada, for the Alhambra was much lovelier and much more Muslim than I had anticipated. I think what pleased me most in the buildings was the subtle manner in which one memorable room or hall led quietly into the next, as if an intricate musical composition were unfolding with always the right notes appearing where they were needed. One moves through this extensive collection of architectural highlights as if he were in a dream, in which one gentle surprise lures him on to the next.

It is not my intention to describe the buildings of the Alhambra, since it has already been well done. I was amused, however, to discover in an alcove of the Courtyard of the Myrtles, with its large reflecting pool, the shell of Santiago used as an ornamental device. There it was: the symbol of the force that would drive Islam from Spain built into the final palace, as if

719
AT THE HEIGHT OF THE
MUSLIM OCCUPATION

Pamplona
Barcelona
Toledo
Lisboa
Córdoba
Sevilla
ENCLAVE
TILL 741

☐ Christian lands
☐ Muslim lands

950
RECONQUEST LAUNCHED
BY LEON AND ARAGON

NAVARRA
ARAGON
L E O N
Salamanca
Toledo
Córdoba
Sevilla
Granada

1035
CONSOLIDATION ACHIEVED
BY SANCHO DE NAVARRA

NAVARRA
ARAGON
L E O N
Toledo
Córdoba
Granada

1214
AT THE DEATH OF
ALFONSO VIII DE CASTILLA

L E O N
NAVARRA
Barcelona
ARAGON
PORTUGAL
CASTILLA
Toledo
Córdoba
Granada

1242
CONSOLIDATION OF
FERNANDO III DE CASTILLA

Pamplona
NAVARRA
Barcelona
ARAGON
PORTUGAL
CASTILLA
Toledo
Córdoba
Granada

1482
ON THE EVE OF THE FINAL
CONQUEST OF GRANADA

NAVARRA
ARAGON
PORTUGAL
CASTILLA
Toledo
Córdoba
Granada

the Muslims had foreseen their own expulsion. And in a room off the Courtyard of the Lions, I found the Star of David, because as I said before, in Spain one finds old memories at unexpected places.

I think the most beautiful thing I saw among the buildings was the passageway leading from the Courtyard of the Myrtles to the Courtyard of the Lions, because here the architect was faced with a universal problem: how to relate two unrelated spaces? He solved it by placing two doorways of radically different widths side by side, then uniting them with one lintel, whose ends dropped down around the sides of the doors, and covering the entire with handsome carving. When I looked at the two doors everything about them seemed wrong; a child could have designed them better, but only a great artist could have juxtaposed them so as to achieve an effect so right and good. I studied them for a long time, because in my own work I have often tried to attain a similar result. It seems to me that any writer should be able to produce 'a well-constructed English novel'; it takes someone like the Alhambra architect to slap together disparate items and make them sing, and if I have not always been successful in my own efforts, I know success when someone else achieves it.

I was surprised at the flimsy construction of the buildings. Is there another structure of comparable importance put together with such contempt for permanence? The ceilings, whose stalactite traceries are so exquisite, are nothing but stucco whose points one could knock off with a knuckle, and the walls of delicate geometric pattern are built up of plaster exactly as one would build up the decoration of a wedding cake and of not much greater permanence. That the palaces of the Alhambra have survived for seven hundred years is astonishing; when one sees how fragile they are, one better understands how vast areas like Medînat az-Zahrâ and caliphate Córdoba have vanished. The surprising thing is that any Muslim remains have survived.

The Courtyard of the Lions was as pure a work of art as I had been told, for here the inventive architects had converted a collection of slim marble columns and filigreed arches into a garden of stone which includes that handsome twelve-sided fountain protected by a pride of granite lions who look more like friendly puppy dogs than jungle beasts.

Turning a corner on one of the upper floors, I came upon the plain notice: 'In these quarters Washington Irving wrote his *Tales of the Alhambra* in the year 1829.' It was easy to visualize the bachelor lawyer, embassy official and future ambassador to Spain ensconced in these rooms with their cloistered balcony of marble columns overlooking the hills and caves of Granada. The workroom looked onto a patio with tall cypresses and a chattering fountain built up from a square inscribed with a circle, and it must have been a romantic place for a man with Irving's imagination; one can understand the flowery visions he entertained here. *Tales of the Alhambra,* composed in a few weeks' time, swept the English-speaking world and made its author famous. Irving was partial to the Muslims as contrasted to the Christians, and his slight tales, often no more than mood pieces, had considerable effect upon subsequent historical judgment; one could not read Irving, especially his more substantial *Conquest of Granada,* without becoming an advocate of Islam and a mourner over its expulsion.

There is no place better, I think, than Irving's rooms in the Alhambra for weighing the moral significance of the Muslim occupation of Spain, and here I tried to reach a judgment. I had always been much disposed toward the Muslims, both in Spain and elsewhere, and I had once written an essay on Muhammad that had gained approval in various countries of the Muslim world. I had lived in six different Islamic countries—Turkey, Afghanistan, Iran, Pakistan, Malaya and Indonesia—and had visited half a dozen others. I had schooled myself in at least the outlines of Islamic philosophy, poetry and art and found myself sympathetic to the Muslim view of life.

I was therefore susceptible to the Washington Irving point of view that Spain had called down upon herself a sad retribution when she expelled the Moors; special damage had been done to her intellectual and agricultural life, and from this she had not recovered. Certainly, post hoc ergo propter hoc reasoning substantiated this: as long as the Muslims were in Spain and making their contribution to Spanish life, Spain stood at the head of nations, but coincident with the expulsion of the Moors, starting in 1492 and ending in 1609, began that long decline which the country has not yet reversed.

In an out-of-the-way inn in a different part of Spain, I had come upon a three-volume book of travels published in 1829, entitled *A Year in Spain* and attributed to 'A Young American.' Who he was I did not know, but whatever college he attended had taught him fine writing; his sentences were some of the longest and most polished I had read and his reflections on the Conquest of Granada were typical of the attitudes which I had inherited:

> Though this victory of Ferdinand and Isabella was a Christian triumph, in name at least, it was not a triumph of humanity; and if the philanthropist or the colder economist, speculating with a view to utility alone, were to inquire what use Christian Spain had made of her dear-bought conquest, and how far the aggregate happiness of mankind and the interests of civilization had been promoted by the extermination of an heroic, ingenious, and industrious people, a picture of fraud, cruelty, and oppression would be presented, as frightful as the world has ever witnessed, and followed by consequences equally ruinous to the oppressors and the oppressed.

(Upon my return to America, I learned through the kindness of the librarian at The Hispanic Society of America that the author of this book

187

was Alexander Slidell [1803–1848], the younger brother of that famous John Slidell of New York City who, after graduating from Columbia College in that city, wound up as United States senator from Louisiana, a post he surrendered when Louisiana withdrew from the Union at the start of the Civil War. As a diplomatic representative of the Confederacy, the older Slidell earned a place in history when the northern navy lifted him from a British ship in which he was traveling to Europe, thus precipitating an incident which nearly brought Great Britain into the war on the side of the Confederacy. Alexander Slidell published his book on Spain at the age of twenty-six; three years later, on August 20, 1832, the Spanish King Fernando VII issued a royal decree banning him from Spain because of intemperate remarks he had made against the country. In 1838 Slidell added the name Mackenzie and was henceforth known as Slidell Mackenzie. In 1842, after three of his sailors were detected in a mutiny, Mackenzie hung the trio from the yardarm of his ship, thus involving himself in a scandal, since one of the hanged men was the son of the Secretary of War. Seven years after the publication of his first book on Spain, he issued a second, *Spain Revisited*, which would indicate that the ban against him had been lifted after the death of King Fernando.)

By training and inclination I was disposed to agree with Slidell Mackenzie's attitude on the Muslim expulsion, but recently I had come upon Bertrand and Petrie's refreshing history, and Bertrand's austere judgments on Muslim Spain derived from his experience and study in the Muslim colonies of French North Africa. Bertrand knew Muslim culture and history in a way that Washington Irving and the anonymous 'Young American' never did, and his acerb views are a corrective to their romanticizing. One of Bertrand's repeated cautions is that we must be suspicious of pro-Muslim writing because its real intention is anti-Catholic; Protestant writers had found in the banished Muslims a convenient club for beating Spaniards: 'To judge Islamic civilization reasonably, it is important not to let ourselves be carried away by the hyperbolical admiration, the preconceptions, and the prejudices of those who exalt Arab-Spanish culture to an exaggerated extent only in order to degrade Catholic Spain in proportion.'

I recommend especially Bertrand's four-page chapter 'The Balance-Sheet of the Arab Conquest,' in which he summarizes his conclusions: Spain owed three positive debts to the Muslims. The concept of the university was Muslim, even though the teaching was 'terrible in its verbalism and almost entirely theological.' Muslim art also exerted a strong influence, as did Muslim poetry. More important, however, were the negative influences upon Spanish character, and these manifested themselves in various ways. The excessive individualism of the Spaniard, his tendency toward anarchy, is a Muslim inheritance 'to such a point that half a dozen Spaniards could not find themselves together in a fort or a caravel without at once forming two or three parties bent upon destroying one another.' Especially destructive to the Spanish character was 'the sinuosity of these Africans and Asiatics,' for from this developed the Spaniard's tendency toward bad faith and the breaking of his word. The bloodthirsty rapacity of the Spaniard and his lust for gold are directly attributable to his contact with the Muslim, as is the custom of keeping women behind bars. The worst of the borrowed characteristics was the parasitism of the nomads whereby living off one's neighbor became an acceptable practice, but almost as bad was the habit of putting the conquered to fire and sword, which the Muslims introduced into the peninsula. Bertrand concludes his dismal summary by citing two influences that were particularly destructive and persistent: the cruelty of the Muslim warrior, which became the cruelty of the Spaniard, and the incapacity of the Muslim to organize a government or to run it methodically. 'The traveler through the mournful solitudes of La Mancha feels only too intensely that the Berbers of Africa have passed that way.'

Elsewhere he makes an additional point of great importance. Conceding that agriculture declined when the Moors were expelled, he warns against interpreting this as proof of Muslim accomplishment, because wherever the Moors went they destroyed agriculture; they did not promote it. The secret was that the good agriculture of the Moorish period was attributable to Spanish farmers using Spanish methods. They had converted to Islam, but when the Moors left, they left too, out of loyalty to their new religion. Bertrand's final comment is unqualified: 'On balance, it can fairly be said that the Muslim domination was a great misfortune for Spain.'

If I were forced to choose between the sentimentalities of Washington Irving and the hard analysis of Louis Bertrand, I would be inclined toward the latter, but I suspect that Bertrand's strictures are somewhat more harsh than truth would dictate, for I detect in his argument more a defense of France's contemporary policy vis-à-vis the difficult Muslims of North Africa than a concern for Spain's historic problems with those same people. It seems to me that Bertrand underemphasizes the artistic accomplishments of the Muslims while overstressing their cruelty; but on one point he is eminently sound and it is one that has not been stressed before: that Spain's proven incapacity to govern herself in the responsible French-English-American pattern is due primarily to her extended experience with Muslims, who fragmented their own holdings into a score of petty principalities and who prevented Spain from doing otherwise until the habit became so ingrained that regional economic separatism became the curse of Spanish life, whether in the homeland or in the Americas. It is this dreadful heritage of anarchy that keeps the Spanish republics of our hemisphere in confusion.

I was restrained from accepting all of Bertrand's conclusions by a curious experience I was having in the Alhambra. Whenever I was tempted to agree that the Moors were as bad as Bertrand said, I would close my books and walk out into the gardens, and there I would find myself face to face with that hideous stone palace which Carlos V had caused to be built in the middle of the grounds and juxtaposed to the loveliest of the Alhambra palaces. One sight of that monstrous edifice, better suited to a cliff along the Rhine than to Granada, satisfied me that although the Moor may have had faults, he also had taste; this castle was so alien to the spirit of the Alhambra that no reconciliation of Spanish ideals and Moorish was possible.

The castle boasts a façade that is grotesquely ugly, as if someone had set out to burlesque the worst taste of the time. Its lower ranges consist of massive stones cut in that style which leaves the central area six or eight inches higher than the edges, producing an effect of brute strength, while the upper portions consist of some of the heaviest and most overly ornamented windows I had ever seen. Since the sides of the building form a square, what one has is an undigested cube of rock, and whoever designed it failed to realize that when plumped down beside the delicate Moorish palaces upon which it encroaches, it could only look ridiculous. There were reasons to forgive the intrusion of the cathedral in the middle of Córdoba's Great Mosque, but the Carlos V castle in the Alhambra can have no justification.

For several days I refused to enter the place, but finally a Spanish friend took me inside and I saw that the interior was a bleak two-tiered circular cloister, unfinished and gapingly open to the sky. This meant that the brutal cube had rooms only around the four sides and these I did not care to see, but my friend insisted, and on the second floor I did find something that made the visit rewarding. I was standing in a royal dining hall, one end of which was decorated by a marble fireplace featuring a medallion bas-relief showing Leda being raped in the most explicit way by Jupiter in the form of a swan, and I said to my guide, "I'll bet a lot of Spaniards spilled their soup in this room,' but he was already leading me to another hall that contained a painting which years ago I had seen reproduced. It was titled 'The Expulsion of the Jews' and was by Emilio Sala (1850–1910), who won a prize with it at the Berlin Exposition of 1891. The guide said, with much enthusiasm, 'It shows us a historic event which occurred in this very city in January, 1492. You see King Fernando on his throne and beside him Queen Isabel. Look at their banner which united Spain with its motto, Tanto Monta. It means that he and she are equal in dignity. Now, who are those two churchmen who seem so excited? The one in crimson, under better control, is Cardinal Mendoza, who served as a general during our Christian victory at Granada. The one in black is the great Cardinal Cisneros. Look at him point with his forefinger as he shouts, "The Jews must go!" You can see that Fernando and Isabel don't want to throw their Jews out, but Cisneros insists.' I was fascinated by the canvas, vast in size, for it was the only one I knew showing the four figures whose histories had become so important to me: Fernando, Isabel, Mendoza and Cisneros, and to see it was worth a trip even through the gloomy palace of Carlos V.

Alas, my enthusiasm was misguided. Long after I had left Granada, I discovered that the agitated figure in black was not my hero Cisneros but rather his predecessor as head of the Inquisition, Tomás de Torquemada, and the scene represented was the famous incident in which King Fernando announced that he had decided not to expel the Jews because they had offered him a bribe of thirty thousand ducats not to do so. Then Torquemada stormed into the room where the sovereigns were listening to the Jews plead for their freedom and he waved on high a crucifix, shouting at the same time, 'Judas Iscariot betrayed our Lord for thirty pieces of silver. The kings of Spain would sell him a second time for thirty thousand. Well, here he is.' With this he threw the crucifix onto the table and disappeared, crying as he went, 'Take him and barter him for thirty thousand pieces of silver.' And the decision to expel was decided upon that day.

In Granada one has conflicting thoughts about Cisneros, for it was as late as 1499, when passions aroused by the Conquest should have subsided, that he ordered the collecting of all Muslim manuscripts in the area and supervised their burning in what has often subsequently been lamented as a major crime against both history and scholarship.

It is appropriate, I suppose, that Fernando and Isabel rest permanently in Granada, the city which had attracted them like a magnet and whose capture became the principal jewel in their crown. In the center of the city, in a royal chapel of florid but pleasing design, lying adjacent to the cathedral, of which it is a part, rest the tombs of the Catholic Kings. The plain leaden caskets lie below ground in a crypt, which can be visited so as to satisfy oneself that the wishes of the kings were respected; they preferred to be buried simply and without undue panoply. But above them, on ground level, a magnificent wrought-iron grille subtends an area which is further enclosed by a plain but handsome iron fence, inside which stand four splendid catafalques, the first pair carved in Genoa of Carrara marble, the second pair in Spain. They represent four royal persons who concern us repeatedly in this book. As you face them, King Fernando V lies to your left in premier position, hands on chest and very regal. Beside him, in second position, lies Queen Isabel I, hands folded and, for some reason I have not been able to discern, looking away from her husband. As we shall see later, he gave her ample reason for dismissing him in this manner, but it was not within her character to do so and I find the tombs disturbing. Beside the great kings, and elevated above them, which seems quite improper, rest two of the unhappiest rulers who ever held a throne in Europe. The young king, who again lies to the left in the premier position, is Philip of Burgundy and Austria, known in Spain as Felipe I of Castilla, recognized in his lifetime as the most elegant of princes and known through Europe as Philip the Handsome. He was a miserable, mean human being, and it is shameful to have him sleeping where he does, for he served Spain poorly, abused the faith Isabel placed in him, fought openly against Fernando and crucified his unfortunate wife, their daughter Juana, who lies beside him. This time it is understandable that the thin-faced, demented woman looks the other way. Hers is a tragic figure, excellently portrayed by the Spanish sculptor, who may have worked from a death mask but also from reports of how the mad queen behaved.

The fact that young Felipe's body is here at all is a compelling story, for the path to this sepulcher was a grim one, but of that we shall hear later. For the present we must fix in our minds the noble panoply of the four kings: Fernando, Isabel, Felipe and Juana la Loca. No kings of Europe enjoy a more gracious mausoleum.

In the sacristy next to the chapel appear two wooden statues which bring the Catholic Kings to life, for here are Fernando and Isabel kneeling on purple pillows as they pray. The wood is polychromed, so that the cheeks of the rulers look as if they had been rouged this morning, and each strand of hair is carved and painted a Spanish black. The statues are delightful and show two pudgy-jowled monarchs in the early years of their reign, with none of the heavy seriousness that characterized them later. They are so appealing that they must be quite popular with Spanish visitors, but I had never heard of them; one look satisfied me that this was the way they appeared to their subjects, and now whenever I think of the Catholic sovereigns, I think of them as these polychromed statues kneeling in prayer. Had they been shown sweating over the problems of government, or leading armies, or haggling with cardinals, or writing snippy letters to the Pope, or deciding what to do with Fernando's regular procession of illegitimate children, the statues would be closer to the truth. These two had but little time for prayer, yet that is how they come down to us.

One day as I was walking through the gardens adjacent to the Alhambra, I came upon a kiosk selling a postcard titled 'Carmen de Manuel de Falla,' a carmen being a rustic house and garden, and it showed an attractive patio with a winding iron-railed staircase leading to the second floor. I knew that Falla (1876–1946) was of Catalan descent but did not know that he had been born in Cádiz and had lived in Andalucía, even though some of his themes appeared to be of that derivation. 'Yes!' the kiosk keeper said. 'Don Manuel had his carmen along that road that climbs the hillside. In the shadow of the Alhambra, you might say.'

I walked along a beautiful road that clung to the hill and provided a fine view of the valley, but soon I came to a fork, and the left path was so narrow that cars could not enter. I hesitated, but a woman cried, 'Is it for Falla's carmen? Along, along.' This trail was even more pleasant than the other and finally I came to an unpretentious house with a garden that climbed up the hill to three different levels, each of which had its unique natural quality. I had not at this point determined whether this was the carmen of Spain's foremost modern musician, but I was satisfied that it was the house of one who loved nature, and it required no imagination to visualize Falla sitting in this exquisite spot as he traced out in his mind the piano passages for his delicate orchestral suite *Noches en los jardines de España* (Nights in the Gardens of Spain, 1916).

Once inside the house one knew that it had belonged to Falla, for it was crowded with mementos of a life to which fame had come abundantly, not only in Spain but also in France. In the bedroom hung the English card commemorating his first communion: 'His death our life. His life our death. June 26, 1886.' For his first confession on June 20, 1884, the card had been in French. Here also were the works of art he had enjoyed: a Goya etching showing the torero Joaquín Rodriguez, called Costillares; a fine Hiroshige print showing two geese, one white, one colored, flying against a full moon with three reeds below. Teófilo Gautier had lived in this street and there was a memento giving his Spanish name. Here Federico García Lorca had attended a testimonial dinner to Falla on February 9, 1927, and farther on was a recollection of Pío Baroja. In these rooms I felt close to Falla, but it was in the wandering gardens that his music came alive.

Standing beside the bamboo trees and looking out across the dry fields and mountains of Andalucía, I could begin to hear those extraordinary rhythms he had used in his four chief works, *Noches*, *El amor brujo* (Love the Magician, 1915), *El sombrero de tres picos* (The Three-Cornered Hat, 1919) and the little-known *El retablo de Maese Pedro* (The Puppet Show of Master Peter, 1920). Here, too, I could understand better how he caught those dark and precise chords so representative of Spanish thought.

To Falla, Spain was important, and the part of Spain he understood best was this hot, impassioned Andalusian section. Contrary to what most believe and many write, he did not introduce folk themes directly into his music, for in his work only two or three instances of such use occur, but he did allow the intention of folk music to infect him, and his re-creation of its purposes is what makes his music so superior to that of colleagues like Albéniz, Granados and Turina. The more I hear Falla the more convinced I am that he was a true original. He is a very clean and honest composer; he speaks with a compact vocabulary and his message is no less profound because it is so brief. I once had the interesting experience of hearing Igor Markevich directing a conductors' school in a baroque church in northern Spain, and for two days I listened to the Radio Madrid Orchestra playing dances from *El sombrero*, over and over again, and two things impressed me: the music never grew stale, for on each repetition I heard some brilliant bit of orchestration or juxtaposition that I had missed before, so rich was Falla's construction; but when the would-be conductors were German or English or Russian, they seemed to fight the rhythms, whereas

*The type of gypsy family
Falla remembered when composing
for El amor brujo in Paris.*

when the conductor was a Spaniard he fell with ease into what Falla intended. Conversely, of course, the other Europeans found Mozart rather easy to handle, whereas the Spaniards treated him too heavily.

Falla is the most important composer Spain has produced since the closing years of the sixteenth century. It is Falla's solid authenticity that appeals to me, the high specific gravity of all he does. His themes are inventive and speak of the Spanish soil; his rhythms are unexpected and although they do not copy the handclapping of flamenco, they derive from it, as in that series of twenty-one staccato chords that closes the 'Ritual Fire Dance' in *El amor brujo* and the seven strange chords that intrude in the Miller's farruca in *El sombrero;* but it is principally his orchestration, as precise as Bizet's, that accounts for the high quality of his work.

That he did not compose much, when compared to contemporaries like Debussy and Richard Strauss, and that he did not attempt large pieces in the great tradition followed by Sibelius are characteristics common to all the Spanish artists of his day. When I was in Granada, wasting lovely hours in Falla's carmen, I had not yet tried to rationalize why the Spanish composers produced so little and I did not yet see this as part of a general cultural malaise; that would come later. For the present I was pleased to have seen the workshop of this notable artist and to have heard again in memory those unanticipated dark notes which García Lorca praised.

Then, as I was driving out of Granada on my way back to Córdoba, I saw on the road map a name which evoked a whole cascade of sound, trivial, to be sure, but sound which I have long enjoyed. The map had a small red arrow pointing to a cul-de-sac and the words Torre Bermeja. I had not known that the Torre Bermeja actually existed, nor had I realized that if it did exist it was in Granada, for this was the title of an unimportant orchestral piece by Isaac Albéniz, another Catalan who chose to write about Andalucía. I had first heard 'Torre Bermeja' (Bright Reddish Tower) as a student attending a concert in London, and even then I had enough knowledge to know that this was not a major piece of music, but it had a captivating lilt and one lambent theme, which Albéniz overworked. But what made the piece important to me was the program note which said that the Torre Bermeja was a Moorish tower, and that was enough to send me daydreaming of a Spain I had not yet seen. I supposed the tower to be some magnificent thing which bespoke its Moorishness to all who saw, and through the years I kept looking for a photograph of what I was sure must be a considerable structure; since I did not know what part of Spain it was in, I never saw it, but whenever I accidentally heard the slow sweet music on the radio I visualized a brooding Moorish tower and felt a strange identification with Spain.

I left the main exit road and headed for the cul-de-sac, which turned out to be a miserable track leading down a hill, the last part of which I had to negotiate on foot. The Torre Bermeja might be a fine structure but it was clear that the people of Granada thought little of it. Then it was before me, this soaring tower of my imagination, and it turned out to be a pair of square, dumpy things with undistinguished lines and little to commend them. 'Is this the Torre Bermeja?' I asked a workman who was hauling out rubble from a nearby cellar and he said, 'La misma' (the same); in Spanish the phrase 'Lo mismo' can have a fine sense of contempt, as if to say, 'Believe it or not, this is it.' An improvised wooden runway led up the side of the nearest tower to a gaping hole, and through this I peered into the interior, but it was even more drab than the outside.

'It used to be a jail,' the workman said. If so, it must have been a dismal one even by Spanish standards, which were never high. I scrambled down the hill to catch the other face of the tower, hoping that there was some point from which the old semi-fortress would look romantic enough to have justified Albéniz's composition, but there was none. I had before me a squat tower built of ugly brick in the worst possible proportions, as far removed in spirit from the music of Albéniz as one could imagine; yet there was about it a fine heaviness, a kind of brutality that was Andalusian. I was glad I had seen it, and had compared it to its music, for although I was not aware of the fact at the time, the experience prepared me for the intellectual adventure I was about to undergo when I got back to Córdoba.

I describe it as an adventure, although I doubt if others would, because it related to the nature of romanticism, and it was my concern with this out-of-date literary style that had first awakened my interest in

Spain. I was about to visit one of the fountainheads of Europe's romantic movement, and this side trip to the Torre Bermeja would serve as a relevant preamble; for what had happened in the relationship between Isaac Albéniz (1860–1909) and this tower was what happened whenever an artist became entangled in the romantic fallacy: a man of creative mind saw something in nature or history with an echo of the past, and around it he constructed an inflated fantasy, often bearing no relation to fact. Much of what had been written about Spain suffered from this fallacy; people looked at old Moorish structures and evoked from them a civilization that simply did not exist except in the imagination. Few things I did in Spain were more instructive than this visit to the Torre Bermeja, for it placed in proper perspective the romantic interpretation from which Spain suffers.

In the preceding sentence, and also in the opening of this book where I refer to the romantic cast of mind and its relationship to Spain, I use the word in its literary sense, referring to the Gothic novel, the tragedies of Victor Hugo, and that artistic movement common to all Europe in which imagination, emotion and introspection were stressed in contrast to classical understatement, and in which extravagant natural settings were chosen instead of arid Greek landscapes. When I returned to Córdoba I was thrown by accident into the heart of this literary romanticism, for as I was sitting one day at a café in the Plaza José Antonio, studying a road map and trying to decide how to get to the marshes lying south of Sevilla, I saw a name which had played a major role in the Romantic Movement: Hornachuelos.

I was surprised to find it a real place, a village of apparently trivial importance off the main road and situated on the bank of the Río Bembézar, which according to the markings on the map ran at this point through a defile. With some excitement I asked whether one could drive to Hornachuelos, and two Spaniards at a nearby table said, 'Fine road. Because farther along is San Calixto, where King Baudouin of Belgium and his Queen Fabiola, who is a Spanish girl, as you know . . .' The men gave a rambling account of how Baudouin had married the beautiful daughter of a Zaragoza family and how their honeymoon at the monastery of San Calixto had been interrupted by a revolution of some sort, '. . . in Belgium, that was, because here in Spain we don't have revolutions any more, thank God,' and how Baudouin had left his bride at dead of night and had sped down the very road I was studying. 'I think the Spanish government built the new road especially for Baudouin and his queen,' one of the men said.

'At any rate,' I interrupted, 'I can use it?'

'Best road in the district,' he said. Then he had an afterthought: 'While you're there, don't miss the Convento de los Angeles.' As he said the words I could hear an opera chorus led by Ezio Pinza chanting the great prayer of the monks as they worship in the Convento de los Angeles.

'You mean there's a real convent by that name?'

'Boys' school now. But it's perched on a site you'll never forget.'

I returned to my map and saw once more that magic name, Hornachuelos. For generations it has captivated operagoers because Giuseppe Verdi's *La Forza del Destino* takes place in and around 'The Inn at Hornachuelos.' I left the café, sought a bookstore, where I purchased a copy of the Spanish classic from which Verdi had borrowed his libretto, *Don Alvaro, o la fuerza del sino* (Don Alvaro, or The Force of Destiny, 1835) by the Duque de Rivas (1791–1865), then went back to the parador and packed my bags.

The road to Hornachuelos led down the right bank of the Guadalquivir and followed the old royal highway to Sevilla, now superseded by a new superhighway on the left bank. After a few miles I saw straight ahead and perched on a cliff overlooking the river one of Spain's most dramatic castles, that of Almodóvar del Río, all crenelations and towers in good repair and as usual abandoned. Some miles farther on, the Río Bembézar entered the Guadalquivir, and this was my sign to turn north along the new road built for the King of Belgium. In a few minutes I saw, off to the right, a bare, whitewashed village nestling on the edge of a cliff at whose feet ran the river. This was Hornachuelos, the epitome of Andalusian villages, as clean and hard as the skeleton of an ox whitening in the sun. At the oak table of an inn that could have been the one in the opera, I took out the play which had served as the Spanish counterpart to Victor Hugo and the German romanticists.

The author was as romantic as his creation, a duque of great inheritance whose liberal convictions had led him to speak out against the royal tyranny of Fernando VII. Surrendering his seat as liberal deputy in the Cortes, in 1822 he suffered banishment and entered upon that long exile in Gibraltar, London, Italy, France and particularly Malta, where he wrote exalted poetry and cultivated his addiction to romanticism. Recalled to Spain when the tyranny of Fernando ended, Rivas entered the government as a minister, and when his tendencies had become less liberal, found himself in charge of putting down a liberal revolution, which when it succeeded threw him once more into exile, this time because he was a reactionary. Again he wandered and again he intensified his commitment to romanticism. In the end he had acquired most of the honors to which he was eligible and was recognized as one of the grand old men of Spain and of European letters.

His masterwork, *Don Alvaro,* is practically a textbook of the high romantic style. A play in five acts, it tells the story of a mysterious young man of unknown antecedents who woos the daughter of an impoverished noble family of Sevilla. The introduction of Don Alvaro is classic and the despair of playwrights who followed. At the end of the Triana bridge in Sevilla a group of townspeople are discussing yesterday's bullfight, and here begins the description of the hero, whom we have not yet seen.

Seventeen-year-old gypsy mother.

SECOND TOWNSMAN: The fight wasn't as good as the previous one.

PRECIOSILLA: Because Don Alvaro, the rich fellow from Peru, wasn't there. And either on horseback or on foot, he's the best torero in Spain.

GALLANT: It's true, he's a real man.

Why wasn't he at the fight? Because he was beweeping the termination of his suit for Doña Leonor's hand; she still loved him but her proud father forbade the wedding: 'My friend, the noble Marqués de Calatrava, is too haughty and vain to permit an immigrant nobody to be his son-in-law.'

Bystanders say of Don Alvaro that he 'is worthy to be married to an empress.' He is generous and tips well. He is valiant. 'In the Old Park the other night seven of the toughest thugs in Sevilla jumped him, but he backed them like sheep against the mud wall of the riding school.' Another recalls that 'in his conflict with the captain of artillery he carried himself like a true gentleman.'

OFFICIAL: Then why doesn't the marqués accept Don Alvaro? Because he wasn't born in Sevilla? Gentlemen can also be born outside Sevilla.

PRIEST: Yes, but is Don Alvaro a gentleman? All we know is that he came here from the Indies two months ago bringing with him two Negroes and much money. But who is he?

FIRST CITIZEN: They say a great many things about him.

SECOND CITIZEN: He's a most mysterious fellow.

UNCLE PACO: The other evening there were some gentlemen here discussing the matter, and one of them said that this Don Alvaro made his money from being a pirate . . .

GALLANT: Jesucristo!

UNCLE PACO: But the other held that Don Alvaro was the bastard son of a grandee of Spain and a Moorish queen.

The priest says that it was proper for the marqués to reject such a suitor, and the official asks what must Don Alvaro do, and for the first time a forewarning of tragedy is struck, the fate that will doom the young man.

PRIEST: He ought to find a different sweetheart, because if he persists in his rash pretensions, he will expose himself to the sons of the marqués when they return to break the skull of anyone who has trifled with their sister.

Because this is a romance, the two brothers are formidable, one a soldier dedicated to defending his honor, the other a hell-raising student at the university. Their sister, meanwhile, has been sequestered at the family hacienda to protect her from Don Alvaro. The stage is set for the entrance of the hero, and this direction indicates how he arrives:

Night begins to fall and shadows obscure the theater. Don Alvaro enters, muffled in a silken cloak and wearing a great white sombrero, half-boots and spurs. Very slowly he crosses the stage, gazing with dignity and melancholy this way and that, and exits by the bridge. All observe him in deep silence.

Where is he going? The observers guess that it must be to try to see Doña Leonor, whereupon the priest whispers in a broad aside to the audience, 'I would be delinquent to my friendship with the marqués if I did not advise him this instant that Don Alvaro has been prowling about the hacienda. In this way perhaps we can avoid a misfortune.' Don Alvaro does go to Leonor's room, where the alerted marqués upbraids him. In one of the best inventions of the romantic theater, Don Alvaro, in a gesture of submission, throws his revolver at the feet of the marqués, but the shock of striking the floor discharges the weapon and its bullet kills the marqués, who, as he dies with Doña Leonor looking on in horror, utters the fatal malediction, 'I curse you.'

The second act takes place at the inn of Hornachuelos, where we hear reports of how the brothers returned to Sevilla, seeking vengeance. The scene shifts to the Convento de los Angeles, then serving as a monastery, and at this point I closed my book and started north to see where the tragedy had culminated. After a few miles a narrow trail branched off from King Baudouin's road and led through a recently harvested cork forest, which in turn led to the edge of a rather steep cliff. After one or two miles of this rather frightening road, I reached the canyon of the Río Bembézar, which lay far below. The road threatened to peter out but finally turned sharp left and ended at the entrance to the ancient convent, wedged in between a mountain to the left and the precipice to the right.

As I studied the site a taxi drove up behind me and a father and mother, he obviously a farmer, descended with a frightened boy of eleven. 'This is your school,' the mother said reassuringly, but the boy drew back and bit his lip to keep from crying. The father tugged on a bell rope exactly like the one that must have hung in that spot centuries ago, and the solemn bell began tolling, perhaps the same bell that under similar circumstances had set aflame the imagination of the Duque de Rivas one day around the opening of the nineteenth century. A friar, such as the duque might have seen, came to the gate and swung it slowly open to admit the small family. He allowed me to enter too, and while he processed the new student I was permitted to wander through the school, and I noticed on three different floors series of posters imploring boys to consider the priesthood as their vocation. The drawings were modern, as if they had been done in some first-rate industrial-arts shop in Milan or Rome; they had humor and color and made the profession of the Church seem a desirable vocation, with problems, defeats, triumphs and great spiritual satisfaction. The fact that three separate series of about a dozen posters each were displayed led me to think that the Church must be having a difficult time filling its seminaries, and it required no imagination to see the young boy who arrived with me electing the priesthood in such surroundings.

I left the old convent and sat on a wall along the edge of the cliff to read the famous stage direction of the third scene of the second act; it had inflamed the readers of its period, including Verdi in Italy, and is still remembered as one of the classic bits of the romantic age:

> *The theater represents a piece of level ground wedged into the declivity of a rude mountain. To the left, precipices and craggy steeps. Facing, a profound valley traversed by a rivulet on whose bank can be seen in the distance the village of Hornachuelos, terminating at the foot of high mountains. To the right, the façade of the Convento de los Angeles, of poor and humble architecture. The great door of the church is closed, but workable, and over it a semicircular window of medium size through which can be seen the shimmering lights from within; closer to the proscenium, the door of the porter's lodge, also workable but closed, in the middle of which a peephole which can be opened or closed and at the side a bell cord. In the middle of the stage there will be a large cross of rough stone corroded by weather, rising from four steps which can serve as seats. All will be illuminated by a brilliant moon. From within the church will be heard the pealing of the organ and the choir of monks singing their matins, while from the left, very fatigued and dressed like a man in a hooded coat with sleeves, a sombrero with drooping brim and boots, staggers Doña Leonor.*

The simple plot is now prepared. Doña Leonor, burdened with the guilt attached to her father's death, will have nothing to do with ill-fated Don Alvaro, who has joined the Spanish army in Italy to seek an honorable death. She is allowed to inhabit a grotto near the convent, disguised as a monk, and plans to spend the rest of her life in a remote cell. Her soldier brother, seeking Don Alvaro, also goes to Italy and unwittingly finds himself in the same regiment as the Peruvian, who saves his life. In spite of this, the brother is determined to kill Alvaro and goads him to a duel. Alvaro kills this brother, whereupon the university student intensifies his efforts to track down the Inca who has betrayed his sister and killed his father and brother, but he has a hard time finding Don Alvaro, because the latter has grown weary of a life so stalked by doom and has decided to enter this same convent as a monk, not realizing that Doña Leonor is living nearby. To this rocky defile the student finally comes and in a scene of wild passion duels with Alvaro and receives a mortal wound, but when he calls for extreme unction he uncovers the fact that his sister and Don Alvaro have been staying in the same holy place. Assuming them to be sharing their guilty love and revolted by the profanation, he stabs his sister to death and himself dies. What happens to Don Alvaro we shall see in a moment.

The play introduced certain conventions of the romantic theater. When the plot reaches an impasse at which the masquerade of the soldier brother must be disclosed if he gives his right name, and when there was no reason for him not to do so, he turns to the audience and delivers these inventive lines:

DON CARLOS: (*Aside*) I think I won't tell the truth. I am Don Félix de Avendaña.

At another point the hero uses for the first time on any stage a gesture which will become traditional furniture on the romantic stage:

DON ALVARO: Woe is me! Woe is me!
(*He presses the back of his hand against his forehead and remains in great agitation.*)

Romantic excess reaches its climax in the closing scene, which became notorious. I have never seen *Don Alvaro* on stage, but I've read several contemporary reports of its reception and this last scene was apparently a shocker. I wish the Spanish department of some American university would stage the play if only that I might see this final scene:

There is a long moment of silence; thunder sounds stronger than ever, and lightning increases as we hear in the distance the chanting of the Miserere by the holy community, whose members come slowly closer.

VOICE: (*From within*) Here, here what horror!
(DON ALVARO *recovers from his fainting spell, then flees toward the mountain. Enter the* GUARDIAN FATHER *and the holy fraternity.*)
GUARDIAN FATHER: My God! Blood spilled everywhere. Cadavers. The penitent woman.
THE FRIARS: A woman! Heavens!
GUARDIAN FATHER: And you, Father Rafael!
DON ALVARO: (*From a crag, completely convulsed in a diabolical smile*) Seek, fool, for Father Rafael. I am the ambassador from hell. I am the fiendish exterminator. Fly, miserable ones . . .
ALL: Jesús! Jesús!
DON ALVARO: Hell, open your mouth and swallow me. Let the heavens crash. Perish the human race. Extermination . . . destruction . . .
(*He climbs to the highest point on the mountain and leaps off.*)
GUARDIAN FATHER and FRIARS: (*Kneeling in diverse attitudes*) Misericordia, Father! Misericordia!

Little can be said in defense of such an ending; in its way it is as bad as the fake classicism it supplanted. Exess in either direction was regrettable, but the grotesqueries of romanticism had the added weakness of being open to burlesque, so when the duke's play had been on the boards for some years a cartoonist offered this spoof: a demented poet, ranting his verses on a night when the moon scuttled between clouds, stands tiptoe on a precipitous cliff, with a rope around his neck, a dagger at his throat, a lion at his rear and a crocodile waiting for him below. The whole extravagance of romanticism is lampooned, and especially the extravagance of *Don Alvaro*. Yet the play was not a waste. It paved the way for realism and for a while provided much pleasure and excitement. It also questioned the nonsense of exaggerated family pride, but I suppose that during the years of its greatest success this parody of pundonor was not so recognized; the landed families of Spain must have seen the play and said among themselves, 'By God, that's the way brothers should act when an upstart meddles with their sister.' In fact, if the play were given in Sevilla tomorrow, I would expect the great families to applaud.

After similar plays of the Romantic Movement had circulated for some time, accompanied by novels and music of like vein, the adjective *romantic* acquired a new definition which stressed not a literary tradition emphasizing nature but a sentimental mélange of sex and adventure summed up in the advertising phrase which has come to characterize Spain: 'Visit Romantic Spain.' This tag is both the damnation and the salvation of Spain and she had better be careful what she does with it. By damnation I mean that it encourages the country to engage in certain abuses solely because tourists from abroad will pay money to witness them. Thus, in recent years in tourist cities like Palma, the bullfight has been burlesqued into a vaudeville show because tourists and uneducated Spaniards prefer it that way. Flamenco, as I have pointed out, has degenerated into a flabby night-club act, because such debasement is profitable. In Spain generally stress is laid on the past rather than the future, because it is the past that is marketable. Romantic carry-overs like the imprisonment of women, the excesses of pundonor and the backward look in the arts are supported. Enough wrong judgments of this kind can destroy a country, and thus Spain's official adoption of romanticism as her international badge is damning.

By salvation I mean that whether one likes it or not, this is the concept available to Spain for peddling to the world at large, and if she does her job well, she can earn needed income from it without corrupting her soul. The enormous building developments which we shall later see along the Mediterranean coast of Spain are there because northern European capital considers Spain romantic; financially, Spain would be ill-advised to alter the image of herself which she circulates abroad. I can best explain what I mean by reference to Hawaii, which is something like five-percent Polynesian, fifty-five-percent Oriental. Some years ago the Caucasian and Oriental businessmen who were putting up most of the money for advertising the islands said in effect, 'It's silly to keep on publishing those photographs of hula girls and ukuleles and grass shacks. We're a modern society with fascinating Oriental customs, a great art museum, a fine university and forward-looking industries. These are the facets we should be stressing.' So they took the hula girls off the advertising and put on the alternatives, and incoming travelers diminished by some startling percent. The rest of the world had decided that Hawaii was the land of the hula girls, and if facts proved otherwise, then to hell with Hawaii. Who would want to spend the time and money to visit islands simply because they had a good university, an art museum and challenging confrontations between the Orient and the Occident? The tourists of the world knew what Hawaii was better than the business leaders, and after a disastrous hiatus, the posters reappeared with hula girls, and everyone has been happy ever since.

Spain, I am afraid, is stuck with the romantic legend portrayed in *Don Alvaro;* people shivering in Sweden and Germany want sun and romance, and Spain has no alternative but to provide them. The neat trick, as the people of Hawaii have learned, is to peddle this romantic illusion to outsiders but not to oneself. For the present, Spain has not yet mastered this trick; however, a few leaders of the country are becoming aware of the facts and they will probably adopt the policy of Hawaii's canny leaders: 'For the tourists hula girls. For the natives IBM computers!'

But even as I was formulating these judgments in the rocky defile of the Convento de los Angeles, I was false to my own conclusions, because when I approached King Baudouin's road I decided to turn right toward San Calixto rather than left toward the highway that would take me to Sevilla; I wanted to see the refurbished monastery where Baudouin and Fabiola had stayed and to compare it with the convent I had just seen. The monastery was nothing, but as I reached it I found that the hunt clubs of this part of Spain had convened for a trial of their packs, and some four or five hundred of the best hunting dogs, lashed two-by-two for safety in transportation, were preparing for a dash across the desolate emptiness of these hills. It was a brilliant moment, with rural costumes, the sound of horns, the yapping of the dogs and on some distant hill the waiting stag. Five hundred years ago men and women exactly like this, with dogs like this, had come here attended by servants no whit dissimilar to hunt over these barren reaches. A thousand years ago, when Moors held the land, these were, of course, cultivated fields supporting hundreds of families, but with the expulsion of the Moors the lands had fallen idle and would long remain so. My companion, listening to the confusion of sound and looking at the huntsmen as they saddled up to chase across the distant hills, asked, 'Isn't it romantic?' It was . . . in both senses of the word.

FOLLOWING PAGE:
From the swamps.

V

LAS MARISMAS

OCEANO
ATLANTICO

MILES
0   100

Barcelona

Maranchón

Madrid

Lisboa

Almonte

Sevilla

Concha y Sierra

El Rocío

← LAS MARISMAS

CABO DE
SÃO VICENTE

COTO
DOÑANA

Sanlúcar
de Barrameda

Cádiz

MAR MEDITERRANEO

One wintry day when storm clouds hung low over Sevilla, I set out on a journey to the south to complete a task I had set for myself some years earlier. I had been planning a novel with a Mexican setting, and because of the Spanish background of one of my characters I required to know something of life on a Spanish ranch given over to the rearing of fighting bulls. I had selected as my prototype the historic and honored ranch of Concha y Sierra (Shell and Mountain Range) and a matador living in Sevilla had agreed to show it to me. He respected the Concha bulls because of their heroic performance during the past eighty years.

'The ranch lies in the swamps,' he warned me as we set forth, and this seemed an unlikely statement, since one visualizes a bull ranch as occupying hard, rough soil which strengthens the bull's legs. 'A common misunderstanding,' the matador assured me. 'It's the nature of the grass, the minerals in the water . . . something in the essence of the land and not its hardness. That's what makes a good bull. Anyway, the Concha y Sierras live in the swamps.'

We drove south to the end of the road. Parking our car in the rain, we set out on foot along a narrow earthen path that might have been passable in the dry season but which was now so muddy that going was difficult; if we stepped off the path on either side we were in swampland, not the green-covered stagnant swamp of fiction but an interminable area extending for miles in all directions, consisting of completely flat land covered with grass and two or three inches of water. 'These are the swamps of the Guadalquivir,' the matador said, and for the first time I looked out upon the infinite desolation which was to attract me so strongly and in so many ways.

Lean matador, chunky author trudging home after a day studying the bulls.

The storm clouds swept rain squalls ahead of us which beat down upon the brackish waters to bounce back in tiny droplets, so that it seemed as if there were no horizon, as if sky and earth alike were made of mist and grayness. For two reasons that first day persists in memory. The immensity of the swamps astounded me; I had not realized that Spain included so large an area of primitive land, a retreat given over primarily to wildlife, where birds from all parts of Europe and Africa came in stupendous numbers to breed; this swamp, lying so close to Sevilla, was as wild as the seacoast of Iceland, as lonely as the steppes of Russia.

What I remember most vividly, however, is that on this introductory day, for reasons which no one has been able to explain, as the matador and I walked a flock of swallows stayed with us, perhaps a hundred in all, and when we took a step they swooped down to the tips of our shoes, then off into the sky, one after another, so that we moved in a kind of living mandorla such as encloses the saints in Italian religious painting. At times the swallows came within inches of our faces, swooping down with an exquisite grace past our fingertips and to our toes, flicking the swamp water with their wings. This continued for about half an hour, during which we seemed to be members of this agitated flock, participants in their spatial ballet, which moved with us wherever we went. It was one of the most charming experiences I have ever had in nature, comparable I suppose only to the day when I first skin-dived to the bottom of the coral beds off Hawaii; there was the same sense of kinesthetic beauty, of nature in motion, with me in the center and participating in the motion.

Why the swallows stayed with us for so long, I cannot guess; once during the walk I wondered if our feet, to which they seemed to be paying most attention, might be kicking up insects too small for us to see but inviting to the birds; but I had to dismiss this when I saw no evidence that the swallows were catching anything. There was also the possibility that our steps were throwing up droplets of water which the birds were taking in the air, but again there was no evidence that we were doing so, and I concluded that they were simply playing a game. This was not unreasonable, for obviously they were enjoying our walk as much as we were. At any rate, they served to remind me that these swamps existed as a realm for birds and that in entering it I was trespassing on their terrain.

The area is called Las Marismas (The Tidelands, in this instance a twofold tide, one coming in from the Atlantic Ocean direct and a more important one creeping up the Río Guadalquivir to spread out over an immense area). Las Marismas is roughly forty miles from north to south, thirty-five miles from east to west, but it is not square and has an area of less than a thousand square miles, or about six hundred thousand acres, of which only about three hundred thousand could be called swampland proper, the rest being equally flat and bleak but free of water most of the year.

I was fortunate in visiting Las Marismas for the first time in winter, for this was the rainy season and I was thus able to see the bull ranch in maximum swamp condition; it seemed to me that about seventy percent of its land was either under water or was so water-logged that if I stepped on what appeared to be a solid tussock, it collapsed beneath me with a soft squish, so that my feet were again in water. It was on such land that the Concha y Sierra bulls flourished, but it was not until the matador led me to the dry area on which the ranch buildings stood, and I saw the famous brand of an S inside a C scrawled on the side of a corral, that I was ready to believe that this was the territory of the bulls about which I had read so much.

The Concha y Sierra bulls had a brave history, and many a noble head had gone from the bullring to the taxidermist's and from there to the wall of some museum, with a plaque beneath to inform the visitor as to what this bull had accomplished before he died.

On June 1, 1857, the Concha bull Barrabás participated in what the books describe as 'one of the most famous accidents in the history of bullfighting' in that, with a deft horn, it caught the full matador Manuel Domínguez under the chin and then in the right eye, gouging it out. It was assumed that Domínguez would die, for his face was laid open, but with a valor that had characterized his performance in the ring he survived, and three months later was fighting again as Spain's only one-eyed matador, having stipulated that for his return the bulls must again be from Concha y Sierra. For another seventeen years he fought with only one eye and

Concha y Sierra brand painted in whitewash on a wooden shield in the testing ring. The horn scratches remind the visitor that the bulls of this ranch have given tremendous glory to some bull-fighters and have taken the lives of others.

enjoyed some of his best afternoons with Concha bulls. He is known in taurine history as Desperdicios (Cast-off Scraps, from the contemptuous manner in which he tossed aside his gouged-out eyeball).

On August 3, 1934, the Concha bull Hormigón (Concrete) verified his name by killing the beginning bullfighter Juan Jiménez in Valencia, and on May 18, 1941, in Madrid the gray Farolero (Lamplighter) killed the full matador Pascual Márquez, thus ending the career of a young fellow of great promise. On August 18, 1946, the Concha bull Jaranero (Carouser) killed young Eduardo Liceaga, brother of one of Mexico's best matadors. And so the story goes, with the great gray bulls of Concha y Sierra defending themselves valiantly in all plazas.

The matador and I left the ranch buildings and on horseback set off across the marshes to see if we could find any of the bulls in pasture, and after we had ridden for some time in the direction of the Guadalquivir, that meandering, desultory river of such force and quietness, the matador suddenly cried, 'Look!' and off to our left, rising from the reeds and thistles like an apparition, loomed a gray bull, his horns uptilted, his ears alert. We stopped the horses. He stopped. We stared at each other for several minutes, and then we saw, gradually appearing from the mists behind him, the shapes of fifteen or twenty other bulls, and slowly they moved toward us, not in anger but rather to see what we were doing. They came fairly close, much too close for me, but the matador said, 'They won't charge as long as they're together and we stay on the horses,' and so we stayed, among the bulls who had materialized from the swamps, and after a while they gradually drifted away and the mists enveloped them.

It was while wandering in this fashion in Las Marismas that I became aware of the Spanish seasons—the rain and the drought, the cold and the heat, the flowering and the harvest—and I decided that if I ever wrote about Spain, I would endeavor to cover each of the seasons. I have never spent all of any one calendar year in Spain, but I have visited each major area except Barcelona during at least two different seasons so as to see the effect of the passing year upon it; so far as I can remember, the only month I have missed is February, and it is possible that one of my Easter visits started in late February, but if so, it could have involved only a few days, and I do not remember it. I have seen Las Marismas in all seasons, never as much as I would have liked but enough to teach me a few facts about the land of Spain.

Spain! It hangs like a drying ox hide outside the southern door of Europe proper. Some have seen in its outlines the head of a knight encased in armor, the top of his casque in the Pyrenees, the tip of his chin at Portugal's Cabo de São Vicente, his nose at Lisboa, his iron-girt eyes looking westward across the Atlantic. I see Spain as a kaleidoscope of high, sun-baked plateaus, snow-crowned mountains and swamps of the Guadalquivir. No one of these images takes precedence over the other, for I have known fine days in each of these three contrasting terrains. That snow should be a permanent part of my image may surprise some, but Spain has very high mountains and even in the hottest part of July and August, when the plains literally crack open from the heat and when the blazing skies described in Spanish fiction hang everywhere, snow lies on the hills less than thirty miles north of Madrid. In the middle of August not long ago I drove across the mountains that separate the Bay of Biscay from the city of León and saw snow about me for mile after mile; at another time, when I had come to Spain in midsummer for my health, doctors in Philadelphia asked, 'Is it wise to visit Spain in July? Won't you suffocate?' But my plans took me to the high north, where during much of the summer I needed a topcoat at night.

But now we are speaking of Las Marismas, in the heart of the

The ancestors of this fighting bull, standing along the banks of the Guadalquivir, were brought up the river by Romans more than two thousand years ago

southland, and to appreciate it, and the land of Spain in general, we must watch it through one whole year, and if in doing so I seem to be speaking primarily of birds, that is appropriate, for here is one of the great bird sanctuaries of the world, as if nature, realizing how difficult it was going to be for birds to exist in a constantly encroaching world, had set aside this random swamp for their protection.

WINTER

The Guadalquivir itself never freezes, of course, but occasionally areas of shallow water with low salt content will freeze to a thickness that would support a bird but not an animal. In winter the tides run full, and even if no additional rain fell they would be sufficient to fill the streams that crisscross the swamps; but rains do fall, most abundantly week after week, and the tides are reinforced, so that water stands on the land. The sky is mostly gray, but when storms have moved away, it becomes a royal blue set off by towering cumulus clouds moving in from the Atlantic; Las Marismas is a product of the ocean; it is not a somnolent offspring of the Mediterranean Sea.

Maximum flooding occurs in January, and then one can move by boat across large segments of the land, and in this boggy, completely flat wilderness life undergoes conspicuous modification. Animals like the deer and lynx have taken refuge by moving to preselected higher ground, and in their place come several million birds from northern Europe to prepare for breeding. Three hundred thousand game ducks have moved in to winter, ten thousand large geese. In January untold numbers of coots arrive to breed. Through a hundred centuries they have found in Las Marismas a plentiful food supply, for the marsh grasses provide seeds and roots and the shallow waters teem with swimming insects.

Toward the end of winter the birds begin to settle upon specific clumps of grass, testing them for strength and protection, and in March they begin weaving nests which will house them for the important work ahead in spring. Where do they get the material for the million or more nests they must build? From all imaginable sources but particularly from the weeds themselves. However, in the nests I have seen feathers, bits of mouse fur and even strands of hair from cattle.

In the winter men leave Las Marismas pretty much alone. Along its edges, of course, towns have grown up and in them live skilled hunters who know all the footpaths that cross the swamps. Here also are herdsmen who pasture their cattle on the grassy portions in the summer, and fishermen who work the Guadalquivir. And there are, I am glad to say, a handful of men who simply love the bleakness of the swamps and study it year after year, as they would a book, but in winter even they stay mostly at home.

Río Guadalquivir.

Over the vast area one sees mostly the movement of birds, thousands upon thousands of them, birds that have known Siberia and the most remote fjords of Norway, that will spend their summers on the moors of Scotland and in the forests of Germany. They live in tremendous families, each associating with its own kind, but a single area of marshland may contain fifty different species, waiting through the long winter till their summer feeding places in the north have thawed.

On the thirteenth day of January each year, in obedience to one of those unfathomable rules that govern birds, storks fly north from Africa to their chimneys of Holland and Germany and continue to do so for some weeks, so that the Spanish have a saying which could be translated as:

> At the day of St. Blas
> The storks do pass.

Why they go north in midwinter has never been explained, but in midsummer they will go south, as if their calendar were askew.

But there are also, in these months, the birds that live permanently in the Spanish swamps, and in some ways these are the most interesting because they are the ones that we shall see in all seasons, like old friends. There is no more beautiful small bird in Europe than the goldfinch of Las Marismas, a tiny gem of color and design. I have watched a group of goldfinches for an entire morning and have never tired of their display, the flash of their color against the brown swamp, the chattering of their family life. Large numbers are trapped here and sold throughout Europe, for they make fine pets, and whenever I saw them caged in other parts of Spain, I thought of Las Marismas, for they seemed to take the swamps with them.

At the opposite end, so far as size is concerned, was quite another bird. I remember one day, when I was on the Atlantic Ocean edge of the swamps, seeing a huge creature fly into the crown of a tree. It was slightly smaller than a griffon vulture, which are common throughout Las Marismas, and of a different character. Since it remained motionless in the tree, I was able to study it at leisure, but it was not a bird with which I was familiar; later I learned that I had seen an imperial eagle, the noblest inhabitant of the swamps. There are partridge, too, and magpies, and crested coots, and purple gallinules, and a species of owl.

The resident bird which dominates the scene in winter is the cattle egret, a snowy-white bird with yellow legs, a long yellowish bill and a silhouette much like a heron's or a small stork's. They get their name from their habit of feeding not only with cattle but on them, so that if you are wandering through Las Marismas it is not unlikely that you will see a sleek and coiffured little egret riding like a debutante between the horns of some massive fighting bull as he grazes in the swampland, and I have often watched a herd of bulls and a flock of egrets as they blended together in such harmony that one would have thought they had been created as halves of a symbiosis. Certainly they form one of the most attractive features of the year. Regardless of where one sees them, the egrets are winsome birds, delicate in motion on the land and unforgettable in their broad-winged flight. They range far from the swamps and can often be seen in the fields near Sevilla, looking for insects, but no matter where they spend their days, at night they return to the swamps in flocks that number in the hundreds. They can be seen in all seasons but are most appreciated in winter, when they have least competition, as the total bird population is then at its smallest.

Primarily, winter in Las Marismas is a resting time, for the birds, for the animals, for the seed plants and for the men; but to see the swamps in this season is an intellectual challenge. Can you imagine what they will look like in summer? I failed the test, for I was unable to visualize this watery world, this endless waste of tussock and salt, becoming other than what it then was. I could not imagine the transformation it was to undergo.

SPRING

The rains cease. Evaporation begins, and with each inch that the water falls, grass springs up to take its place. What had seemed, only a few weeks ago, seventy-percent water, now seems ninety-percent grassy meadowland, but if one steps off established paths, he sinks in up to his knees, for the underlying water will remain until well into June. As the waters recede, the swamps cease being attractive to ducks and geese, who fly north in huge flocks to the thawing lakes of Russia; but as seed grasses appear, with their assurance of food, large numbers of terns and coots arrive to set up housekeeping, and the men of Sanlúcar de Barrameda, the town at the mouth of the Guadalquivir, prepare their boats for one of the strangest harvests in Europe.

It begins when grass has fairly well covered the swamps, so that horses and cows can be let in to forage. They eat such grass as shows above the water, in which they stand up to their knees, but as they feed they leave behind shreds of grass that float on the surface and these the terns and coots collect for their nests, which they build on circular flat constructions that float on water and stretch in all directions for miles.

Now comes the harvest. In these semi-floating nests the birds lay large quantities of eggs, and for as long as men have lived along Las Marismas they have poled their flat-bottomed boats into the marsh in spring, collecting these birds' eggs. They work in teams of six or seven men to a large boat, from which small skiffs, each bearing a single man, set out to explore tiny rivulets, gathering eggs which will later be sold for food. Year after year they rob the nests of hundreds of thousands of eggs, but the bird population seems not to suffer, for enough eggs are overlooked to ensure the perpetuation of the species.

Only once did I see a team of egg collectors in action. They came, as usual, from Sanlúcar, one of my favorite towns in Spain, a sun-baked, miserable dump of a place that looks much as it did in the days of Columbus and Magellan, who knew it well, a most authentic remnant of old Spain. Five men entered the area in a large boat painted blue and boasting an outboard motor. In the boat they carried a small skiff which they launched in the marshes. The man who poled it through the shallow waters was indefatigable, for he moved swiftly from one floating nest to the next, scooping up enormous numbers of eggs. How many did he gather in the short time I saw him? Probably five or six hundred, and he had touched only a small portion of those available to him. The men in the blue boat were drinking wine and encouraging him, and I never understood what the division of labor was supposed to be. Perhaps the man in the skiff was the only worker; the others may have come from Sanlúcar for the ride.

A flight of cattle egrets returning to roost in Las Marismas at end of day.

As the grasses grow and the land begins to solidify, small land birds begin to crowd Las Marismas in flocks of such magnitude that most Americans have no experience with which to compare them. Many arrive from Africa and the Holy Land, and I shall never forget my astonishment, one spring day when I had arranged a picnic in Las Marismas for a group of friends, at seeing, near the clearing in which we ate, two of my favorite birds from Israel, the long-billed, inquisitive hoopoe and the brightly colored bee-eater. 'Are they native here?' I asked an expert who was sharing our picnic. 'No, they migrate from Africa but they arrive so regularly each year that we think of them as native.'

Even in spring, when the swamps have begun to look like land, it is the water birds that one remembers best, for now the avocets arrive, those delicate, long-legged birds with the upturned bills; I had not known the avocet until I spent some time in Colorado, where they were common, but the Spanish ones seem larger and more colorful. The stilts come now, too, and the slender-billed terns, so that what lakes remain are crowded with fascinating life, even though the spectacular ducks and geese have gone.

SUMMER

Summer is something to see in Las Marismas! Even though storm clouds occasionally hang over the Atlantic, the sky over the land becomes an incandescent arc producing temperatures that go well above a hundred degrees in the shade, if any can be found. Day after day the sky hangs there, motionless, relentless, drying up the waters and bringing the grasses to seed. What few streams remain are covered with golden pollen, and even their banks are barren for yards on each side. Young birds are everywhere, feeding on fallen seeds and slapping their awkward feet on the baked earth as they look for water. Jack rabbits appear in large numbers; they attract fox and lynx, who hunt them constantly, but it is from an unexpected source that the food supply becomes abundant.

As the accidental streams that crisscross Las Marismas dry up, multitudes of fat carp search frantically for the permanent rivers which will sustain them through the summer, and in great numbers they move in obedience to faulty instinct from one evaporating fragment of water to the next, until at last they perish in vast numbers on dry earth. At times their glistening bodies completely cover what had lately been a lake, but before they have a chance to rot and thus contaminate Las Marismas, flocks of kites and vultures, sensing the impending tragedy while flying over North Africa, swoop in and help the local birds clean up the carcasses.

The bird that seems to represent summer at its best is the heron. The large white ones appear in flocks of up to six thousand at one time, the smaller in flocks of twenty thousand, ranging over the entire area in white dignity. How can so many birds find food? They eat fish when they find them, and frogs, lizards and the larger insects. They scour the dried earth for remnants of the carp and uncover so much food that they prosper where other birds would fail.

A bizarre tragedy now occurs and one that I would have thought improbable had I not seen it. Among the hordes of aquatic birds that resided here in the spring, and I am speaking not of hundreds but of hundreds of thousands, most have left, but there are some who nested here, and they seem unable to believe that these watery lands are going to dry up, so in spite of mounting evidence in late June and early July, they linger on. Now the remorseless drought of late summer catches up with them and for some weeks the three-month-old ducklings search frantically for ponds which they knew existed in a given spot only a month before, but they find only sun-baked earth. Sometimes they march on webbed feet,

Man of Las Marismas.

three or four thousand in a small area, searching vainly for water, and one
by one they perish.

Now the raptores move in on silent wings to kill off the survivors. The
sharp-eared lynx darts out from his hiding place to catch his supper, while
the fox and the rat keep watch. The mournful pilgrimage continues for the
better part of a week, this noisy march of hopeless ducks trying to find
water, and then Las Marismas is silent once more.

The extraordinary thing about this season is that in drying, the
once-muddy areas of land become a perfect highway for automobiles—flat,
even, undisturbed and so hard that cars throw no dust. I have several
times driven far out into the summer swamps at thirty miles an hour, and
when something interesting loomed ahead, at forty or even forty-five, and
in this way have covered twenty or thirty miles with no inconvenience but
with a sense of flying low in an airplane over a placid bay. Of course, the
driver must have some general knowledge of where the permanent water-
ways are, for even if the water has evaporated, as is sometimes the case,
the vanished rivulet leaves such a depression that the car could not cross
it. Except for this limitation one can ride for hours across Las Marismas
and see the skeletons of carp.

If one were to see Las Marismas for the first time in midsummer he would find it difficult to believe that the place should be called a swampland, for there is certainly no evidence to justify such a name. Perhaps *marshland* would be a better translation of the Spanish, or even the Scottish *moorland*, because when dry, Las Marismas has many characteristics of the latter; but considering the area as it exists throughout four seasons, swampland is not an inappropriate description.

In summer many men come into Las Marismas, some to tend cattle, others to hunt and still others to wander through the wilderness as their ancestors have done for generations. The immense expanse of sky and the weirdness of the absolutely flat landscape exert a powerful appeal to these men, and one of their delights is to shoot a rabbit, skin it and then spread-eagle it on a structure made of three sticks tied together in the form of a Cross of Lorraine. The upright member of the cross is left long, so that it can be used as a handle for holding the rabbit over a fire of hot coals until the meat is hard and crisp. Salt is rubbed on the finished meat, which is cut into thin strips and mixed with raw tomatoes, peppers, much onion, garlic, olive oil and vinegar. 'Maybe the best salad a man can eat,' those who live along Las Marismas claim. For as long as men can remember, huntsmen who prowl the swamps have been entitled to shoot all the rabbits they need for food; the most recent estimate is that about eight thousand are taken each year.

But as the knowing men cross the hard-baked swamp they are careful to watch out for a menace which through the years has taken the lives of many animals and occasionally even of men. This is the ever-present ojo (eye), which stands invitingly here and there in attractive spots, a kind of minute oasis with a central eye of water, perhaps a swampy spring or well, and surrounding green grass and shrubs and sometimes even small trees. On the great arid swamp these ojos are most tempting, for they promise both water and shade, but they are treacherous because they also contain quicksand of a most virulent sort, and once it grabs hold of a leg it rarely lets go. Domestic animals wander into the ojo alone, get stuck and never break loose. If they die, they do so beside the carcass of some boar or deer that got stuck in exactly the same way a week before. Within a few hours the bones are white; vultures keep watch on the ojos.

No matter how well one knows Las Marismas he occasionally meets with surprises. One day as I was riding past a section of the swamp I saw long rows of what looked to be human beings, each bent forward from the waist as if gleaning a field for some lost object. I stopped and crossed the intervening land to see what they were doing; much of the land was under water but ridges had been left as footpaths, and after I had walked along these for a few hundred yards I saw that the bent-over people were women,

On the banks of the Guadalquivir rice planters work at one of the relatively high-paying occupations of Las Marismas.

Apparition in Las Marismas.

with heavy nets over their heads and faces, and that they were engaged in transplanting rice, digging handfuls of young rice plants from the seed bed, where they grew in close profusion, and carrying them to the larger fields where they would be transplanted, one stalk at a time in the mud. The women were thus required to stand in water and bend over the soggy fields for eight and ten hours at a time, exactly as other women were doing in Asia.

The nets over the face served two purposes. If a woman bent close to the water on a sunny day for extended periods, the reflected rays of the sun would bounce up at her face and produce a sunburn that might in time cause cancer. More immediately, the nets kept away the hordes of mosquitoes that infested Las Marismas in summer, making it at times almost unbearable. 'If you're going into the swamps,' Spaniards told me repeatedly, 'take along some 612.' This was a potent insect-repellent that worked.

And occasionally as one penetrates the swamps he sees on the horizon a strange brown animal larger than a bull and thinks for the moment that his eyes are deceiving him. Then the animal moves, in an undulating manner, stops, twists his long neck and raises his long-nosed face. It's a camel. His ancestors were brought over from Africa in the latter part of the eighteenth century for use among the sand dunes around Sanlúcar; they adapted well to Spain, but peasants protested that they frightened them and that if God had wanted such ungainly beasts on Spanish soil He would have seen to the matter. Men interested in working the area tried to explain that the camels were harmless, but to no avail. In 1828 all those in the Sanlúcar area were rounded up, transported across the Guadalquivir and set free. There cannot be many left, and I suppose that within another decade they will have disappeared.

The kangaroos that were introduced somewhat later than the camels have already vanished, as have the monkeys which were brought to Sanlúcar from nearby Gibraltar. So far as climate and food are concerned, there is no reason why monkeys should not have prospered in Las Marismas, but once more the peasants of Sanlúcar, who must have been an unusually suspicious lot, protested that the almost-human faces of the monkeys scared them at night, and that if God had wanted such beasts . . . The last monkeys were killed off about fifty years ago.

More rewarding than the camels that one occasionally sees are the melons, which are among Spain's best. They grow luxuriantly wherever sandy soil remains soft enough during the early summer to permit the vines to mature; most often the blazing sun absorbs all moisture and the plants wither, but if they survive, the fruit they yield is delicious. Apart from the rice, it is the only edible thing grown here commercially.

But whatever the season, Las Marismas is primarily the residence of birds, and what happens to men or camels or melons is a secondary concern, and so as summer ends one looks again to the sky and sees aloft the great bustards, accompanied by their cousins the little bustards, coming in to glean the hard ground for seeds and bees and insects. They fly in splendid circles and land in two or three hops. Their quick eyes scan an area in seconds to determine where the good feeding will be, and they pick the land clean, quarreling among themselves as to who saw which first. When they take their short hops and rise again into the air they see below them only a parched earth, blazing in heat as great as that of a desert, with the somnolent Guadalquivir wandering southward through the middle of Las Marismas, and at its mouth the sunburnt adobe of Sanlúcar de Barrameda, blistering in the sun as it did in the days when Columbus stopped there.

AUTUMN

The best time of year, for me, in Las Marismas is autumn, because three things happen to make it both bearable and exciting: the dreadful heat diminishes, so that temperatures become quite pleasing; the first rains come and with them a new color in all living things; and the movement of birds is captivating. As for the heat, Las Marismas, which in midsummer seems as hot as tropical Africa, stands at about the same latitude as San Francisco (Sevilla 37°, 27′N; San Francisco 37°, 40′; Richmond 37°, 30′, Wichita 37°, 48′). Therefore, when autumn comes and the baleful effect of winds blowing in from Africa and the Mediterranean has gone, the temperature is delightful; one wears loose clothing during the day, a substantial jacket of some kind after dark, and if one wishes to ride over Las Marismas at midnight to spot wildlife, a sturdy coat. I would suppose that anyone who loved the outdoors, and especially the tracking of birds in their larger migratory movements, would find Las Marismas in autumn almost irresistible, for then nature changes its aspect daily, and what has been a barren wasteland marked by whitened carcasses becomes a meadow which will sustain millions of birds in their migrations.

The change begins with the first rain. Year after year it arrives sometime between the twentieth and twenty-fifth of September, as if it had been waiting for summer officially to end. This is only a slight rain, not even enough to heal the cracks that mar the land, but it is followed in desultory fashion by one or two others. On Columbus Day, October 12, celebrated throughout the Spanish world as El día de la raza (The Day of the Race), the people who live along the edges of Las Marismas enjoy their last guaranteed clear day and their picnics are apt to be gay, for with strange regularity, on October 13, comes the first drenching rain of sufficient duration to soak the ground, but even though enormous quantities of water fall in this and subsequent storms, there is still not enough for any to collect. No lakes re-form and the permanent rivers are no higher than they were before; this water seeps into the dried earth. In doing so it reactivates plants, and even before the swamps re-form they look as they did when water was plentiful.

Now a few courageous ducks and geese begin to arrive from Scandinavia, and they must be sorely frustrated by what they find, for there are no lakes and food is bitterly scarce, for seeds of autumn have not yet fallen and the water plants on whose roots the birds exist have not matured. There is even trouble in finding a lake on which to rest; most are dried basins, their cracks just beginning to heal. And even when some accidental lake is found, its water is extremely brackish and unable to provide the swimming life which ducks and geese use to supplant the seeds and roots. But these first arrivals struggle with their problems and no living thing in Las Marismas must welcome subsequent rains with more excitement. One day I watched as a group of land-bound geese wiggled and cried with delight as rain came down upon them; it was the promise of a fruitful autumn.

These newcomers face an additional problem, for when they are kept from their normal feeding and hiding grounds, they lay themselves open to attacks by the imperial eagles, who now move in for easy kills. Perhaps easy is the wrong word, because the eagles have to exercise real skill if they want to catch a graylag goose who has protected itself in the north for the last six months. No eagle flying alone has ever been seen to take a goose except by sheer accident, for although the eagle is stronger and has powerful talons, he cannot overtake a goose in full flight; pursuit is useless. Therefore, the eagle finds himself a partner and as a pair they become formidable. One flies rather high, in the fly-space of the goose, and somewhat awkwardly, so that the target gets the idea that he can outfly this enemy. The other eagle flies low and well behind the first, and as the awkward eagle maintains altitude on the goose and makes a series of futile passes at him, the big bird takes the easy way out and with adept spirals evades the eagle by dropping to a lower altitude, where the second eagle sweeps in with terrifying talons.

There is other death in Las Marismas now. The cattle who have been browsing all summer on the safe flat lands begin to withdraw to higher ground as the rains start to engulf them, and by following paths long established, they retreat, but often one stumbles into an ojo, now camouflaged by growing grass and shrubs, or he waits too long and is trapped on an islet, where he dies, or the long trek weakens him. In any case, he is carefully watched by the vultures who scout the vast expanses day after day. In Las Marismas nothing rots.

For human beings in the region the autumn is as exciting as it is for the birds and animals, because this is the season of the vendimia (vintage) when the first fruit of the vine is pressed to the accompaniment of week-long celebrations. If one wanted a single painting of Spain to remind him of the best of the country, he could do worse than choose Goya's exquisite painting of the vendimia, now hanging in the Prado in Madrid, in which idealized peasants bring in the grapes while a nobleman, his pretty wife and their little boy, dressed in green velvet and red sash, taste them. Spaniards love this unpretentious work, for it speaks to them of the land, the rich, hard land of southern Spain when the harvest is under way.

In Sanlúcar the vendimia is celebrated with the same rustic vigor that it has been for the last thousand years, but at nearby Jerez de la Frontera, from which sherry takes its name, occurs the most renowned vendimia. Then the world-famous families who make and sell sherry—Domecq González, Byass, Osborne—set up kiosks where wine is served. Countrymen arrive to promenade in carriages drawn by six horses. There are bullfights and celebrations that last through the night. All around the rim of Las Marismas there is festivity in which Catholic Spain remembers pagan rituals and combines the old religion and the new in fascinating juxtapositions.

Now, too, is the time when huntsmen concentrate on the swamps, for the latter contain two enormous herds of deer, an indigenous red deer with

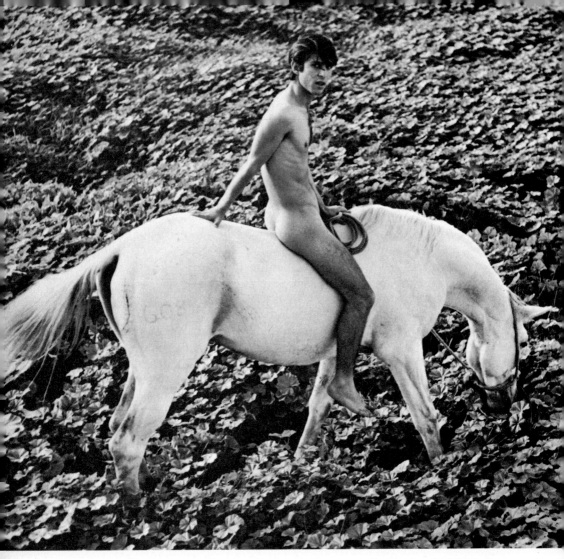

No. 608, whose deep horn wound on the right flank proves he is a horse that works the bulls at Concha y Sierra, comes out of the Guadalquivir after his bath in the late afternoon.

pointed horns, which is held to be an honorable target for the huntsman, and the grosser-formed fallow deer with palmated horns imported from Asia in the early 1900s, and not allowable as quarry for a gentleman. One autumn I was in a car filled with huntsmen speeding over the macadam-hard swampland, scouting for deer, and because I wear rather strong glasses I could see farther than my companions. 'Buck!' I shouted with some excitement as I spotted a handsome animal with large horns off in the distance. The car slowed down; the men looked; and there was silence as we drove on. I concluded that I had mistaken a doe for a buck, but shortly thereafter I spotted what could only be a buck. To my eyes he was majestic, with a spread of antler exceeding any I had seen before. 'Buck!' I cried, this time with firmness. The car stopped; the men looked; and in embarrassed silence drove on. On the third spotting, for I was still seeing animals before the others, I cried, 'Goddamn it, that's a buck.' This time the car did not even bother to slow down, but one of the Spanish gentlemen did whisper, 'Michener, look at the horns! No gentleman would shoot a beast like that.' I had been spotting fallow deer, and they didn't count. After a long silence I saw a herd of perhaps sixty deer, and they were different, red instead of spotted brown, pointed horns instead of palmate. 'Buck!' I shouted for the fourth time, and there stood a series of noble beasts with proper horns. My alarm caused some excitement, and the gentleman at my side whispered, 'Well done. Those are deer.'

I am not a huntsman, except with camera, so to me the deer-stalking of autumn was less exciting than the subtle transformation of the land. I have never seen Las Marismas in late autumn when the water system of winter is fairly well formed, but I have seen it twice in early autumn when the rains have begun to take effect, and to see lakes quietly come into being, to watch dead rivers creep back to life and above all to see the surface of the land begin to collect its water and soften itself from concrete into mud, with grasses and flowers gently appearing, is a profound experience. I wouldn't be able to say when the swamps had fully reestablished themselves, perhaps by the first weeks in December, but at any stage in the process they afford an insight into nature that one cannot obtain elsewhere. How beautiful this transformation is, how simple: the land was barren and a raceway for the wind; it is now a meadow and a home for birds.

As always, it is the birds that inspire. A cold wind comes down from Madrid and next day all the migrants from Africa have taken flight. Remember, it is hardly five hundred miles from Las Marismas to the first deserts of Africa, and beyond them it is a couple of days' flying time to the warmer regions in which the birds are accustomed to spend their winters. The bee-eaters, the hoopoe birds and some of the egrets depart, and in their place come the robin and woodcock and widgeon. For a short period the swampland seems relatively depopulated, for the birds that have fled were conspicuous in size and color whereas the newcomers are markedly less brilliant, but after a few weeks of emptiness the damage is repaired, for now the real flocks of ducks begin to appear, so that a lake that was empty one day may have a thousand birds the next, and as the waters replenish themselves, the birds do likewise, and the poetic year of Las Marismas draws to a close.

It would be difficult to say where the capital of Las Marismas was, because the Guadalquivir cuts the area into two parts, the larger lying on the right bank, the more productive on the left. The right bank contains no major settlement, although, as we shall see, it does have the two major features, a shrine and a palace; the left bank contains one of the most memorable towns in Spain, and so far as I am concerned, it is the capital.

Sanlúcar de Barrameda is a dirty, low-lying settlement located at the mouth of the Guadalquivir, a seaport partaking of the nature of both the ocean and the river. When I first saw it, only one street was paved, and it poorly. The bullring was built in the ancient Moorish style, with onion-bulb gates and crescent windows. On the small hill that rises in the center of the town a ruined castle perches; it houses a tribe of gypsies and four families of peregrine falcons that fly out each morning to hunt the swamps. In its alleys, incredibly dirty in comparison with the rest of Spain, I saw many more horses than automobiles, and the only industry I could spot besides fishing was the lonely salt bed in which overflow from the ocean was trapped and allowed to evaporate, leaving behind a brownish deposit, half mud, half salt. In one of the bars a man said, 'You're in the best town in Spain. Real spirit here. This is where we make manzanilla.' If this was true, Sanlúcar deserves more fame than it has received, for manzanilla is one of Spain's noblest wines, a sherry so pale and dry that it seems hardly to be a liquid but rather a delicate spirit. I had not imagined it as having come from a miserable spot like Sanlúcar.

But the more I came to know the town, the more attractive it grew. In the old days every treasure boat from the New World was required to drop anchor in these roads so that government officials could go aboard and check the bullion. 'The men in Sanlúcar you could trust,' a Spaniard explained, 'but if the gold once slipped through to Sevilla unweighed, there wasn't an official who was honest.' It was from this dreary little port that Christopher Columbus set sail on his third voyage to the New World. He had a difficult time in Sanlúcar, for reasons unconnected with the town, as we shall see shortly. It was also from here that Magellan set sail to circumnavigate the globe, and it was to Sanlúcar that one of his ships returned three years later, but without him.

Noble families distinguished in Spanish history had their seats in Sanlúcar, though why, I shall never know, and in the middle of the last century the sun-baked little town became rather prominent; Queen Isabel II's younger sister married a son of the King of France, and when apprehension arose lest he try to gain the Spanish throne, he and his bride were banished to Sanlúcar where they could do no harm. Only a few years ago another noble, with vague claims to the throne, died here in Sanlúcar, and as I wandered through the streets I tried to visualize what royal exiles did to occupy their time in this backwater. In their letters they usually spoke of Sanlúcar with affection; in recent years adventurous American naval officers who work at the submarine base not far away have rented fifteenth-century homes on the hill and have lived there without electricity or running water. 'The best town in Spain,' they report unanimously. 'It has character.' If I were to live in the south for any period, I think I would elect Sanlúcar. It has quality and lies near Las Marismas.

In the heart of the swampland there was a building which I scarcely expected to find in such a place, a stone church which served as a shrine for a dramatic cult centering upon a wooden statue of the Virgin, known formally as Nuestra Señora del Rocío and popularly as la Paloma Blanca (the White Dove). Around the church has grown up an extraordinary village of some six or eight tree-lined streets with cottages on each side, so that the place looks almost as much English as it does Spanish. The village is unusual in that it is empty for fifty-one weeks each year; it is the fifty-second week that counts.

To appreciate the significance of El Rocío one must go far back in history to a time prior to 711, when the Visigoths still ruled Spain after having converted it to Christianity. There must have been in those days many churches in Sevilla and other settlements along the edges of Las Marismas and each contained a stone or wooden statue of the Virgin, who even then was popular in Spain. In 711 the Muslims invaded from Africa and within a few months overran the southern areas of the country and threatened the others. Then Christians, terrified by this unknown enemy who crushed any army that confronted him, grabbed the statues from their churches and buried them in remote spots to protect them from profanation by the infidel. As it turned out, their apprehensions were unjustified because Islam, even though it sought converts, preferred that conquered peoples remain Christian, for if they did extra taxes could be levied. Thus churches were not only permitted to continue but were encouraged to do so.

When the relatively benevolent nature of the new order was discovered, many of the buried statues were dug up and returned to their niches, but others remained where they were and were forgotten. Perhaps the man who had buried a given statue was the one who embraced the new religion when he saw that it was economically profitable to do so; if he had converted, it was unlikely that he would dig up a statue relating to his old faith. At any rate, when four or five centuries of Muslim occupation had passed and Christians began regaining their lost territories, it became fairly common for shepherds, who lived under the open sky year after year with little to occupy them, to uncover by accident in some remote spot one of these long-buried Virgins. Word of his discovery would flash across the countryside and before long would reach the bishop in the capital. Investigations would be launched, but by this time the simple act of uncovering the statue would have been clothed in heroic or spiritual garb. 'For three nights running Juan the Shepherd saw a light hovering above a rock.' Or 'While Tomás was tending his sheep he heard a voice speaking to him.' Thus a miracle was born.

In my travels through Spain, I was to come upon at least eight of these miraculous appearances of the Virgin, but none with a more appealing history than the finding of the El Rocío statue in Las Marismas. More than a century had passed since the area had passed from Muslim control to Christian, and one day a hunter from the town of Almonte was looking for game when his dogs assumed a point before a thicket. He verified that there was no game in the brush, but the dogs continued their point, so he investigated and found hidden in the hollow of a tree a statue of the Virgin. He abandoned his hunt, took the image in his arms and set out for Almonte, but with his burden he became weary and fell asleep, only to awaken and discover that the image had disappeared. He returned to the tree and was overjoyed to find that the statue had returned there and was once more in the hollow, where he left her to report the miracle in Almonte. A group of villagers, doubting his story, walked the long distance to the tree to see for themselves, and when they entered the thicket they found the statue hiding in the tree. Again they tried to carry her to Almonte and again she insisted upon returning to the tree, whereupon the men ran back to the village and informed their priest, who explained that by this gesture she meant to tell them that it was there that she wished to be worshiped. Accordingly, they raised a hermitage on that spot, which accounts for the remote location of so famous a shrine. She was at first called, after the place of the apparition, Nuestra Señora de la Rocina, a name which was later altered by the villagers, no one knows exactly when or how, to the simple and poetic Nuestra Señora del Rocío (Our Lady of the Dew).

As for the village that has grown up about it, a full-scale settlement with many cottages wholly furnished for one week's occupancy a year, the fame of the Virgin of El Rocío became so widespread that each spring an enormous pilgrimage is organized throughout southern Spain, when families in traditional two-wheeled carts decorated with banners and flowers and drawn by oxen similarly decorated take the long trek to El Rocío to pay homage to the stubborn Virgin who knew where she wanted her home to be. In special years as many as eighty thousand pilgrims ride over dusty roads to enjoy as wild a weekend as Spain has to offer.

Unfortunately, I never saw El Rocío in fiesta, but friends introduced me to Don Luis Ybarra González, the forty-year-old son of a distinguished Sevilla family that specialized in all things relating to olives. Their commercial empire became so extensive that they were required to put together their own shipping company, and this in turn encouraged them to enter collateral fields. Señor Ybarra was a well-known amateur naturalist with whom it was a pleasure to roam Las Marismas, except that he entertained so many foreign visitors, each speaking a different language, that in self-defense he referred to birds and animals only by their Latin names. 'The only sensible way,' he told me. 'Birds are the same everywhere. It's the countries they visit that change.'

He was cousin to the Conde de Ybarra and knew well the history of the region, especially that of El Rocío. 'It's a great pity you couldn't have seen it during celebrations,' he said. 'You won't get much seeing it this way.' And I must admit that as he drove me across the swamps to a large grove of eucalyptus trees I could not visualize eighty thousand pilgrims converging on this lonely spot, for there was nothing to commend it, neither natural beauty nor buildings of interest. When we reached the village itself I was astonished by its emptiness; we were like characters in a romance who had come upon a sleeping town. Here were the houses, street after street of them, and the stores, and a church and all the appurtenances of a village except people. It was uncanny, and I asked, 'It's empty like this all year?' He nodded and pointed to one of the larger cottages. 'My family's. We've come here one week a year for as long as I can remember. Beneath those eucalypts there will be tents for ten thousand. Farther along many refreshment bars. No roof, no walls. They will serve thousands of snacks. Over here beer stands. More than you could count.'

As he spoke, I wished that we were in one of those movies in which, as the hero begins to explain something, the scene he is describing begins to take form. I should have enjoyed seeing this deserted village spring to life for its one wild week, and I was lucky to find, in a small town on the other side of the Guadalquivir, an unusual Englishman who had settled there years ago as the Volkswagen representative for southern Spain, and he turned out to be both an El Rocío enthusiast and a spirited raconteur and it was through his account of adventures on the pilgrimage that I gained some sense of what it must be like.

He was John Culverwell, a handsome bull-necked fellow with a petite wife from the English Midlands who was fluent in Spanish and a fine horsewoman. Without repeating the questions I asked to keep their commentary flowing, I should like to report on their experiences in undertaking a Spanish pilgrimage.

'Cecilia and I had been so often that three years ago our community came to us and said, "Señor Culverwell, you and your wife are as good Spaniards as any of us, so when the grand parade is formed to ride past the Virgin next week, we want your wife to ride at the head of our column and carry the flag of our village. You are to ride at the end of the parade and carry the standard of the Virgin of El Rocío." You can imagine that this struck us as something of an honor, because I can't recall another instance when a foreigner was invited to carry the flag of his community at El Rocío.

'The pilgrimage occurs each year at Whitsunday, which if you were a Catholic you'd call Pentecost, the seventh Sunday after Easter, that's the fiftieth day, when something or other important happened. From our side of the Guadalquivir you can get to El Rocío only on horseback, so early in the week we arrange for our horses and at sunup on Friday we leave home and ride to Sanlúcar, where we meet with hundreds of horsemen who have collected from towns around here. We ride down to the river's edge, where barges wait to ferry our horses across to the other side, and after delivering them we walk to a different pier, from which we are taken across in small boats. On the opposite bank we recover our horses, saddle up and head for an adventure you'd never believe if you hadn't seen it.

'Did you know that on the other side of the Guadalquivir there are first pine forests, then sand dunes for eight or ten miles? Yes, big, flowing, beautifully sculptured sand dunes with hardly a tree or shrub. During the trek to El Rocío horsemen frequently get lost in these dunes. I don't know whether any have died in recent years, but I do know that a couple of years ago I got separated from Cecilia and the others and it was rather touch-and-go before I got back. A wilderness of white sand with desert birds you won't spot elsewhere.

'Well, we ride for many hours through the dunes and it's difficult to believe that we're in Spain, but toward evening we come in sight of the palace . . . Yes, there's a full-scale palace hidden away in the loneliest part of Las Marismas, off beyond the dunes. I'll explain some day why it's there. Anyway, we ride up to this palace and there we spend the first night among so many birds you'd not credit the number. My chief delight these days is studying birds, and I doubt if there is a better place in the world to do this than at the palace, for there you get land birds, sea birds, swamp birds, dune birds . . . everything a man could want to see. Whether you ever get to El Rocío or not, you really should try to see the palace.

'On Saturday morning we rise early, saddle our horses and cut off along the edge of Las Marismas, past the famous heronries and into the eucalyptus groves and to El Rocío itself. It's about a seven-hour ride as we take it, because we stop to check on how many birds are nesting. You can see, I would suppose, several thousand nests without much searching, but toward midafternoon we come in sight of El Rocío. You can tell where it is because of the enormous cloud of dust that rises over it. Thousands of oxcarts converging on the shrine. We spur our horses, dash into the village, go straight to the chapel and from outside salute the Virgin, then make a couple of circuits to inform the world that our contingent has arrived.

'El Rocío! If you haven't been there I can scarcely describe it, but imagine a convocation of thousands of people, hundreds of gypsies, and drums and flutes, guitars, hand-clapping and a world of two-wheeled carts from the last century, and no sleep.

'No sleep! You arrive Saturday afternoon and until late Monday there's no sleep. If a man begins to nod, somebody wakes him up. He couldn't sleep anyway. The noise is too tremendous. Bang, bang, bang! A clatter such as you've never heard before. Naturally, tempers get a little short. In fact, the game is to make the other fellow's temper explode. You kiss his girl or steal his wine. But if he makes one move to hit you, everybody shouts, "¡Viva la Paloma Blanca!" As soon as this is said he has to laugh, shake hands and share a drink with you. One year I watched them badger a chap beyond endurance. He was about to clout his chief tormentor when we all shouted, "¡Paloma Blanca!" He went ahead and busted his enemy in the eye and shouted, "¡Paloma Blanca! ¡Ojo negro!" (White dove! Black eye!)

'Each community in this part of Spain owns one of the cottages which it dresses up for Whitsuntide and it serves as your headquarters. Here you get free drinks, meet your friends, leave your wife when you want to raise hell somewhere else. But late Saturday evening you must report back, for now the formal parade of horsemen in honor of the Virgin is about to begin. As I told you, our group, which contains some of the best horsemen in the south, was to be led by Cecilia.

'About nine o'clock at night there's one hell of a noise. Flamenco music and shouting and general brawling. And then on all sides of the central plaza, the Real del Rocío, the parade forms, and for more than three hours we ride past the chapel of the Virgin and pay our respects. It's something to see, a recollection of old Spain, but the best part comes after the formal parade breaks up, because then gangs of riders rip and roar through the village all night. When I am in England and try to recall why I love Spain so much, I think of two things. The birds at the palace and the night-riding at El Rocío.

'On Sunday morning at ten o'clock something happens you wouldn't believe. The Real is crowded with people who have come to celebrate a field Mass in which a portable altar is set up. Riders attend on horses, as they did in cavalry days, and when they dismount to kneel, it's something to see.

'Sunday night is a sort of bleary time, a sentimental wandering from one community house to the next. Men you wouldn't bother with in normal business suddenly become good friends, because they took the trouble to visit El Rocío. The singing continues all night, and if there is someone who simply can't take the noise any longer, he sneaks out into Las Marismas and sleeps under the stars.

'Monday is the day! Early in the morning the Virgin, the original statue about which all this fuss is being made, is brought out of the church atop a rather large wooden structure like a float in order to make a paseo so that she can bless the pilgrims who have come to do her honor. Honor! That's the word. By tradition her float is carried only by the men from Almonte, because it was they who first did so when they took her from the tree. But the rest of us are free to volunteer, but if we do the men from Almonte push us away.

'So how does a man win the honor of helping to carry the float? By gouging, kicking, pulling and clubbing whichever men have her at the moment. A shirt lasts about three minutes. I have seen fights in the shadow of this Virgin that make one of your sales at Macy's look puny. I've seen men so eager to touch the float that they rear back, take six running steps and torpedo themselves headfirst into the face of the man who was holding the float. You'd think the man who was hit wouldn't have a tooth left in his head. He'd stagger back and want to fight, but someone would shout, "¡Viva la Paloma Blanca!" and he'd wipe his mouth and grin.

'How long does the brawling last? Four or five hours. Maybe more. The Virgin moves a few yards at a time, trembles, teeters, almost falls in the dust, but hands always catch her at the last minute and keep her erect. The fighting continues at fever pitch because as soon as anyone is exhausted and has to withdraw, someone fresh plunges in determined to capture the float.

'By late afternoon Monday the two-wheeled carts begin to drive back along the roads to sanity. The battered Virgin is restored to her quiet niche in the shrine and the community houses are slowly boarded up for another year. The stores that have been opened to serve the pilgrims are shut down. The gypsy bands move on to another fiesta and everywhere you look you see tired men and women sleeping on porches or under trees. Horses that have not rested for days sleep standing or graze along the edges of the swamp.

'On Monday, Cecilia and I ride back to the palace, and believe me the birds are a welcome change from the madness we've been sharing. On Tuesday we return through the dunes and come to the edge of the river. On the other side we see the low roofs of Sanlúcar and wonder if the ferry will ever spot us and come to fetch our horses.'

In the spring of 1498, when Christopher Columbus proposed to sail from Sanlúcar on his third voyage of exploration to the New World, he was forced to delay the departure of his six ships until the thirtieth of May, 'because his sailors had gone off to El Rocío and would not return.' When the five ships of Magellan assembled at Sanlúcar in 1519, prior to setting out for their circumnavigation of the globe, the season of El Rocío was well past, for it was mid-August, but most of his sailors from the Sanlúcar district would have made the pilgrimage earlier, for the Virgin looked after her devotees.

'She's a wonderful Virgin,' Señor Ybarra assured me as we stood under the eucalypts in her deserted town, 'and she'll forgive me if I say that the best single thing about El Rocío is the honey. Until you've tasted our honey, you can't know what Las Marismas is.' I asked him why he spoke of 'our honey,' and he said, 'Each Whitsuntide my father drives here in a carriage and opens the cottage as his father did before him. We send ships all over the world, but El Rocío is our spiritual home. Taste the honey.'

We had stopped at the only store which keeps open throughout the year, a thoroughly beat-up shack with earthy peasant proprietors who looked after the cottages during the silent months, and the wife brought us a kilo of dark honey in a glass jar that had once housed peanut butter made in California. How it had reached El Rocío, I could not guess, but the honey, when I tasted it on a piece of hard bread, was all that Señor Ybarra had predicted. I've sampled honey in most of the areas where it is made and have had some very fine brands, especially in Japan and India, but the heavy, dark El Rocío honey gathered from flowering weeds in Las Marismas was finer than any I had previously tasted. Señor Ybarra summarized its quality precisely when he said, 'Tastes like Spain, doesn't it?' If Spain has a taste, it would be either that of El Rocío honey, or a dark red wine from Rioja, or a fish zarzuela from Badajoz or the anchovies of Barcelona or perhaps the incredibly good bread of Arévalo, which we shall meet later. Certainly this excellent honey would be one of the components.

Like the honey, Señor Ybarra was a heavy, dark man with a graying mustache who spoke rapidly with both a lisp and a marked southern accent, but the subjects with which he dealt were so interesting that I found myself understanding him better than I did most Spaniards. 'The unique flavor of El Rocío honey comes from the rosemary and eucalyptus on which the bees feed, and also from the swamp flowers.

'One thing you must see while you're here is the new chapel we're building for the Virgin. Look! She'll have a throne of pure silver. What a change from the tree trunk in which she used to rest. You ought to take a set of the El Rocío tiles home with you.' He showed me the nine orange, blue and yellow tiles which when cemented side by side in a wall would create an image of the Virgin enthroned and surrounded by a grand halo of sixteen gold disks. 'Our legend says that the statue was carved in Italy and sent to North Africa to help convert the heathen. She wound up in Morocco, and after converting that land, was brought to Spain to save us. When the Moroccans changed to Islam they wanted to take her back lest she bring us good luck, and that's why Spain was invaded.' In bemused silence she sits in her old shrine waiting for the new one to be finished, as profoundly loved as any Virgin in Spain, in a strange, wild way.

The more I was with Señor Ybarra the more impressed I was with his affection for the land; again and again he returned to this topic. 'My father had a great love for the Guadalquivir, probably because he saw it in such majesty here in Las Marismas. Anyway, he said, "There's nothing another river can do that our river can't." Somebody said that the Volga could produce caviar, and my father took this as a challenge. He remembered that even in Roman times the Guadalquivir was famous for its sturgeon. There was an old Roman coin found at Coria del Río which showed the sturgeon. So he searched through Europe to find Russian émigrés who knew how to make caviar and finally found an expert living in Cape Town. Brought him here in 1929 and within a year my father was producing all the caviar sold in Spain. You go into a fine hotel and ask for caviar . . . Well, a lot of people do. You get Guadalquivir caviar and even the experts can't tell the difference.'

It was unusual to find a Spaniard who spoke with such love of rivers and meadows and mountains, for Spain more than any other European nation has abused its land. It is in this respect that Spain is guilty of the charge that Frenchmen so often make against her, that she is not a European nation but an African: 'Africa begins at the Pyrenees.' Demographically this is not so; in the abuse of natural resources it is.

The nearly eight centuries during which Spain waged intermittent war against African invaders, 711–1492, created a type of gentleman to whom the maximum good in life was knightly behavior in war, which was not in itself destructive, because for different reasons similar values were respected in all European countries, but in Spain a contempt developed for anyone who worked with his hands, especially farmers. It became an actual disgrace, from which a family could not cleanse itself, for a member to work at agriculture; inevitably, the land suffered.

What was worse, a system grew up whereby gentlemen who were not allowed to farm were allowed to herd the highly profitable Merino sheep, so long as the animals grazed at will over vast territories rather than on a single farm owned by one man. A gigantic cooperative developed, the Mesta (The Group of Proprietors of Sheep), and because only gentlemen were allowed to join, it won special privileges from the Spanish kings and flourished as a major economic agency in Spain from about 1300 through the first quarter of the 1800s.

Its flocks were so huge that in one poor year the census showed 1,673,551 sheep, ceaselessly in motion, like a great pendulum of destruction oscillating between the northern limit of the central plateau and the southern. In this heartland of Spain where a rational agriculture should have been developing, fencing off was not permitted; fields had to be kept open for the passage of sheep, and any settled farmer who tried to protect his crops from the vagrant sheep was hauled not before a magistrate but before an officer of the Mesta who traveled with the sheep, dispensing a harsh and arbitrary justice. Before 1585 there was no appeal from a decision of the Mesta judges.

Many books have been written about the terror that possessed Christian settlements in Spain when the Muslims came up from the south; others have dealt with the fear engendered by the Inquisition when it was probing into private lives, but I suppose the best book that could be written, the one that would tell more about day-to-day Spanish life than any other, would be the story of some village whose farmers watched in dismay as the outriders of the Mesta crossed their fields, warning them that the sheep would soon follow. Then the farmers had to retire, remove obstacles, make no effort to protect their crops and wait in their huts until the all-powerful sheep had passed.

Why did this extraordinary condition prevail? Partly because sheep-herding had become recognized as an occupation for gentlemen but mainly because the kings of Spain had discovered that in the wool from their Merinos, which under pain of death could not be smuggled out to other lands which did not have them, they possessed a commodity which other nations would pay for at a price that Spain would determine. Merino wool was recognized as the best available and the Spanish economy was geared to produce Merino and to protect the men who tended the sheep that grew it. The Mesta existed as a mobile feudal kingdom, ravaging the best land and inhibiting its proper utilization. By the time the Mesta declined, an irreparable damage of two kinds had been done: the land was depleted and the ordinary agricultural processes which English, French and German farmers had mastered through the centuries were not known.

The capricious nature of this division between acceptable sheep growers and unacceptable farmers should not disturb the reader, for many other societies have made similar distinctions, equally impossible to justify. Thus in the American west it was the cattleman who was acceptable and the sheep man who stood outside the pale; I have been present when a self-respecting Coloradan entered a restaurant, took one sniff of the cooking odors, turned on his heel and stalked out, growling, 'They're serving lamb in there.' It was in Hong Kong, however, that I observed arbitrary categories at their best. A long-time English resident, having volunteered to help me buy a watch, took me to a shop called something like Ledyard's, and when a satisfactory deal had been concluded, he said, 'Good fellow, Ledyard.' In the street he reprimanded me for having said, 'Mr. Ledyard.' 'The man's in trade,' he pointed out. 'Should never be addressed as Mister. Couldn't possibly be a gentleman.' When I asked why, my friend said, 'Ledyard could buy and sell me seven times over, but by God, in nineteen years I've never called him Mister.' While I was in Hong Kong a convivial chap who ran a bar was finally admitted to one of the exclusive clubs, to which he had sought admission fruitlessly during many years; the club had not changed its rules excluding men who were in trade, but the saloon owner had that week sold his bar and gone into wholesale distribution of beer and whiskey, and that, according to British tradition, was not trade.

But if all nations have similar peculiarities, few have suffered from theirs as much as Spain has from hers. Hundreds of perplexed travelers during the last three hundred years have commented on the fact that the country was filled with virtual paupers who maintained their classification as gentlemen by refusing to work; they starved but they remained gentlemen. Although such a system had deleterious effects on farming and manufacturing, it had the virtues of not being based exclusively on money or big houses; a man with one room and one suit, if he carried himself properly, could be just as much a gentleman as a man with a palace, and this universal eligibility has permitted a friendship between economic classes which has not existed in other European countries. The impoverished Don Quixote, and many of them exist today across Spain, feels no sense of embarrassment in addressing as an equal the duque or conde or

It was the inherent surrealism of Spain that produced a painter like Salvador Dali.

marqués with whom he comes in contact, while to the recent millionaire he feels superior.

The effect of all this upon the land has been tragic, and I remember one hot summer day riding through the heart of the Mesta territory, northeast of Madrid, and coming upon the village of Maranchón, so typical that it could represent all that had grown up in the sheep country. How beautiful and quiet this place was, with majestic old houses crowding each side of the somnolent main street. How enticing were the views I caught of the narrow streets that led off to right and left as I passed. Here was the inevitable sign, 'Correos,' plus an arrow, indicating that down this alley there was a house serving as post office. Another sign, common to all villages, read 'Telégrafo' and a third said 'Teléfono.'

In Maranchón I saw one shepherd, but he had no sheep. I caught sight of a woman ducking into a doorway and then I was in the outskirts of the village, but when I came to the little bullring, 'Erected 1915,' I had an overpowering desire to know more about this town, so I wheeled my car about and parked on the main street. I walked up the grass-grown Calle Generalísimo Franco, to where it met Calle Calvo Sotelo, and I stayed there for some time just looking. Almost no one moved, for Maranchón was largely deserted. The fine houses were shuttered and the doors over which family shields had been carved were locked.

Where had the men gone? 'To Germany, señor. They have all gone to Germany.'

But these houses held women, too. Where are they? 'They've gone to Barcelona, señor. The lucky ones are in Barcelona.'

But your fields are rich. Why aren't they tilled? 'The men have gone to Germany, señor. There they can make a living.'

Maranchón lives in my memory as a permanent symbol of Spain, even more lasting than the depopulated villages of Extremadura, because it was more beautiful and in its day had known a more complete life. How really lovely that main street was! If it could be transported bodily to California it would be one of the treasures of the United States and artists would fight for the privilege of renting the rooms that stand behind its plain, perfect façades. Where have all the people gone? If Maranchón itself could speak, it would say, 'For five centuries my people were abused by the Mesta, whose courts used to sit in that hall over there, sentencing farmers unjustly. Any man who had a good idea about caring for his land was muzzled. The fields that could have been so productive have gone to waste and the boys who once ran in these streets have gone to Germany and Barcelona.'

It seems uncanny that a nation which made the miserable mistake of chasing after Mexican and Peruvian gold instead of developing manufactures should in the field of agriculture have made an equally destructive wrong choice, electing the quick money of the Mesta rather than the sustained productivity of an orderly system of farms. Just as the gold damaged the country instead of helping it, so the Mesta destroyed the land instead of making it productive. As I say, it is unusual to meet a Spaniard like Don Luis Ybarra, who understands the land, especially when he is a distinguished gentleman.

'At the palace,' he said one day, 'we're taking steps to correct our indifference.'

'What is the palace? Culverwell mentioned it too.'

'I'd like to show it to you.'

The prospect of seeing a fresh section of Las Marismas under Señor Ybarra's guidance was so inviting that we made plans to visit the secluded place. We left El Rocío and drove south toward the Atlantic Ocean west of Sanlúcar and soon were in the kind of sand-dune country that Culverwell had described. When we had about reached the seashore we turned back north on a miserable track and for the better part of an hour crawled along, trying to keep out of the watery ditches on either side. When we escaped them we found ourselves stuck up to our hubcaps in drifting sand, and if bushes had not been plentiful, so that we could tear off their tops to throw under our spinning wheels, I doubt that we would have made it. At last, however, we broke through and found ourselves in a wild and barren land with a chain of small lakes off to our right.

'Look!' Ybarra cried. 'Eagles!' We stopped to watch two imperial eagles chasing a goose who must have had experience with them, for he not only dodged the upper eagle but did it in such a way as to stay well clear of the one waiting below. We cheered the clever goose and with this appropriate introduction I entered one of the rare spots of Europe, or the world either for that matter, the Coto Doñana (Wildlife Preserve of Doña Ana). We turned a corner in the road and saw a lake on which there must have been a thousand ducks. Ybarra said, 'They're back! Early, but they're back.' When we had passed this check point I saw ahead of me a compact, very old three-story stone building rising mysteriously out of the swampland, a true fifteenth-century palace set down here God knows how, a refuge inhabited in times past by kings who sat for Velázquez, by the Duquesa de Alba, who is said to have posed here for Francisco de Goya, and by the man whose spirit seems to haunt the place, King Alfonso XIII, who came here in his impeccable hunting suits and was driven over the swamps and dunes in a 1922 Citroën fitted with tank tracks. This was the palace of Coto Doñana, and in the past fifty years almost every leading naturalist in the world, if his specialty was birds, has caught his breath with excitement as he came upon this unbelievable building in the marshes.

The Coto Doñana is a large area of wilderness consisting of part marisma, part sand dune and much water in the form of semi-connected lakes strung together like the beads of a rosary. On the north it reaches almost to El Rocío, on the south and west almost to the shoreline of the Atlantic and on the east almost to the Guadalquivir. It has many oak trees, not huddled together in a forest but standing each one by itself, with gaunt branches suitable for supporting nests. It also has a copious supply of shrubs and low grasses which produce seeds. It is thus an almost perfect haven for birds of every sort, from the eagle that needs a tall tree to the widgeon and coot that require water and grass. Since sometime around the year 1500 it has been known as a hunter's paradise, because in addition to a bird life of unimaginable fecundity, it has also contained very large herds of red deer, and, since their introduction in the early 1900s, of fallow deer as well. When I say large I mean that in an average walk across six or eight miles of the Coto one may see forty different herds of deer, each containing fifty or sixty animals.

For several centuries the Coto was set aside as a hunting preserve where bears and wolves and wild boars were protected from poachers, hence its name, and where the elite of Spain came on quite primitive safaris, as much to enjoy the wilderness as to hunt game. Kings and dukes, famous bullfighters and actors, visiting nobility and merchant princes made it to the Coto and stacked their guns in the racks of the palace. The area was owned by noble families living in the Cádiz region and was held by them for the enjoyment of their guests.

Very early in the Coto's history its owners realized that some kind of permanent building was going to be necessary, not only for the yearly guests but also for the gamekeepers, so the palace was built. How were these stones brought over land with no roads? How could a building of this excellent quality have been erected in such a wilderness? The records of its construction are lost, but it is known to have existed in the sixteenth century. Hundreds of peasants must have labored a long time, hauling materials on their backs from dumping grounds at the edge of the Guadalquivir. Or perhaps the stone and timber came by boat to the open beach along the Atlantic, from which they were hauled in two-wheeled carts over the sand dunes. At any rate, the old palace was finally completed, centuries ago.

It is not, as Señor Ybarra warned me, 'a palace palace.' It's more like the fortress palace one finds in rural Italy, a large rectangular block resembling more an oversized farmhouse than an urban palace; but when one comes upon it after a trek over the dunes or the swamps it has a palatial grandeur, so that the name is not amiss.

Among the noble hunters who occupied it in the last years of the nineteenth century and the early years of this were some who forgot the herds of deer and the lynx and fox and began to look at the bird life, and through them the fame of the Coto as a bird sanctuary began to spread. Throughout Europe naturalists who wanted to study the birds of England or Denmark or Russia found that to complete their information they must come to where their birds came, the Coto Doñana in southern Spain, and as so often happened in such matters, it was a group of public-spirited Englishmen who brought the Coto to the attention of the world at large and formulated plans for its acquisition by an international body that would protect it permanently as a wildlife preserve.

Under the leadership of the Duke of Edinburgh, Lord Alanbrooke (of World War II fame) and Prince Bernhard of The Netherlands, aided by Frenchmen and Germans and perhaps an American or two, including Roger Tory Peterson, the bird expert, the World Wildlife Fund was established to preserve areas where birds and animals take refuge, and one of its first acts was the purchase of the Coto, which was saved just in time from the inroads of modernization. The Fund has offices throughout the world, but its spiritual home is the palace. One of its principal assets in Spain is the talented man chosen as director of the Coto, the ornithologist Dr. José Antonio Valverde, who keeps an office in Sevilla. He is a learned and very amusing man, and anyone wanting to visit or support the Coto should seek him out.

'Ah!' Señor Ybarra cried as our car came to a halt under the eucalypts which surrounded the palace. 'Our welcoming committee.' A bedraggled nanny goat appeared to greet us, followed by a tame red deer with only one horn who made straight for me. Since it is not often that I get a chance to play with deer, I stepped forward to scratch my friend's nose, but Ybarra grabbed me and drew me back. 'Watch out for Bartolo! He was suckled by that goat and now thinks he's one. That horn can raise hell.' As he spoke, Bartolo took a leap at me, lowered his head and came right at my stomach with his one sharp horn. Ybarra kicked him away just in time, and he stood off to one side, his head cocked. Later he came at me more properly and we had the first of many fine visits. Ybarra was right. He thought he was a goat and even ate odd things the way his foster mother did.

On my first night at the palace I met a widely informed Spaniard who was to serve as my principal mentor in Spain, although neither he nor I was aware of this fact at the moment; it was not until I had come upon him again in Madrid and in the various cities of the north that I appreciated what an unusual fellow he was, how wise and well-intentioned. He was an ardent patriot, had a keen appreciation of what was happening in Spain and would discuss it frankly. Had he known of any adverse comment on Spain that I intended including in this book, he would have stayed up all night trying to argue me out of it; if on the other hand I report upon certain aspects of Spanish life with affection, often it is because he instructed me about them.

He was introduced as Don Luis Morenés y Areces, an avid huntsman from Madrid. He was about my height, somewhat on the heavy side but surprisingly light on his feet. He had a head much larger than that of the average Spaniard and heavy dark hair with slight streaks of gray, even though he could not have been more than thirty-five. His features were large: broad-set eyes, a substantial nose, a large, mobile mouth, a heavy neck running into shoulders that sloped like an athlete's. He loved the outdoors and had a keen eye for all natural phenomena. He was a born huntsman and loved guns, which I do not, but in all else his interests and mine coincided; particularly, he had a boisterous sense of humor, a really rollicking Sancho Panza type of Spanish laughter, and as in the case of most good storytellers, a fair share of the yarns he told were at his expense, for he was in no way pompous. He spoke English and French with little accent and had what I especially appreciated, an almost total recall of places we had seen together or conversations we had held, often years before.

The first question I asked him was typical. 'Who was the Doña Ana after whom the Coto was named?' and his meticulous reply was representative of thousands that I would receive in subsequent conversations: 'There are three theories on that. Some say it was Ana, the Duquesa de Medina Sidonia. The family that produced the admiral who led the Great Armada against England in 1588. They come from down here and had an important seat at Sanlúcar. But Señor Ybarra believes it was Ana, the Condesa de Denia y Tarifa. The big family over by Gibraltar. They owned the place for a while. I'm of the personal opinion that it must have been named after Ana de Austria. Ah, but which Ana of Austria? The fourth wife of Felipe Segundo and mother of Felipe Tercero? I don't think so. More probably the second wife of Felipe Quarto. She was his niece, you know, and the mother of Carlos Segundo. This Ana loved the hunt and often came to the Coto, which in honor of her visits was named Coto de la Reina Doña Mariana de Austria, to give her full name. This was contracted to Coto de la Reina Doña Ana, and then to Coto de Doña Ana, and finally to Coto Doñana. You would be interested to know that it was this queen who gave her name to the Marianas Islands in the Pacific Ocean.'

He told me something else that seemed logical though surprising. 'The Coto played an important role in the history of India. Some British officers stationed at Gibraltar during the years when Spain and England were allies against Napoleon were invited here as guests of the Spanish king, and while staying at the palace they saw him hunt boar with a lance from horseback, and when they were transferred to India they introduced the sport there. So Errol Flynn and all the other Bengal Lancers got their start here.'

Don Luis then solved a problem for me. 'You asked how the stones for this palace reached here? You wouldn't believe it. They came from quarries north of London. When the English discovered our sherry wine and started to import huge quantities of it, their ships could think of nothing to carry back to Spain on the return trips. So for ballast they loaded up with granite blocks, but no one in Cádiz or Jerez wanted the stone, so they dumped it on the shore and men hauled it in handcarts to build this palace.'

In the pause that followed, Señor Ybarra queried Don Luis concerning a girl who had made herself a depositada, and Don Luis said, 'She's doing as well as you'd expect.' He then turned to me and explained. 'In our country, getting a girl of good family married sometimes involves a lot of problems. Suppose that José, age twenty, wants to marry Rosita, age seventeen. In the eyes of the law and the Church they were old enough to do so when he was fourteen and she twelve, but until Rosita reaches the age of twenty-one she must have her parents' permission. If they approve, okay. If they object, Rosita must wait till she's twenty-one. Then she can marry José whether her parents like it or not.'

I pointed out that many countries had similar rules. 'Ah, yes!' Don Luis agreed. 'But what they don't have is our depositada process. The girl is free at twenty to marry only if she leaves her parents' home. If for any reason—and when good families are involved this is usually the case—she continues to live with her parents in order to win from them a dowry, she cannot marry without their consent until she is twenty-five, but a recent law has dropped that age to twenty-one. Nor can she become a nun without their permission. It is in the interest of family continuance that this law exists, and we observe it. But it is also in the interest of Church and state that girls marry young and bear children while they are able. So a compromise is necessary, and here it is. A girl who cannot get her parents' permission to marry can throw herself upon the mercy of the court, which will deposit her, hence depositada, in the home of a relative or friend so that others can inspect the young man and supervise the courtship for a period of somewhat less than six months. At the end of this cooling-off period, as we call it, if she still insists upon marrying her young man, the family into which she has been deposited acts as her parents.

'Now, if young José fails to win permission from his parents, he can't marry either, but what he can do is send his father, through the offices of a judge, a registered letter setting forth the reasons why he intends to marry, and at the end of a reasonable time if he proves to the judge that his father did not respond to the letter, the court will grant him permission to marry. Again there's been the cooling-off period.

'There's one more way out. If at any time young José and Rosita, regardless of their age, can steal away and find some priest to marry them, they're legally wed—except that neither has a right to a share of the other's inherited property—and their parents can't do a damned thing about it except to organize a hunting party and go out and shoot the priest. It's rather impressive how many priests are willing to run this risk. The Church tends to favor early marriage, and if a couple are truly in love the priest can usually detect it, but on the other hand, they don't abuse the practice because they know that if the people of the countryside felt that they were going too far, the Church would suffer. Besides, the new law of April 24, 1958, has liberalized the system. It's still complicated, like much in Spain, but it works.'

Señor Ybarra asked if it was working in the case we had been discussing, and Don Luis said no.

Don Luis had come to the Coto by special invitation and for a particular purpose. The herds of deer about the Coto had grown so numerous that they were endangering the sanctuary's food supply, so a few huntsmen like Don Luis had been called in to kill off some of the bucks. 'Would you like to join me?' he asked, and we set off in a Land Rover at thirty miles an hour over the parched marismas. We passed about a hundred and fifty fallow deer but by now I had learned not to comment on them. However, Ybarra asked, 'Are you going to thin out the fallow deer?' but Don Luis said, 'I'd prefer not to bother with them.' Later I spotted a herd of at least a hundred red deer, but they were much too far away. Apparently they knew this, for they grazed quietly and took little notice of us except to look up now and then to stare across the cracked earth.

The sun was beginning to set and Don Luis said he was afraid we'd not be able to approach any of the herds in the time remaining, but very far in the distance I spotted a group of about forty red deer in good position, and we drove to within a quarter of a mile of them, then descended to try to creep up on them. When we had reached a point from which I could not yet be sure that the herd contained bucks, Don Luis said, 'This is about right.' I asked if he intended shooting from there, for the deer seemed to me to be almost two football fields away, and he said, 'Why not? Anyway, they won't let us get much closer.' As a matter of fact, the outlying watchers had already detected us and were alerting the herd, but as one handsome large buck stopped to sniff the air, Don Luis took careful aim and with one shot dropped him. Unable to believe that a hunter could be so accurate from such a distance, I stepped off the measurement, a yard a step, and it came to one hundred and seventy yards. The bullet had struck the deer in the head and death had been immediate.

I felt uneasy about sharing in the killing of an animal on a game preserve, even though I could see from the size of the herds that it was necessary, so I was gratified when we turned from deer to the inspection of the lakes to which the aquatic birds of the north were beginning to arrive. This brought me into the activity of the Coto and I saw the useful role it played in European conservancy.

The significance of the Coto is best expressed in what one of its directors told a Danish hunting club which had been solicited for funds and had been hesitant: 'Gentlemen, if the lakes of the Coto are allowed to disappear, within five years there will be no ducks in Denmark.' The money was forthcoming, and the same appeal had proved effective elsewhere in northern Europe. Consider merely the birds I watched while I was there.

From Denmark came the graylag goose; from England the robin; from Scotland the woodcock; from Sweden the mallard; from Siberia the widgeon; from Germany the starling; from Holland the avocet; and from France the stilt. From Africa and Asia, too, the traffic was considerable. From Ethiopia came the bee-eater; from north Africa the hoopoe; from south Africa the stork; from west Africa the egret; from central Africa the kite; from various parts the spoonbill; from the Sahara the ruddy shell duck; from the Congo the purple heron. Destroy the Coto, and the life patterns of these birds and hundreds of others which I did not personally see would be altered, perhaps with serious consequences.

To cross this apparently barren and remote area at night, with flashlights probing the low cover to spot the lynx or the fox or the silent herds of deer, is to see nature in one of its most impressive forms, because wherever you look you see evidence of wild things living in a precarious balance of water and grass and dune and tree. By some extraordinary accident these components are preserved here, in an area that man has not spoiled.

In a quiet pool in Las Marismas a European pochard rests on his flight north from Africa.

Next morning Señor Ybarra started introducing me to the nesting areas of the Coto, explaining the wildlife in Latin phrases which he later interpreted into English by means of Roger Tory Peterson's handbook. In his infectious lisp, highlighted by fascinating stories of bird behavior, he introduced me to several birds I had not known before and two for whom I developed a considerable affection. Before speaking of them I should like to relate some of the surprises Ybarra showed me.

Along the ground at the edges of the swamps, in trees and higher shrubs, we frequently saw a gray-brown bird with a camouflage that could only have been developed as a mask for the bird as it perched among leaves. The disguise was well-nigh perfect, and sometimes I would stare at a branch for some moments without realizing that the leaves I thought I saw consisted mainly of this bird. 'Observe its huge mouth,' Ybarra said. '*Caprimulgus europaeus*. Flies almost blind, with its big mouth open like a seine for trapping insects.' It was the nightjar, a bird peculiar to Europe and known popularly as the goatsucker because of the widespread belief that that is how it feeds.

He also showed me a splendid bird of the *Circus* family, a hen harrier we later decided it was, which flew like our hawks in graceful sweeps, its black wing tips and white under-feathers making it a fine sight in the sky. I grew fond of watching its swift movements and concluded, perhaps incorrectly, that it attained higher speeds than the hawks with which I was familiar.

I asked if the Coto had any peregrine falcons and after this was translated into Latin, *Falco peregrinus*, Ybarra said, 'One pair! Would you believe that on land which used to nest dozens of pairs, only one remains? The reason? Too many chemical poisons spread on the grounds where they used to feed. Also, the old castles in which they nested are being torn down or renovated. This rare bird is almost gone from this part of Spain.' I told him of seeing four pairs in the ruined castle at Sanlúcar, and he said, 'Yes, in a few of the old ruins you can still find them.'

In happier vein he told me of the bird-banding experiments carried on in the Coto. 'We banded thousands of little egrets. And what do you suppose? Two of them wound up in the Caribbean. One in Trinidad. One in Martinique. If we understand correctly, this is the first time in history that we can prove birds to have emigrated naturally from the Old World to the New over the full width of the open ocean. And do you know what those clever birds did? They followed the same course as Columbus. Who taught whom?'

At the lakes we had an exciting time watching hundreds of coots and purple gallinules; the latter were the more beautiful, with subdued colors that shone in the sun, but the coots were the more fun. They were a heavy, blackish, ducklike bird with snow-white beaks and white foreheads, and they obviously enjoyed the water, diving and splashing like a bunch of children. They were aware of our presence, and if we made an unexpected move, they would take off in large numbers, tiptoeing across the waves as if in secrecy but making a huge clatter with their wings; I was surprised at the distance they required to get airborne, some thirty times their length. After they had been aloft for a while and were satisfied that we were not going to harm them, they returned to the lake and landed like reluctant auks, their feet acting as brakes amid a noisy screeching. 'The best water birds we have,' Ybarra said. He preferred them to the showier ducks that would arrive later from Siberia.

The first of the two birds that captured my affection was the kestrel. '*Falco tinnunculus*,' Ybarra said. 'A true falcon but smaller than the ones you've seen in America.' It was a bird that was handsome in any posture. When perched on a tree at the edge of the marsh, it was a compact, medium-sized bird about a foot long with a fine reddish speckled body and a bluish head and tail. For some reason which I could not explain, it carried itself with a sense of confidence and was so common throughout the Coto that I had adequate opportunity to study it. All things considered, it was the most enticing bird I saw in Spain. In flight the kestrel is magnificent, swooping in large arcs through the sky or hovering almost motionless above some suspected quarry. Seen from below, its wing tips are delicately speckled, so that they reflect light coming up from the lakes, and its tail has a sharp, clean bar near the tip. It looks much like the land of Spain, but Señor Ybarra told me that it is equally at home in England, where it is highly regarded.

It was not surprising that I should have liked the kestrel, for it resembled the hawks which nested near my home in Pennsylvania, so that I was in a sense prepared for it, but if anyone had predicted that I would find my second choice in Las Marismas so appealing, I would have laughed at him. When I first saw this creature, for it was only with difficulty that I could accept it as a bird, it was standing in a meadow across which we had been riding in the Land Rover. It was enormous, with a wingspread when it waddled over the ground of about eight feet. From its clawlike feet to the top of its apparently bald head it would have measured another three feet. 'In English it's the griffon vulture,' Ybarra said. 'It flies up here from Africa, and without it Las Marismas couldn't exist. It's the scavenger that keeps us cleaned up.' When we moved in on the first griffon I had ever seen, we found that it was hacking away at a dead rabbit. Later we found a dead calf at which some thirty or forty were feeding. Ybarra said that sometimes as many as a hundred and fifty descend on the carcass of a steer, but I never saw that.

The griffons were so common in the Coto that I came to know them as friends, and the more I learned about them the more respect I had for them. They are a sandy brown, with a head that is always described as bald but which is covered with a silky down that wraps around to protect their face and neck as well. A circle of white feathers about the neck creates the impression of some drunken Velázquez noble in ruffs, for when they move on land, which they do constantly, they lurch and roll as if intoxicated. They are a noisy lot, quarreling, gouging at each other with hawklike beaks and pushing for the best position at the feast. Since their heads are much too small for their bodies, they look grotesque; they are awkward in all they do but possess a quality of stubborn endurance which makes them as interesting as any bird in the Coto and more useful than most. They serve an essential purpose, and if one dismisses them because they are ugly, as I used to do, he misses a major point of nature. They too are much like the land of Spain: awkward, formidable, sometimes repellent but always fascinating.

While Señor Ybarra was instructing me on birds, Don Luis was setting me right on a famous fable attached to the Coto. From various books on Goya, I had gleaned the information that he often visited the estate at Sanlúcar de Barrameda owned by the Duque de Alba and that while there had fallen in love with the duquesa, with whom he had gone to

Griffon vulture.

the Coto. Certainly in the Hispanic Society of New York there is a portrait of the duquesa standing near a lagoon which has been identified as one in the Coto, but it was two other supposed portraits that gave rise to legend, the notorious 'Maja desnuda' and the 'Maja vestida' (Flashy Woman Nude, and Dressed).

'Not a word of truth to the legend,' Don Luis protested. 'Both the previous Duque de Alba, who was ambassador to London, and his successor have presided over conferences of savants who have totally demolished that libel. Spanish historians have proved that the supposed love affair could not have taken place and art experts have demonstrated beyond question that the 'Maja' could not have been the duquesa. Three distinguished medical men, Blanco Soler, Piga Pascual and Pérez de Patinto, have proved in their book that she did not die from poisoning, as the legend claims. Please do what you can to silence this silly tale which has brought so much offense to one of Spain's noblest families.'

One afternoon Don Luis took me to the second floor, where a row of windows looked out upon the flat lands of Las Marismas, and said, 'At these windows King Felipe IV stood with his arquebus . . . Like the one his son carries in the painting by Velázquez . . . And while he stood here the peasants down below drove a herd of deer past the window and he blazed away. After several tries he bagged one.'

What interested me most among the many things Don Luis showed me was a long row of carefully framed photographs covering the years from about 1890 to 1931. Judging from the excellence of these shots, it was customary for hunting parties to bring along professional photographers, so that today the gallery of the palace contains an enviable visual record of those last days of monarchy. Duques, condes, famous bullfighters and occasionally some burgeoning industrial magnate fill the photographs, dressed in costly hunting clothes from London and driving even more expensive automobiles from Paris, but the unquestioned hero of the series is a tall, slim, impeccably dressed man with aquiline nose, long mustaches and imperial bearing. He is King Alfonso XIII, last of the Borbón rulers and probably the most regal and handsome king of this century.

He was a vapid young man interested only in hunting. It is doubtful if he ever read a whole book, and when he was required by custom to visit a university it was understood that no professors or students with serious interests would bother him; a few noble youths experienced in hunting were to surround him so that he could speak of things he understood. The handsome photographs at the palace prove that in the hunt, at least, he was expert and that his love for the outdoors was both sincere and inexhaustible.

One of the pictures I liked best showed him in a suit which only a king would be brave enough to wear: the background cloth was a quiet gray, beautifully cut to fit his austere build, but into it was woven a series of huge brown diamonds five inches tall, their points standing vertically. At first sight the king looks like an advertisement, but as one sees him in various poses and in the company of others, one realizes that he selected this suit on purpose, for when it appeared in a crowd, its wearer stood out as majesty.

After I had seen a score of the Alfonso photographs—he must have been a frequent visitor to the Coto—I began to realize that my guide, Don Luis, must have come from a family that knew the king personally, for he spoke of details which otherwise he could not have known: 'It is these three portraits which have the deepest meaning. Here is Alfonso in the last days of his reign. He's more serious now. His troubles have begun and it's sad to think that soon after this was taken he deemed it prudent to leave Spain, to which he never returned. He loved the Coto and during his exile he must have longed for it. Here's a fine photograph of his family taken in Madrid a few years before his departure. His English queen . . . She was a granddaughter of Queen Victoria . . . A splendid woman and very loyal to him. This is the oldest son, Don Jaime, who would have made a fine king except that he was removed from the succession because he was a deaf-mute. This is Don Alfonso, the unfortunate son who married a Cuban commoner and died in an automobile crash in Miami in 1938. This is Don Gonzalo, the youngest son, who also died in an auto crash.' He pointed out the children one by one, ending with a handsome young man. 'And this is Don Juan de Borbón, who now lives in Estoril, near Lisboa in Portugal.' He said no more and I was unable to ascertain his opinion of Juan; it would have been improper for him to express one, because Juan, as the legal heir of Alfonso XIII, who died in 1941, ought to become King of Spain when Generalísimo Franco goes, except that powerful forces, including Franco, prefer that Juan's son, Prince Juan Carlos, take the throne. There could be trouble between father and son, and prudent Spaniards are reluctant to tell foreigners whose side they support. Pointing to the last of the three photographs, Don Luis said, 'And this is Don Juan by himself . . . photographed in Portugal, where he lives in exile.' He was an attractive fellow and others in Spain told me that he would make a fine king, but what Don Luis thought of the matter, I was not to discover.

Wherever I turned among the photographs I found some aspect of Spanish history which attracted my interest. Here was the dictator Primo de Rivera standing over a wild boar which he had just killed with a lance. Over here was the Conde de Tarifa, who once owned the Coto, at the wheel of the Citroën swamp wagon he had bought for the use of Alfonso. This handsome woman was the Duquesa de Medinaceli, from one of the noblest families in Spain, standing with the man she had invited to the Coto, the famous matador Rafael Guerra, called Guerrita; the photograph must have been taken around 1910, when Guerrita was in retirement. This solemn-looking man was the Duque de Cádiz as he appeared in 1908; of his home city in that year it was said, 'It has three hundred and sixty-six churches and no library.' In 1966 a resident told me, 'Today things are better. We have three hundred and sixty-five churches and one library. But mostly it's closed.' In this corner is Alfonso, clean-shaven and just as good-looking that way as with his Kaiser-like mustaches; but the photograph which lives in my mind showed him ready for the hunt, a dashing king with enormous mustaches and a rifle cradled in his arm. He wore heavy peasant trousers with pronounced vertical stripes, English leather boots, and over all zahones, which formed a heavy leather apron divided down the middle and tied securely about each leg. He was an archaic figure, best suited to the seventeenth century; how admirable a subject he would have been for the brush of Velázquez. The camera barely does him justice.

I am constantly fascinated by this empty-headed, charming fellow, because there is a strong possibility that he was a part-American whose name should have been Alfonso McKeon. Clearly he was the son of King Alfonso XII and Queen María Cristina of Austria; no one questioned that, but who Alfonso XII might have been was another matter. He was the son of Spain's notorious Queen Isabel II, probably the most lecherous crowned head ever to rule in Europe, man or woman; if she is in second place it is only to Catherine the Great of Russia, and this I doubt. Obligated by dynastic reasons to marry her cousin, impotent and a homosexual, she said of him, 'What can I report of a man who on his wedding night wore more lace than I?'

Since she and her impotent consort had numerous children, of whom five lived to become fine persons, each birth became the occasion for a good deal of open speculation as to who the father might have been, and since Isabel took a bewildering series of lovers in rapid succession, the guessing sometimes became confused. The father of her first child could have been any one of four: a general, an opera singer (tenor), a marqués or a young colonel in the army. This child died. Who the father of her second baby was no one cared to state, for this time there were six putative fathers, but the little girl, who lived to become one of Spain's gentlest and noblest ladies, beloved by everyone, was generally known as Arañuela, after her mother's prominent lover at the time, an ordinary soldier named Araña.

The next child, who also died, was attributed to either Obregón the singer, Arrieta the composer, Puig-Moltó the soldier or an unspecified marqués. Regarding the parentage of her later children the guesses were fantastic, for preceding their births Isabel had what might be termed a catch-as-catch-can series of lovers from all ranks of society, although she always maintained a preference for musicians and soldiers. What concerns history is the parentage of her first surviving male child, the boy who later became King Alfonso XII. Prior to his birth the queen's favorite had been the soldier Puig-Moltó, who enjoyed a longer stay at the palace than most, but there is reason to believe that he could not have been in attendance when the child was conceived; he was absent on maneuvers. The honor of siring the future king probably went to an itinerant American dentist named McKeon, who, the gossips said, 'did a lot more at the palace than fill teeth.' For more than a year he was the royal favorite and this during the time when the future king was conceived. The extraordinary fact about Isabel's children is that regardless of who their fathers were, each looked a true Borbón, while Alfonso XII and his son Alfonso XIII actually had Habsburg chins!

When Don Luis and I finished our tour of the portrait galleries, Señor Ybarra suggested that we go out to see a remarkable oak tree. I replied that in America we had oaks of all kinds and there were further photographs on another floor that I wished to see, but Ybarra said, 'Oak trees you may have, but none like this.' So I went with him to a part of the Coto I had not seen before, and in the distance I saw a large oak whose branches and trunk were almost completely white. As we approached, I saw that it contained many nests, each about the size of a small table, built of hundreds of fairly good-sized sticks laid crossways like the nest of an eagle.

'How many nests would you say?' Ybarra asked.

There were clearly more than a score, and when I started to count only those on one branch I saw that the total must be over a hundred. 'About three hundred and fifty,' he said.

'Eagles?'

'No. One of the most beautiful birds to nest in Europe. The *Platalea leucorodia*, spoonbill.' In fact, so many spoonbills nested in this particular oak that their droppings, made acid by the fish they ate, had not only colored the tree white but were also causing its death. The one thing that might operate against the Coto's continuance as a sanctuary, for certain kinds of birds at least, was the constant killing off of the bigger trees by the birds themselves.

'We don't know what to do about it,' Ybarra said. 'We're especially concerned about the spoonbills, because they began to come here only in 1959. Two pair appeared that year and apparently enjoyed their experience, because just as a satisfied customer at a summer resort spreads the news, they told their friends and next year we counted two hundred and fifty-five pairs. I wouldn't like to guess how many we have now. Twenty or thirty large oaks like this one, each with hundreds of nests. They're about the loveliest bird we get, spectacularly beautiful.'

The spoonbill reminded me of another bird, and I asked whether the Coto attracted any flamingos, who have been known to breed in Europe, and a knowing smile came over Ybarra's lips. 'Do you really like birds?' he asked; and when I nodded, he said, 'It's not generally known even yet, but some years ago in a series of pools leading off from the Rhone in southern France a large colony of flamingos bred for about twenty years. Of course, naturalists heard about it right away. A sensation in bird circles. But we kept it a secret among ourselves. Perhaps two hundred men in eight or ten different countries. Because if the general public knew, they would swarm to watch the birds, and inevitably some damn fool would shoot them. He wouldn't be able to help himself. So we kept it a secret and in due course the flamingos left their French lagoons.'

He hesitated for a moment, and I suggested, 'And they came down here to the Coto?'

'Yes, but not to breed. However, they do come to ———,' and he mentioned an area not far from the Coto where a substantial colony of perhaps the world's loveliest bird, certainly its most dramatic, had been breeding for several years with an apparent prospect of continuing for many more. Experts in London and Paris and Stockholm know about this phenomenon and it is watched with care, because many of the flamingos' normal breeding places in Africa are being destroyed, so that within a hundred years perhaps the African flamingo may cease to exist, as may other rare species that now use the Coto as a breeding ground.

'All sensible men, who cherish the world as it has been,' said Ybarra, 'are engaged, whether they wish to be or not, in a crusade to keep whole species from being exterminated. If our human population continues to explode at its present rate, and I see no reason to suspect that the rate will diminish, the pressure on open land like the Coto will become unbearable. In our lifetime we'll see it.'

'It's begun,' Don Luis told us at dinner one evening. 'In Madrid there is much agitation, even among men who love the outdoors, to dam off the overflow waters of the Guadalquivir and drain the swamps of Las Marismas. It could be done with relatively little effort, and all the land Michener has seen north of here could be converted into rice fields and wheat.'

'Why do that?' I asked. 'Spain's got ample food.'

'The phrase is "social necessity." Spain wants entrance to the European Common Market, but as long as we must be classified as a backward country economically, it is not attractive to the other countries to admit us as an equal partner. If we reclaim our marshes and increase our food supply, then we stand in quite a different light and the other nations may want us. We may have to drain the marshes.'

Don Luis was speaking as if he were attached to the government, and I started to ask what job he held in Madrid, but talk turned to other matters and Ybarra said, 'The irony of the situation, and its danger, is that the Coto Doñana is viable as a truly great sanctuary only so long as Las Marismas exists out there. Because then our birds have a substantial feeding area and the millions of birds that live off Las Marismas form a kind of biological unit with the ones in the Coto. Destroy Las Marismas, and you destroy at least half our effectiveness.'

'But doesn't the Coto already control a good deal of Las Marismas?'

'A common misunderstanding. We own so little that you'd hardly believe it. Considering our entire area . . . dunes, lakes, dry land . . . we have only seventeen thousand acres altogether. And of that, only about five hundred acres are marismas . . . and not the best. You see, in the old days Las Marismas was so enormous, so useless, that everyone said, "It'll always be there. For the Coto we'll buy only the good land." So now we have good land and almost no marismas. And suddenly, with the prospect of draining the swamps, Las Marismas has become very valuable, far beyond our means to acquire it. Within five years, if men worked energetically with bulldozers and dams, they could make Las Marismas disappear.'

I left this gloomy talk and walked out beneath the eucalyptus trees. Bartolo, the tame deer, ran up to nuzzle me, accompanied by his nanny goat, and in the shadowy distance I could see the forms of fifty or sixty wild deer that always moved in close at night. Beyond lay the flat lands of Las Marismas in whose depths the camels wandered still free and birds nested without number. As far as I could see there was only flatness and the slowly returning waters that would soon make of the area an enormous lake a few millimeters deep in which substantial rivers would mysteriously form and islands where the fighting bulls would congregate and rabbits and foxes and the endless herds of deer. It was an area that I had seen in all seasons, whose dreamlike transmutations I had followed from north and east and south. In its heart and along its perimeter I had organized a dozen picnics so that I might know it more intimately; I had seen it from Sevilla and from across the river at Sanlúcar, that grubby little town I loved so well. Instructed by Las Marismas, I had come to know birds that I would otherwise have missed, the gape-mouth nightjar winging past to trap insects, the clean and fiery kestrel, the spoonbill and the vulture, that handsome and repulsive thing. Was it possible that within my lifetime this concentration of natural wonder was doomed? I could not believe it, and yet on the previous day while roaring across the hard-baked marismas I had seen a ridge of earth, a rather simple one about six feet high that a bulldozer had thrown up with no great effort, and after we had followed it for some miles I asked, 'What's the ridge?'

'It's an experiment,' Ybarra said. 'To see how difficult it would be to prevent water from coming into Las Marismas.'

'Does it work?'

'When they seal off the other end, over by El Rocío, they'll have dried out about twenty thousand acres.'

The land of Spain! For the last three thousand years it has been a challenge and on its relentless bosom men have made one ghastly mistake after another, as the moribund village of Maranchón demonstrates, but within the last decade there have been signs of hope. In the barren reaches of Extremadura, where flood waters used to rage three years in ten, and in many other parts of the country, large earthen dams are being constructed which will irrigate once-useless fields and bring them into productivity. In the mountains hydroelectric systems are proliferating at a surprising rate. Perhaps Las Marismas will have to be drained, out of deference to opinions in Paris and Berlin, but there is a possibility that it can be done leaving strips or areas where the old conditions can continue. Knowing the greediness of men, and especially the greediness of Spaniards, I doubt that any of Las Marismas can be saved and I would expect it to have vanished by 1985. The Coto Doñana, because it has fallen into careful hands, has a chance to continue, but only if its custodians are vigorously supported by those who love nature and appreciate its subtle influence on man. However, if Las Marismas vanishes, many of the birds who now use the Coto will no longer have reason to do so; perhaps even the vultures will stop coming when animals no longer die on the flat lands, but I suppose the Coto lakes, filled with rich animalcules, will still attract the ducks.

To have seen Las Marismas and the Coto while they were still at their peak was to have seen the best that Spain can offer the naturalist. For the immediate future these areas will continue to be available for those to whom ecology is at least as sacred as eschatology.

FOLLOWING PAGE:
Sculptor's studio in Sevilla.

VI

SEVILLA

OCEANO
ATLANTICO

MAR MEDITERRANEO

MILES
0   100

Barcelona

Madrid

Lisboa

Almendralejo

Córdoba

Jaén

Huelva   Sevilla   Granada
                     Almería
Jerez de la
Frontera   Málaga
Cádiz

One of the top experiences a traveler can have in Spain is to visit Sevilla for Holy Week, which ends at Easter, and the feria that follows. I suppose there is nothing in the world to surpass this, not Mardi Gras at New Orleans nor the Palio in Siena when the exuberance of the Renaissance is re-created. Carnival in Rio de Janeiro is an epic of noise and color, and for sheer celebration it would be hard to equal Bastille Day in Tahiti, when the island goes mad for two weeks; but these events lack spiritual depth.

In Sevilla each spring one finds combined within the span of a few weeks six major diversions: the world's most profound religious spectacle plus a rustic fair recalling those of a thousand years ago, plus a congregation of circuses drawn from all parts of Europe, plus a bizarre open-air carnival, plus a daily program of social events and stunning promenades on horseback, plus a series of first-rate bullfights conducted in Spain's most beautiful plaza. And these six features are encapsulated, as it were, within the confines of an ancient city studded with handsome buildings, narrow streets where only pedestrians are allowed and exquisite vistas along riverbanks. At any time of year Sevilla is a distinguished city, but during Holy Week and the days that follow, it is without peer.

I have attended several of Sevilla's spring celebrations, and when I try to recall the essence of what I saw I picture myself standing at four o'clock in the morning at the entrance to the tobacco factory where Carmen spun her smoky web to entangle a soldier. I am in a very old city and it is dark, for winter has only just ended and the early rising sun has not yet returned, but along the horizon to the south a dull glow is visible, as if fields were being burned off before the planting.

No prudent farmer accounts for those fires. In a tree-lined park on the edge of the city, Sevilla is holding revelry and the lights will continue until dawn and for half a dozen dawns to follow, and if one listens closely he can hear, coming to him over the intervening space, the muffled sound of carnival and circus, of promenade and castanets.

But it is neither this beautiful glow on the horizon that I remember as the characteristic of Sevilla when I am away from the city nor the sound of the revelry. It is the shadowy approach of figures looming out of the dusk as they wander past the tobacco factory on their way home from the festival. They come like ghosts of ancient Spain, from Roman times or Visigothic or Arabic or medieval Christian, moving in stately silence until some member of the group begins softly to clap his hands. And it is then that the sound of Sevilla, the sweet memorable sound of this most dramatic of the Spanish cities, overtakes me.

The hands I hear do not clap as they would at a football game nor even at a flamenco party. They tap in a seductive night rhythm, with variations which a person reared in Massachusetts or Stockholm could not devise. They tap out the beat of some old song, well known to all in the crowd, and before long a woman walking through the night adds her staccato. Others follow, and soon one has along the broad street before Carmen's tobacco factory a dozen or so persons clapping out this strange rhythm.

No one sings. No one chants the words of the mute song. There is only the soft clapping of some dozen pairs of unseen hands, but I get the impression that the participants are softly repeating the words to themselves as they pass me by. No one speaks, and when the group has gone the sound of clapping hangs in the night air for a long time as the revelers proceed to some point near the cathedral, or in back of the bullring, or at the beginning of the narrow street called Sierpes (serpents), where they break apart, each member going to his own home to sleep for a few hours before the next day begins.

But before the first group has reached the point of separation, other groups have come along the lovely dark street, which in the growing twilight looks much as it did in the days of Carmen, and they too clap softly in the night. And for more than a week, for almost twenty-four hours each day, the visitor to Sevilla will hear this compelling tattoo. It is the sound of Sevilla in spring, one of the most persuasive sounds I have ever heard.

To savor the six-part spectacle you must set aside several weeks and plan to arrive before Palm Sunday. Depending upon the date of Easter, the six parts can cover from three to five weeks. Some travelers skip the first three and arrive only in time for the final crescendo, but this is a miscalculation which robs them of the spiritual preparation necessary for the full enjoyment of the spectacle. It is like listening to only the fourth movement of Beethoven's Ninth Symphony, since that is where the human voices appear, and missing the preparation which Beethoven has laid out in the preceding three movements, when only the orchestra is playing.

For the heart of Sevilla's spring celebration is a religious experience, and it throbs through the city for an entire week. Beginning with Palm Sunday an atmosphere of sanctity settles over the towers and the alleys of Sevilla, permeating every crevice of the city, and so it will continue for the seven days which recall the passion and death of Jesus. Bells start tolling from dozens of steeples scattered through the city. Even across the river, in the gypsy quarter of Triana, ordinary noises stop. Citizens dress in their best black clothes, men and women alike, and at selected parishes scattered through Sevilla two radically different types of men begin to assemble at church doors: the religious men and the laboring men. Spectators, who may number in the thousands, gather in the streets outside the churches to watch these men, for they are about to become the most important in Sevilla. Let us follow one man from each group.

Don Francisco Mendoza Ruiz is a cautious man who works in a bank and lives with his wife and three children in a fine little house in the old Jewish quarter, where no automobiles are allowed. After church on Palm Sunday he invites us to accompany him home, where he takes down from a closet a set of boxes from which he unpacks a costume that looks as if it had come from the Middle Ages.

'Heretics condemned by the Inquisition used to wear costumes like this,' he says. After stripping down to shirt and trousers he massages his feet prior to putting on a pair of heavy-soled black shoes. 'I shall be walking, walking,' he says. Then he puts on a tunic which covers everything from neck to shoe tip. Each parish church will have for its members a distinctive color. Don Francisco's is purple, and over it he throws a white cape which reaches to his knees. About his waist he ties a sash eight inches wide made of an expensive damask and allows its ends to fall free.

'Now comes the good part,' he says as he takes from a long, thin box a stiffened purple hood about three feet tall with a tip at one end and a broad cape at the other. There are two very small slits for his eyes, and when Don Francisco puts on the hood, pulling the cape end far down over his shoulders, he transforms himself into a mysterious figure with only his eyes showing.

'To you norteamericanos,' he says apologetically, 'I must look like a member of your Ku Klux Klan.' He is right. During Holy Week whenever members of the confraternity (in Spanish cofradía) assemble they will look like a bunch of Kluxers on the rampage through some bayou village. 'Thus do rascals appropriate the robes of the just and contaminate them,' Don Francisco says, and again he is right, for the Ku Klux Klan did borrow its costume from the religious procession of Sevilla. Señor Mendoza next takes a six-foot candle, which he bought a few days ago, and stands with it at an angle to his hip. 'I am now a member of the confraternity, ready to march.' There are fifty-two confraternities in Sevilla, each connected with a parish church. Like a lodge or brotherhood they meet throughout the year to collect funds for their church and particularly to arrange for the processions of Holy Week.

As the sun sets, Don Francisco says, 'It's time for the church,' and as we pick our way through the crowd we recognize other men dressed in his colors: purple tunic, white cape, purple hood; but we also see a few who wear different colors, and they are on their way to join up with some other confraternity. At the church there is much confusion. Outside, a huge crowd has gathered to watch the beginning of this first procession, which will be followed by others for each of the next seven days; inside, the two floats sponsored by this church are being given their final inspection. They are strange and wonderful things, each twenty feet long by nine feet wide by fifteen feet tall, and the route they will follow through the city streets was laid out more than a century ago and will require twelve hours to complete. The float to the left shows Christ at the Crucifixion surrounded by Roman guards, and it will go out first. The float to the right, and much the more important of the two, contains the Virgin Mary in glory. She is life-size and every effort has been taken to make her seem alive. Her eyebrows are made of real hair; her cheeks are delicately rouged; six glass tears run down her cheek; her hands are manicured; she wears a wealth of jewelry.

'Oh, darling Virgin!' people cry when she appears.

'Sweetest Virgin, if you're real, toss me some of those jewels.'

'My Virgin! My Virgin! You make the other Virgins of Sevilla look like a bunch of putas [whores].'

She is greeted as a living person, a blend of queen and popular singer. 'I throw you a kiss, lovely one,' a man shouts.

Don Francisco, beneath his mask, does not participate in this frivolity, for he takes religion gravely. It is, he says, the most important aspect of his life. 'I serve in the confraternity,' he explains, 'because I am convinced that a good Spaniard must give part of his life to the Church and all of his devotion to the Virgin. For me the year comes to a head with Holy Week, and this year is special.' In a few moments we shall see why, but as the day ends let us move to an old river-front warehouse to meet our second man.

He is José (Pepe) Gómez, a tattooed stevedore, twenty-nine years old, and he too is about to march in the procession, but the religious ideas expressed by Don Francisco Mendoza are alien to him. 'I leave church to the priests. My father was a Communist and during the Civil War he was shot.' We ask him why then is he marching in the procession, and he says, 'Because I get paid. And because my Virgin is the best damned Virgin in Sevilla.' His actual words are more profane than that, but they reinforce a

basic fact about the Holy Week processions. To many of the marchers the carved Virgins and Christs are real people: the Virgin of this parish who has looked out for her people for the past century, the particular Christ who loves the children of this parish.

Pepe Gómez dresses in the only suit he owns, a pair of white trousers and a torn shirt. He wears no socks but does have a pair of new rope sandals, supplied by Don Francisco's confraternity. He also has a canvas bag about the size of a pillowcase, and this he partly fills with a mixture of sand and sawdust, placing it on his head in such a way that the sand falls to the end of the bag that is over his shoulders. A fellow stevedore hammers the bag to see whether it is taking up the shock, and Pepe says, 'Good. Let's go.'

We leave the waterfront and walk through the narrow streets to the church where Don Francisco and his confraternity have assembled about the float of the Virgin. When Gómez appears, along with thirty-five other laborers similarly dressed and with bags of sand and sawdust resting on their heads, the treasurer of the confraternity pays each worker one dollar and ten cents, whereupon the stevedores prepare to crawl under the float, which has been built upon a large table with legs that keep it about four feet off the ground when it is rested. The space between the float and the ground is masked by a heavy brocade skirt which will hide the feet of thirty-six stevedores below. Thus, when the workmen march, the float will seem to move by itself and the men inside will do their work in sweaty darkness, turning the float only as a captain directs from outside.

A float may weigh as much as half a ton, so that the task of bearing it through the streets for twelve hours is not a light one. A few extra stevedores go along to provide occasional relief; also, during the twelve-hour march the float may be stopped by a traffic jam or by reaching an intersection when another float is passing in a different direction. When such things happen the stevedores lower the float and scramble out for air, and one of the amusing sights of Holy Week is that of a beautiful Virgin Mary temporarily deserted by her bearers, who have ducked into a bar where someone is standing drinks.

When they do move, the floats sway gently from side to side, giving the wooden figures a kind of poetic life. A float never seems static. Along the course, which winds in and out through all parts of the city, each float having its own route, which does not necessarily follow that of any other, citizens note with approval any new statues or repainting introduced during the past twelve months. I once heard a man remark to his wife as the float of his church went by, 'I think our new head of Jesus is the best in Sevilla.'

Pepe Gómez and his fellow stevedores now pull up the brocaded skirt and crawl into position beneath the float. Adjusting their bags over their heads and about their shoulders, they test the weight and try to find

269

positions which will be comfortable. Outside, the captain waits for a signal from the priest, then slaps the corner smartly.

'One.' The unseen stevedores brace their heads and shoulders against the floor of the float.

'Two.' They rise to a standing position, and the Virgin seems to ascend of her own accord.

'Three.' The stevedores move slowly forward and the first float for the Holy Week parade is under way. From balconies people cry ecstatically, 'Oh, sweet Virgin. Come back to us, you little beauty.'

It is incredible with what skill the stevedores move this huge float. At the doorway there is a clearance of about four inches, and as the Virgin moves through narrow streets there will be many points where encroaching buildings seem to make progress impossible, but through obedience to signals the men move their burden an inch at a time and rarely scrape a doorjamb or a wall.

The hooded members of the confraternity, their long tapers held at an angle from their hips, fall in line before the float as if to give it protection, but Don Francisco is not among them. He told us earlier that for him this year was to be special, and now he sits on a chair in his church and takes off his shoes. From beneath his hood he says, 'In February I faced a crisis at the bank. It could have been disastrous. But I prayed to the Virgin and she rescued me. I told her, "Save me and I will do penance." It was a promise.' When he is barefooted he lashes chains about his ankles and the heavy links drag behind him for six or eight feet. He lays aside his candle to take up a heavy, full-sized wooden cross. Then he rises and steps into the street, where his chains jangle on the cobblestones. He is prepared to drag his cross through the streets of Sevilla as Jesus dragged his through the alleys of Jerusalem. 'Blessed Virgin,' he mutters with intense devotion, 'accept my penance.' For twelve hours he will march barefoot with half a dozen others who have made similar vows to this Virgin. The confraternity does not appoint these men to their task; they are volunteers who feel that some aspect of their lives requires atonement, and the punishment to which they submit themselves is not light.

I followed Don Francisco most of the twelve hours, and it was morning before the Virgin returned to her church, where at least two thousand people waited to watch her come home. As long as the Virgin was in the plaza before the church their cries of welcome were such as a man might give his betrothed on her return home, but when she entered the portals, inch by inch, the greetings were those of children to their mother. Thus the Spanish Virgins fill a dual role.

'Jesucristo, that was a hard night,' Pope Gómez admits as he crawls out from under. Tomorrow he will carry a float from another church, and so on throughout the seven days.

Don Francisco's words are quite different. As he lays aside his cross and unbinds his chains, he says with his mask off, 'I feel that the Virgin was very close to Sevilla this day. I could sense her nodding as she accepted my penance.'

Each day from Palm Sunday through the Saturday before Easter this procession will be duplicated, but Don Francisco's confraternity will not march again, for Sevilla has many parish churches and the days must be parceled out among them. In 1967 the processions were as follows:

Day	Confra- ternities	Mary Floats	Jesus Floats	Mary and Jesus Floats
Sunday	7	7	8	1
Monday	8	6	6	1
Tuesday	7	6	8	0
Wednesday	7	6	4	3
Thursday	7	6	7	1
Friday morning	6	6	6	0
Friday evening	7	5	4	3
Saturday	3	3	2	1
Total	52	45	45	10

Some of these hundred floats leave their little churches at one in the morning to march all night and stagger home at noon. Others go out at dawn and wander through the streets till sunset, but on Good Friday two sets of confraternities go out, one early and one late, and it was to one of these that Don Francisco took us at four in the afternoon to watch the departure of a float showing Jesus and the Roman soldiers whose parade would mark those solemn evening hours when Christ died of his Crucifixion.

'Marching barefoot with the Virgin is an honor that no man . . .' Don Francisco says as he watches the Friday parade. He stops. He is in his late forties and is an important businessman in the city, hefty, dark-haired, amiable. He wants to explain what Holy Week means to him but is afraid a Protestant would not understand. 'It's an honor,' he says quietly, 'but to march with one of the Jesus floats on Good Friday . . . You'll understand when you hear the tremendous silence. Señor Michener, when this float comes through Sierpes, Jesus Christ himself is in that street.'

The Jesus float is much different from the one that Don Francisco attended, for in the latter the Virgin sat in awe-inspiring splendor with a hundred and fifty tall candles as the major piece of decoration. The Jesus float, on the other hand, is a tableau centering upon a life-sized figure of Christ on the cross, each element of his agony depicted in minute detail. Beads of sweat stand on his forehead. Ruby drops of blood run down his side where the spear has pierced him. His feet are turning blue from the nail, and his crown of thorns brings blood. This particular statue was carved some ninety years ago to replace one that came originally from The Netherlands. It is accompanied at the four corners of the float by life-sized imperial Roman guards in resplendent uniform. Each carries one of the implements of the Crucifixion and they form a terrifying and brutal group. Similar Roman soldiers will appear on many of the floats and one of the greatest Virgins will be preceded by a marching company of live men dressed as Roman legionnaires. If the rest of the world has sometimes been perplexed as to who was responsible for the death of Jesus, some blaming Jews, others Romans, the confraternities of Sevilla are not confused. Their statues show Romans in the act of villainy.

In addition to Jesus and the four soldiers, our float contains about a dozen additional figures, some large, some small, and over the years whenever a given statue has worn out or been damaged, it has been replaced by a new one. Or if a tradesman of the parish prospered he might one day announce, 'I will give a new Roman soldier to the confraternity.' Thus, of the figures on our float, all might be of different age, yet all combine to present a harmonious picture of Christ in his last hours.

The oldest figures on the hundred floats date back to the seventeenth century. In the intervening years well-known sculptors carved figures which gradually supplanted originals, and in the nineteenth century there was a general refurbishing, at which time the emphasis was on strict fidelity to the living figure. It was then that the glass teardrops and the specks of ruby blood became common. The twentieth century has been the age of adornment and most of the ultra-luxurious costumes date from this period.

The most extraordinary, and by far the best loved, are those like the one we saw first which simply present the Virgin Mary throned in glory, dressed in gorgeous robes and with a crown of silver and gold encrusted with hundreds of precious stones. Of the forty-five floats presenting Virgins alone, two are preeminent and the subject of such veneration that even the most casual observer must reflect on the fact that Holy Week, which commemorates Christ's passion and death, has become in Spain a celebration in which he plays a secondary role, with his mother becoming the central figure. The first is La Esperanza, the Virgin of Hope, from the gypsy quarter of Triana across the river. She became famous as the patron Virgin of the bullfighter Juan Belmonte and remains the focus of much popular affection. The second is La Macarena, named after an Arabian princess, and she was preferred by another great matador, Joselito, and to see her leave her parish church of San Gil at one in the morning of Good Friday or return later in the day is held by many Sevillanos to be the most important thing that can happen during Holy Week.

Late at night one Holy Thursday I went to watch La Macarena leave her small white church, and an hour before the time of her departure all

Roman soldiers preparing
for the execution of Christ.

streets were jammed. Not far from the church, devotees of this Virgin have built a permanent arch of triumph, a delightful little stucco affair with seven Moorish towers, the only one of its kind in Sevilla. I was standing in a throng near this arch when the float left the church, and it seemed miraculous that the stevedores behind the curtain could maneuver this immense structure so delicately through the doors.

The float was in some ways the most ornate I had seen, with a baldacchino of gold and an edging of silver; but it was also the simplest, for it contained only the Virgin clad in white dress, green and gold cape and red sash, and wearing a corona featuring sixteen silver stars and a diamond cross. She was a majestic figure, with tears on her cheeks and a pearl necklace wrapped about her left hand. In place of the subsidiary figures that accompanied most floats stood several score of tall wax tapers, and she was preceded by a confraternity dressed in white satin robes and emerald hoods. Like the other great Virgins of Sevilla, she carried no child.

When she appeared the crowd reacted with joy, bestowing upon her a love which has no counterpart in other countries. It required about forty minutes for her to inch her way from the church and through the arch, even though they stood only a few yards apart. The crowd would not give way; everyone wanted to stand as close to the wonderful Virgin as possible, and we were behind schedule when we finally set out through the darkened streets for the traditional passage of La Macarena.

After proceeding by herself for some hours, La Macarena, like all the other floats that were out at this time, began heading for the center of the city, and by the time the sun rose, they had coalesced into a long official procession that would pass before the town hall and end at the cathedral. At no time during this preliminary activity was any float unattended. Its approach was heralded by two or three men carrying wooden staves from which dangled iron rings. When the staves were pounded down against the paving of the street, a harsh jangling sound warned beholders to draw back. Some sort of band accompanied the float, beating out a somber half-step which had the effect of a funeral march. Then came the confraternity followed by the float, which during the night was illuminated by flares. Finally there were the penitents, marching barefoot over the stones with their burdens of chain and cross. It is this whole unit that creates the noble impression, forcing the observer to reconsider any prior judgments of religion.

In reviewing mine I was confused by three extraneous elements that helped make up the parade. First, each float was escorted by a company of soldiers in full military regalia including loaded rifles, and they marched with such solemn ferocity and proprietary interest that no one could ignore the fact that in Spain the principal job of the army was to defend the Church; this had been its preoccupation from the time of its war against the Moors and apparently it would always be. That is why on the left wall of the shrine of La Macarena stands the tombstone of General Gonzalo Queipo de Llano y Sierra (1875–1951) with the ominous date '18 July 1936,' which was when he exercised the brutalities that earned him the title among Republicans of 'The Butcher of Andalucía,' and among Franco men of 'The Savior of Sevilla.' I spoke to a Spaniard about this and was told, 'Why not? Queipo de Llano saved the Church in Andalucía. In the old days we'd have made him a saint. Now we have to be content with his tomb beside our Virgin.' If the parades of Holy Week were religious processions, they were also military ones, and one day Don Francisco said to me, 'We Spaniards cannot understand that strange thing that happened in the United States army. One of your artillery colonels devised a banner and a slogan for his gunners, "For God, for country and for Santa Bárbara." But atheists protested and your government made him stop. Everyone knows that Santa Bárbara is the patron saint of bombardiers.' I tried to explain that in the United States we subscribed to a separation of Church and state and to us it was offensive to confuse an artillery unit and a female saint, to which he replied, 'You must indeed be confused. If Santa Bárbara watches over your gunners in battle, why not admit it?'

Second, at frequent intervals units of the Guardia Civil appeared in full uniform and heavily armed. They stared with what I thought at the time was a menacing gaze, but which I suppose was only an impassivity, at the spectators, as if daring them to make any move against the Church. If the Holy Week procession was partly a military manifestation, it was also a police function, for the two elements were never far separated.

Third, when the parade had formed and it was time to march through the center of the city, political leaders of the community slipped into position, some as penitents lugging crosses, some as members of the confraternity but with their faces exposed, and some as honored marchers in morning coats and top hats; it was clear that no politician could hold office in Sevilla who did not conform to the observances of the Church. The presence of these officials was made conspicuous; they were preceded by bishops and soldiers and bands and guardia; they were accompanied by hushed and approving whispers from the crowd; they were clothed in a kind of extraterrestrial glory and formed as significant a part of the parade as any of the floats, the capstone, as it were, of the religious-military-police-political edifice that was Spain.

Of course, some years later I witnessed exactly the same kind of exhibitionism in New York City when I watched the St. Patrick's Day parade along Fifth Avenue and saw that any Jewish politician who hoped for favor with the Irish electorate had better put in an appearance on that day. A few years after that, when I was myself running for Congress in a different part of America, my advisors warned me, 'There is one thing a politician must do. March in the St. Patrick's Day parade or else.' I was as warmly received in my community as were the Sevilla politicians during their obligatory parade. In Sevilla it was only the appearances that were different. As a matter of fact, one year when Adlai Stevenson was in Sevilla for Holy Week he was invited to march with a confraternity, and as a wise politician he did so.

When I had watched the floats, supervising their exits and returns, I felt that I understood something of the spiritual quality of Holy Week, but it was two unplanned experiences which brought me close to the heart of the matter. The first had occurred on Palm Sunday, when I had been following Don Francisco's float for more than ten hours. We stopped for some unknown reason in a small plaza, and the stevedores came out from under their boards and lounged about with beer bottles in their hands, for it was now daylight and the sun was growing hot. The soldiers, the guardia and the politicians had left us, for we were in the backwaters of the city far from the formal parade route; we were in a sense on our own and some members of the confraternity removed their hoods, and it was then that I came face to face with Don Francisco Mendoza Ruiz, so exhausted and beat down by the weight of his self-assumed cargo that I thought him close to fainting.

For a long, long moment we stood facing each other, and the mark of pain was so visible in his face that I had to acknowledge that here was a man who had truly assumed the burden of Jesus Christ in the moments of the passion. This was neither the play-acting of the men who carried the iron-ringed staves, beating them about as if they were marshals, nor the parade heroics of the armed soldiers looking as if they were about to enter battle, nor the posturings of the politicians as they exhibited their public spirituality. This was the face of an ordinary man who had assumed a burden that was almost more than he could bear; he was undergoing a religious experience that I had not ever come close to, and when I gave him a drink from my bottle he thanked me with an expression of ecstatic gratitude. I have never forgotten his face; he was not of the procession; he was the procession, standing at its very heart, and he was accepting as much of the passion of Jesus as any man could comprehend.

The whistles blew. The captain shouted at the workmen. The lines re-formed. And the staves thundered against the roadway. 'One, two, three,' came the signals, and slowly the Virgin rose into the sunlight, wavered unsteadily for a moment, then resumed her soft undulation as the huge structure moved forward once more. And behind the Virgin, so richly dressed and so wooden with her face staring straight ahead, struggled this weary barefooted man bearing his cross.

My second insight occurred on a street far removed from the little plaza. In the center of Sevilla, running from the commercial headquarters to the government buildings, is a narrow pathway which in ordinary circumstances would be an alley but which in Sevilla has become a major pedestrian thoroughfare. Its shops are the richest in the city. The big plate-glass windows behind which lounge the principal men of Sevilla, like a coterie of lesser gods on a lower Olympus, here seem more formidable than elsewhere. The pretty girls who throng the street are more relaxed. The corner restaurants are busier and the quiet bustle of the little pathway is more exciting.

Because of the manner in which this slim, beautiful street lies stretched out in the sunlight, it has for many centuries been known simply as Sierpes and has been termed by many 'the loveliest street in Europe.' To justify this, one must accept certain special definitions, for Sierpes cannot compare with a boulevard in Paris or with one of London's wide streets. How little it is! I once measured its width at the Restaurante Calvillo and it was exactly fifteen shoe lengths across. To see Sierpes at its best is to understand the saying: 'The three finest pleasures a man can know are to be young, to be in Sevilla, and to stand in Sierpes at dusk when the girls are passing.' I would add a fourth: 'And to stand in Sierpes during Holy Week when La Macarena is passing.'

The first evening I ever spent in Sierpes was when the floats of Holy Week were going by and even then I sensed that this must be the high point of the parade, for it was in their passage down this brilliant street that all participants tried to do their best. The rope-sandaled men stifling under the boards moved cautiously so as not to scrape the walls. The cries of the captains became whispers. The bands played in better rhythm and the professional soldiers marched with increased precision. At the entrance to Sierpes additional politicians slipped into line, so that they could be observed during the march past the city hall, which stands beyond the exit from Sierpes, and those penitents who were uncovered straightened up so that their faces might be seen. In those moments Sierpes became the focal point of Spain, for although similar processions were under way in Madrid and other cities, this was the famous one.

I now understood what had determined the width of the floats, because there were several tight spots in Sierpes where the tableaux of Jesus and Mary had to be borne just so in order for them to slip between projecting walls. Not many spectators could crowd into Sierpes; on the other hand, since it was the culminating point of the procession, as many as possible jammed in, chairs being sold at a premium. Directed by a group of young Spaniards, I had slipped in and wedged myself against a wall, where the floats passed me by at a distance of inches rather than feet. It was exciting to be so close to the carved figures and to see the nuances of their expressions; there was also a kind of animal pleasure in seeing now and then beneath the protecting curtains the softly moving feet of those who bore the floats and to hear their whispers, as if the spirits of the statues were speaking.

But as an insight into religious experience it did not compare with my earlier confrontation with the penitent; that had been a true revelation and this spectacle in Sierpes could be no more than a well-conceived parade. However, on Good Friday evening, as I was watching in Sierpes, I heard from a balcony projecting over the street the high, piercing scream of a woman. '¡O Dios!' she cried, and all movement along the pathway stopped. '¡O Dios!' she repeated, and when the throng was silent she launched into the most strange and impassioned song I had ever heard. She had a deep effect upon the emotions of those who listened, for her voice alternated between throaty cries of pain and soaring evocations of ecstasy. She continued thus for some four or five minutes, pouring forth a personal song of devotion to Jesus Christ, and her performance was so powerful that all in Sierpes, marchers and witnesses alike, paid her the homage of silence, so that her voice rang out like a bell, floating over the massive crowds. She paused. No one moved. Then she entered the passionate coda of her song, with her voice ascending in spirals and fury until at the end she was possessed. Then silence, as if the crowd wanted to consider her song, then the sounds of the soldiers and the police and the clanking chains and the rustle of the float, as all resumed their march toward the city hall.

The woman had been chanting a saeta (arrow; in plural, ecstatic religious outcries), which would be heard throughout the city on this day. My Spanish friends tried to tell me that such songs were spontaneous outbursts of persons overcome by religious experience, but I found it hard to believe that this woman was an average person overcome by her identification with the passion; she was a professional singer if ever I heard one, and I thought that I was fortunate to have had her as my first saeta performer because she introduced the form in such a flawless setting that I have ever since been a devotee. A great saeta, well sung, is something one can never forget. But I felt sure she had been planted on that balcony with instructions as to when and how to sing for maximum effect.

Some hours later, on Good Friday night, when I had wormed my way to a different segment of Sierpes, across from a corner bar which had closed in honor of the procession, I watched as an ordinary man pressed in against the wall shook himself free when one of the great Virgins approached. Staring as if transfixed by the statue, this man threw back his head and poured forth a simple, unadorned song in praise of this Mother. It was an extraordinary song, more moving than the first, for it was uttered rather than sung professionally. It was an offering from this man to this intercessor and it was volunteered in humility and deep feeling. Its authenticity impressed the marchers and they stood at solemn attention as the singer's voice grew stronger and his cry more fervent. Then suddenly he stopped and returned as if in embarrassment to his former position against the wall. The wooden staves with their iron rings beat against the pavement of Sierpes and the procession continued.

At the far end of Sierpes the floats exit to a large square along whose side stands the city hall, and it is here that the procession reaches its temporal climax, for on the wooden grandstands are seated the official families of the political leaders who have been marching down Sierpes. Now the various bands explode into a roar and additional soldiers and police slip into the parade. Very bright searchlights illuminate the scene and there is no place here for the singers of saetas.

From the city hall to the cathedral is a short distance along Sevilla's main street, and here large areas of chairs have been rented out by the city government. Here also the parade prepares itself for the spiritual culmination of the procession, the entrance to the cathedral. This is much more impressive than it sounds, for Sevilla's cathedral is one of the most enormous in Europe. Its aisles are so broad that the floats are able to pass through more easily than through Sierpes. I suppose all the Holy Week floats could fit into the cathedral with ease. As one astonished Frenchman wrote home: 'I am sorry to tell you that Notre Dame could fit inside this cathedral without causing much stir.'

It stands in the center of the city and can be seen from miles out in the countryside. It is a barnlike structure and only in size does it compare with Toledo's Gothic masterpiece, but it does have two features which make it unique. At one corner rises a graceful Moorish tower which once belonged to a mosque that was torn down to make way for the cathedral. This tower is called La Giralda (Weathervane), after the female figure representing faith which tops it, and it has become the symbol of the city. I have often seen it from points many miles away as the driver of my car would call, 'Ah, La Giralda. Home at last.' The second feature is less conspicuous but perhaps even more lovely, a large walled-in garden with cathedral cloisters at one end and long rows of orange trees which spread their fragrance through the area. It is called the Patio de los Naranjos (Court of the Orange Trees) and at any time of the year is worth visiting.

It is to this massive cathedral that the floats finally move. They leave the street, pass through the cathedral door and stop for ecclesiastical blessing. The hooded confraternity kneel and the penitents drag their chains before the altar, some with ankles bleeding from the irons. In silence the float leaves the cathedral and the politicians duck away. The stevedores wait for the first stopping point, then crawl out and head for the nearest bar to refresh themselves before the long march back to their home church.

One would miss the spirit of Holy Week if he saw only the solemnity. In the silent crowds are groups of young girls who would otherwise not be allowed on the streets, and boys follow them. There is much pinching and bumping and hushed giggling, and for many girls their first fumbling introductions to sex come at this time. As Pepe Gómez told me, 'We don't always crawl out from under the boards to get a drink or listen to a saeta. It's fun to look up the girls' dresses as they stand on the balcony.' The excitement is keenest in those moments when some popular Virgin passes, for then the boys and girls press together without supervision and give meaning to the cry that will later be shouted to the Virgin as she returns to her church: 'Oh, dearest Virgin! How I remember you!'

On Sunday two significant things happen. The faithful gather in the cathedral to celebrate the resurrection of Jesus, but not much is made of the matter, for Sevilla in spring is concerned mainly with the Crucifixion. And promptly at five in the afternoon Holy Week ends in the blare of a brass band whose lively tempos herald the beginning of the Easter bull-fight, first of the season.

In the weeks that follow, depending upon the year's timetable, activity begins in two widely separated quarters of the city. The first is the more important historically; the second is the more significant today. Many centuries ago a channel was dredged connecting Sevilla with the Río Guadalquivir, which flows some distance to the west, and this enabled Sevilla to function as the major port of the south, even though it lay many miles from the ocean. On the flat land that lies between the channel and the river, gypsies now begin to gather and are in the process of erecting a tent city with restaurants, bars, trading points and other appurtenances. They appear to be preparing a traditional gypsy fair, with spiced foods, crooked horse races and beautiful fortunetellers.

That is not their intention. For as one studies the strange town he sees an uncommonly large number of horses, mules and donkeys. From outlying rural areas come peasants who would normally have little association with gypsies; the processions of Holy Week were not attractive enough to lure these peasants, but the gypsies do. Experts from France and Portugal also arrive, and the last time I was there three tall gentlemen from Texas appeared in spurs and sombreros.

For this is the famous horse fair of Sevilla, dating back two thousand years to the days when Romans came here to buy horses for their generals. Some think that it was this primitive trading that later called forth the processions of Holy Week; certainly it formed the vital nucleus around which the rest of the present complex fair was built.

When I was in Las Marismas, watching birds with Don Luis Ybarra González, we had discussed Sevilla's horse fair, and at that time he had explained, 'The fair probably goes back to Roman days, but sometime in the eighteenth century it was discontinued. In 1847 my great-grandfather, the Conde de Ybarra, was serving as mayor of Sevilla. He loved horses, had a bull ranch of his own and one day got the idea of having an old-style fair. So in its present form it dates only from 1847.' To it come horse traders from all parts of southern Spain, eager to test their trading skill against the practiced gypsies. There is much bargaining, much riding of horses back and forth across the dusty plains, much noise.

If a man likes horses, this rough-and-ready market with no rules and little order would delight him. It is conducted under a blazing sun and has

At the great horse fair a young man studies a possible purchase.

about it a strange and ancient quality. I have attended at three different times and found it difficult to believe that I was in the twentieth century; always I have thought it regrettable that most visitors to Sevilla miss the horse fair, because in many ways it is one of the most authentically Spanish parts of the spring celebration.

Last time I was there a gypsy boy of eleven was showing a donkey to a suspicious farmer from a vineyard north of Cádiz. Boy and man studied the donkey for more than an hour, and if they found anything unusual in the beast, I did not. The boy kept stressing the good points of the animal while the man parried with his suspicions about the wind, the hooves, the obviously weak back, the splayed foot and the visible sore near the tail.

Hoping by some dramatic gesture to conclude the sale, the boy took the donkey's halter and cried, 'But observe how he runs.' The beast would not move. Repeatedly the boy urged the animal to show his unusual skills, but apparently the donkey had none. All this time the farmer stood aside in contemptuous silence until finally the child screamed at him, 'Sir, you have bewitched him!'

Two hours later I observed the same boy with the same donkey arguing patiently with the same farmer. During the whole of the horse fair one can see such bargaining taking place along the banks of the Guadalquivir.

I once spent the better part of a morning with a tall gypsy named Antonio Suero Varga from the Extremaduran town of Almendralejo. He was broad-shouldered, had dark hair and very dark eyes and carried the badge of the gypsy horse trader, a rattan cane with which he conducted most of his business. 'Look at that horse. Have you ever seen finer legs for heavy work?' With his cane he would point out the special features of the animal he was trying to sell, but after I had been with him for a while I heard him say, as he jabbed at a mule with a weak back, 'You expect an honest man . . . Let's say a farmer who has to earn his living . . . You want him to buy a mule like that?'

I asked, 'Are you buying or selling?'

'Either.'

'Where are your horses?'

'Mine?' he laughed. 'I have no horses. I'm a comprador [purchaser].' He went on to explain that he made his living by attending fairs and bringing suspicious farmers who wanted to buy into contact with other suspicious farmers who wanted to sell. 'The Spanish farmer is a suspicious creature. He'll never trust himself or another farmer, so he has to trust a gypsy. He hires me to do his bargaining for him.'

I had been with Antonio Suero for some time when he was approached by two fine-looking young farmers from a village near Almendralejo. José Gallardo and his brother Juan farmed a profitable wine and olive plantation of a thousand acres. 'We already have three tractors,' José told me, 'but we'd like to buy a good mule to do the close-up work.'

'Why don't you just buy the mule?'

The Gallardos looked at me as if I were insane. 'Us? Buy a mule?' I judged I had offended their pundonor and wondered if I should apologize, but José said, 'A Spaniard can't go to another Spaniard and argue with him about the price of a mule. Well, it just couldn't be done. Nor would the man with a mule to sell want to haggle with me. It would be beneath his dignity. So we hire Señor Suero here to do it for us.'

At this point José and the gypsy withdrew to discuss terms, and I asked Juan, 'Do you trust him?'

'Suero? He's famous for being the best bargainer in these parts. We have to trust him. Watch.'

The gypsy, having learned what the Gallardo brothers wanted and what they would pay, left them and ran like a young boy from one group of men to another, waving his rattan cane and cursing. Once I heard him bellow, 'For that mule? My friend, I have two gentlemen who know mules. I'd be ashamed to take that animal before them.' Before long he came running back, waving his cane in the air. 'My God!' he cried. 'I've found the finest mule ever to reach Sevilla.'

He brought with him an old, suspicious, mean-tempered farmer in a broad hat and chaps who was leading what I took to be a very average mule, but as I watched, Suero put on one of the finest bits of acting I was to see in Spain. He laughed, he wept, he cursed, he pleaded, he cajoled and he swore as heaven was his witness that this was a good mule and that the price was just, but apparently he had not yet received a firm price from the seller, for as the bargaining proceeded the latter changed his price, where-upon Suero began reviling him as a thief for trying to sell this spavined beast to a decent man. Then, as soon as a firm price was determined, he became the seller again. Taking José Gallardo's hands in his he became a wise and understanding father. 'Believe me, Don José, I knew your father, I knew your uncle, and fine men they were. How many animals did I find for them, tell me. And did I ever recommend one that was faulty? Take my word for it, Don José, you'll search this feria on your knees before you find a mule as good as this one.'

According to the tradition of the feria the gypsy's job was to make the Gallardo brothers produce a hundred-peseta note, which he would then hand as a token to the seller, and the deal would be closed on the word of the two men. Suero, therefore, took José's hand in his right hand, the dealer's in his left and brought the two together, pleading with José to produce a hundred pesetas as a token. Tears came to his eyes; his voice broke; he could only mumble; then be began to speak like a machine gun and it seemed to me that about ninety percent of what he said was irrelevant. Slowly Gallardo produced a note and placed it among the four clasped hands, at which Antonio Suero gave a deep sigh.

'You have bought yourself a great mule,' he said, and with this he turned his attention to a farmer who had been tugging at his sleeve. To my surprise, it was the suspicious wine grower from Cádiz who had been haggling with the boy over the donkey. Apparently the two had remained locked in an impasse and now sought adjudication from Antonio Suero Varga. 'Coming, coming!' the gypsy cried as he ran off, waving his rattan cane, to solve this new problem. Later he would return to collect his commission on the Gallardo purchase.

It was during the horse fair some years ago that I stumbled upon a rewarding acquaintance. I had ridden a bus out to the Guadalquivir to spend the day with the gypsies and had eaten, at one of their kiosks, a mixture of grain, chopped meat and gravy, and now I returned on foot to the heart of the city. I rested for some time in the Court of the Orange Trees, using the stone slabs provided there, and then went into that fine street along which the Holy Week procession ends.

Spanish police are notoriously abrupt with pedestrians who try to cross other than at traffic lights, so I waited in line for the green to show,

The white dove of Spanish poetry rests easily on the shoulder of the arrogant gypsy.

because I wanted to spend the rest of the day wandering in the area by the bullring. I happened to look across the street at the people waiting on the other side and saw there two handsome young men whom I judged to be in their late twenties. One of them, a tall slim fellow with unusually fine features, I was sure I had seen somewhere before; these were the days when Hollywood was beginning to produce many films in Spain and I supposed he was an actor. Then it came to me. I had seen his picture in an American paper. And his name, for some curious reason, leaped to mind. He was John Fulton Short. And he came from Philadelphia. And he was a bullfighter.

We met in the middle of the street and I said, 'Aren't you John Fulton?' which was the name he fought under. He nodded and I introduced myself. He nodded again in much the manner that a Spanish grandee nods to the baker peddling bread from a barrow. 'Good luck, Matador,' I said, using the traditional Spanish phrase, and we crossed over, each headed his own way.

I learned later that the young man with him that day was Jerry Boyd, an aspirant writer from America who happened to be married to the daughter of one of my favorite artists, the fine Jewish Shakespearean actor from Budapest and London, Abraham Sofaer. It was Boyd, I later learned, who told Fulton, 'My God! If that's who he said he was, he's from Philadelphia too. Maybe we better see if he'd be interested.' John Fulton, in the manner of matadors, knew nothing of books and had no special desire right then to meet anyone from Philadelphia, for he was conspicuously down on his luck, but he allowed Boyd to double him back, and after a short walk, for I was moving slowly, they overtook me near the bullring.

'Are you from Philadelphia?' Fulton asked. I replied that I was and he gave me his card: 'John Fulton, Matador de Novillos, Hernando Colón, 30, Sevilla, España.' He smiled and said, 'Why don't you drop around?' But Jerry Boyd intercepted the card before I could take it and asked, 'You did say your name was Michener, didn't you?' When I nodded, he asked, 'And you do write books?' I nodded again and he let me have the card, and it was through this chance meeting that I embarked upon those adventures of the spirit which led to the writing of this book.

John Fulton, art student and would-be matador from Philadelphia, had a small second-floor apartment on a side street which debouched into the Court of the Orange Trees, and here, during a period of some six or seven years, came most of the Americans who got as far south as Sevilla. Maharajas stopped here and dozens of actors making movies in the area and writers and newspapermen and artists from England. The hospitality that John Fulton extended during the years was astronomical and he offered it while being stone-broke and trying to make his way in one of the toughest professions in the world. To be a bullfighter in Spain requires from even the Spanish youth an endurance that most men cannot visualize; but to be an American trying to crack that vicious and closed society demands absolute courage.

How Fulton supported himself during those bleak and wonderful years, I do not know. Most of us who trespassed on his hospitality managed in some way or other to leave behind donations: one brought the wine, another the anchovies, another the cheese. Hemingway made his contribution by check; a delightful woman from Cleveland made hers by throwing memorable flamenco parties at which she gave John a fee for his professional help; I made mine by commissioning Fulton to paint me a picture, for I judged that he had more chance to succeed as an artist than as a matador.

I was right. He was an excellent artist and subsequently made a name for himself as an illustrator of children's books; for his paintings he also acquired a distinguished list of patrons, including Adlai Stevenson and the Baroness von Trapp. But whenever I talked with him about the desirability

FOLLOWING FACING PAGES: *John Fulton and Antonio Ordóñez at the entrance to a small-town bullring. They wear the traditional Andalusian cowboy costume used in non-formal fights.*

of his attending art school somewhere and applying himself to that profession, he replied, 'I am going to be a matador.' His dedication never faltered, in spite of doubters like me, and I watched with sorrow as he beat his head in futile rage against the indifference of Spanish promoters. This handsome young fellow from Philadelphia might want to be a bullfighter, but the impresarios of Spain did not intend to help.

Those were marvelous days in Sevilla. In the afternoon we ate at a small restaurant called El Mesón (The Inn), where substantial food was served at reasonable prices in an atmosphere of bullfight posters and butchered pigs hanging from the ceiling. Food in Sevilla during the spring festival is apt to be dismal; some meals served in the major hotels are shocking, but at El Mesón we ate well. It was there I first tasted three fine Spanish items which together made a meal. First we had a tall pitcher of sangría, a drink made of harsh red wine, cognac, seltzer water, quartered oranges, lemon juice, some pineapple squares and red cherries, sweetened with not too much sugar and served with lots of cracked ice and cinnamon. It was delicious, and travelers who learn to like its different taste prefer it to other Spanish drinks.

For our second course we had gazpacho, an ice-cold soup which can be compared to nothing. If you ever travel in Spain and come upon a restaurant that serves gazpacho, take it, because no other dish in the country will you remember with such affection. Once when I had been out of Spain for some years, a neighbor found in a gourmet shop in Princeton a shelf of canned gazpacho, but since she could not be sure whether it was any good or not, she bought only one can, plopped it in her refrigerator and when it was ice-cold, called us over. When she served it with some chopped onion, cubes of cucumber and bits of tomato, tears of joy came to my eyes, something she had not been able to achieve with flamenco records or colored slides of Spain, and next day I drove all the way to Princeton to buy up the remaining cans. For gazpacho is Spain. The cook at the Mesón told me how to make it.

Take two stale rolls and reduce them to crumbs. Soak in water until they form a thick paste and set aside. Into your blender put two pounds of tomatoes, one large pared cucumber, two large green peppers, a quarter-cup of pimientos and two small sweet onions. Season with pinches of salt and pepper. Now comes the tricky part. To this mixture you must add olive oil and vinegar, which are the heart of the soup. A Spaniard will use one cup of the former, a tablespoon of the latter. Americans, of whom I am certainly one, prefer not more than a quarter-cup of oil and four tablespoons of vinegar. At any rate, reduce all ingredients except the bread to a liquid, then mix in the bread by hand and put the result in a covered wooden bowl and place in the refrigerator for six hours. Serve ice-cold and pass a serving tray containing separate dishes of chopped tomatoes, cucumbers, onions and small cubes of bread. No part of this strange recipe sounds very good, but taken together and properly blended, these ingredients produce a soup which is as distinctive as vichyssoise.

For dessert we had membrillo and Manchego cheese. The latter is the only good cheese Spain produces, a salty, coarse-grained product from the Don Quixote country. When eaten along with membrillo it makes a spicy dish, for membrillo is a grainy gelatin-like dessert made of quince. It is both sweet and acid and has a delicious chewy quality. Burnt orange in color, it is served in generous slabs as if it were a cheese, and at the Mesón was extra good, brought in from a small town near Córdoba which specializes in its manufacture; I believe that it too can sometimes be bought in the United States, but I haven't tasted it yet. However, the waiter warned me, 'Be careful where you buy your membrillo. Some of those other restaurants make theirs of sweet potato.'

At night in this in-between period we would rout out a near-blind flamenco singer, Gafas (Spectacles) they called him, and in the old days he could chant flamenco with as great an artistry as anyone in Spain, but now his voice was gone. We used to rent an attic in the medieval part of town, import a set of dancers and drag in a keg of wine, some bread, cheese and anchovies, and dance till morning. It was with Gafas singing in his cracked, wine-heavy voice, which no one could call beautiful, that I learned his version of that haunting song whose music I had first heard in Valencia years before, 'Petenera,' about the forbidden Jewess who brought disaster to her village and herself:

> Where are you going, beautiful Jewess,
> All dressed up and at such an hour?
> I am going to meet Rebeco,
> Who is now in the synagogue.
>
> Whoever named you Petenera
> Didn't know how to name you.
> You should have been named
> The perdition of men.
>
> If you hear the bells,
> Don't ask who has died,
> Because you will be told
> By your own remorse.

One would like to know the origin of that last verse. Is it an authentic Spanish statement anticipating John Donne? I suspect it's a late addition reflecting the popularity of Ernest Hemingway.

Whenever Gafas sang 'Petenera' to the rather banal music that accompanies it, I felt that I was in medieval Spain, as I do today when I hear it. In time this unimportant little song, to which each singer had his own dozen verses, including usually the three given above, came to represent for me the best of flamenco, and even though it is not one of the great songs, I would rather hear it sung well by a peasant voice like that of Gafas, tired and world-weary at the end of the day, with the guitar flying in mournful accents, than the finest formal chanting I have so far heard. It is in a very real sense my particular song of Spain; in the years when I worked submerged in Jewish materials I would often recall its phrases, and they came to me not in the syllables of the various recordings I had purchased, nor in the poetry, which is of good quality, but rather in the cracked and reedy voice of Gafas as he sang in the attics of Sevilla in those good days. Shortly after I heard him for the last time he died, leaving behind no recording of his 'Petenera.'

At John Fulton's there was much talk of art, but as I have said, I got nowhere trying to convince him that he should apply himself to painting. In his apartment when I knew it, one found Mexican matadors, Chilean painters, Minnesota architects and Vassar philosophy majors in Spain for their junior year. The visitor who gave me the most trouble was a Danish schoolteacher from Copenhagen; she was in her late twenties and no beauty, but she had a wonderfully soft quality about her and obviously loved children, to whom she imparted her strong sense of values. She taught, if I remember correctly, chemistry, which seemed an odd subject for a quiet girl like her, but she explained, 'There's an unusual need for chemists today. Especially in Denmark. And those of us who have any skill in the field are kept busy.' I judged that her pupils received good instruction.

But one meets many schoolteachers in Spain. What set this admirable young lady apart was the fact that on a previous vacation she had conceived a grand passion for a young Welshman who, like John Fulton, was determined to become a bullfighter. The fellow had no prospects whatever, insofar as I could determine, yet he hung on, year after year. At the beginning of each summer his Copenhagen schoolteacher appeared on the scene, with her savings from the term before, and together they moved from one fair to the next, she blond and he swarthy, clinging to the fiction that one day he would become a great fighter, one day they would marry. The illusion kept them going, and I was with them at the end of one season when the little Welshman actually got an invitation to fight in the fair being put together by an impoverished village.

It would be more accurate to say that he had been invited to participate in the fair, because it wasn't going to be a formal bullfight; the Welshman would be welcomed if he paid for his suit, for his assistants, for a horse to be ridden by his picador and for part of the bullring expenses. In return he would receive no wages at all but would be allowed to test himself against an overage, overweight, wily old bull who had already in previous fights sent two men to the hospital.

This offer presented a serious dilemma to the schoolteacher. Obviously the funds required of the Welshman could be provided only by her, and if she laid out this substantial amount she felt that she ought at least to attend, especially since there was a strong likelihood that her matador would be wounded, if not killed. But to attend the fracas, for that's what it shaped up to be, would require her to miss the opening of her school in Copenhagen. She asked me what I thought she ought to do, and I, as a conservative who used to teach school myself, taking it very seriously, said without hesitation, 'You take the next plane to Denmark.'

Apparently I brought her to her senses, for she put down the money for the fight, canceled her flight to Denmark and accompanied her hero to the village festival. On the way she explained, 'They can't fire me. Chemistry teachers are hard to come by.' I asked if her school board knew that she was spending her vacations in Spain, living with a bullfighter. She replied, 'I suppose they know. At least the children do. They think it's rather sporting.'

We got to the village, a Welsh bullfighter with a Danish manager, a Portuguese assistant, a Mexican picador and an American cheerleader. As so often happens, there was no fight; the local impresario had collected funds to buy the two bulls and had then absconded.

It was in this world of broken promises, venal arrangements and utter corruption of all principle that John Fulton struggled. How he maintained his good humor I will never know, for he was humiliated by the numbers. One, promise him a fight. Two, wheedle him into designing the handbills. Three, make him agree to fight overage bulls. Four, make him employ my brother-in-law as his picador. Five, postpone everything. Six, abandon everything. Year after year this continued; year after year he either told me or wrote me: 'I will be a matador.'

Gradually, as I visited him more often, I became aware of a quiet young man who seemed to be sharing the apartment and to be decorating it with photographs of high quality. For long periods, when the talk was on subjects in which I had little interest, I would study the photographs, excellent works in very dark blacks and pure whites, and I became convinced that the man who had taken them understood Spain.

The quiet young fellow with well-fitted suits and conservative haircut was Robert Vavra, from California, a nature photographer. He had been working for some years on a book of text and pictures describing in detail the life and death of the fighting bull, and from the first moment I saw his work in sequence I was convinced that here was a man who could photograph the movement and sense of animals; but I was equally impressed by his shots of people. He seemed to catch the spirit of things in repose; there was little artiness about him and I began to look forward to my visits to the apartment: I wanted to see what Vavra had done recently.

There followed a chain of unforgettable days in Las Marismas, tracking bulls, watching wildlife and marking the migration of birds to Africa. It was on such trips that I renewed my acquaintance with the bee-eater, that spectacular bird which was to become so important to me when I worked in Israel. Here, too, I saw my first hoopoe bird, which would be even more important.

Then one day, as I studied a batch of Vavra's photographs and listened to his plans for a series of children's books in color, a project which has happily come to fulfillment, I happened to see a chance arrangement of some twenty or thirty fine photographs depicting the people and life of Spain: they were not the usual body of material, for there were no cathedrals, no medieval houses and no flamenco dancers. There was simply the look of Spain, static and yet persuasively alive, and in that moment not far from the Court of the Orange Trees this book was born.

Because I was burdened with a heavy schedule that would keep me busy for some years, I could not then speak to Vavra of my incipient plans; but when my work was completed I went back to Sevilla, and in that same quiet and delightful period between Holy Week and carnival, when the gypsies were again preparing to trade horses on the riverbank, I proposed that we do this book together.

I remember the commission we agreed upon: 'Vavra will go over Spain guided only by his own eye, completely indifferent as to what Michener may write or think or prefer. Shoot a hundred of the very finest pictures he can find and make them his interpretation of Spain. If he can succeed in this, the pictures will fit properly into any text. But Vavra must avoid trying to guess what someone else wants. Make others see what he has seen.'

For the capacity to see a foreign country is extremely rare; hardly one person in a thousand can do this, so that all the vast sums of money spent by Pan American and Air France in their enticing advertisements—'See Lebanon. See Egypt. See Brazil'—are largely wasted, because the people who fly forth to see these places rarely do. Vavra can see.

When the religious parades have ended, when the horse fair on which the spring activity originally centered has started to convene, and when old friends have had a chance to renew acquaintances during the time of relative rest, the real Sevilla fair, as most people think of it today, convenes. Now the night clapping begins to echo through the city.

In a spacious park lying at the southern edge of Sevilla, and within easy walking distance from the center of town, three separate but connected areas have been staked out, each the size of a small pueblo. For the next week these three areas will become the heart of Sevilla to charm the visitor as few other fairs in Europe can.

In the first area, improbable as it seems, five different circuses, each complete in itself, have gathered from various parts of the continent. There's a Swiss circus, with famous clowns, an Italian one, a brilliant Chinese one featuring acrobats and Oriental girls, a Spanish one and, best of all, a large German circus with four different wild-animal acts.

To one who loves circuses, the Sevilla fair is unique: one can spend three days moving from one tent to the next and even then he will not be able to see all the acts. There is something quaint and even nineteenth century about these European circuses; occasionally a family will work in one for forty or fifty years, and no effort is made, as in America, to keep all the women beautiful. In these tents one sees whole families growing old surrounded by events they love. For example, I have never seen another animal act so utterly delightful as the one in the German circus in which a hefty woman in her late fifties, dressed in bespangled tights, put a cageful of tigers through their paces. It was charming in the way sadistic old fairy tales are charming.

In the area adjoining the circuses noise is king. Here you will find more noise than the human ear can absorb or the sane man imagine, because this is the carnival space, filled with rides, games, shooting galleries, half a hundred outdoor restaurants, loop-the-loops, trips to Mars and a near-score of other rides. Apparently it is obligatory for each business to own a microphone and five or six of the loudest loudspeakers. 'Come here!' bellow the shills. 'Mothers, take your children through the mysteries of outer space!' The call of '¡Churros!' is popular, for these greasy fritters served laden with sugar, are the delicacy of the fair. But no one cry predominates, for wherever you stand you are assailed by at least twenty loudspeakers relatively close to your ears.

One night I took a friend from America to the middle of the carnival area, and he stood in admiration at the frenzy around him. 'The Spaniards are to be congratulated,' he said. 'They've discovered noise incarnate.'

Yet the area is not vulgar. It too has a controlled Spanish charm and a much wider variety of booths at which to spend money than I have been able to indicate. Merely to stroll through the lanes and sample food at each of the booths would require, I suppose, a couple of days, and to ride on each of the wheels and whips would take another two. The section is clean, brightly lighted and constitutes a little fair by itself, a swirling concentration of revelry.

It operates, of course, twenty-four hours a day. At four one morning I wandered among the tents, checking to see how many features I had missed on previous visits, and I came upon a large field jammed with nothing but trucks and wheeled caravans that had hauled this weird collection of rides and restaurants to Sevilla. Painted red and green and gold and blue, the trucks huddled together like a collection of bizarre animals assembled from all parts of Europe, and in almost every cab some man or woman was sleeping. Now when I think of the carnival part of Sevilla's fair I remember not the noise but rather that silent, slumbering collection of gaudy vehicles.

In spite of the richness of the circuses and the flamboyance of the carnival, it is the third section of the park that captivates most people, and

This mother-and-daughter fruit-selling team expresses the gracia of Sevilla.

it is true that of a hundred foreigners visiting Sevilla for the spring festivities, a good ninety see only the area I am about to describe. They miss the Holy Week, the horse fair, the circuses, the carnival and even the bullfights, but what they do see makes the trip worthwhile.

This part of the fair has been laid out along a grid of unusually wide streets, the main ones forming a massive capital H with top and bottom closed. Along the sides of the streets forming this enormous H, and along lesser contributory streets as well, the citizens of Sevilla have been accustomed for the past half-century to build each spring small wooden structures whose walls and roofs consist of brightly striped canvas. They are called casetas (little houses), and each has a wooden floor, electric lights, running water, perhaps a refrigerator, a table and at least two dozen chairs. Each caseta stands jammed against its neighbors, and to see a quarter of a mile of such little houses, each with its distinctive and gaudy color system, is delightful to the eye.

It is in these casetas that the well-to-do people of Sevilla will spend most of their time during the fair, returning to their homes only in time to catch a few hours' sleep between five and eleven in the morning.

What happens in the casetas? When the front canvas wall has been rolled up so that passers-by can see within, specially invited guests stop by for refreshments, drinks and light conversation. Entertainment is provided by amateurs and by troupes of noisy flamenco dancers imported from across the river in Triana. With music and dancing, with sherry wine and churros, with laughter and flirtation the long nights drift by. Young couples sometimes wander away from the caseta to the carnival area or even to the circus, but by one in the morning most are back where they belong. A special feature of the casetas is the presence of children between the ages of four and twelve, beautifully dressed in folk costumes and dancing flamenco patterns until two or three in the morning. It is incredible how much music there is in these lines of gaily colored casetas: one night at two o'clock I made a casual count and came up with sixty-five different orchestras.

And the songs! In one tour of the casetas I heard amateur performances covering the complete range of flamenco, from the so-called deep songs to the little songs. One jazzy folk song intermixed with the flamenco had a standard opening verse and a rather startling conclusion:

> If a brunette is worth a duro
> Any blonde is worth two.
> But I go to the low-priced love,
> The love of my heart.

> My Virgin of Macarena is brunette,
> Oh, she's a real brunette!
> She comes from Sevilla
> And is sweeter than the morning star.

When the real morning star appears the father of the family rolls down the canvas wall facing the street. A son runs off to summon a horse-drawn carriage. The gypsies are paid off and the refrigerator is locked. The tired family piles into the carriage and drives off through the morning twilight. From the carnival area nearby come volumes of sound, for the rides and restaurants are still busy, and as the family rides homeward through the darkened streets they hear the sound of muffled clapping coming from other groups who are walking home. At dusk next evening the family will return to its caseta, and for a whole week this procedure will be repeated. During the fair Sevilla gets little sleep.

In addition to the small family casetas, at which no stranger is welcomed unless specifically invited, so that many Americans spend an entire week at the fair without ever being inside one, most companies doing business in Sevilla operate their own large casetas, and some of these are public. By paying a small fee one can sit at a table, listen to professional flamenco and drink beer or champagne.

Among these large casetas stands one with special importance. It belongs to the Aero Club and its membership is so highly restricted that it constitutes, during the season of the fair, the focus of Spanish society. Here congregate those especially handsome people who form the apex of Spanish life: the duques, the condes, the grandees of Spain. And they are a forbidding, impressive lot, perhaps the most conspicuous nobility operating today.

In daylight hours the side curtains of the Aero Club are rolled up, so that passers-by can observe the great figures taking a light lunch or drinking their Tío Pepe along with a handful of roasted nuts. Condesas, accompanied by leading bankers, sit at tables looking out into the street; duquesas share their tables with famous bullfighters; at one table it's all pretty women and racing-car drivers. At night the curtains are lowered and two different bands alternate from six in the evening till four in the morning. During two fairs I held honorary tickets to the Aero Club, and I would judge the Spanish leaders I met to be among the most carefully groomed people I have ever seen. It is difficult, as one observes their old-fashioned gentility, to believe that they are part of this century.

To observe this manifestation of Spanish society one does not require a ticket to the Aero Club, entrance to that establishment costing some forty dollars. Each day at noon an informal parade starts through the wide streets of the H and in it participate most of the leaders of Sevilla society. As twelve o'clock approaches, in all parts of Sevilla horses are saddled up and handsome young men appear dressed in formal riding habit. They wear fine jackets with five buttons on the sleeve, dark riding trousers covered by large hand-tooled leather chaps, white ruffled shirts with lace at the throat and front, and flat, wide-brimmed hats. When they have mounted they adjust a pillion behind them, from whose rear projects a small leather handle which passes under the horse's tail. It is on this pillion that the gentleman's girl companion will ride, perched sideways across the rear of the horse, one hand passing about the man's waist, the other gripping the leather handle. Since the girls are dressed in resplendent gypsy costume, gold and blue and red predominating, the couples form attractive images as they ride forth. When three or four hundred begin to converge in bright sunlight on the caseta area, a parade of lovely dimensions is under way. For some three hours they ride back and forth along the tree-lined streets, halting now and then to chat with fellow riders, dismounting occasionally to visit with friends in the casetas and displaying to good effect both their fine costumes and their well-trained horses. The girls resemble a convocation of butterflies, they are so colorful.

At the same time other couples are about to join the parade, and these are much different. The men's suits are more subdued. The horses' garnishings are more expensive, as are the horses themselves. And the

*In her palace stands
the Duquesa de Medinaceli,
most betitled woman in Spain.*

women, who this time will ride alone, each on her own animal, are stunning beyond compare. They are the gentry, the social leaders from the Aero Club, and all are dressed in formal black or charcoal gray or very dark brown. The women's suits are of whipcord; their hats are slimmer and flatter than the men's; their heavy leather chaps are apt to be trimmer than those we saw before. They ride with the reins lightly held in the fingers of the left hand, their right hand turned in against the waist, and invariably their hair is done with austere plainness. With little or no make-up they ride forth, as handsome a group of women as one can find. In some strange way, in their somber mien, they make the pillion riders, despite their rainbow colors, seem drab.

But even these beautiful women are overshadowed by a phenomenon of this fair: ornate carriages pulled by two or four beribboned horses, driven by two coachmen in antique costume and bearing four or six girls in colorful dress, accompanied sometimes by gentlemen. These delightful carriages, looking like some procession that had driven into Sevilla from the eighteenth century, ease themselves into the files of horsemen, and around the streets of the H they go, back and forth for three or four hours. Sometimes as many as a hundred carriages, each of different size and quality, move along under the trees, the occupants laughing and visiting with their friends; half the parade moves clockwise, the other half counter-clockwise, so that on any one tour, if that is the proper word, one meets half the paraders, and since it is permissible to reverse one's direction after having made a couple of circuits, by the time the huge promenade has ended, one has met up with most of the participants.

I cannot describe how lovely and quiet and satisfying this parade under the broad trees and along the casetas is. Even if one has no horse and saddle of his own, nor access to the expensive carriages, he can still join the parade, for at any corner he can hire a kind of horse-drawn taxicab and for surprisingly little money ride back and forth along the majestic streets of the H. Where do they come from, these hundreds of carriages for hire? How can a modest city like Sevilla find so many horses?

Whenever a horseman reins up before a caseta owned by his friends, courtesy requires that both he and his lady be handed small glasses of sherry. Without dismounting, the riders drink, return the glasses and thank their hosts. Once I was left in care of a caseta while the family joined the riders in a carriage, and not then knowing the custom of the sherry I stood by while a particularly vivacious couple reined up before me. They waited. I waited. Then, in disgust, the man snapped in Spanish, 'At this damned caseta the hospitality flows like lead.' I understood enough to catch his meaning and in my broken Spanish asked what had gone wrong. When he realized that I was a stranger he jumped from his horse, showed me where the sherry was and flagged down all his friends. That night he took me on a tour of his favorite casetas, and we hired our own band of Triana gypsies, and the boisterous flamenco we provided with our company of fifty is still spoken of.

A feature of the parade is that select band of carriages which are pulled by eight horses, the postillions being dressed in robber costumes from the eighteenth century. Not only are the carriages worthy of respect and the horses a delight because of their matched appearance, but a ninth horse in front seems not to be attached to the carriage in any way, nor to the other horses. He moves by himself, guided by invisible wires attached to his bit and by words called by the driver, who rides a considerable distance behind. It is something to see such a carriage coming down the avenue, surrounded by a hundred riders and meeting dozens of other carriages, with the lead horse quietly picking his way without apparent assistance.

Thus the great fair of Sevilla continues, day after day. Toward dawn on the last night I stood at the entrance to the Aero Club as members of the nobility departed for the last time, and in the street stood an old man leading a donkey. He was not the kind who would own a caseta, nor a horse to ride in the daily procession, nor even a job in one of the carnivals. He was a rural peasant come in with his donkey to see the sights, and as he watched the ending of the fair he sang:

> 'Yo soy un ánima infeliz,
> Perdida en este mundo atormentado.'

(I am a miserable spirit lost in this tormented world.) And as he wandered off, singing to himself, the tents of the five circuses were coming down, the parking lot where the carnival trucks waited came back to life and electricians were disconnecting their wires from the multitude of little casetas, which would soon vanish.

As I stood in the darkness that night I reflected upon the strange development of Spanish history which permitted the nobles to play so important a role without suffering the limitations to their power that overcame their fellows in England, France, Italy, Germany and Russia. In Spain a conde is still somebody and a duque is a near-god. In the year 1400 the arrogant nobles of the major European countries were about equal in the power they exercised, but one by one the other European nations, in the order named, underwent revolutions of fact and spirit which cut back the absolute power of their nobles and transferred that power to a new and educated middle class, from which would come the political and industrial leaders of the future. In Spain this did not happen; on the contrary, the nobles arrogated more and more power to themselves, so that as late as the nineteenth century they dominated Spanish life, especially in the countryside. They told priests what they might and might not preach; they terrorized schoolteachers; they put newspapermen out of business; they exercised control over the cabinet, the army, the Church hierarchy and agriculture. Even today, as we shall see later when discussing a typical business operation in Madrid, they dominate Spanish life. No other nobility in the world compares in power and wealth with Spain's, and as one watches it in operation the only parallel he can find is the operation of the Hungarian nobility in the late 1700s.

If the Spanish nobility had exercised a leadership commensurate with its privilege, as was frequently the case in England and France, Spain would have prospered, but that did not happen. When Spain needed industrialization, the nobles said no. When Spain required a first-class army and navy to defend its empire, the nobles insisted upon using these services as their private playthings, with one general for every ten or fifteen men, and so abused the army that it fell from being the best in Europe to the worst. When the Church should have been doing what it did in all other major countries, adjusting religion to a changing world, the nobles, through their occupancy of high positions, refused to allow speculation. No nation in Europe, except possibly Hungary and Rumania, has been so badly served by its upper classes as Spain. With the intellectual and moral capacity to govern, they refused to do so; instead of seeking the common good they sought their own preferment, and the gap between them and the people became tragically wide.

I think the best light one can throw on the problem of the Spanish nobility is an oblique one shining from Peru, Chile, Paraguay, Venezuela and other Spanish countries of America. In the capitals of Europe one of the standard figures is the exile bearing a name like Juan Jiménez López. He was born in one of the Latin countries of South or Central America and was either elected or appointed to office, which he held for about five years, during which time he stole every peso or bolivar he could and sent it to a numbered account in Switzerland. Señor Jiménez caught the last plane out, said goodbye forever to his homeland and now lives happily and with a certain flair in Europe. Never in his upbringing did he catch a glimpse of what public service meant. Reared on a mixture of pundonor and Viva yo, he had no option but to do what he did, for he felt no obligation to his homeland other than to use it as his milk cow. The defect lay not in Jiménez but in the fact that the Spanish upper classes, from which he at least spiritually sprang, have never undergone indoctrination in the principle of noblesse oblige.

There was another contributing factor. During the critical years, say 1500–1815, when the nobility of England and France were being either educated or eliminated, Spain was governed in a spirit of absolutism not known in the other major countries save Russia by a series of kings who were not Spanish, and under their system of rule most of the best administrative jobs went to foreigners. Forget the fact that these foreigners stole the country blind, one after another retiring to his homeland with a fortune; forget the savage mismanagement and forget the subversion of law; the important fact was that the Spanish upper classes were thus deprived of the schooling in government which might have modified their insularity, arrogance and general incompetence. Other nations have suffered foreign kings. If Flemish not Spanish was spoken at the court in Toledo, so German not English was spoken in London; but the English upper classes would not permit their German kings to import outside ministers; indeed, it was sometimes the presence of the German king that spurred the English upper classes to greater energy and a more resolute defense of national prerogatives. Therefore, in the period when new lessons were to be learned, the English upper classes were in a position to learn them and the Spanish were not. Later, when it was necessary to make crucial decisions on which the fate of the social order as well as the empire rested, the English had been trained to make those decisions; the Spanish had not and the series of disastrous wrong choices followed.

The choices were wrong only for the nation and the general welfare. The upper classes looked out for themselves, so that each year the chasm between the very rich and the very poor became greater, until it seemed that all Spain was divided between these two extremes. No region of Spain is better equipped to exhibit this differential than Andalucía, which includes both Córdoba and Sevilla, for here the extremes are even greater than in Extremadura. The poor of the two regions are equally poor, but the rich in Andalucía are much richer; Extremadura has produced few noble families and those not of top power. When one speaks of a 'grandee of Spain' he visualizes primarily the great families of Andalucía: aloof, arrogant, powerful, indifferent.

This was illustrated one hot afternoon as I was driving from Sevilla to Córdoba and was accosted by a workman who said he must get to the latter city. He said, with no reluctance before a stranger, 'It's dreadful for a poor man to live in Andalucía. We starve. The rich ones don't live out here, you can be sure of that.' When I asked where they did live, he pointed contemptuously over his shoulder at La Giralda. 'Huddled together in the city where the police and the army and the Guardia Civil can protect them.' When I asked him why, he said, 'Because if they lived out here they'd be killed in their sleep. That's why.' It is this legacy of bitterness which one sometimes glimpses during the spring feria that otherwise seems so gay. It recalls the perceptive statement made by a Frenchman: 'Spain has had many revolutions but it has always missed the revolution.'

In recent years the feria has acquired an international cast which it did not formerly have. So many famous people arrive and so many motion pictures are shot in the surrounding area that the Alfonso XIII, a grand hotel situated not far from the cathedral, the casetas and the bullring, becomes during this period the jet-set capital of Europe. Orson Welles holds court here and American visitors are impressed by the reverence in which he is held by Europeans; he is judged to be one of the six or seven most significant Americans. Audrey Hepburn lends gracia to the old hotel, while Rita Hayworth and Juliette Greco add piquancy. In 1966 the two American princesses, Jacqueline Kennedy and Grace Kelly, stole the show as they paraded their crystal beauty at the various exhibitions. Spaniards were especially pleased when Jackie Kennedy rode through the park dressed in a faultless costume of Andalucía topped by a flat-brimmed hat. They were surprised at her fine horsemanship, and several members of the noble families expressed the hope that she might want to settle permanently in Spain. 'She is one of us,' they said. 'She'd find our way of life congenial.'

The daily schedule during feria is a demanding one:

11:00 A.M.	Get up. Breakfast on hard roll and coffee.
12:00 NOON	Dress in riding habit and join the parade.
4:00 P.M.	Leisurely lunch.
5:00 P.M.	Walk to the bullfight.
8:00 P.M.	Visit with friends and talk.
11:30 P.M.	Leisurely dinner.
2:00 A.M.	Drive to the Aero Club for dancing.
5:00 A.M.	Nightcap with friends, then off to bed.

The above is of course the schedule of a cautious man who prefers to take things easy. If at dawn there is excitement on one of the bull ranches or if Don Angel Peralta is giving an exhibition of horsemanship at his ranch near Sevilla, the true devotee skips the sleep.

As to the bullfights, one evening I dined with Orson Welles, that scowling giant who in his youth had trained to be a matador, and he said in his rumbling voice, 'What it comes down to is simple. Either you respect the integrity of the drama the bullring provides or you don't. If you do respect it, you demand only the catharsis which it is uniquely constructed to give. And once you make this commitment you are no longer interested in the vaudeville of the ring. You don't give a damn for fancy passes and men kneeling on their knees. There used to be this fraud who bit the tip of the bull's horn. Very brave and very useless, because it played no part in the essential drama of man against bull. Such tricks cheapen the bull and therefore lessen the tragedy. What you are interested in is the art whereby a man using no tricks reduces a raging bull to his dimensions, and this means that the relationship between the two must always be maintained and even highlighted. The only way this can be achieved is with art. And what is the essence of this art? That the man carry himself with grace and that he move the bull slowly and with a certain majesty. That is, he must allow the inherent quality of the bull to manifest itself. Today in Spain we

Grand entrance of the bullfighter.
at Sevilla's Maestranza
the La Scala of bullfighting

have many vaudevillians and you won't waste your time completely if you watch them. We also have men of bravery and it's always rewarding to observe this rare commodity in action. But of the true artists who comprehend the fruitful relationship that ought to exist between man and bull there is only one, Curro Romero. And until you have seen him, my friend, you have seen nothing. For this young man, handsome of face but round of body, can launch passes which are the essence of bullfighting. He is really so good that it's difficult to believe that this age produced him, for he has the style of the past, when vaudevillians had little place in the arena. Some day you'll see this boy at his greatest, and I'll be there, and we shall nod to one another across the intervening people, and you will thank me for having insisted that you go to see him.' Unfortunately, Curro Romero did not fight when I had tickets, so I had no chance to see him.

If Córdoba is the apex of the Romantic Movement because of *Don Alvaro, or The Force of Destiny,* Sevilla is the popular capital because of the works which have used this city as their locale. The story of *Carmen* takes place in Sevilla and one needs no imagination to see the gypsy lounging in the doorway of the old tobacco factory, second largest building in Spain and now used as part of the university. Spaniards profess to be irritated by the attention given *Carmen* throughout the rest of the world and claim that it damages the image of Spain, but I have noticed that whenever a Spanish impresario needs a full house, he puts on *Carmen*. One of the greatest performances came in the bullring at Sevilla; when the brigands filtered onto the stage they came with lanterns from all parts of the ring, and in the gala scenes carriages with prancing horses and three hundred extras filled the ring. Say the Spanish intellectuals with resignation, '*Carmen* is the cross each Spaniard has to bear.' But others confess, 'We're just bitter that it took two Frenchmen to invent her.'

Naturally, it was here that *The Barber of Seville* plied his trade and went forth to conquer the theaters of the world. Many other works of a romantic turn have centered on this city, but the most seminal was a curious play which appeared in print, without fanfare, for the first time in 1630, although it may have been on the boards for as long as fifteen to twenty years. Since then many people have wished that they could have been in the audience on opening night, whenever it was, to see the birth of what has become the most ubiquitous legend in world drama, yet one whose significance has never been adequately explained.

This fateful play was *El burlador de Sevilla y convidado de piedra,* and I have left the title in Spanish because of the difficulty English translators have faced with the second word. Obviously we are speaking of the standard hero of the play, and he was a burlador, or one who engages in burlas. Any standard Spanish-English dictionary shows that a burla is a joke, a jest, a trick, a sneer, a gibe, a mockery, a taunt, a scoff, so we are here dealing with what we might call a prankster, and this accounts, I think, for the erroneous titles which English-speaking translators have used: *The Rogue of Seville,* or Mocker, or Rake. Actually, in Spanish daily life a burlador is a seducer of women and the title should only be *The Seducer of Seville,* which is not only alliterative but also pertinent to the action. Why English translators have shied away from this simple word, I do not know.

Who is this seducer? We meet him at the medieval court of the King of Naples, where his uncle serves as Spanish ambassador. He is leaving the bedroom of a duquesa whom he has seduced in the royal palace by posing as her future husband. This incurs royal displeasure, so he flees to Spain, where he is shipwrecked on the Catalan coast and saved by a lovely fishergirl who nurses him back to health and whom he seduces with promises of marriage. He moves on to the court of the Castilian king at Sevilla, where his father is chancellor and where his servant announces that for the good of all maidens a public crier should precede his master with the proclamation, 'Let all beware of a man who deceives women and is the seducer of Spain.' The king has learned of the Naples escapade but forgives him, with the stipulation that he marry the duquesa, but before this can be arranged he enters by trickery the house of a noble lady loved by a friend of his and attempts to seduce her. When her father, the Comendador de Calatrava, rushes in to protect her honor, the seducer kills him. He now flees to a nearby town, where he thrusts himself into the midst of a local wedding and, with a violent promise of marriage, seduces the intended bride. As the duquesa and the fishergirl appear at court to complain to the king, the seducer returns to Sevilla, and chancing upon the tomb of the Comendador, with a show of bravado seizes the stone statue by the beard and invites it to dine with him that night, which explains the second part of the play's title: convidado de piedra (guest of stone). To his astonishment, even though he has had a table set as his part of the bargain, the statue appears, eats, then invites the seducer to dine the following night in its chapel, on which they shake hands. Although the seducer notes a certain unearthly quality in the handshake, his pundonor obligates him to keep the appointment. At the conclusion of the meal, which has consisted of scorpions, vipers and wine of bile and vinegar, the statue extends its hand, which is taken, whereupon host and guest sink down amid sound and fury into the fires of hell.

Thus appears for the first time in the theater Don Juan Tenorio, hero-villain of demonic proportions. Imagine the reincarnations he is to have. In France, Molière (1665) and Corneille (1677) will produce plays on his life, while at a later date Mérimée, Dumas and De Musset will base stories on his legend. In Italy there will be several versions, the best being Goldoni's (1730). In England, Shadwell (1676) will construct a play on the subject, which Purcell (1676) will use as the basis for an opera, and Byron (1819) will borrow the theme for his major poem. In Germany three distinguished musical versions will appear: Gluck (1760), Mozart (1787) and Richard Strauss (1889). In Spain the recensions will be numerous, until in 1844 a dramatist of whom we shall speak later will construct of the legend a play which will become Spain's national drama, a kind of *Hamlet* and *Faust* combined.

I cannot recommend too highly the original version of this legend. It was written by an ingratiating friar, Tirso de Molina, nom de plume of Gabriel Téllez (1571?–1648), thought to be the illegitimate son of some noble family and the author of four hundred plays, of which nearly ninety are extant. In many ways Friar Tirso's account of Don Juan excels anything that followed, even Mozart's *Don Giovanni*, because it is a hard, clean, unsentimental play with terrific impact. It is realism ahead of its time; ironically, it was to serve as the source of much romanticism. The scenes move rapidly and with a grand fatality; the character of the seducer develops properly and those about him are well differentiated; and the device of the marble statue is used with stunning effectiveness. The style of writing is most attractive, a lean statement not overburdened with simile but filled with salty observation. One matter is of particular importance: although this original version was written by a friar, it does not, like some of the later accounts, end in an orgy of religious reconciliation. Don Juan dies a cynical, tough rogue. At the final banquet with his stone host he dares retribution to overtake him:

> 'What do you call this dish, Sir?'
> 'Scorpions and vipers. These are our foods. Aren't you eating?'
> 'I'd eat it if it were all the asps in hell.'

His only concession comes in his next to last speech, and it was on this that the later versions built their scenes of redemption: 'Then let me call someone to confess and absolve me.' To which the statue replies, 'You have thought of it too late.'

Tirso's version has a classic dignity. It was apparently written about the time of Shakespeare's death (1616) and shows Tirso to have been rather less inventive and poetic than his English contemporary, but in the use of characters from everyday life he is as good. Actually, the form of the play and its development remind one of Racine and Corneille, who followed him. It makes a strong impression on stage, the flow of scenery and costume being particularly attractive, but it requires a strong actor to carry the role of Don Juan. He cannot burlesque it or play it as a dandy; he must be more like the resolute hero of a western movie than a fancy gentleman in lace and ruffles. He is, indeed, the archetype of the hero-villain and should be played as such.

Excellent as the Tirso original was, so far as Spain was concerned it remained merely one more good play among the hundreds produced in this period and it appeared in the theater no more often than any of the minor

works of Lope de Vega, who died just about the time when Tirso's play was published. But in 1844 something happened, of itself of no significance but of great accidental importance. A romantic playwright named José Zorrilla y Moral (1817–1893), the darling of the theater at that time, produced *Don Juan Tenorio*, a metrical version in full-blown romantic style. It was a sloppy play filled with so many improbabilities that any critic could tear it apart, as many did. The author himself termed it 'the greatest nonsense ever written' and listed the dozen or so points at which it violated dramatic canons and psychological reason. And yet it was touched with flashes of true poetry that tugged at the sentiments; it was flamboyantly staged and excited the imagination, and in some curious way that has never been explained, it evoked a sense of Spain, and in its bombast people of all degrees could see themselves. It leaped into prominence and has ever since retained a hold on the Spanish imagination, both in Spain and in the New World.

Zorrilla's Don Juan is an astonishing man to have become the hero of a nation. Before attempting to guess why this has happened let me assert briefly that it has; intellectuals today in Spain will try to pooh-pooh the idea and say, 'Don Juan Tenorio? No one takes him seriously any more,' but I have talked with too many Spaniards to accept that easy dismissal. Toward the end of October, for reasons which I will describe later, newspapers across Spain carry full-page analyses of Don Juan and find a surprising number of public figures to admit that he is their hero. 'Tenorio lives the way a hero should, not giving a damn for anyone, and when it comes time to die he dies like a man.' 'Tenorio is Spain. I feel very much like Tenorio. I hope I can stand up to adversity the way he did.' 'Estupendo! I vote for Don Juan.' 'What I like about Tenorio is the way he was willing to fight anybody for any reason. The bit about the girls? Well, a man couldn't get away with that today. At least not so much, but men are fundamentally like that. He's my hero.' The statements go on and on. I have more than fifty before me as I write, and some are much more revealing than the commonly heard ones which I have quoted. Today Zorrilla's Don Juan has practically the same power over the imagination of the Spanish male, at least certain males, that he did when he first appeared in 1844.

What changes did Zorrilla introduce to account for the popularity of his hero? Well, the setting remains much the same but the time has been advanced from the indiscriminate fourteenth century to the heroic 1550s, when Carlos V was king and Spain was on the move. In the play there is a sense of Spain's new greatness and some of this rubs off on Don Juan.

This time the curtain rises on an inn in Sevilla, where Don Juan sits writing a letter to his intended bride, Doña Inés, on whom he has not set eyes, since according to custom she has been hidden away as a novice in a convent. He is masked, for it is carnival, and is awaiting the arrival of his friend Don Luis Mejía, with whom he made a wager a year ago 'as to which could commit in a year more evil.' This is the night for casting up accounts. Unexpectedly Don Juan's father and the Comendador de Cala-trava, father of Doña Inés, arrive separately, also masked, and take chairs in a side room so as to overhear what this disreputable young man is up to. Don Luis appears; the bettors unmask; and they proceed to report on their behavior. Don Juan says that he chose Italy as his theater of operations and in Rome fixed the following notice to his door:

> Here is Don Juan Tenorio,
> For anyone who seeks anything of him.

When forced to flee from Rome because of his evil reputation, he repaired to Naples, where he posted another sign:

> Here is Don Juan Tenorio
> And there is no man his equal.
> From the haughty princess
> to the lowly fisherwoman
> all women are fair prey;
> and he will undertake anything
> if it involves gold or valor.
> Let troublemakers seek him out;
> let gamblers crowd around him;
> let anyone who dares come forth
> to see if anyone can best him
> in gaming, dueling or making love.

When his extended list of accomplishments is compared with that of Don Luis, it is seen that Don Juan has won, with thirty-two men murdered in duels and seventy-two women seduced. Don Luis admits himself the loser but points out that Don Juan's list lacks one type of seduction to make it strictly first-class, that of a novice about to take vows as a nun. Don Juan leaps at the challenge and says that for good measure he'll add an additional category, the intended bride of some good friend. Don Luis proposes a time limit of twenty days, but Don Juan says that six will be sufficient, because he does not require much time per woman:

> One to make love to them,
> another to enjoy them,
> another to get rid of them,
> two to replace them,
> and an hour to forget them.

With supreme arrogance he climaxes his boast with the announcement that the bride whom he will ravish shall be none other than Doña Ana, Don Luis' betrothed. At this dreadful statement the two men in the side room have heard enough. The comendador, convinced that his intended son-in-law is a monster, announces that Don Juan's engagement to Doña

Inés is ended, whereupon Don Juan says that the novice he must seduce shall be Doña Inés. At this blasphemy his father disowns him with the words, 'You were never my son.'

Don Juan succeeds both in seducing the novice, Doña Inés, and the bride, Doña Ana, but at his country house, to which he has taken the former, he discovers that she is madly in love with him, in spite of his treatment of her; overcome by her pure innocence, he awakens to the fact that he loves her. His change of heart comes to nothing because at this moment the comendador and Don Luis Mejía break in, seeking satisfaction for their injured honor. Don Juan kneels before the comendador, begs his forgivenness, and tries to convince him that he is a new man, but to no avail. When the comendador seeks to engage Don Juan in an honorable duel, the latter whips out a pistol unexpectedly and shoots the old man dead. He then kills Don Luis, too, and escapes to continue his rampage of destruction. He has proved false to his love, whom he has seduced and abandoned, to his father, whom he ridicules, to his religion, which he has debased, and to every generous impulse save bravery alone.

What can a foreigner make of a nation which elects such a man its national hero? Before trying to explain we must look at the surprising conclusion of Zorrilla's play. Years later Don Juan returns to Sevilla to visit his family home but finds it converted into a cemetery, one corner of which is a mausoleum in which a sculptor is at work putting finishing touches to a group of life-sized statues representing the victims of Don Juan. To the latter's surprise, he notices among the dead a beautiful standing statue of Doña Inés and he learns that she died of a broken heart. When the sculptor has left, the don addresses the effigy of his lost love and confesses that he did truly love her. Overcome with grief, he leans weeping upon her tomb, and when he opens his eyes he finds that her statue has disappeared from its pedestal. In a dream sequence the ghost of Doña Inés appears and tells him that since she has chosen to remain faithful to her satanic lover, God has condemned her to the purgatory of her tomb to await the return of Don Juan, both of them to be saved or lost together. Don Juan dismisses her appearance as an illusion and his old bravado reasserts itself. As in the Tirso play, he invites the statue of the comendador to dine with him; subsequently he dines with the statue in the cemetery. Again the statue offers its hand, and Don Juan feels himself pulled down toward hell. 'Lord, have mercy on me,' he cries, but the statue replies stonily, 'It is too late.' But now Doña Inés takes a hand in the proceedings, and the stage directions for the final scenes explain better than the dialogue what is happening:

> *Don Juan falls on his knees, stretching toward heaven the hand that the statue leaves free. Shades and skeletons are about to throw themselves upon him, but at this moment the tomb of Doña Inés opens and she appears, taking the hand which the don stretches upward.*

Flowers open and little angels issue forth, surrounding Doña Inés and Don Juan, scattering over them petals and perfume, and to the sound of a sweet and distant music the scene is diffused with the light of dawn. Doña Inés falls on a bed of flowers instead of in her tomb, which disappears.

Don Juan falls at the feet of Doña Inés and both die, but from their mouths issue their souls, in the form of two bright flames, which disappear in space as music plays and the curtain falls.

This Mercy of God and the Apotheosis of Love, as the last act is subtitled, can be quite moving if well staged and if no one laughs; it has made the play acceptable to believing churchgoers in spite of Don Juan's execrable list of crimes in the first two-thirds of the play. *Tenorio* thus becomes a sardonic morality play, demonstrating the doctrine that even the most flagrant advocate of Viva yo can attain salvation. In fact, God seems to approve of Don Juan and, through him, of Spain as well. Also, the engaging figure of Doña Inés—and she can be one of the most appealing heroines in drama—as she saves the rakehell through the purity of her love, is attractive to women. I have seen the play four times in Spain, twice in Mexico and twice on television, and each time as it ended the women around me were crying. A friend once explained, 'Every Spanish woman sees herself in Doña Inés. By her love alone is her husband saved.'

One of the reasons why *Don Juan Tenorio* is so popular is accidental and relates to cemeteries. Because Zorrilla introduced in his concluding scenes a mausoleum containing marble statues of the don's victims, a tradition was established for Spanish cities to offer *Don Juan Tenorio* in the week of November 1, the eve of All Souls' Day, which is the Spanish Memorial Day, when families traditionally visit cemeteries. This aspect of the play's acceptance is of course irrelevant and childish.

But Zorrilla's *Don Juan* is much more than an accidental cemetery prank. To understand the strange grip it has on the Spanish audience one must remember what was happening in Spain when it appeared. It was 1844, a time of chaos, when knowing men already suspected that Spain was in permanent eclipse. The empire was falling apart; the internal government was inept; the economy had failed; the storms of liberalism and conservatism were beginning to rip the country; and here came a figure who recalled the days of glory when Spain ruled Europe. (Remember that numerically most of Don Juan's adventures took place in Italy, not Spain, and those of Don Luis in Flanders, along with Germany and France.) He was a kind of challenge to the rest of the world, the brave, arrogant man who would surrender to no adversary. He was Spain entrapped; he was Spain fighting against great odds; and in the end he was saved, partly because of his tremendous intransigence.

Don Juan is also the exemplification of male values in Spanish life. From what I have said of his career one might suspect that Spanish women would hold him in contempt, but that is far from the case. He is their hero as much as he is the hero of their husbands and sons. His love scenes are never gross; he woos with tremendous passion and with a poetry that explodes in symbols and verbal fancies; he is no cruel Bluebeard but a devoted lover; that is, during those two days that he can allot a woman. He is also manly in a general sense, quick with the sword, swift to resent insult and brave beyond challenge. On stage he is enormously attractive; Enrique Guitart, one of the actors who specialize in portraying him, wears a large variety of brocaded capes, which he has learned to flourish in beautiful sculptured circles much as a matador does when fighting a bull, although better because the stage capes are bigger and their flourishes more unexpected, cutting wide swaths of astonishment.

Finally, say the critics, Don Juan is more than a man, more than a hero. He is all humanity, and like humanity he seeks ideal solutions. He is not chasing women; he is seeking the perfect woman. He is not a cowardly murderer; he is mankind faced with the inescapable responsibility to kill in warfare. And in the culminating scenes of apotheosis he becomes all guilty men throwing themselves on the benevolence of God and finding themselves saved because of their submission to the female principle of love. All these things Spain believes of herself; redemption is possible. I spoke a few paragraphs ago of how I have seen women weep during the scene in which Doña Inés rescues Don Juan; I have seen just as many men weep in an earlier scene in which Tenorio, learning for the first time that Doña Inés died after he stole her from the convent and abandoned her, utters a heartbreaking sob and acknowledges that he did truly love this girl. 'At this moment,' a friend explained, 'each man in the audience remembers all the pretty girls he kissed years ago and didn't marry, and the passage of time and the closeness of death become very real.' My friend had tears in his eyes as he spoke. Without question, this strange and poorly written play evokes in the Spaniard a memory of Spain and of lost opportunities.

My own interpretation of Zorrilla's play is that it epitomizes the union of pundonor and Viva yo. At a dozen places Don Juan affirms the principle of pundonor. In defense of his peculiar definition of honor he would die, kill his best friend, duel his closest associates, challenge the marble statue or oppose God. He is almost a burlesque of pundonor, but not quite, because both he and the audience take his challenges seriously. At the same time he is the epitome of Viva yo. No other national hero is so self-centered as Tenorio. Faust is concerned about human values and is hesitant about ignoring the rights of others until Mephistopheles goads him to do so. Hamlet constantly weighs the good and evil which his actions might impose on others: the king praying, the queen's right to remarry, Ophelia's future. Don Juan Tenorio indulges in no such soul-searching, not even when it is forced upon him by his father, whom he spurns abusively.

And this makes him attractive to the Spaniard, who feels the same way about his country. The visitor to Spain is often shocked by the fact that what he holds to be a cause for condemnation is judged by the Spaniard to be a cause for congratulation. Later when I speak of Queen Isabel the Catholic, I shall make it clear that I find her one of the notable women rulers of all time, probably greater even than Elizabeth of England, but I have always regretted two acts which tarnish her reputation: her sponsorship of the Spanish Inquisition and her expulsion of the Jews. I was surprised to find that Spaniards are apt to love her *because* of those reasons: 'She showed the rest of the world that she was boss and that Spain was Spain.'

Before ending this adventure in romanticism run wild I must point out that among young Spaniards the cult of Don Juan is being subjected to analysis and sometimes to ridicule. One newspaper in 1966 asked its readers whether Don Juan still existed in Spain: 'Yes, and in today's world he's contemptible.' 'Sure, in the cinemas. He's masquerading as James Bond.' 'Of course, in the Spanish gallants who swarm the beach at Torremolinos, trying to seduce Swedish girls.' 'Yes, the gamberros [hoodlums] and the ye-ye crowd [rock-and-rollers].' It was generally agreed that Don Juan was hanging on, especially in small towns, where men took seriously their obligation to be lady killers. 'He exists in every real Spanish man. We all dream we are brave, honorable and death to ladies.' But one young woman warned, 'I've got news for Don Juan. He may exist but girls like Doña Inés are no more. I don't know any girl who's going to swoon because some man looks at her.' Another girl said, 'Doña Inés is still around but today she's comical.'

If one were preparing for a visit to Spain it would be profitable to learn the language; it would be more so to see a performance of *Don Juan Tenorio*, for with mere words one can go only so far, but with the vocabulary of this play one can speak of central matters. To prowl the streets of Sevilla with Don Juan in cloak and poignard is to explore permanent Spain.

Even if Sevilla had no Don Juan and no feria, it would still throw down a unique challenge. Outwardly it strikes the visitor as a congenial place, but inwardly it permits no stranger to penetrate its secrets. It is not a city of contrasts; it is a city of contradictions, enticing but withdrawn, alluring but arrogant, modern in appearance but eighteenth century in attitude. In Madrid or Barcelona the stranger has some hope of forming friendships which will uncover something of the workings of Spanish life, but in Sevilla this happens so infrequently as to constitute a miracle when it does. The symbol of Sevilla is the caseta, brightly illuminated and with its front wall removed so that the passer-by can observe the festivity of a

FOLLOWING FACING PAGES: *During feria the young women of Sevilla appear at their most seductive. And always in the background, iron bars of tradition.*

closely knit family group. If he is lucky enough to own a horse, he can even rely on a traditional sherry if he stops outside. But to enter the caseta and to participate in the mystery that surrounds the family of southern Spain seems almost impossible.

Sevilla is a feminine city, as compared to masculine Madrid and Barcelona, but if one finds here the ingratiating femininity of grillwork on balconies and grace in small public squares, one finds also the forbidding femininity of a testy old dowager set in her preferences and self-satisfied in her behavior. It is not by accident that Sevilla has always been most loyal to movements that in the rest of Spain are in decline.

For example, at repeated points in history Sevilla has been faithful to the crown when other cities have not; the symbol of Sevilla is the rubric NO-8-DO, in which what looks to be an 8 is really a skein (madeja), so that the whole reads: 'No madejado' (She has not abandoned me), referring to a time when a king in trouble appealed to Sevilla for help. The city also adheres to an older interpretation of religion and to feudalism. As we have seen, in the countryside surrounding Sevilla the relation of noble to peasant is much the same as it was in England in 1400. Laws of course proclaim otherwise, but custom prevails.

Sevilla is ancient and as a city of importance nearly two thousand years older than Madrid. It was an important Roman center, and near its present site stand the excavated ruins of a considerable city named Itálica. But Roman occupation of the area left little imprint on Sevilla, although Sevilla made considerable impression on Rome, having contributed two of the principal Caesars, Hadrian and Trajan. Sevilla was also a major capital of the Moors, having been occupied by them in one capacity or another for 536 years, yet today one finds in the city even fewer of the Muslim memories that make Córdoba and Granada such noble testaments to the Moorish influence in Spanish history. Even the graceful Giralda has had its Moorish origin submerged in Christian additions, while in the nave of the massive cathedral the Moorish pillars are lost in heavy Gothic shadows. Whenever a conqueror departed, Sevilla quickly reestablished itself as a Spanish city, jealous of its prerogatives and marvelously insular in its attitudes. If one seeks a whole body of people who have refused to acknowledge the advent of change, few can compare with the citizens of Sevilla.

Of all the cities involved in the Spanish Civil War, Sevilla was modified least by the experience; the governors required only a few hours to make up their minds as to which side they were on, and after an initial slaughter of six thousand, took over the place for General Franco and his troops. Avoiding the agonizing indecision that paralyzed and even doomed other cities, the people of Sevilla almost avoided the war. Little of moment happened here and the return to peace was accomplished more quickly than in any other city of comparable size. To Americans, whether from

north or south, Sevilla is of special interest because although the colonies
of Spain were conquered by Extremadura, they were governed from Sevilla; the cargoes of gold from Peru and Mexico were brought up the
Guadalquivir to the docks where the bullring now stands, and the nobles
who were to rule the distant lands either well or poorly sailed with their
commissions from this port. Scholars have long believed that one day the
inexhaustible depositories of Sevilla will produce hitherto unknown documents relating to the early history of the Americas, and they expect maps
to be uncovered which will alter our present understandings, for to Sevilla
came reports from all parts of the world. Here also centered the branches
of the Church dealing with America and the administrative cadres, both
civil and military, responsible for the actual governing. Sevilla might
properly be termed the historic capital of the Americas; during some three
centuries it was the nerve center which controlled all.

If a stranger could inspect but one city in Spain and if he wished to
acquire therefrom a reasonable comprehension of what the nation as a
whole was like, I think he would be well advised to spend his time in
Sevilla, for this city, even though it is too individualistic to be called a
microcosm of the whole, is nevertheless a good introduction to classical
Spanish life. I was familiar with the rest of Spain before I saw Sevilla, but
nothing I had learned elsewhere taught me so much about Spanish behavior. Others have reported a similar experience, for Sevilla does not have
ambiente; it is ambiente, and nowhere has this been better expressed than
in a lyric by Manuel Machado, written in this century, which is quoted
constantly throughout Spain. It is a litany of Andalusian names, each
described with its most typical appositives except one, for which no adjectives or nouns suffice:

> Cádiz, salada claridad,
> Granada, agua oculta que llora.
> Romana y mora, Córdoba callada,
> Málaga, cantaora,
> Almería, dorada.
> Plateado Jaén.
> Huelva, la orilla de las tres caravelas.
> Y Sevilla.

(Cádiz, salt-laden brilliance/ Granada, hidden waters that weep/ Roman
and Moorish, silent Córdoba/ Málaga, flamenco singer/ Almería the
golden/ Silvery Jaén/ Huelva, the shore of the three caravels [of Colum-
bus]/ And Sevilla.)

No part of the spring feria was more enchanting to me than the way
it ended. As dawn breaks following the last night of the fair, or perhaps at
six or even at seven o'clock, when there is no longer any hope of encoun-
tering late revelers, and when the sound of clapping has finally died out in

Time and tradition pass very slowly. It is the people who age rapidly.

the streets, drivers of horse-drawn cabs assemble informally at the southern edge of the city. There, from whatever bottles of wine they have
reserved for this moment, they drink together and stare back at the
outlines of Sevilla as it becomes visible in the morning twilight. Then they
climb onto their seats, whip their horses gently and begin a single-file trek
to the south.

Here comes a carriage with arms blazoned across the door. Behind it
moves a pair of white horses pulling a cab which today bears no paying

passengers but only the driver, his wife and their three children, all five sleeping as the horses jog slowly homeward. Here come two more cabs with their drivers asleep, for many of the cabbies have not been to bed for more than a week; during the fair cabs are busy twenty-four hours a day. In quick succession three businesslike cabs pull out of line and overtake the others, for their drivers hope to gain additional fares by reaching home before nightfall. And at intervals one sees highly polished carriages being driven by boys not much older than ten or eleven; the rightful drivers have gone south by bus so as to get in a full day's work at some regular job, leaving the cabs to be brought home by their sons.

For fifty miles this extraordinary parade stretches out, a hundred carriages or more, so that if you travel this day along the eastern edge of Las Marismas you will see fine vehicles all the way to Jerez de la Frontera and even on toward Cádiz. For these are shrewd men whose ancestors learned more than a hundred years ago that if a driver can somehow get his carriage to Sevilla during the fair he can pick up a good deal of money from the excess of strangers who crowd the city at that time. It is worth making a drive of sixty miles or more each way to qualify for a chance at this money, and now the cabs are heading home.

If any reader should want to see the feria for himself, he'd better hurry. On my last day in Sevilla I asked Señor Ybarra, whose ancestor had revived the fair in 1847, if there was any truth in the rumor that the fair grounds had been sold for industrial buildings, which would mean the end of the circuses, the carnival and the casetas, and he said, 'We've been told that the land has been sold. It's economically impossible to keep so much land near the center of the city lying idle eleven and a half months a year so that people can ride horseback for one week. But don't worry. Plans are under way to move the whole thing out to the river lands where the horse fair is now held.'

I cannot imagine Sevilla in the spring with a fair so far away that I could not easily walk to it. I cannot imagine the nights without groups of people passing beneath my window on their way home. I am sure the new fair will be approved by many, but not by me.

FOLLOWING PAGE:
La zarzuela.

VII

MADRID

From the first moment when as a boy I read of Spain, and in high school when I studied my first Spanish short stories, and even in college when reading simplified novels, one corner of Spain always preempted my affection, as during recent centuries it preempted the affection of Spaniards. Poets wrote verses about this part of Madrid; novelists laid some of their most powerful scenes within sight of its buildings; painters depicted it at various times of day; and on frequent occasions the ordinary people of Spain erupted into its confines to launch either protest or revolution. Scenes of the most dreadful savagery had occurred here, but scenes of compassion and love were not uncommon.

It was appropriate that the first literary work I read in Spanish was *El capitán Veneno* (Captain Poison, 1881) by Pedro Antonio de Alarcón (1833–1891), in which a gruff and surly captain is wounded in one of the frequent uprisings of the time and thereafter takes refuge in the house of an impoverished woman and daughter who live in the vicinity of the Puerta del Sol.

Gate of the Sun! Eastern Gate of Madrid, from which road distances in Spain are measured. Beloved of Madrileños for centuries and focus of their life in a way that the popular squares of other European capitals could not equal. I was a young man filled with unrealistic visions of Spain when I first saw it, and from an inconsequential hotel which stood nearby I began those quiet explorations and investigations which brought my preconceptions of Spain into some kind of harmony with the facts. I could have wished little better for myself than the experience of seeing the Puerta del Sol as I did in the days before its significance began to decline as sharply as it has done in the past thirty years. Then it was a summary of the Spanish history of the nineteenth century, preserved like a museum

into the twentieth, and to wander in its surroundings was to walk intimately in the alleys, if not the grand halls, of Spanish memory.

What was the Puerta del Sol? In my day there was no portal or gate as
such, although in earlier centuries there must have been. There was,
however, an intimate plaza shaped somewhat like a half-circle, around
whose curved side stood a collection of sturdy, symmetrical beige buildings
of almost classical charm. Along the flat side stood government buildings
of some sort, but these never attracted my attention. A total of ten streets
debouched into the plaza, which explained how, in time of riot, it could so
swiftly fill with people. The Puerta itself contained no shops that interested me, but in the warren of streets and twisting alleys which fanned out
from it were some of the most enticing businesses in Spain. Here one could
find almost anything he desired and, as we shall see later, almost any kind
of restaurant.

How utterly lovely the Puerta del Sol was in those days, how exciting
for a foreign tourist! This word has come into ill repute in recent years,
because so many tourists have gone abroad with no preparation which
would enable them to appreciate what they were about to see and no
humility to make them approach the country on its own terms. In Spain I
have always been a tourist and have been rather proud of that fact. This is
the book of a tourist and the experiences described herein are those which
are open to any intelligent traveler. If, as I once heard an Englishman say,
'to be a tourist is to stand gape-eyed with love,' I have been one, and never
more so than in my first days in the Puerta del Sol.

Because I wanted to stay as close to the heart of Madrid as possible, I
took a room in the old Hotel París on the Calle de Alcalá, a room as dark
and confined as any I have ever stayed in. There was no reason why a
sensible young man would remain in such a room a minute longer than
necessary, for my lone window looked into a ventilation chute and the
bathroom was so far down the hall that I could not luxuriate in the tub. It
was rather like the bunk on a submarine, a place which one uses only
when in a state of utter exhaustion. Thus I was thrown into the Puerta del
Sol for as long as I could walk and then into the public rooms of the Hotel
París when I had to rest.

In the plaza I met wonderful people who enjoyed talking with a
norteamericano. In the hotel I met considerate men and women who
wanted to be sure that I saw the best in Madrid. 'Have you been to the
military museum?' they would ask, or, 'Have you tried the seafood restaurant in the Calle de los Cuchilleros [Cutlers]?' And they talked with me,
abiding my poor Spanish but recognizing my enthusiasm. It was with
strangers from this hotel lounging room that I first saw the Prado Museum
and stood 'gape-eyed' at the plethora of greatness it contained. It was with
a family that was bored with its room as small as mine that I went to the
Teatro de la Zarzuela to resume my study of what I had liked so much at

the theater in Castellón de la Plana. With these congenial strangers I saw the parks, the boulevards, the bars of the grand hotels and the music halls, but always we came back to the Puerta del Sol, that magic plaza along whose edge the trolley cars ran to all parts of the city. In my travels I have sometimes been disappointed in sights which publicity has built up; at other times I have been surprised by the excellence of things I had not previously heard about; but I believe the most pleasant experience is to find something like the Puerta del Sol which is exactly the way the poets, historians, novelists and musical composers have said it was. Now, of course, it is much diminished; the burgeoning growth of Madrid has dragged the center of the city to other quarters and the tourist will no longer find in the Puerta what I found there. I went down the other day and it looked much like an open square in New York or Mexico City and it was difficult to believe that this was the spot which had had so strong an effect upon me years ago. The Hotel París still stands and in its rooms travelers with small funds still stare at ventilation shafts, but the glory of the Puerta del Sol is dimmed.

The same can be said, I think, of that really noble area that stands just off the Puerta del Sol, the Plaza Mayor, a huge thing rimmed with classical buildings and massive stone arcades. A rather fine equestrian statue in the middle of the plaza carries a plaque which summarizes the history of the place:

QUEEN ISABEL II, AT THE REQUEST

OF THE GOVERNMENT OF MADRID, ORDERED

TO BE PLACED ON THIS SITE THIS STATUE OF

KING FELIPE III

SON OF THIS TOWN, WHO RETURNED THE COURT

TO IT IN 1606 AND IN 1619 CONSTRUCTED THIS

PLAZA MAYOR

1848

An eighteenth-century engraving shows the great plaza prepared for a bullfight in which four mounted noblemen were to participate, and the caption, written at the time, states that 'the Plaza Mayor on this day showed seven hundred balconies and contained fifty-two thousand spectators.'

The plaza is linked, in the minds of those who read Spanish history, with Spain's most unfortunate king, Carlos II (1661–1700), known as El Hechizado (The Bewitched) because of his twisted and incompetent body and mind to match. He was the last of the Spanish Habsburgs and the inheritor of all their weaknesses; a substantial case could be made that he was insane, but he reigned from the age of three, and it was his childless death that brought the Borbón rulers to the Spanish throne and the war of the Spanish succession to Europe.

When Carlos was eighteen he caused much excitement at court by finally expressing an interest in something. Overhearing that the Inquisition's jails in outlying districts were crowded with heretics whom the judges had found guilty but had not yet burned, he announced that it was his pleasure to hold in the Plaza Mayor a sumptuous auto-da-fé at which a hundred and twenty condemned would be brought forth for sentencing. With real excitement the slack-jawed monarch organized a spectacle of which the English historian John Langdon-Davies has said, 'There can be no denying that the show staged on June 30th, 1680, in the Plaza Mayor of Madrid, must have been one of the most dramatic, the most moving, conceived by the mind of man since the days when Christians and wild beasts fought one another for the amusement of decadent Rome.' Carlos spent a month formulating the complex ritual for the exhibition and running through a series of dress rehearsals. On the day itself fourteen uninterrupted hours were spent preaching at the heretics and reading their sentences, after which one hundred and one were dismissed with lesser sentences, like flogging or a term in the galleys, while the remaining nineteen were prepared for the stake.

It is not my intention to recite the details of this grisly day; anyone wishing to know what was entailed in an auto-da-fé—for some curious reason this particularly Spanish institution has always been known in English in its Portuguese spelling, instead of the Spanish auto de fé (act of faith)—should consult Langdon-Davies' *Carlos, The King Who Would Not Die* (1962). I am more interested in that author's researches as to how the king who had organized this spectacle for his personal edification had become the way he was, and what Langdon-Davies has to say on this subject throws much light both on Spanish history and on the decline of the Habsburgs.

Spain had had two crazy queens. The second we have already met, lying in state in the mausoleum in Granada, Juana la Loca (1479–1555). The first was her grandmother, Isabel of Portugal (c. 1430–1496), whom we shall meet more fully in the next chapter. It was through these two unfortunate women that the madness of the Spanish Habsburgs was transmitted; had their offspring married outside the family it is highly probable that the faulty strain would have been submerged. Instead, look at what happened to produce a near-idiot like Carlos II:

> A man's ancestors in the third, fourth and fifth generations comprise eight, sixteen and thirty-two relationships respectively. Thus Carlos' parents, like everyone else, each had fifty-six such relationships in their family trees, or one hundred and twelve between them.
>
> These one hundred and twelve relationships in their case were shared between only thirty-eight individuals. Of Carlos' mother's fifty-six ancestors,

The Rastro, Sunday morning.

forty-eight were also ancestors of his father. Of the thirty-two women in the fifth generation, that is the sixteen of one parent and sixteen of the other, twelve were descendants of mad Isabel of Portugal.

In the two family trees the name of Juana la Loca occurs eight times, the names of her two sons nineteen times. Seven out of the eight great-grandparents of Carlos II descended from Juana la Loca. No wonder he was bewitched.

Today the Plaza Mayor is a vast empty area in which little happens. The many balconies still lend the place an architectural charm, but even when I first knew it the predominant echoes were tragic, for history has passed it by and it is only in the lesser streets surrounding it that the life of Madrid moves with its old vigor. I first became aware of this one Sunday morning when I saw large numbers of people leaving the Puerta del Sol and heading for what I supposed was the Plaza Mayor, but I was wrong, for they passed right by this empty square and sought another set of streets leading to a narrow plaza watched over by a heroic statue of Eloy Gonzalo, a bearded soldier who had conducted himself with glory in the Spanish-American war in Cuba. What stretched out at the foot of the statue was something that was difficult to believe. Thousands upon thousands of people had convened, as they did each Sunday, to see what bargains they could pick up in the junk stalls of the Rastro (Slaughter-house), and I was later to discover that no traveler can feel like a real Madrileño unless he can announce at dinner or when entertaining friends, 'You must see the wonderful purchase I made in the Rastro last Sunday.' Some of my friends have furnished their whole apartments from hand-some odds and ends acquired in this way; one man bought in June six bronze candlesticks, each seven feet high, for three hundred dollars and sold them in August to a New York antique dealer for three thousand. Renaissance pictures, empty Coca-Cola bottles, antique needlepoint, Chevrolet carburetors, Roman coins, damaged Goya etchings and positively anything a human being could want or which in normal circumstances he would throw away can be found in this amazing market. It operates in diminished size the rest of the week, of course, but the Sunday outpouring is something to see.

And so in my early visits to Madrid I stayed at the Puerta del Sol, wandered in the Plaza Mayor, absorbing history, and refreshed myself with the mobs in the Rastro. When I had saved a few pesetas I followed the advice of a gentleman I had met at the Hotel París and took my meals in either of those two fine restaurants that lie just off the Plaza Mayor, Botín's dating back to 1725 and The Caves of Luis Candelas, a rambling affair named in honor of Spain's Robin Hood, who was a great favorite in Madrid. When I first encountered them these restaurants were well known; now they are world-famous and worthy of their reputation.

In 1966, as I approached Madrid once again as a tourist, intending a long stay during which I hoped to clarify my ideas about Spanish politics, I began to reflect upon the changes whose development I had observed during the last fifteen years, and I think the city will be more meaningful if I describe it in terms of those changes, which any tourist could have noticed.

In a sense no visitor can ever be adequately prepared to judge a foreign city, let alone an entire nation; the best he can do is to observe with sympathy. But certain recent experiences had qualified me to look upon Spanish life with better than average understanding. Spain was a theocracy, and I had lived in Israel and Pakistan, which were also theocracies, and the problems of such governments tend to be the same, whether the theocracy is Jewish, Muslim or Catholic. Spain was also a dictatorship, and I had recently come from the Soviet Union and could compare what happened in Spain's relatively relaxed tyranny with what happened in a hard dictatorship like Russia's. 'We no longer have a dictadura, a dictatorship,' a Spaniard told me, 'but rather a dictablanda, a bland dictatorship.' And what was most instructive, I had known Japan, and it, like Spain, was feudal, ritualistic, devoted to honor and committed to maintaining a closed society. In fact, I found Spain to be the Japan of Europe, and at many points I was able to fathom the incomprehensibility of Spain only because I had first met the similar incomprehensibility of Japan.

In 1950 Madrid was one of the most delightful world capitals to visit, for then I could debark at the airport, ride quietly along beautiful streets to the center of town and choose at will from some twenty good hotels, where I would be welcomed; *now* Madrid is grotesquely overcrowded so far as tourists are concerned and I have learned to steer clear unless I have confirmed reservations. In 1963 I could not find hotel space, but that was understandable because I had come in May, when the fair of San Isidro was under way. In October of 1964, when nothing was under way, I was absolutely unable to find a room in any hotel and had to scrounge around among my friends. In May of 1965 I invited an American to stay with me in Madrid, and all the services of the air line, the police and my friends could not find him accommodation. He had to sleep on a cot in a hallway. And in September of 1966, in the real off-season, I could find not one hotel room, and it was only when Don Ignacio Herguete, whom we met in Trujillo, interceded that something was provided.

Then Madrid had one of the most charming trolley-car systems in Europe, and on it I wandered through the various sections of the city, watching as people of various types clambered aboard to argue with the conductor. Getting about the city was not only easy but positively pleasant, for Madrid had the characteristics of an overgrown country town, with unexpected nooks at the end of each trolley ride; *now* the trolleys have largely vanished and I have to go by subway or cab, and no other city has so miserable a taxi system. There are not enough cabs; they do not serve the proper centers; and they will not respond to phone calls. After the theater, or a bullfight, or a football game or dining out one must wait forty or fifty minutes to catch a cab, and even then he must walk eight or ten blocks to reach a point where cabs will stop. At least five times on each trip to Madrid I swear, 'I'll never come back to this city . . . the humiliation is too great.' The government is aware of the problem but can do nothing about it, for reasons which have been explained to me but which I cannot understand.

Then Madrid was a compact city of one million, six hundred thousand; *now* it is a sprawling metropolis of more than two and a quarter million.

Then its buildings looked as if they were at least two centuries old; *now* the new growth startles me whenever I have been away as long as six months.

Then Madrid was a city of little traffic, for cars were few; *now* it is a perpetual traffic jam, not yet as bad as Florence or Nice but bound to get worse because within ten years the number of cars will double.

Then Madrid was a puritan city, with police watching for any display of modern life such as short dresses on women, or hand-holding between lovers or flashy dress on men, and the crackdown could be embarrassing. I saw English women thrown out of churches because their bare elbows showed, and German men visiting the Mediterranean beaches were arrested for not wearing tops with their swimming trunks; *now* the city is like a delightful garden in which young people in love kiss openly, girls wear pretty much what they want, and the only women who bother about covering their heads when visiting churches are self-conscious American Protestants. It is difficult to believe the transformation that has occurred in less than a decade.

Then if an American woman traveling alone wished to eat in a restaurant at night, even inside her own hotel, the head waiter would place before her a small American flag to warn the Spanish dandies that this one was not a prostitute, even though she was eating alone in public; *now* women frequent cafés alone, a thing quite impossible even five years ago. I was in one of the famous bars when unattended women began to appear, and one would have thought the roof had suddenly collapsed, but in late 1966 it was not uncommon for business girls to meet in threes and fours after work to drink beer.

Then on church doors across Spain appeared notices, which were taken seriously, warning females against wearing anything but skirts, and these of a dignified length; *now* minifaldas (miniskirts) and slacks are popular.

Then young people had few places to go; *now* it is quite different. On

This modern mother and daughter run a fashionable boutique.

my last trip I stopped for dinner in what had once been a fairly good Chinese restaurant and was shocked to find in every booth a young couple locked in a public embrace. The owner no longer ran the place as a restaurant because he could earn more with less work running it as a cock-tail bar for young people who worked. When I asked about this, a friend told me, 'But all those girls still have to be home by nine o'clock. A lot of Spanish families are discovering to their amazement that girls can become pregnant between seven and nine in the evening, as well as between one and three in the morning.'

Then Madrid was a dark city with few street lights; *now* it is a lovely place in the early evening, brimming with light. The Avenida José Antonio is one of the most pleasant I know and its fountains are a joy. I have lived at one time or another in about six different parts of the city and they were not only varied but also charming. This is a city of much beauty.

Then prices for things like men's suits, women's gloves, leather goods and Spanish-style jewelry were low and represented the best buys in Europe; *now* there are no bargains, but quality is good and what you pay for you get.

Then there were few elevators, and if you wanted to do business with the average Spanish company, you had to climb, climb, climb; *now* each new building has its elevator, and sometimes it works.

Then the newspapers of Madrid were the worst one could read in any major capital, so fantastically bad that it would be painful to describe them. I happened to be in Spain during three different international crises and from the available newspapers I could obtain no logical or sequential news. Imagine how impossible it was to discover anything about Spain itself. Once I brought home with me three sample Madrid dailies to prove to my unbelieving friends how awful they were. The front page usually had a bombastic picture of Generalísimo Franco dedicating a dam. The second page carried a sentimental essay by some hack professor about how Cervantes represented the soul of Spain. The third contained an article on Bishop So-and-So and his belief that Spanish women, when they attend church regularly, are the noblest in the world. On the fourth page appeared a selection of news items ingenious in their ability to say nothing. I remember two complete items. 'Today General Eisenhower made a star-tling change in his cabinet.' 'General de Gaulle announced today that from here on the French government will pursue a different policy regarding Algeria. The general said that the old policy has not succeeded.' On the following days there was no development of the story and no attempt was made to explain why Eisenhower had shifted his cabinet or what France's new policy was to be. The last three pages provided as good sports coverage as I could have found in London or New York. *Now* the Madrid newspa-pers have escaped somewhat from the heavy hand that held them down, and from them I can get a sensible idea of what is happening in the world.

During one American election there were extensive analyses of the senatorial race in Illinois, the influence of Robert McNamara on national policy and the shifting popularity of President Johnson as the Viet Nam war intensified. I could find out almost anything I wanted to know except what was happening in Spain. Although censorship of Spanish news had not been relaxed, a salient difference between the Spain of two decades ago and now is the improvement of the newspapers.

Then television was nonexistent; *now* it dominates Spanish life and most of the Madrid homes I visited had a set. Since American shows are popular, magazines regularly offer articles such as 'What Was the Real Eliot Ness Like?'

Then Madrid was a fairy-tale city in which one rarely dined before eleven at night and could go to the theater for the second show at one . . . in the morning, not the afternoon. There was an infectious charm about long afternoons in which luncheon was served at four if anyone was in a hurry, at five if not, and no one acquainted with Madrid in those indolent days will ever forget the gracious city; *now*, although the eleven o'clock dinner is still popular, one can eat at nine or even earlier, and the theater begins at ten.

Then wine was the drink; *now* beer is popular.

Then anything like a cafeteria would have been an insult to the Spanish way of life. A few were attempted but they were derided as American abominations; *now* grab-and-run restaurants are not only popular but essential, because the noontime break in offices is being shortened from three hours to two or even one. The most popular medium-priced restaurants in Madrid today are chrome-brightened places with names like California, Nebraska, Iowa and Samoa, the American name having become an asset rather than a liability. 'You can trust such places to serve good food, clean food and quick food,' a Spanish secretary told me as she had a hot dog while I had gazpacho.

The biggest social differences between then and now is the radical change effected by what a Spanish man called 'the revolution of the Sueca.' I had better let a Madrid businessman explain: 'I'm not joking when I say that the Sueca has had an effect in Spain somewhat greater than the atomic bomb on those atolls in the Pacific. We had been taught for centuries that any woman who allowed a man to touch her before marriage, and I mean touch literally and not as a euphemism for sexual intercourse, was damned. Society was rigid and allowed no deviations from the central rule. Life was hard and anyone who transgressed was doomed. It was what you call in the United States puritanism, but much stronger than yours because our whole society supported it. Then came the Swedish girls, Suecas we call them, young, blond, laughing, the most beautiful girls in motion anywhere. Of course, there were also Finns and Norwegians and Danes and Germans, but we link them all together as the

Suecas. They discovered Spain and flocked down here by the planeload. Their first impact was on the beaches, and once they stripped down to their bikinis and we saw what the human body could be, the old laws simply could not be enforced. You couldn't tell a Spanish man he had to wear a top with his trunks when those damned Suecas were on the beach. He wanted them to see his pectorals.

'Well, the first result of the Sueca invasion was cataclysmic. I can't tell you what a thrill swept over the manhood of Spain when they discovered that such girls were on our beaches looking for sun . . . and romance. In the old days the proudest boast of a Madrid dandy used to be "I know a bullfighter" or "I'm having an affair with an actress." Now it's "I have a Sueca down at Torremolinos." To have a Sueca as your mistress, tall and leggy and blond, is the best thing that can happen to a man these days. I know half a dozen of my friends who have Suecas, and their lives have blossomed like lilac bushes in spring.

'Take this fellow Agapito. A very conservative vice-president of a bank here in Madrid. When I visited Torremolinos, here comes Agapito dressed in old blue dungarees, with a tattoo on his arm, a ring in his ear and a beard. I say, "Agapito! What the hell has happened?" and he says, "Sssssssh! I dress this way every vacation and tell the Suecas I'm a sailor from Alicante. They think it's romantic and I'm doing better than ever." I asked him, "But, Agapito, what do you do when your vacation ends?" and he said, "I throw a party at a restaurant and tell everyone sadly that my ship is sailing from Alicante and I must be off. They cry. I cry. Then I drive to the next town and shave my beard and come back to Madrid." You know what I think, Michener? I think that one of these days some Sueca is going to go into his bank to cash a traveler's check and there's going to be hell to pay.'

This gentleman also told me that the Sueca invasion has yielded two unexpected results. 'It's been rather hard on the traditional Spanish gallant to whom courtship is a series of set positions, as it were. In church he stares at the girl. At the grille he sighs deeply. In the cinema he is allowed to hold her hand for three minutes . . . each show. He has his set speeches, arranged in order of passion, and these he delivers on schedule over a six-month period. It's all been set out for him by custom and if he omits even one step the girl feels he isn't properly ardent. Imagine what happens when such a system runs up against a Sueca who has paid a lot of money to get to Torremolinos, has a limited vacation and doesn't have much time to waste. When our Spanish gallant starts to go into his set act she's liable to say, "Sure, where?" I've seen a lot of Spanish men completely thrown over by such a response. They don't know what to do. They're unnerved and they run away.

Although Madrid is the youngest city we shall visit,
its Retiro Park, with its stone royalty,
has a classic beauty.

'But a more lasting effect has been the psychological. As I said, we've been taught that if a girl allowed a man to touch her, she was proscribed, but we see the Suecas come down, live with men, have a marvelous time and go home as good as they were when they arrived. In my group the enlightenment came when we saw in a newspaper that Birgit So-and-So, whom we had all known at Torremolinos, had married a Swedish official. One of my friends yelled, "But I used to sleep with her!" What he meant was that if a girl had slept with a man she was condemned. But here was this Sueca marrying an important man. It didn't seem fair. But slowly the Suecas have revolutionized our thinking. Not all the world needs to live the way we do in Spain. I cannot begin to tell you how profound this revolution has become. Its effects will be greater, in the long run, than those of the labor unions.'

He then added an interesting afterthought. 'It has many ramifications. Especially regarding you norteamericanos. We see your beautiful girls at our university here, or visiting the military bases. And we see that they are as free sexually as the Suecas. It's fun for us and we have some great times. But then the nagging question comes up. "Should we respect the norteamericano for his manufacturing, his successful democracy, his rich way of life . . . if he can't even protect the honor of his own daughters?"' I asked him if he thought the Spanish way was better, and he said, 'In the long run, yes. Women should not appear in bikinis at Torremolinos. Or stay out at night the way your girls do in Madrid. Women should be kept closely guarded at home.' Then he looked wistfully across the avenue and said, 'But the Suecas have ruined all that. Because our women have begun to study the Suecas too.'

One aspect of Madrid remains unchanged, then or now, the Prado. This collection of paintings has such a plethora of riches that I know travelers who plan any trip to Europe in such a way as to have a couple of days in Madrid, not to see the city but to stroll once more through this forest of masterpieces. If I want to see eight top paintings, I go to Venice. If I want to see eighty, I come to the Prado.

I was therefore excited as I walked down the avenue one morning in 1965 and saw this stalwart, unimaginative building waiting. The miniskirts, the traffic, the restaurants might change, but the Prado remained permanent and unique. It is a family museum, most of its paintings having been acquired because some specific king or queen loved art and bought a specific painting. Here there was no buying of already assembled collections formed in Paris or London, the way the Romanovs gathered the paintings in Leningrad's Hermitage. Here there was no robbing of museums in cities defeated in war, the way Napoleon robbed to fill the Louvre in Paris. The Prado began as a private collection formed for the most part by the people of one continuous family, at first Spanish, then Habsburg, finally Borbón, and it was never enriched by theft or expropriation. From 1492, when Queen Isabel I the Catholic was making her first cautious purchases, to 1868, when Isabel II of Borbón ended her reign, the pictures were bought one by one, and what we see today are the family heirlooms of this extraordinary sequence of rulers.

Of course, when the Prado was opened as a public museum other Spaniards contributed pictures, and some were very good, but essentially the museum reflects the taste of Habsburg and Borbón.

Among the royal donors, three kings stand out. Carlos V regarded Titian (1477–1576) as the best painter in Europe and commissioned several portraits. In the best of these the emperor appears in full armor astride a black horse caparisoned in purple. In a stormy landscape the setting sun illuminates the small, bearded king as he appeared during the notable victory of Spanish forces over German at the battle of Mühlberg in 1547.

The second of the great collectors was Carlos' son, Felipe II, whose portrait by Titian shows him as a young, intense and capable man. Felipe was known as an ascetic, yet if one segregates the paintings he brought into Spain one finds that he was responsible for the glowing nudes of Titian and Rubens (1577–1640); he also added the wonderful sex-filled paintings by Hieronymus Bosch (c. 1450–1516) to the collection and other lush canvases from Venice and Brussels.

The third of the master collectors is as familiar to us in appearance as one of our own family, for Felipe IV, grandson of Felipe II, was painted numerous times by Velázquez (1599–1660) on horseback, or standing in lace ruffles, or half-length in austere black, or even as seen in a mirror while having his portrait painted. This king stares back at us with heavy-lidded eyes, huge curling mustache and that enormous chin which characterized the Habsburgs. His family is also known to us through many Velázquez portraits: his two wives, his handsome son and above all his adorable little daughter.

The relationship between Felipe and Velázquez was one of the most rewarding in art history, for not only did the royal family provide the artist with some of his finest subjects, but Felipe also commissioned Velázquez to travel in Europe and buy paintings on his behalf. Twice he toured the continent, and many of the choice works in the Prado are there because in riding back and forth between Italian cities he came upon canvases which he thought the king might like.

Today the royal collections are housed in a dark and handsome building located in the center of Madrid. The Prado was originally built in 1787 as a natural history museum but in 1814 was converted for its present use. I had hoped that I might see it in company with Señor Don Francisco Javier Sánchez Cantón, who has been associated with it for many decades and has been responsible for its catalogue. Museum people in other countries hold him in high regard, but each time I reported to his office he was engaged elsewhere, so I missed meeting him, but his secretary provided me with a guide who in many ways was even better, because with Sánchez Cantón, I would have seen merely paintings; with José María Muguruza, I saw everything else.

He was a tall, scholarly Spaniard in his mid-sixties, outspoken and enthusiastic. In the circular tower room which he used for his office he said, 'Everybody knows me because of my brother. A really great architect. He did lots of the buildings Spain is proud of and I suppose I got my job because of him. He died young, you know. I'm an architect in charge of the Prado and you might like to see some of the crazy things we've been doing.'

I said, 'I'm familiar with the changes. The new wings, the way you've converted empty courtyards into new exhibition rooms.'

'Those things are nothing!' Muguruza said. 'Are you game for some real excitement?' I said I was, and he grabbed a cane which he would use for pointing out details of what had taken place. 'From the outside does the museum look any different from when you first saw it?' I shook my head. 'But from the inside! That's a different story!'

I did not know what he was talking about, for as I had said, the inside changes had been no different from what take place in any good museum, but what I was about to see was unique. Dr. Muguruza led me up a steep flight of stairs, then another and another, until we stood on the roof of the old building. There, in Madrid sunlight, he said, 'In the building below us,' and he kicked on the roof, 'we have a collection of paintings which are beyond value. What would they bring? Supposing they could be sold? A billion dollars, two billion? And if they were lost, the damage to the human spirit would be incalculable. So we couldn't risk keeping them in an old building put up a hundred and seventy years ago.'

'That's where they still are,' I said.

'That's where you think they are. Come inside and see.' He led me to a crawl space under the roof and showed me how the vaulted ceiling of the old museum had been left intact, as had the roof on which we had been standing, but between them had been inserted a steel-and-concrete shell nearly a foot thick and invisible from either within or without. The old vertical walls had also been left as they were, and the exhibition walls on which the pictures were hung, but between them new walls of steel and concrete had been inserted.

'We never closed the museum one day,' Muguruza said. 'Working quietly, where no one could see us, we built a concrete cocoon which encloses every area. We have made the museum as fireproof and as burglarproof as possible, because you can't get into it without penetrating this cocoon.'

I could scarcely believe that this transformation had taken place during the years that I had known the Prado. How had the massive girders and the tons of concrete been slipped into position? 'We were satisfied to work slowly,' Muguruza said. He jumped up and down on one of the mammoth concrete vaults and asked, 'What do you suppose is below us right now?' I didn't know, and he said, 'Room XII,' and I visualized that finest single room of the world's museums, a room whose twenty-six paintings represented one of the chief treasures of history.

'Jump up and down on it,' Dr. Muguruza cried, and I did so. The concrete shell did not even reverberate, but I felt uncomfortable jumping on top of Room XII of the Prado.

When I climbed down from the roof and studied the museum from street level I could find no mark that betrayed its renovation, and I reflected that much of modern Spain was like this, heavily reconstructed but with few external marks showing, because the comfortable old appearances had been retained.

How good is the Prado collection? Because of the personal manner in which it was assembled, it has to be uneven. Since the kings of Spain considered Dutch painting plebeian because it portrayed scenes of everyday life, the Prado has practically no Dutch school, and since they cared little for English painting, none were there until a few years ago when a New Yorker who had grown to love the museum unexpectedly gave a Gainsborough and a Lawrence, which look quite out of place. The French school is poorly represented, with no moderns at all, and several of the major Italian schools are ignored. In comprehensiveness the Prado does not begin to compare with great collections like those in the national galleries of London and Washington.

But where it is strong, it has no equal. Thanks to Carlos and Felipe it has the world's top collection of Titians. One room alone contains sixteen prime works by the Venetian, a staggering collection of portraits, religious subjects and nudes. As if that were not enough, in the next room hang eleven more, each good enough to be a major item in an ordinary museum, and in the storeroom hide an additional dozen!

Equally rich is the Rubens collection. In room after room the visitor finds those choice canvases crowded with nudes with which he has been familiar for years without realizing that they were all in Madrid.

That we can still enjoy these nudes of Titian and Rubens is something of a miracle, for although they were among the favorites of the early kings, by the later they were judged scandalous, and toward the end of the eighteenth century were condemned to be burned. Plans were made to destroy every nude in the collection, but in 1792 a group of men, at considerable risk to themselves, hid the offending pictures in a back room of a lesser museum, where they stayed unseen for more than thirty years until it was safe to bring them forth again.

The museum contains many Italian masterpieces. Raphael's (1483–1570) 'Portrait of an Unidentified Cardinal' is here, staring at us coldly from beneath his red hat; scholars have suggested seven different churchmen as the possible sitter, but he remains a mystery. Here also is Paolo Veronese's (1528–1588) radiant little jewel, 'The Finding of Moses,' probably the best painting this polished artist ever did.

My favorite among the Italians is Correggio's (1494–1534) exquisite 'Noli Me Tangere' (Touch Me Not), about as fine a work as the late Italian school produced, for the figure of Christ with arms extended has the quality of supreme religious painting, while the Magdalene in her rich brocade represents humanity at its most enchanting. The landscape, showing as it does the hour of dawn, is faultlessly done and all parts combine to make a most gratifying work.

One of the surprises of the Prado is a series of small rooms on the second floor, so unpretentious that many visitors miss them. Here are displayed the Flemish and German paintings collected by Felipe II and his contemporaries, and to understand the work of these schools one simply must visit the Prado. Two works easiest to grasp are the powerful self-portrait by Albrecht Dürer (1471–1528) and the exquisite little blue painting by Gerard David (c. 1450–1523) showing the Holy Family resting on its way to Egypt. It is one of the purest of paintings, a jewel perfect in all parts.

The picture here that no one should miss is, of course, Hieronymus Bosch's 'Garden of Delights,' in which the precursor of surrealism presents a teeming canvas flanked by two wings in which the delights of sensuality are portrayed with heavy but not offensive emphasis on sex. The central panel is divided into three parts: at the top a lake on which fantastic pleasure boats appear and over whose rivers nightmare bridges rise; in the middle a pool in which lovers swim and around which ecstatic couples parade on all kinds of beasts, including unicorns, griffins and camels; at the bottom a bewildering maze of persons engaged in various delights, such as lovers entrapped in a giant clamshell, dancers whose heads unite to form an owl and a pair surrounded by an evanescent soap bubble.

The curious thing about the 'Garden of Delights' is that it was a favorite picture of Felipe II, and we know that it occupied a place of honor in his palace, but this particular Bosch is only one of several in the Prado, for the more the men of Felipe's time brooded over religious matters, the more they appreciated these lusty pictures from the north.

The most important picture in the Flemish section, however, is of quite a different kind. Many critics have held it to be one of the four or five most significant paintings in the world, and I know two experts who deem it the best canvas ever painted. It is of particular interest to anyone visiting the Prado, for it illustrates better than words can explain the peculiar quality of this collection.

Early in his life Felipe II heard that in a small chapel in Louvain, dedicated to the Confraternity of Crossbowmen, there stood an altarpiece by Roger van der Weyden (1400?–1464) depicting the body of Christ being lowered from the cross. Visitors familiar with the marvelous painting reported to Felipe, 'It is the greatest of the north.' In vain the king tried to buy it, and when this proved impossible he sent a court painter to copy it, and with the copy he was content for several decades. Later his aunt, the Queen of Hungary, succeeded in acquiring the painting for her collection, and remembering how much her nephew desired it, gave it to him as a present.

In the depiction of the ten differentiated figures, in their placement, in the use of color, design and space, and above all in the symbolization of religious emotion, this marvelous stark painting is one of the major accomplishments of western culture. The best painting in the world? That is too strong. One of the four or five best? Without question.

The lasting glory of the Prado lies, however, not in these importations from foreign lands but in paintings from the Spanish school. In this field the Prado has no equal or even any close competitor.

Leave the Flemish rooms and walk down the long corridor housing the works of the Spanish school, and see for yourself the incredible richness of this collection. To take only one example, near the rotunda you will find not one elegant Murillo (1617–1682), 'Immaculate Conception,' with Mary, surrounded by angels, standing on the defeated crescent of Islam, but three separate versions. The third and finest has a strange history: when Napoleon conquered Spain in 1808 to place his brother Joseph on the throne, his general in command of the invasion, Marshal Soult, packed up this Murillo and hauled it back to Paris with him, where it found a home in the Louvre. More than a hundred years later, in 1941, the Franco government in Spain arranged a deal with the Vichy government in France whereby the Soult Murillo was returned to Madrid in exchange for a Velázquez which went to the Louvre, whereupon certain Spanish art critics said, 'To trade a Velázquez for a third copy of a Murillo! We Spaniards must be crazy!' A kinder judgment would be that the Soult Madonna is superior to the other two versions, and to have three such Murillos together in one spot, while other museums have none, demonstrates how lucky the Prado is where Spanish painting is concerned.

Leading off from the Murillos is the long, specially lighted room on whose ceiling I had been jumping. It is known simply as Room XII and has no equal in other museums. Many travelers who schedule their trips so as to see the Prado come only to see this room.

It contains twenty-six paintings by Velázquez, works so varied and magnificent that of themselves they comprise a museum. One Spanish guidebook says bluntly, 'In this room and those nearby hang all the best Velázquez paintings in existence.' Certainly, if one wants to understand this master he must come to Room XII.

I have spent so many hours here that they must add up to days or even weeks, and even yet I don't know how to view it properly. First, of course, one looks at the huge 'Lancers' on the end wall, a painting, like Rembrandt's 'Night Watch' in Amsterdam, so complete that one either perceives its majesty at once or misses it. Words cannot help. There it is, a mammoth canvas overflowing with vitality and perfection, and some people are content to spend their time with it, ignoring the other paintings.

I prefer, however, that series of three powerful canvases in which Velázquez portrays ordinary Spanish life: the weavers, the blacksmiths, the winebibbers. Any one of these paintings, given a room to itself in some museum in London or New York, would be the gem of the collection, but in Room XII it is merely one among twenty-six.

Most visitors to the Velázquez room stand a long time before the two portraits of a young prince named Baltasar Carlos, for these are two of the most engaging and tragic child portraits ever painted. They are engaging because in the first we see him at the age of four or five, dressed as a knight astride a pudgy brown pony set in an idealized landscape. In the second we see him at the age of six—the canvas tells us that was his age—posing as a hunter, cap awry, attended by two brilliantly painted dogs.

The pictures are tragic because of what happened to Baltasar Carlos. The son of Felipe IV, he was a handsome child, apparently intelligent, and Spain was relieved to know that the throne one day would pass into his hands. As he matured he became even more attractive, and Velázquez painted him at various ages, showing him finally as a young fellow of sober bearing with a conspicuous Habsburg chin. But from fifteen on, the young heir fell into debauchery, from which at seventeen he died. The throne passed into the hands of his near-idiot half brother, whom we saw at the auto-da-fé of 1680, Carlos the Bewitched, and the Spanish Habsburgs were doomed.

Women visitors to Room XII linger before the graceful portrait of a little girl, Velázquez's personal favorite, the Princess Margarita, who would grow up to marry the Emperor of Austria. Velázquez painted her many times; several European museums contain versions showing her standing in extremely wide dresses made of lace and satin, and in a moment we shall see that his masterwork also focused on her. By all accounts the little princess was a charmer who matured into a responsible empress, but like her brother Baltasar Carlos, she died prematurely, at the age of twenty-two. That Velázquez loved her strange mixture of imperial dignity and childish charm there can be no doubt.

Some years ago a group of art experts in Florence became irritated by the publicity given the fact that Rembrandt's 'Aristotle Contemplating the Bust of Homer' had sold for $2,300,000, and they issued a statement estimating that the famous first room of the Uffizi, with its three versions of the Virgin enthroned by Cimabue, Duccio and Giotto, would bring $25,000,000 if offered at auction. What would the contents of the Prado

Room XII bring? For the 'Lancers' I suppose a bid of $5,000,000 would be only an opener. For any one of the three genre scenes the price would have to be around four or five million. For the great portraits? I suppose the final figure for the room would be well above $80,000,000, which was one reason why I was somewhat apprehensive about jumping on it.

In an isolated room not far from Room XII hangs in solitary majesty a Velázquez which has attracted attention since the day it was finished. On a special plaque set into the wall nearby, the curators of the Prado describe it as 'The culminating work of universal painting.' It is 'Las Meninas' (The Maids of Honor) and it unfolds on many planes, one behind the other. Six conspicuous ones are, first, a lifelike dog; second, little Princess Margarita attended by her maids of honor and a well-known dwarf; third, Velázquez standing back from his easel on which he is painting a picture which we cannot see; fourth, a man and woman observing the scene; fifth, a wall containing a mirror in which we see that Velázquez is painting the portrait of Margarita's father and mother, Felipe IV and Queen Mariana; sixth, seen through a doorway, a flight of stairs up which a chamberlain is walking.

The picture is unbelievably complex, a kind of exercise in dexterity that only an established painter would attempt in order to prove that he could do it. The various planes are indicated by perspective, the interplay of light and dark, and a clever use of colors. The figures are well done and breathe vitality, but the essential mystery of this work lies outside such considerations. It is a moment of family life caught in suspension, and the groups represented are as real today as when Velázquez painted them.

For visitors interested in modern painting, that is to say the work of artists like Cézanne, Manet and Van Gogh, two small pictures in one of the lesser Velázquez rooms attract most attention. These two unimportant landscapes show the gardens of the Villa de' Medici in Rome and were done on one of Velázquez's scouting expeditions to Italy. The first landscape appears finished and shows simply the façade of a wall of some kind, tall cypresses, a hedge and two male figures. The second, and more important, shows a comparable scene except that the wall is replaced by an archway beyond which rocks and landscape can be seen. Three male figures populate this picture, which might seem unfinished except that this was the way Velázquez intended it.

It is an extraordinary work. It could have been done by any of the modern artists mentioned above, or by Renoir or Pissarro. The subtle brushwork, the spare use of color, the impressionistic drawing and the manner in which space and planes are indicated combine to make this small canvas one of the gems of the collection. It speaks directly from the age of Velázquez to the present, reminding us that all artists face similar problems.

As one would expect, the Prado contains superior works by a host of other important Spanish artists like Ribera (1588–1652), Zurbarán (1598–1664) and El Greco (1541–1614), but it is the paintings by Goya (1746–1828) that astonish. So rich is the museum in works by this artist that a major room on the second floor is given over to them, plus a series of rooms on the first. In the former is found that intriguing pair of portraits which we discussed when visiting the Coto Donaña, 'Maja desnuda' and 'Maja vestida.'

It is in the downstairs rooms that Goya's work seems most impressive, for only here can one see this virile, tough artist at his best: his etchings on the horrors of war, the bullfight series, the famous black paintings. Here also are those exquisite scenes of picnics and parties in the outskirts of Madrid, and the little landscapes that seem to be from another artist, so delicate and poetic are they.

The most famous of the Goyas are those showing the brutality of life, and none excels 'The Third of May,' in which soldiers are shooting down unarmed citizens against a leaden sky showing the spires of a nearby town. This powerful work might almost be termed a summary of Goya's social philosophy, but it is also a masterful work of art.

Concerning the black Goyas, I am embarrassed. On my first visit to the Prado, years ago, I was repelled by this series of fourteen gloomy works in which dark paint predominates. I had not heard of them before and was unprepared for their power. On my second and third visits I also failed to appreciate them, but then I read an essay by Dr. Sánchez Cantón (this was one of the things I had wanted to speak with him about) and I began to understand why experts praised these works so highly; today a painting in comparable style, 'El Coloso o El Pánico,' has become one of my favorite Goyas. It shows a brooding landscape with turbulent sky, a low mountain range flecked by purple clouds, and a valley down which cattle and covered wagons and people are fleeing in obvious panic, driven onward by a terrifying apparition. At the head of the valley, his legs hidden behind the mountains, rises a colossal nude figure, bearded and with enormous arms which he brandishes boxer-style. He is thousands of feet high and is obviously infuriated by some unseen thing which has attacked him. With one hand he could crush all the fleeing people. The total scene is so bizarre and the flight so headlong that the picture remains a masterpiece of terror, as psychologically bewildering as it is artistically exciting.

There are many such Goyas in the Prado, some so revolting as to repel the average viewer, but when one is surfeited with them he finds a small painting, perhaps the last that Goya did, a beautiful work in grays and blues depicting the young French woman who used to deliver milk to his home when he was living at Bordeaux. It was painted, the signature states, when Goya was eighty-one, and like the 'Medici Gardens' of Velázquez seems as modern as any work by Cézanne or Renoir. It is a marvelous thing, a true portrait of one real milkmaid, yet an evocation of all the women Goya loved throughout his life.

Whenever I visit the Prado I am tantalized by the fact that in 1870, during a troubled period, some dozen top-quality Goyas were stolen from the museum. They have never been recovered, but Spanish experts believe they are in existence somewhere. So at any time some lucky seeker, rummaging through old stacks of paintings, may discover one of the missing Goyas and find himself half a million dollars richer.

I end each visit to the Prado by going to a remote room on the ground floor which houses a mysterious statue. It shows a young woman, handsome rather than beautiful, wearing a curious headdress, and was found in 1897 buried on a farm near Elche in eastern Spain. In some way that has not been explained to me it reached the Louvre, where it was recognized as a major work of art, probably the best statue ever carved in Spain, but remained unidentified. When was it carved? Not a clue, but it seems unquestionably old. Who carved it? Not a clue, but guesses have oscillated between a pre-Roman artist and a pre-Renaissance. Who is the woman? Not a clue, but she must have been a person of rank, for the headdress is extraordinary. The statue found its way back to Spain as part of that deal in which the Louvre traded its Soult Murillo for a Velázquez, and as the significance of this statue becomes recognized, critics begin to modify their earlier objections: 'It's still true that to swap a Velázquez for a Murillo is insanity, but if you get the Dama de Elche thrown in, it's not so bad.'

Present judgment inclines toward a theory that this enigmatic statue was carved by Iberians either a few centuries before Christ or a few after, and I have inclined toward the former, but I was startled by the most recent speculation: 'Probably not a woman at all. More likely a young king dressed in ritual battle gear.' When you're next in the Prado, judge for yourself. It will be worth the effort, for this is one of the world's most compelling statues.

In my wanderings about Madrid I kept running into a gentleman who intrigued me. I did not know who he was, but at the bullfights there he would be. In the cafés, at the theater, strolling along the promenades he appeared, always grave, bald, handsome. He looked like a Spanish Charles Boyer and conducted himself in the same courtly manner. He never seemed to make noise but he did exert an authority which was acknowledged by those who came within his circle. I often wondered who he was, for in his combination of studied dress and casual manner he seemed to me Madrid's essential man-about-town, and I knew I would enjoy meeting him.

I did so in a curious way. Front-row tickets for the special series of bullfights held in May were impossible to get, but a Spanish friend showed me how to butter up one of the attendants—fifty pesetas a day, whether anything happened or not—and this fellow would keep an eye on the front row and slip me into any seat left vacant. Some days it worked; some days it didn't; but at one important fight there were two seats vacant and I was summoned to one of them. The man who got the other was this gentleman I'd been seeing about the city.

'I am Manolo Torres,' he said quietly. So this was he, Madrid's legendary bon vivant, a man with a most unusual reputation. Everyone knew him. I'd read three or four long newspaper stories telling how he was held in affection by different strata of Madrid's society, but the thing that all remembered best was that he made flan (egg custard).

'I read about your flan,' I said.

He smiled with genteel embarrassment. 'I do most things poorly,' he said, 'but flan I make as only the angels do.'

It had become a custom in Madrid for Don Manolo to make up a large batch of his special flan each noontime, and there were many important figures who had developed the superstition of never making a significant decision before having had a good-luck flan with Don Manolo. Was a bullfighter flying to Mexico for six fights? Better share a flan with Don Manolo. Was the impresario opening a new musical comedy? Better ensure good reviews by taking a cup of Don Manolo's flan. Cartoonists, politicians, athletes and especially those in the theater relied on Don Manolo's magic, to bring them luck.

'How do you make it?' I asked between fights.

Don Manolo's face became ecstatic, one of the few times I was ever to see him betray enthusiasm. 'If when you return to América del Norte you wish to make true Spanish flan, proceed in this manner. In each of six molds put a spoonful of sugar and melt it over the fire until it covers the bottom and almost reaches the point of caramel. Take it off the fire. In a bowl beat three whole eggs and the yolks of three more. Grate some lemon rind. Mix one soup spoon of sugar, not too full, for each of the egg yolks, in this case six. Add milk sufficient to fill the molds, which you now put in the Mary's bath.'

'The what?'

'Baño de María. It means you don't put the molds directly against the heat but with their feet in water. And the flame mustn't be too strong. It should be low. When the mixture seems to have become like gelatin, that is, after about an hour, put the molds in the oven or even better in a little electric stove so you can brown the crust. Then move them to the refrigerator, but don't eat them until you have a guest who has a delicate palate. Estupendo!'

It was a strange thing. I came to know Don Manolo and also read a lot about him but never discovered what he did for a living. It was known that from the age of twenty-four he had gone to the theater every night save when kept in bed by illness. 'Cinema, opera, comedies, tragedies,' he said. 'It's been all the same to me. I am afflicted with the theater. But especially zarzuela.'

I caught my breath. Ever since that first night in Castellón de la Plana, when the man working the barges had taken me to the theater during feria and I had seen my first zarzuela, I had wanted to talk with

some expert who knew something of this unique musical form, but in all the years of casual inquiry in both Mexico and Spain, Don Manolo was the first I had met. It was not possible that day to speak with him as much as I would have wished, but later I was able to do so, and I will share his comments in a moment.

The Spanish zarzuela was one of four distinct yet comparable theatrical forms which grew up spontaneously during the last half of the nineteenth century, only to subside in the twentieth, and each seems to have arisen in response to a similar need, even though the four audiences voicing the need were dissimilar.

In England it was the evening of music-hall acts which developed, with its broad mixture of comedy, dance and song. In Vienna the same impulse gave birth to the operetta, which utilized the above three ingredients but added a story. In the United States the best we could do with these ingredients was the sui generis minstrel show. It was in Madrid that this type of popular art found its artistic apex in the zarzuela, which was a playlet, half spoken, half sung, with dancing, comedy and delightful music.

I have often tried to find the name of that first zarzuela I saw in Castellón, but with no luck. All I know is that it had a lasting effect. When the curtain opened and a costumed chorus sang about how pleasant it was to live in Madrid, I settled back for a typical evening of Viennese operetta, but soon a soprano sang an aria of startling dimension, and she was followed shortly by a contralto and a tenor who sang a duet that could have been written by Verdi. But just as quickly the chorus took over to chant something about taking a walk in the park, and I heard no more opera. In other words, in each of the best zarzuelas two or three operatic numbers will explode through the theater for several minutes, after which things subside to routine comedy or folk tragedy.

Most Americans who enjoy good music remain ignorant of the zarzuela, and that is a pity, because Spain today offers more than eighty different zarzuelas in recordings, including some in stereo if preferred. There are also a few records of high quality offering anthologies of choral numbers, the best duets or the best solos for various voices, and these are excellent. For example, if one heard fifteen or twenty of the best duets he would be confused as to their origin; they are equal in intensity, drama and vocalization to the best of Italian or French opera. It is difficult to convince Americans of this, but two summers ago when André Kostelanetz wanted to introduce some sparkle into his series with the New York Philharmonic he offered a soprano singing selections from *La revoltosa*, and the New York audience was delighted. The singers of zarzuela are also of top operatic quality. One year I heard Pilar Lorengar doing zarzuela in Madrid, the next year *Don Giovanni* in Tel Aviv. The tenor Alfredo Kraus has made a similar jump. Not long ago in a zarzuela in Toledo, I heard a soprano who was eligible for work in any opera house in Italy or Germany.

It is in the lack of scope and sustained musical narration that zarzuela suffers when compared to opera, and this deficiency takes some explaining. The composers demonstrated that they could write as good music as their competitors in other nations; the librettists often wrote better; and the performers were as good. I suppose it was the public that was defective, preferring the brief and incidental to the sustained and generic. There is also a noticeable lack of mature dramatic themes—all Donizetti and no Wagner—so that today the typical zarzuela seems as old-fashioned as an antimacassar.

'I like it that way!' Don Manolo says. 'I don't want some clever hack to update the jokes or to place the action in modern Barcelona. The zarzuela is nineteenth-century Madrid and its charm lies in its authenticity. Leave it alone.'

I asked him if he enjoyed zarzuela as much today as when he first saw it. 'Of course! It's engrained in my life. It's me and I respond to it.'

When I asked him what had arisen to take its place, since it was so dated, he became angry and said flatly, 'The zarzuela will never be replaced by anything. In its day it was Spain, and Spain is not replaceable.'

I pointed out that since zarzuela is not presented much any more, something must have taken over the theaters which it used to occupy. What did Don Manolo think of the modern revue? 'Please don't ask me even to attempt such a comparison. The real zarzuela was music, book, setting, a bite of real life. The revue? Beautiful girls and snappy jokes.'

I asked what it had been in the zarzuela that had pleased him most, the dramatic action or the music, and he said, 'There you have the secret. Zarzuela was a perfect blend of each, and any that were deficient in either have died out. I would, however, grant that even if they alter the words too much you can still enjoy the music.'

Then came the two questions which I had been wanting to ask someone for so long: What zarzuelas had he liked as a boy? And which of the old classics still had most life in them? Of those he had seen when he was beginning to attend the theater two stood out, *Molinos de viento* (Windmills) and *Los cadetes de la reina* (The Cadets of the Queen). I had not seen either, but judged from the titles that they had played in Don Manolo's growing up the role that *The Student Prince* had in mine, except that the music was better.

Of the classics, Don Manolo mentioned four which among them cover the main aspects of zarzuela. *La viejecita* (The Little Old Lady, 1897) represents about two-thirds of the plays in that it is merely a frothy entertainment which cannot be taken seriously except for the lilt of its music. In this case it is Brandon Thomas' *Charley's Aunt* (1892) set to music, and is a frolic because it calls for the hero, an infantry officer, to be played by a beautiful soprano so that later on she can masquerade as the old lady. Spanish theater has many roles in which actresses appear as men, to the delight of the audience; since Spain is so essentially a man's country and since the honor of manhood is so stressed, audiences find it refreshing to witness scenes in which mere girls can be better men than the pompous males. I am sure there must be something darkly Freudian about this, but when set to music it is fun.

La revoltosa (The Rebel, 1897) is typical of those zarzuelas which offer a cross section of life in the Madrid streets; of the dozen best zarzuelas, I suppose eight or nine deal with such subject matter, so that the zarzuela could properly be said to be a product of Madrid. This version deals with a high-spirited girl growing up in a Madrid semi-slum and with how she defends herself from the older men who bear down upon her while she tries to decide what to do with the young man who wants to marry her. Some of the music, especially the duet between Mari-Pepa and Felipe, is of high quality.

Gigantes y cabezudos (Giants and Big-headed Dwarfs, 1898) represents the zarzuelas which were not content to mimic Madrid life but which went afield to report on the local color of Spain's various regions. There are those who feel that when the zarzuela does so wander it loses quality, but this one is something quite special and lovely. A good translation of the title, since it refers to figures who appear during festival, might be something like *Halloween*. The action occurs in the northeastern city of Zaragoza, where an illiterate girl who works among the vendors in a marketplace receives letters from her soldier-lover in Cuba. A rascally sergeant from Andalucía makes believe that he too has received letters from her soldier and reads them to her, inventing a series of outrageous lies about the young man—he has married a girl overseas, he has been killed in battle—intending to win the girl for himself. The whole thing works out, of course, but what endeared this zarzuela to the Spanish public was the time and circumstance of its birth. It was the tragic year of 1898, when Spain's military, shot through with corruption, came face to face with a well-disciplined opponent at Manila Bay and Cuba. Suddenly the façade of Spanish life broke away to show the crumbling structure beneath, and the shock would never be forgotten. Symbolic of the trauma that jolted Spain was the fate that overtook the hero of the Cuban war, Eloy Gonzalo, whose statue we saw at the Rastro. After defying Yankee guns with rare bravado he died senselessly of malaria. In that doleful year the theatergoers of Madrid trooped out to see one more new zarzuela, *Gigantes y cabezudos*, and the first scene was the light comedy to which they were accustomed, but then came a brief entr'acte. The stage was empty save for a painted backdrop depicting the Río Ebro, behind which could be seen the outline of La Seo, Zaragoza's unique Moorish-looking cathedral. Onto a bridge came a group of soldiers straggling back from defeat in the New World. They stopped, looked at their beloved cathedral and sang.

Their words tore at the hearts of the befuddled audience, for they spoke of patriotism, love of home, fidelity to old beliefs. The zarzuela swept over Spain, and choruses everywhere sang this chant of the repatriated ones. I have seen it only twice, but when that entr'acte curtain falls, now old and dusty, and when the defeated soldiers reiterate their faith, something happens.

> At last I look upon you, famous Ebro—
> today you are wider and more beautiful.
> How I wondered if I would ever see you.
> After long absence, how happily I look upon you;
> only on your banks can I really breathe again.
> Once more I tread the soil of Zaragoza;
> there is the Seo and there the Pilar.
> For the fatherland I left you, woe is me,
> and with longing I always thought of you there.
> And today, mad with joy, ay madre mía, I am here.
> Very bitter waters are those of the sea;
> I learned the reason when I went away.
> So many sorrows sail over the sea that
> they make it bitter from so much weeping.
> Ay, my Aragonese maid, I have not forgotten you.
> I return to your side, full of faith,
> and I shall nevermore leave you.

The strange thing about this chorus is that the music, which falls into three parts, is as inventive as the words are moving. One naturally compares it with Gounod's 'Soldiers' Chorus,' from which it was probably copied, but the zarzuela is better. One feels that Gounod and his librettist said, 'Let's have a good chorus as the wooden soldiers come back.' In the Spanish version a group of defeated real men have come back to a specific city and the difference is tremendous.

By common consent, the masterpiece of zarzuela is a work bearing the curious three-part title *La verbena de la Paloma, o El boticario y las chulapas y celos mal reprimidos* (The Fiesta of the Virgin of the Dove, or The Apothecary and the Flashy Dames and Jealousy Ill-repressed, 1894). I do not find the word *chulapa* in any of my dictionaries; it is Madrid slang for tarts, hot numbers or, as I indicate, flashy dames. The genesis of this satisfying work helps explain why it is so loved by Madrileños.

There was a poet in Madrid who had such bad handwriting that when he wrote his zarzuelas the print shop sent him, by means of a young man who worked as typesetter, an extra set of galleys for his corrections, and on the Eve of the Virgin of the Dove this young man arrived at the poet's home in foul humor. When the latter asked what was wrong, the boy gave a distraught account of his love affair with a girl who was 'as precious as an ounce of gold,' except that she kept playing around with a dirty old apothecary who gave her such presents as a lace shawl and a silk dress. When the poet asked the young man what he proposed doing about it, the latter said, 'For one thing, I'm going to tear the verbena apart in a way they'll remember forever.'

The poet said later that on this clue alone he visualized a complete zarzuela, which he dashed off in the space of a few days, having the additional good luck to find a composer who inclined toward grand opera. At the first performance the audience realized that they were seeing the kind of work which comes along once in a generation. Curtain calls lasted for half an hour, and both the poet and the musician were carried through the streets till dawn. The excitement has not even now subsided, for *La verbena* is accidental perfection.

It is hardly what you might expect. The scene opens with a city character discussing aimlessly with a lecherous apothecary the merits of various laxatives: 'Castor oil isn't bad if you take it in capsules, but purgative lemonade isn't worth a damn.' Slowly, speaking a wonderful Madrileño argot, the various actors wander in, an untidy lot, some of whom appear only briefly. There is a haunting moment as a young singer advises the crowd that since she has no mother, do not look for her at home; her home is in the streets. Briefly a night watchman appears, almost too drunk to negotiate but willing to explain to two policemen the government's attitude on the social question. From within a building a disembodied voice summons the watchman with the name 'Francisco!' to which the latter reacts in a variety of ways, all to the most delicate night music. Belatedly the main action is set in motion by the apothecary, who is over seventy but who finds pleasure in keeping two girls simultaneously, one blonde, one brunette, and in scandalous song explains the advantages of doing so. The two girls appear and also Julián, the young man who loves the brunette. The girls' aunt is a bawdy old witch with a voice like a bullfrog which she exercises frequently. In desultory but enchanting action the zarzuela develops, broken frequently by songs bordering on opera, until the emotional climax is reached in an unexpected and natural way. Susana, the brunette, and Casta, the blonde, are on stage with their apothecary, and Julián, without looking at Susana, begins to sing softly:

JULIAN: Where are you going with Manila shawl?
              Where are you going with Chinese dress?
SUSANA: To show myself off, to see the fiesta,
              and afterwards home to bed.
JULIAN: And why didn't you come with me
              when I begged you to so much?
SUSANA: Because I'm going to assuage in the drug store
              all that you've made me suffer.
JULIAN: And who is this lad so handsome
              you're going to carouse around with later?
SUSANA: A fellow who has vergüenza, pundonor,
              and all a fellow needs to have.
JULIAN: And what if I just took a notion
              that you shouldn't go arm in arm with him?

SUSANA: Why, I'd go with him to the fiesta anyway
and then to the bulls at Carabanchel.
JULIAN: Oh, yeah?
SUSANA: Yeah.
JULIAN: Well, we'll see about that right now.

The words are sung to the hesitating music of youth; Julián becomes all young men bewildered by love, Susana is the timeless flirt, yet there is something typically Madrid about the duet. It is one of the highlights of the zarzuela, not pyrotechnical in its music but perfect in its style.

What happens? Nothing much you could put your finger on. Julián wrecks the verbena, is arrested, released on the pleas of his neighbors and wrecks the verbena all over again. The closing words of the zarzuela are uttered by a policeman: 'Ladies and gentlemen, please don't cause any further scenes at the Fiesta of the Dove.'

If one were to arrange in order of artistic merit the four popular forms that appeared at the end of the last century, it would be zarzuela, operetta, music hall and minstrel show, with little constructive to be said for the American entry. It is strange, therefore, that in spite of the zarzuela's excellence it has not traveled well to other countries. It has been too specifically Spanish, and sometimes too Madrileño, to be appreciated abroad, except of course in the Spanish countries of Latin America, where it still evokes a powerful nostalgia. It is not presented much in Spain any more, although most large cities will offer a short season now and then, but modern young Spaniards would no more think of bothering with zarzuela than American university students would with a minstrel show. On the other hand, zarzuela seems to have a vital life on records; from time to time on the good-music radio stations in America zarzuelas are played late at night, and if *La verbena* is offered it is worth staying up to hear.

In the years when zarzuela flourished, an attractive custom grew up in Madrid, which is still observed. In the narrow streets and alleys clustered throughout the district of the Teatro de la Zarzuela were small bars specializing in tapas (hors d'oeuvres) set before the public on long rows of dishes from which one more or less helped himself. Today on the Calle Echegaray, named after the dramatist who won the Nobel Prize in 1904 and whose brother wrote zarzuelas, a taxi can barely pass because of the crowds who come and go from the dozens of tapa bars.

There is a long bar behind which two men in traditional aprons serve cold beer and other drinks. Upon the bar have been arranged some two dozen open dishes crammed with a wild variety of tidbits tastefully arranged and accompanied by glasses of toothpicks, which are used to spear the goodies. The tapa place that I have frequented for many years offers dishes in four categories: first comes the seafood—the anchovies, eel, squid, octopus, herring, shrimp, salmon, five kinds of sardines, five kinds of fish; next come the boiled eggs, deviled eggs, egg salad, potato omelets cut in strips, vegetables, onions, salads; third are the cold meats in great variety, including meat balls, York ham, Serrano ham, tripe, brains, liver in a variety of styles, beef, pork and veal; and finally the hot dishes, which can be delicious. Shish kebab in hot sauce is good but I prefer mussels in a sauce of burned onions and clam broth, but there are five or six other kinds of shellfish which are about as good.

Tapa bars, so far as I am concerned, are divided into two groups, those that serve cocido Madrileño (Madrid stew) and those that don't. This is a heavy peasant concoction made of beans, flank beef, salted ham, sausage, onions, carrots, potatoes, kohlrabi and garlic, allowed to cook for days, with new ingredients thrown in from time to time. A good cocido, with hard bread and red wine, is a real Spanish dish.

The traditional way to enjoy the tapa bar, however, is not to sit down for a dish as formal as a cocido but to gather a group of friends and wander leisurely from one bar to the next, taking from each the one dish for which it is famous. In this area there is one bar that serves nothing but octopus and squid, prepared in various ways, and another that specializes in shellfish. One of the best known is a very small corner place called La Gaditana (The Girl from Cádiz), which advertises 'The largest restaurant in the world. You enter at Cádiz and leave at Barcelona,' those being the names of the streets which form the corner.

One aspect of the tapa bar frightened me. About half the dishes are bathed in a heavy, bright yellow mayonnaise that shimmies like gelatin when you put the spoon in. The finest shrimp, the best eggs, the fresh vegetable salad are drowned in this rich, inedible goo, but with care one can avoid it. However, if you dine with a Spaniard and he sees that your plate contains nothing but wholesome octopus, mussels and anchovies, he will insist upon slapping on a final gob of mayonnaise. Otherwise it wouldn't be a respectable tapa.

At my favorite bar one night a Spaniard who had learned to speak English while working the Venezuela oil fields suggested that I take in the jai alai at the frontón (court) where professional teams of Basques played this swift and exacting game. He was a nut, himself, and an ideal cicerone. 'Don't bother to come,' he warned, 'unless you enjoy gambling,' for the major purpose of jai alai is betting, and to see gambling run wild, one must attend a Madrid frontón.

'It starts with an act of sheer insanity,' my oil man explained. 'At the beginning six players appear on the court but the game is going to be two against two. So how to decide which two will play which two?' He took me to a large board containing the names of the six players and their numbers, from one to six. Bookmakers were taking a flurry of bets which I couldn't understand. 'Simple,' the oil man said. 'At this board we bet on what the composition of the teams is going to be. Suppose you buy that ticket for Team 4–6. It means that you are betting that one of the teams will be made up of Player 4 as captain and Player 6 as his mate. If it works out that 6 is captain and 4 is mate, you lose. As you can see, there are thirty possible teams, so the odds against guessing right are thirty to one, about the same as in roulette.'

'How do they determine what the teams are going to be?' I asked.

'Don't worry about that. Just pick three or four tickets here for the fun of it.' I chose Team 1–2 and Team 3–4 and Team 6–5. 'They're as good as anybody else's,' my oil man said, and we went inside to watch the six players warming up and I was amazed at their skill. Soon they began a round robin, with Player 1 taking the floor against 2 and holding it for as long as he continued to win, after which he gave way to player 3 or 4 or 5. A large scoreboard showed the names, which were part of the fun, long Basque words like Azurmendi, Urtasun, Azcarate and Yrigoyen, and whenever one of the players approached a score of five, excitement grew. Finally Player 2 accumulated five points, and a red star was placed against his name, signifying that he would be captain of the red team. Soon Player 4 scored five, and he was designated captain of the blue team.

At this point the round robin halted and we all trooped back to the gambling board. It was now known that the two teams would be 2 plus somebody and 4 plus somebody, but who their partners were to be would not be known till later. So bets were placed on the eight possible combinations, and since my first tickets had been proved worthless I switched to Teams 2–6 and 4–5. We went back to the arena, where the same six players went at it again. The scores made by 2 and 4 did not count, for they were assured of positions, but soon the excitement grew as the other four players approached scores of five. Finally the teams were decided, 2–5 red, 4–6 blue. I'd picked the right players but on the wrong teams, so once more my tickets were no good.

Now the game proper started and such bedlam I had not heard for years. Inside the screen and facing the audience stood nine husky men in official coats. Each carried a stock of tennis balls with one side cut away leaving a hollow, and as they brandished these balls they bellowed at the crowd, offering bets on the game between Teams 2–5 and 4–6. 'We better bet,' my guide said. He held up his hand, indicating by some signal that he wanted two bets on 2–5. One of the gamblers caught his eye, then looked about for someone who wanted to bet on 4–6. Pointing quickly to the two locations, he confirmed the bet, then wrote two receipts on government forms, stuffed them into two tennis balls, and with lightning accuracy pitched them long distances to the two bettors. The unit in this frontón was $6.40, of which the government took eighteen percent.

I now had my money riding on Team 2–5, but as play progressed toward the game point of 45, my team fell behind. Then the screaming of the gamblers increased, for they offered me a chance to copper my bet at attractive odds, and this I did, but my partner was contemptuous of hedging, so the further our team fell behind, the more vigorously he backed it at generous odds and soon was in a position to make some real money if Team 2–5 pulled itself together. Sure enough, our boys drew the score to 40–38 in favor of the other team and the excitement in our part of the frontón, at least, grew intense, but in the end Team 4–6 steadied and pulled away to a 45–41 victory.

At one o'clock in the morning the frontón was echoing with shouts, but then the games ended. 'Damn you norteamericanos,' my oil man growled. 'In the old days we used to play till three or four, but you've ruined it.'

'How can you blame us?'

'You've preached, "All Spaniards are lazy. They take a siesta." So the damned government wants to look modern. It's outlawed the siesta and everything has to shut down at one o'clock. Hardly worth living in Madrid any more.'

Soccer, known in Spain and the rest of the world as football, appears to be the kind of sport the Spanish government prefers to sponsor; it's international, it's modern, it's out-of-doors, and it's good for children, in that it can be played without expensive equipment. For a series of exciting years, Real Madrid proved itself to be the best football team in the world and Spaniards turned in large numbers to this frenzied sport.

I have often lived in countries that played soccer, but I have never become involved; however, during my last visit to Madrid the World Cup was being contested in London and no one who read a paper or listened to radio could escape being caught up in the frenzy. Spain beat Switzerland in one of the early rounds, and there was joy throughout the city, which closed down to watch on television, but she lost to Argentina and West Germany, and there was gloom. Shortly after, the local papers featured an incident which had occurred in Mogadiscio, the capital of Somalia, where the referee, one Salak Mobarek, made a wrong call against the Public Works team, which proceeded to kick him to death. The report said that because of this action, the Public Works team had to forfeit the game, a penalty which some of my football-playing friends considered vengeful. The Madrid papers went on to recall the number of times in recent years that referees had been killed, and since no plea was added to halt the violence, I concluded that the list was meant as a warning to the local men to watch their calls.

One beautiful moonlit night I went out to Madrid's Estadio Bernabéu to see what this madness was about, and long before I reached the approaches to the stadium I could see that a fair portion of Madrid's population was converging on that spot, for I was trapped in traffic that no longer moved. I finally had to leave my cab and walk about one mile, but it was worth it, because the stadium was one of those new affairs which one enters at street level to find himself halfway up the side of a long graceful

bowl set deep into the earth. The playing field was thus three flights below street level and the topmost seats about three flights above. It was huge, with something like a hundred and ten thousand seats. During the pre-game period it was illuminated by the moon and a group of soft lights, which converted the grassy area into a kind of silver, but as game time approached, four rows of lights around the stadium flashed on, and day-light enveloped the field and the grass turned green. It was the most beautiful stadium I had ever seen.

Barcelona was playing Madrid and the excitement was intense as the players ran onto the field, but as play progressed it grew. At some times all hundred and ten thousand spectators screamed at the referee, and armed police moved into position to repel those who might want to run onto the field. 'We behave better than they do in Brazil,' a Madrid fan assured me. 'There they've had to dig a moat between the stands and the playing field, so that the wild men can't rush the referee, even if they want to.'

Madrid was favored to win, but at the half the score stood Barcelona 1–Madrid 0. The crowd was disconsolate, but the man next to me said, 'Don't worry. Madrid is bound to win. This is the team that used to be world's champion. They have pundonor.'

Their vaunted pondonor did them no good when the second half opened, for Barcelona made a great sally at the goal and scored again, and the men around me groaned as if such a thing were indecent or unlawful. A moment later they were cheering wildly because the referee had disal-lowed the Barcelona goal on some technicality which no one could explain. I thought the decision was fishy and that it had come suspiciously late, and the next day the papers said the same thing. A statistical study had recently been made of Spanish football, proving what everyone had sus-pected, that a disgracefully high proportion of games was won by the home team, the theory being 'If the home team wins, nobody riots.' Tonight the referees seemed determined to prevent riots.

Soon thereafter, Madrid tied the score, then quickly made a second goal, but the referee was so embarrassed at having robbed Barcelona that now he did the same to Madrid. The man next to me really wanted to kill the swine, but a friend reminded him, 'They're supposed to even things out,' and the game ended Madrid 1–Barcelona 1.

Some time later I was in Córdoba when Madrid visited there, and in the days before the game one of the executives of the Córdoba team said in the local paper, 'The reason Córdoba has lost its last two games is that our fans have not been terrorizing the referees the way they do in Palma and Sevilla. Loyal fans are the twelfth man on the field. If you want us to beat Madrid, you must come out and scare the referee.' I attended that game, and the fans did their part. From the opening whistle to the last they created a bedlam, and although they may not have scared the referee, they did me. In the second half, when a bad call was made, a young man leaped from the stands, grabbed a camera from a newsman, rushed onto the field, and swinging the strap in a full circle, cracked the referee on the head with the camera and laid him out on the turf. The crowd applauded and apparently the official got the message, because Córdoba won.

The miracle of soccer as compared to American-style football is that the men who invented it came up with a game in which, because of the low scoring, ties are frequent. This means that if you bet on a game you must take into consideration three, not two, possibilities. Your team may win, or lose, or draw, and it would require a good man to predict accurately all the results of the fourteen games that appear each week on the betting list. The obvious wins and losses are easy, but what about those possible ties?

It is this unpredictable aspect of football that has made it such an ideal gambling game. Today all over Spain you see grubby little bare-window shops with the magic sign 1 X 2. It is to these shops that the people of Spain flock to mark their ballots for the slate of games to be played on the coming Sunday. Each ballot lists the fourteen games, eight from the first division, three from the northern section of the second division, three from the southern section, plus two reserve games to replace any of the scheduled ones that might be rained out or otherwise suspended. Alongside each game are the fascinating figures 1 X 2. If you circle the 1 it means you predict that the home team will win. Circle the 2 and you're betting on the visiting team. But circle X and you back a tie.

If you guess all fourteen correctly, and are the only one to do so, that week, you stand to win a fortune. The twenty-first Sunday in the 1964–65 season saw many upsets and only one man guessed them all, winning 15,364,075 pesetas (about $256,000), but that was exceptional. More typical were the results last year. There were thirty-nine betting days and 808,916,155 bets, of which only 19,129 gained top position, or one in every 42,000. On five of the days no one guessed all fourteen results, so naturally those who hit thirteen won. On one day of many upsets only two people won, and they got about $130,000 each, but on another day 3,836 did and won only $112 each.

Football betting is a mania in Spain and few are the homes with no addicts. Each year the newspapers carry agonized stories about some man who has studied the teams, made form sheets for the players, kept a record of which referees favor which teams and then gotten weather reports on the various playing fields before making out his list. With infinite care he has checked it, tried to anticipate where ties might fall and then decided on his fourteen outcomes. Where games are extra chancy he has bet a second and a third time, or even a twelfth, trying to cover all contingencies. He wins nothing. But his wife gets a first prize with fourteen correct. When asked what her system was she says, 'I took my list to the butcher's. He was cutting up bones, and every time he raised the cleaver I asked, "One, two or tie?" and he would whack the cleaver down and say, "One," or whatever came into his head. Fourteen times in a row his cleaver was right.' An amusing debate runs in the papers, 'Does It Help to Know Anything about Football?' and the consensus seems to be that too much knowledge inhibits freedom in spotting the ties. It is apparently better to wake up some morning and say, 'You know, I wouldn't be surprised if Barcelona ties Madrid.' Few Americans who have lived in Spain for any time have escaped infection: 'Let's throw a hundred pesetas in the pool to see if we come up with something.' Spoken like a Spaniard.

One fact about the pools astonished me. On those rare Sundays when no games are scheduled in Spain, the pool is based on some league in Italy that no one ever heard of and about which he can learn little. The betting is just as active as on a normal weekend and everyone seems to have about the same amount of fun.

I was able to resist the betting until I stumbled into the zany world of books written on the higher mathematics of the subject; then I became a sucker for each new theory and came home with half a dozen intricate systems based on permutations and combinations. I found there was a Norwegian system which would protect me against ties and an Italian system based on identifying a few sure wins, eliminating them and covering myself three ways on tricky games. Like thousands of Spaniards, I became fascinated by the pure mathematics of the thing; for example, supposing you are morally certain of the outcome of twelve games but have no clue as to how the other two will go. To cover yourself, you'd have to bet nine columns with the two dubious games marked thus:

Game A:	1 1 1	X X X	2 2 2
Game B:	1 X 2	1 X 2	1 X 2

If you did that, you couldn't lose. (If you are interested in either mathematics or gambling, draw up a table showing that to ensure yourself against all contingencies when eleven games are certain and three uncertain, you will have to bet twenty-seven columns.) Tables have been prepared whereby you can ensure yourself mathematically against any contingency, but the insurance is costly. For example, suppose you know the outcome of seven games, are completely confused about five and reasonably certain about the remaining two, you would bet the seven games in one column, the five confused games in three columns and the two chancy games in two columns, but to do this properly would cost you the betting fee for 972 columns, and one unexpected tie in the supposedly sure games would ruin everything. I favored the wild system worked out by Alejandro Abad, who gave personal consultations like a psychologist. He sold a large book of tables showing how to bet on one hundred and forty-four different columns properly arranged and get a sure win . . . unless something unforeseen happened. Other counselors, whose books sold for as much as ten dollars a copy, advocated other systems, but in spite of them a disconcerting number of top prizes still went to the women who sought advice from their butchers.

My visits to Madrid were made pleasant by the fact that I had been invited to attend a well-regarded tertulia which met at four-thirty each afternoon in the Café León (on the signs, Lion, from the French Lion d'Or), across from the post office. Here, around old tables kept scrubbed by the courtly waiter Mariano, a group of men convened, as their counterparts had in Badajoz, to discuss everything except religion and politics. They saw no reason to discuss the former because all were Catholics and had nothing to argue about; they avoided the latter because they had found it wise in Spain to do so.

The membership was distinguished. José María de Cossío, of the Royal Spanish Academy, attended, and one who knew anything about bullfighting recognized him as the authority, his four-volume *Los toros* being the ultimate reference in argument; I was surprised to find that a man whose reputation I had known for so long was still very much alive. Camilo José Cela, another Academician, whose *The Family of Pascual Duarte* and other novels were respected in all Spanish-speaking countries, was there. The Conde de Canilleros, a historian from Extremadura, had strong opinions, as did Gerardo Diego, poet and member of the Spanish Academy.

The tertulia was held together by the strong personality of its founder, Antonio Rodríguez Moñino, Spanish bibliographer of world-wide fame and now a professor at the University of California at Berkeley, who spends his academic leaves in Madrid. In addition to the Spanish members, the tertulia also attracted a goodly number of the Spanish professors from the United States and other countries who came to Spain on scholarships or sabbaticals. My favorite was a valiant debater named Ramón Martínez López, a Spanish professor at the University of Texas, for he had strong and hilarious prejudices on everything, which made him a delightful conversationalist.

If I had wanted to explain to a stranger how a tertulia operated, I could have contrived no better experience than what happened accidentally one October afternoon in 1966. The group was seated in the leather-upholstered chairs about the marble-topped tables and I had asked them, 'What percentage of Spaniards use the Castilian pronunciation I learned in college as opposed to the Andalusian or South American pronunciation?' The question was good for about an hour of discussion as the men recalled their experiences and the opinions of their friends.

'Figure it out this way. Years ago somebody convinced the intellectual community in the United States that gentlemen speak only Castilian. The word veces must be pronounced *vay-thayce* with a th and not *vay-sayces* with an ese. Well, in Spain itself we divide this way. In Cataluña nobody uses the th. In Galicia, maybe one-third of the people. In the islands, one half. The Basques, one half. Andalucía, none. Valencia, half. So you see, it's restricted mainly to the Castillas and León.'

'Percentages? Perhaps one-third of Spain uses Castilian.'

'In Spanish America no one uses it except immigrants from Spain who want to lord it over the locals.'

'And actors.'

'That's right. Because of some curious tradition, you must speak Castilian on stage. The way in Minnesota you try to speak Oxford English on stage.'

'They were making this movie about Jesus Christ in Mexico City and the big hassle was, how should Jesus speak? They took the problem all the way to the cardinal, and he said, "It would sound sacrilegious if our Lord spoke anything but Castilian. But it would be pompous for a mere tax-

*Two immortals. The tertulia has seven
participants who are also members of the
Spanish Royal Academy. Here famed
critic Guillermo Díaz-Plaja explains
a point as José María de Cossío listens.*

collector like Matthew to do so." That's how they made the picture—Jesus
Castilian, the disciples Mexican. And everyone said, "Sounded just right." '

'I knew García Lorca and he never spoke Castilian. He said you
couldn't write poetry in it.'

'He was right. I speak only Castilian. But the th sound was a late development. Probably not known before the sixteenth century.'

'There was this university in the United States. Had on its faculty the
best student who ever graduated from Texas, and they wrote me asking if I
could provide them with a head for their department of Spanish. I wrote
back and asked, "What's the matter with López? There's nobody around

better than he." And they wrote back and said that López didn't speak Castilian and they'd feel uncomfortable with him.'

'When Fernando de los Ríos from the Ronda region was elected to the Royal Academy he announced to the members, "Now that I'm an Academician I promise to speak respectable Spanish, and I've tried to say *civilización* the way you do, *the-vee-lee-tha-thyóhn*. But I'll be damned if I can get that third th out. So you'll have to be satisfied with *thee-vee-lee-tha-syóhn.*'

And so the discussion went, as it did day after day, but this time there was to be something different. By sheer accident an American professor visiting the tertulia dropped a bombshell by identifying a date as the year in which Magellan circumnavigated the globe.

'What did you just say?' Dr. Martínez López of Texas snapped.

'I said it was when Magellan circumnavigated the globe.'

'Magallanes!' one of the professors cried, using the Spanish version of the great explorer's name. 'My God, man, are you out of your mind?'

'In 1521. When he circumnavigated the globe.'

'My dear man! There is no reputable scholar in the world today who thinks that Magallanes was the first to circumnavigate the globe.'

'I do.'

'Apparently. But no one else I've heard of in the last hundred years has had such an idea. Does anyone in this tertulia think for a moment that Magallanes was first around the world?'

With some temerity I raised my hand, and the Spaniards turned to look at me with the compassion they would have directed to an idiot. 'Have you never heard of Juan Sebastián Elcano [in English del Cano]?' they asked.

'No.'

'My God! He was the first around the world. And he was Spanish.'

'Wait a minute!' the American professor cried. 'Magellan . . .'

'My good man,' Dr. Martínez López said, 'King Carlos himself gave Elcano a coat of arms showing a globe inscribed with those glorious words, Primus circumdedisti me (You were the first to circumnavigate me).'

The other Spaniards confirmed this, but the American was not overawed.

'Merely because a king made an error . . .'

'Carlos Quinto did not make errors.'

And so the debate went on. On succeeding days the Spaniards lugged books and citations to the tertulia, including an Italian encyclopedia, proving that whereas Magellan (in Portuguese Magalhães) had started the voyage around the world, he had died in the Philippines, leaving its completion to his Spanish assistant, Juan Sebastián Elcano. The evidence was impressive and I began to think that here was a corner of history about which I was uninformed, but then the American lugged in his evidence, which was hard to ignore.

'If in your insularity,' he said, 'you wish to maintain that a man could circumnavigate the globe only if he started from Spain and ended in Spain, then Elcano is your man. But if going around the globe means going around the globe, or, in effect, proving that the earth was a globe that could be gone around, then Magellan, who had already traveled to and from the Philippines by the eastern route and then had returned to the same point by the western route, was the first around.'

'My good man,' the Spaniards argued, 'one day a group of ships set sail from Sanlúcar de Barrameda and one of those ships, the *Victoria*, went in an unbroken journey around the world, and when it had completed its journey Magellan was not aboard. Juan Sebastián Elcano was. What, in all decency, can you conclude from that?'

The American replied, 'Merely that the *Victoria* was the first ship, and Elcano the second man, to circumnavigate the globe.'

The debate extended over a full week, and by the time it ended, with no satisfactory resolution of the point, everyone participating understood the facts and their implications. No one in the tertulia would admit then that he had changed his mind, but I would suppose that in their subsequent writing and teaching they would at least allude to the position contrary to their own.

In the winter of 1967 the tertulia came into momentary prominence when one of its members held a press conference in Boston which reverberated around the world. When Dr. Jules Piccus joined the tertulia he appeared to be merely one more visiting American professor, this time from the University of Massachusetts at Amherst. He was a young man, bearded, prematurely gray, lively in manner and quick in argument. Members of the tertulia knew him mainly as a scholar searching the archives of the Biblioteca Nacional, and there had been many like him in the past, but on February 13, 1967, Dr. Piccus announced that one day while looking for a medieval manuscript he had found instead two manuscripts by Leonardo da Vinci which had been catalogued in 1866 by B. J. Gallardo but which had subsequently been misplaced. One was a notebook, the other a set of sketches obviously intended for publication. They should have been filed at numbers AA-119 and AA-120, but a century ago someone had carelessly tucked them away at numbers AA-19 and AA-20, and there they had remained. The announcement of their recovery launched a storm. 'Why should treasures of a Madrid library be introduced to the world at a Boston press conference?' was merely the most temperate of the Spanish headlines. 'If you speak of this matter,' Dr. Piccus told me one day at the tertulia, 'please be sure to state clearly that I recovered the manuscripts. I did not discover them. The Spaniards had always known they were in existence. I happened to find out where.' Not everyone took the misadventure of the Leonardo so seriously. Mingote used the subject for one of his finest cartoons. Against a wall which was adorned by the 'Mona Lisa,' freshly painted, sat Leonardo in his traditional cap, beard and long robe.

Angus Macnab.

He was writing the last page of a manuscript and saying these v.ords: 'Well, I've written it backwards so they can't read it. Now if I could only think of some place to hide it.'

My life in the tertulia, which was one of the most instructive things that happened to me in Spain, was marred by envy, because although this was the most prestigious tertulia then operating in Madrid, there was another which met in an opposite corner of the café which fascinated me and I longed to join it, but that would have been impossible. It was composed of six or eight elderly men, caricatures of Spanish gentlemen, in tweed trousers, hunting jackets, mustaches and with low rumbling voices. 'It's a huntsmen's tertulia,' one of my group explained. When I asked what they talked about, he said, 'Horses, dogs and things they've shot.' What impressed me most about this tertulia was that for long periods the members would sit just looking straight ahead and saying nothing. Occasionally one would mumble something about wild boars or stags and the others would nod. I was assured that it was a most exclusive tertulia and that its members looked on our group as young radicals who read books, something which none of them did.

In Madrid I met an unusual man whose friendship was to mean much, the dour and salty Scotsman, Angus Macnab, who wrote about Spain with such insight that I wondered how an outsider had managed to penetrate so acutely the Spanish mentality. 'Simple,' he said, drawing on his pipe and speaking out of the corner of his mouth, 'I'm a Spanish citizen.' After knocking about in various countries, he had found Spain the most congenial and had decided to make it his home.

'I like the cautious form of government, the rocklike stability of the people. Mind you, there are many things wrong, but none that hard work won't mend. And it's a marvelous place to bring up children.'

Through visiting Macnab, I came to know the new suburbs whose spectacular proliferation had allowed Madrid to increase its population so sharply. 'Is there another city in Europe which has built so high a percentage of new homes in the last decade?' he asked, and I could think of none. Scattered about in all directions, eight-story apartment buildings had spread over the countryside, not a dozen here and there, but hundreds in clusters. Architecturally they were bleak, and some were beginning to crack after only six years of life, but they were homes. Macnab, his lively wife and children lived in such a colony out beyond the bullring, and as I visited him through the years I could watch the sudden manner in which sixty or seventy great buildings appeared during a ten-month absence.

'Last time I was here you were on the edge of the country,' I said. 'Now it's a new city!'

Macnab said, 'You must keep this in mind when you ask why so many Spaniards support the government. It has built homes and it's given them to us at reasonable rates. You were complaining about the fact you can never find a taxi when you want to come here. Why can't you? Because the rates are kept so low that any workman in Madrid can afford a taxi. Here the good things are not restricted to the rich.'

Macnab's apartment in one of the new buildings was comfortable and well arranged. 'A home for a workman,' he said proudly. 'That's what I am. I work in the foreign office.' He did not tell me what kind of work he did, but he was such a skilled linguist that I assumed it had to do with international documents.

'Didn't you go to Oxford?' I asked one day.

'Indeed yes. Some of my chums from those days would be surprised to see me here, spending my years as a Spaniard. But this is a good country . . . a good country.' He spoke with such conviction that I felt certain he had found in Spain a depth which other Anglo-Saxons missed.

'Mind you,' he said, 'out in the suburbs like this we have our young hoodlums, just as you do in America. But our police don't coddle them.' Macnab showed me many aspects of modern Spain that I would otherwise have missed, but the point he made repeatedly was that it was an excellent place to raise a family. 'Here the emphasis has always been on the family. It's the fundamental fact about Spain, and if you miss that you miss everything.' On picnics he would point out the families; when we discussed education he would stress what it meant to family life; and often when we were just wasting time gossiping about things Spanish he would revert to this matter of stability. It was obvious that he loved Spain and felt it deep in his bones. One day I accompanied him to Toledo, where he had lived for some years following his arrival in the country, and I remember how, when we reached the church he had attended, people of all ages ran out to greet him as if he were a member of their extended family. I thought it strange that a Scotsman with an Oxford education should have been adopted so easily into Spanish life; perhaps it was through the Macnab

Even the most modern buildings in Spain are apt to be enclosed by traditional fences whose beautiful geometry sets the pattern for the cities.

children that this acceptance came, for they were Spaniards and indistinguishable from the others.

'There is a profound permanence in Spain,' Macnab told me one day, 'and if you're lucky enough to identify with it, you have found yourself a very stable home.' He knew the regions of Spain, and certain of the cities I chose for my tour, those that might not attract others, were chosen because of his recommendation. 'You'll like that city,' he would say. 'It has an honest quality.' Talking with him convinced me that he had chosen Spain as his permanent home because of this honesty.

Twenty-eight miles northwest of Madrid lies a vast and gloomy building off to itself, El Escorial (The Slag Heap), a strange pile of gray-black stone set among foothills and the subject of much debate. I find it not only impressive in an overpowering sort of way, but also representative, in its heaviness and simplicity, of the essential Spanish characteristics. El Escorial is Extremadura carved in rock, the barren plains of Castilla set in order by an architect.

Others who know Spanish architecture better than I condemn the building as an alien monstrosity. Where, they ask, is the beautiful ornamentation of plateresque? Where is the echo of Romanesque or Gothic, two styles that made themselves at home in Spain? And where in this enormous rectangle is there even a hint of the fact that Spain was for seven hundred years Moorish? These critics charge that the mausoleum, for that is what El Escorial is now principally restricted to, is a poor rendition of an Italian idea and about as appropriate to Spain as a replica of King Victor Emmanuel's wedding-cake monument would be if it were translated from Rome to the plains of Castilla.

The traveler must make up his own mind in reference to his own experiences, and since most foreigners visiting Spain see the Gothic, the Romanesque and the Moorish and come to think of them as representing Spanish values, El Escorial must be a disappointment. Those like myself who have identified with Extremadura, and Las Marismas and the lonely plains of Castilla, have developed different visions of the country, and to these El Escorial conforms.

What is it? Four things, interrelated and enclosed within common walls: a palace from which kings ruled Spain; a grandiose mausoleum holding the sarcophagi of many kings; a monastery; and an enormous church. It came about because the death of Carlos V at Yuste in 1558 followed closely upon a signal victory of Spanish troops at St. Quentin on the tenth of August, 1557, which day happens to be the feast day of St. Lawrence (in Spanish San Lorenzo). During his last illness Carlos had directed his son to assume responsibility for burying him wherever Felipe thought appropriate, and the latter had the happy idea of building a monastery of unprecedented dimensions which would serve as a mausoleum for the Habsburgs. He scouted the countryside and found this hill onto which mining scoria had once been dumped, whence the name El Escorial, and there he caused work to begin. St. Lawrence had been martyred by being roasted alive on a gridiron, and whether by conscious design or not, when El Escorial was finished, it resembled a rectangular gridiron, complete with handle.

The building has four severe façades whose rather pleasing lines derive from the multitude of windows set into the otherwise bleak walls. The main façade has an entrance marked by twelve Grecian columns and two bronze doors to which the dead kings of Spain were brought for sepulture.

'Who seeks entrance?' the monks asked.

'The Emperor of the Spanish empire.'

'Who seeks entrance?'

'The King of Spain.'

'Who seeks entrance?'

'The man Carlos.' Only then did the gates swing open to admit the dead man to his mausoleum.

Today it is one of the most provocative spots in Spain, an octagonal room deep in the lower reaches of the building. In tiers of four sarcophagi each, the kings of Spain lie as if on file in a library, waiting to be lifted down. At the top of one group lies Carlos V, below him Felipe II, then III, then IV. In other tiers the queens rest, but since some of the kings had three and four wives, only those who gave birth to children who inherited the throne are interred here. Associated with the main mausoleum are others reserved for the royal heirs who died in infancy and for the royal bastards, of whom there was a plentiful supply. In this last room lie the reassembled remains of Don Juan of Austria, who even today has the power to attract more visitors than the legitimate rulers.

El Escorial contains much more: galleries of art, tapestries by Goya, long halls covered with pictorial maps, a fine library and the living quarters of the ancient rulers. It is so immense that when one has seen all this, the complex of the monastery remains to be explored, for this is a town set within walls.

I am embarrassed to report that it was not until my third visit that I discovered El Escorial contained, hidden away in its capacious interior, a church much bigger than many cathedrals. I had wandered through the halls for two days, vaguely aware that off to one side stood a chapel of some sort, but I was preoccupied with other areas and so missed a building of mammoth dimension. How could such a thing happen? When I travel I am wary of guides, preferring always to look at things for myself. I find that if I do not see an object fresh, on my own terms as it were, I often never see it except through a haze of verbalism. Guides, I find, are trained to reduce all things to a common level, and their flow of words weaves a net over the whole, so that one sees only through the interstices and never clean. Furthermore, the things they point out that I might otherwise have missed I would often have been well advised to miss. When I visit a site I want to see three or four things at most and am never loath to ignore others that might have little interest for me. Sometimes my plan causes me to miss something I should have seen, as at El Escorial; I must be the only visitor ever to have missed so large a church.

As if to rub it in, it was a professional guide who finally pointed it out to me, and I was surprised at how clean and beautiful it was. The Patio de los Reyes, the enclosed area before the entrance to the church, was big enough for army maneuvers, while the interior vistas, all severely neo-classical, were much more spacious than I would have guessed. When imprisoned inside the church and unable to see the expanse of the surrounding building, I felt it to be totally un-Spanish, and even when I came to the two groups of statuary for which the church is famous, I found them also alien, which was not surprising, since they were cast in Italy by Pompeo Leoni.

They are delightful and were described to me by an Englishman as 'poor art but pure heart.' Facing the high altar on the gospel side is a group of five life-size figures, three kneeling in prayer, two standing in the rear. They are Carlos V, accompanied by his faithful wife Isabel of Portugal—not to be confused with the earlier Isabel of Portugal, who went mad—his two queenly sisters, María of Hungary and Leonor of France, and his daughter María, who married Maximilian II. The group is ranged behind a beautifully draped table carved in bronze and topped by a pillow whose tassels are so real they seem ready to flutter should a breeze come unexpectedly through the church. I liked especially the bronze robe worn by Carlos and decorated with the Habsburg eagle and panels from the lives of saints. The whole group is sized so as to fit comfortably in the towering spaces of the church and placed so high that it is not dwarfed, a delightful Italian version of a Spanish royal family.

Poised opposite, on the epistle side, is a matching set, also of five figures, also ranged behind a draped table and a pillow, but this shows Felipe II, brooding spirit of El Escorial, and it has a certain quality of arrogance befitting that prince. Where the eyes of Carlos are downcast in prayer, those of Felipe stare straight forward, as if daring God to touch him. He is surrounded by three of his four wives—Maria of Portugal, Elizabeth of Valois and Ana of Austria, with his second wife, Mary of England, appropriately absent, for she had always been difficult for him to handle—and by his heir, Don Carlos who is shown as a thin-faced, intelligent young man of sixteen or seventeen.

If I had missed the hidden church, I wouldn't have lost much, but if I had missed these two sculpture groups I would have missed a view of Spain that I could have acquired in no other way. I had always felt kindly toward Carlos, but the austerity of Felipe repelled me, proving that I was guilty of the grave error which Spanish critics charge against most Anglo-Saxon writers, that I had been contaminated by the Black Legend, that body of charges assembled by non-Spanish scholars, especially Protestants, to discredit Spain and Catholicism.

In recent years much has been written about the Black Legend and its genesis. A personal enemy of Felipe's fled Spain and supported himself for the rest of his life by peddling lurid rumors involving the Spanish court. William the Silent, of the rebellious Low Countries, saw a chance to unite his fractious countrymen by creating in Felipe an object of terror and scorn, so he added to the rumors and gave them circulation. Protestant apologists saw in the charges a chance to defame Catholicism, so they added their inventions, but the worst damage was done by fellow Catholics, the Italians, who wanted to create a political counterbalance to Spanish influence in Italy and did so by spreading existing rumor and creating new. As I read these new studies deflating the Black Legend, I found that they were directed at people like me, for I was almost the archetype of the person corrupted by the legend. It consisted of these postulates: 1. Catholicism captured Spain and adopted a policy of keeping the country in darkness. 2. Using Spain as a base, Catholicism intended to enslave the world. 3. In order to police its conquests, Spanish Catholicism invented the Inquisition, which it proposed to install in subdued territories. 4. The archpriest of these evil designs was King Felipe II. 5. He was personally evil and committed many crimes in furtherance of his aims.

A special emphasis in Spain's refutation of the Black Legend has been the charge that it was promulgated in the first place by a conspiracy among Protestant scholars who had consciously engineered a campaign to defame Spain and had manipulated historical facts to do so. Phrases like these were common in Spanish writing on the subject: 'una fobia contra España' (a phobia against Spain) and 'un complot contra España' (a plot against Spain). Certainly my initial experiences with the legend supported these Spanish charges, for I became aware not only of manipulation of fact but also of a phobia against Spain. I did not come to believe the legend by accident; I was taught it by professors. I remember how my sixth-grade teacher created in me a long-lasting ambivalence toward Spain by first teaching us that western civilization owed Spain much, in that she had saved Europe by preventing Islam from moving north of the Pyrenees, and that if she had not done so, we would all now be Muslims. We then analyzed how horrible life would be in our little town if we had mosques instead of churches, and it was fifteen years before I lost my fear of Islam. Shortly, however, this same teacher showed us how Europe was saved in 1588 by the English fleet that drove off the Armada. This time we were told, 'If the English had not defeated the Spaniards, we would now all be Catholics,' and we analyzed what our town would be like under those conditions, and it was equally bad.

My problem was simple: 'How could Spain have been civilization's savior in the fight against Islam and only a few centuries later the villain in the fight against England?' The answer was also simple: 'Felipe II was an evil man.' Thus the Black Legend was promulgated.

I was so fascinated by the ominous character of Felipe that I read all I could find about him, and when the normal histories were exhausted, a librarian dug up the only book in my life that I wish I had not read. I once heard a spellbinding gospel preacher in Colorado shout that as a young man he had read a filthy book which had so contaminated him, he would gladly cut off his right hand if he could erase having read the book; I was amused at his ranting, because I'd read such books and they hadn't hurt me much. But I have often wished that I had not as a boy read Rider Haggard's *Lysbeth, A Tale of the Dutch* (1901), because it imprinted on my mind so evil a picture of Spain in the age of Felipe and the Duque de

Alva, who represented him in The Netherlands, that it was fifteen years before I was able to counteract it. No other book had so baleful an influence on me, nor one so permanent, partly because it confirmed what my teacher had said about Spain, partly because it carried a series of prejudicial pictures. Two remained with me, as vivid now as when I first saw them. Two Dutch Protestants were reading the Bible furtively at night while a spy from the Inquisition peered from behind a door, and such an air of terror was engendered that I required to know no more about Spain than that. The second picture was more direct. One of the leaders of the Protestants was captured by the Spaniards, and when he refused to betray his fellow Bible readers, he was locked in a room containing a small barred window and there starved to death . . . but not just any room. This one overlooked the kitchen, whose sights and odors came to him as he starved. This was so diabolic, so typically Spanish, it was not until years later that I realized Rider Haggard was merely a storyteller in need of detail who had invented the room and the kitchen.

I had read *Lysbeth* fifty years ago and wanted to check whether it was as virulently anti-Spanish as I remembered, but I was unable to find a copy of the book; in its day it had been widely read but was no longer in print or on library shelves. However, my town librarian located a copy in Minneapolis and borrowed it for me, and in the introduction I came upon the first phrase I remembered: 'By an example of the trials, adventures, and victories of a burgher family of the generation of Philip II and William the Silent, the author strives to set before readers of to-day something of the life of those who lived through perhaps the most fearful tyranny that the western world has known.' I found the book as intemperate now as it had been terrifying half a century ago; the Spanish were real villains, especially the clergy: 'Before he answered the priest threw off his dripping hooded cape . . . revealing a coarse, wicked face, red and blear-eyed from intemperance.' The Dutch were invariably heroic: 'This was William of Orange, called the Silent, one of the greatest and most noble of human beings who ever lived in any age; the man called forth by God to whom Holland owes its liberties, and who forever broke the hideous yoke of religious fanaticism . . .'

The story was well plotted and contained two figures whom I still remembered with fascination, a hideous witch called Martha the Mare and a giant red-bearded Frisian named Red Martin. The purpose of the plot was to provide opportunities for Spaniards to demonstrate how cruel they were. The sin of the Dutch stemmed from their Bible reading:

> 'What has he done?' asked Lysbeth in a low voice.
> 'Done? My dear lady, it is almost too dreadful to tell you. This misguided and unfortunate young man, with another person whom the witnesses have not been able to identify, was seen at midnight reading the Bible.'

'The Bible! Why should that be wrong?'
'Hush! Are you also a heretic?'

One of the highlights of the yarn came when the hideous Mare climbed into a pulpit and disclosed the infamy of the man who had made her look the way she now did:

'You call me the Mare,' she went on. 'Do you know how I got that name? They gave it me after they had shrivelled up my lips and marred the beauty of my face with irons. And do you know what they made me do? They made me carry my husband to the stake upon my back because they said that a horse must be ridden. And do you know who said this? THAT PRIEST WHO STANDS BEFORE YOU.'

As the mob surged toward the culprit she reminded the cowering priest who she was: 'I was once called the Lily of Brussels. Look at him now. He remembers the Lily of Brussels. He remembers her husband and her son also, for he burned them.' The crime so infuriated the Dutchmen that they hanged the priest, preparing the way for the central paragraph of the book:

Thus ended the life of the Abbé Dominic at the hands of avenging men. Without a doubt they were fierce and bloody-minded, for the reader must not suppose that all the wickedness of those days lies on the heads of the Inquisition and the Spaniards. The adherents of the New Religion did evil things also, things that sound dreadful in our ears. In excuse of them, however, this can be urged, that, compared to those of their oppressors, they were as single trees to a forest full; also that they who worked them had been maddened by their sufferings. If our fathers, husbands and brothers had been burned at the stake, or done to death under the name of Jesus in the dens of the Inquisition, or slaughtered by thousands in the sack of towns; if our wives and daughters had been shamed, if our houses had been burned, our goods taken, our liberties trampled upon, and our homes made a desolation, then, my reader, is it not possible that even in these different days you and I might have been cruel when our hour came? God knows alone, and God be thanked that so far as we can foresee, except under the pressure, perhaps, of invasion by semi-barbarian hordes, or of dreadful and sudden social revolutions, civilized human nature will never be put to such a test again.

As I approached the climax of the story, where the Spanish villain was about to condemn the Dutch hero to death by starvation, the horror that I had experienced at first reading came back to me:

'Now might I trouble you so far as to look out of this little window? What do you see in front of you? A kitchen? Quite so; always a homely and pleasant sight in the eyes of an excellent housewife like yourself. And —do you mind bending forward a little? What do you see up there? A small barred window? Well, let us suppose, for the sake of argument, that a hungry man, a man who grows hungrier and hungrier, sat behind that window,

375

watching the cooks at their work and seeing the meat carried into this kitchen, to come out an hour or two later as hot, steaming, savory joints, while he wasted, wasted, wasted, and starved, starved, starved. Don't you think, my dear lady, that this would be a very unpleasant experience for that man?'

'Are you a devil?' gasped Lysbeth.

But as I finished the passage a strange thing happened. I looked for the illustration, so indelible in my mind, and it was not there. It had never been there. The verbal description of Spanish perfidy had been so real to me that I had imagined the illustration; I can see it yet in perfect detail, yet it never existed. Nothing could better exemplify the persistence of the Black Legend and its deleterious effect on the rest of the world's relations with Spain. If the average educated American wanted to approach Spain afresh, he would have to cleanse his mind of many illustrations imbedded there without reason.

Felipe II has suffered much from the embroidery of the Black Legend, and not all the wrong can be charged to aliens. One nineteenth-century Spanish dramatist summarized Felipe thus: 'Cowardly where his father was brave, cruel where the other was generous, and fanatical where Carlos was religious, no crime frightened Felipe when it was a matter of his security, his revenge, or the misunderstood interests of his religion.' His reputation was especially damaged by Friedrich Schiller's poetic drama *Don Carlos* (1785), which portrays him as an insanely jealous king who orders the murder of his own son because he thinks the boy not only is turning Protestant but also is involved in an incestuous relationship with his stepmother, Felipe's third wife, Elizabeth of Valois. Felipe comes out of this play poorly, and no better from Verdi's operatic version, *Don Carlos* (1867), in which he again orders the murder of his son and a bloody auto-da-fé to celebrate the death. But bit by bit the truth regarding Felipe is coming to the fore. He did not launch the Inquisition, nor was his version of it as harsh as that of his predecessors. He was a good husband to Queen Mary of England, who was eleven years older than he and his full cousin, and he did not adopt covert or immoral strategies to trick England into becoming part of Spain. He was a devout Catholic and naturally he tried to convert the people of the Low Countries to his religion in accordance with the principle of *cuius regio, eius religio* (whose country, his religion), and if the Armada had been victorious he would surely have tried to bring England back to the religion from which under Henry VIII and Elizabeth I it had strayed. There is now grave doubt that Felipe murdered his son out of sexual jealousy or suspicion of the boy's incipient Protestantism. Nor is there any proof that he ordered the poisoning of his half brother, Don Juan of Austria, for fear of dynastic rivalry; on the contrary, it was Felipe who generously rescued his much younger brother from obscurity and gave him positions of command. The other murders charged against him do not withstand investigation, and he seems on balance to have been a pedestrian but capable administrator, a just ruler and a king who sought peace more often than war.

The one charge that can truly be laid against him is one which the Black Legend did not make. Felipe ruined Spain. When he was through with it the once-great kingdom was finished, and over the sprawling empire lay the seal of death. The trouble started with Carlos V and his siphoning off of Spain's wealth into bottomless European adventures, though if one had told the old man this when he was pottering about the monastery at Yuste, he would not have understood. 'Look at the territory I have brought Spain,' he would have said, and the new map of Europe would have borne him out; but what he should have been looking at was manufacturing in Spain, agriculture, the decline of the army, the encrustation of incompetence. That balance sheet was dreadfully against him. He knew that something had gone wrong, but he blamed the wrong forces. From Yuste he wrote: 'Of all the goods that arrive from the Americas at the port of Sevilla, ninety percent goes into contraband that does the nation no good.' Smugglers had not stolen Spain into poverty; Carlos himself had done the job.

He left Spain bankrupt, so that many of the failures which finally engulfed Felipe were not of his making and were, by that time, inescapable. But he could have avoided others had he comprehended the changes overtaking Europe. Again and again, in his bitter and narrow way, he turned his back on the present and tried to maintain in Spain a type of life and government that should have been allowed to vanish. Industry, the prerogatives of a middle class, a rationalized army, a Church responsive to modern trends and an educational system based on merit he ignored, and in doing so, sealed the ruin of his country. Solely because of the headstrong policies pursued by Carlos and Felipe, the cost-of-living index rose as follows: 1500—100; 1521—150; 1550—200; 1590—315, reflecting the fact that supplies of foodstuffs and manufactures were declining. If ever the principle of divine right of kings aborted, it was in the case of Felipe II, for he may have had the divine right to rule Spain, but he did not have the right to ruin it.

It is for this reason that I find El Escorial so moving; it is a fitting monument to Felipe, a vast, dark building to commemorate his monolithic soul. He caused it to be built. He selected the architect and approved the design. In the hills back of the building you can still see the seat carved in rock where he used to sit and watch the progress of the construction, and it was he who conceived the happy idea for the two groups of bronze statuary in the church. There is a small room in El Escorial where Felipe used to sit, his foot propped up to relieve the unbroken agony of his gout, and here he spent his last days surrounded by deepening woe. He had survived the death of his insane grandmother Juana, his father, his mother, his first three wives, his heir Don Carlos, his half brother Don Juan and many of the advisors who had been close to him. From the

loneliness of this room he could peer down into the church through a little window and eavesdrop on the progress of the Mass. Here also he met his couriers and studied by candlelight the reports they brought him from all parts of the world. I suppose no other king in history applied himself so diligently to his paper work as Felipe, for the margins of his documents are cluttered with his minute and often pertinent observations: 'He should be hung.' 'The ships should be sent south.' 'The governor must be changed.' Energy, dedication, devotion, constancy and courage Felipe had, but sympathetic intelligence he did not, and in the end it was this lack that undid him.

From El Escorial I traveled over the mountains to Alcalá de Henares, the ancient city known to the Romans as Complutum, where Cardinal Cisneros had built his famous university. It had long since been abandoned, for reasons we shall inspect in the next chapter, but I wanted to see what buildings remained, and I was directed by a policeman to a former residence hall now converted to a public hostel. The doorman said, 'You are welcome to see the ruins of the university,' but this was hardly what I was looking for. The guard understood. 'You want to see the building of Cisneros! Ah, it's on the other side of the square.'

There, shaded by trees and set back from the road, I found the stately building which had formed the core of the university. From the outside it was dignified, with a façade of carefully balanced items; from the inside it offered as noble a cloister as I was to see in Spain, three-tiered and marked off by thirty-two half-columns. In the park facing the building stood a statue of Cisneros, showing his intense, small face, his high cheekbones and his penetrating eyes. His military adventures behind him, the burning of Islamic treasures forgotten, he stands as a churchman with a book and stave in his left hand, a heavily knotted cord in his right. Nearby, in an old chapel, rests his modest tomb, so different from the bombastic one of Cardinal Mendoza in the cathedral at Toledo.

In Cisneros' university great things had been accomplished. The cardinal had insisted that his students be trained in the most advanced theories of their day, and Alcalá became a center of liberalism. In one stroke Cisneros established thirty-three full professorships, 'according to the number of years of Our Lord,' including some in subjects new to Spain, such as recondite ancient languages, new concepts of philosophy and a chair for that abstruse intellect, Pedro Ciruelo, who claimed that theology could be understood only if studied in conjunction with mathematics. Three of the professors personally selected by Cisneros had been born Jews, even though he was at the time head of the Inquisition; when suspicious Catholics protested, Cisneros defended his nominations and said the men were needed for a major task which only they could fulfill.

In 1513, when King Fernando inspected the university to see if there was truth in the condemnatory rumors which had reached him, Cisneros said calmly, 'Sire, it is your job to gain kingdoms and make generals. It is mine to build those men who will honor Spain and serve the Church.' The roster of great men who acquired their education here has seldom been equaled: Lope de Vega and Calderón, to name two of the writers; Tomás de Villanueva and Ignacio Loyola, to name two who attained sainthood.

As we saw earlier, Alcalá was famed internationally for its *Biblia Poliglota Complutense,* a particular brainchild of Cisneros. It provided the first printing of the Hebrew text ever to have been compiled by Christians and the first Greek text to have been printed anywhere. Both remained standard till well into the nineteenth century; the compilation as a whole has been termed 'the first scientific work of the modern world.' Books were being printed in Spain at least three years and probably nine before William Caxton published his first work in England, but the *Poliglota* was long delayed because Cisneros had to encourage his Spanish paper makers to produce pages of the size and thickness he required and his imported French and German type founders to cast Hebrew, Aramaic and Greek type faces. In an edition of six hundred copies, Volume Six appeared first, in May of 1514, followed by Volume Five a month later. The first four volumes appeared at intervals, the last on July, 10, 1517, four months before the death of Cisneros. The completed volumes were not put on sale till 1520, for the Spanish government was apprehensive about distributing them prior to their having been approved by the Pope. In the interim the university generously allowed scholars from other countries to consult the finished volumes, and in this way much of the original work was published elsewhere before it appeared in Spain. Cisneros would not have minded, for his memorial existed not in printed books but in ideas.

Forty-five years after his death an event occurred in his university which has ever since preoccupied historians. To Alcalá for their education had been sent three young men: Don Carlos, son of King Felipe II; Don Juan, the bastard brother of the king and therefore half uncle to Don Carlos; and Alexander Farnese, nephew of the king and thereby cousin to Don Carlos. They were not regular students at the university, for they had private tutors, but they did attend classes and participate in university life.

Their regimen, as laid down by King Felipe, was strict, but on the night of April 19, 1562, young Carlos slipped out of his room to visit the attractive daughter of a porter, and in creeping down the darkened stairs he failed to see that the fifth step was broken and pitched headlong downward, so that his forehead struck a closed door. He was found stretched out unconscious and the matter was reported to the king.

Fortunately, young Carlos made an easy recovery and the escapade was forgiven, but on the tenth day alarming symptoms suddenly appeared and it looked as if he were going to die, presumably from pressure on the brain. Nine specialists were summoned, among them the Fleming Andreas Vesalius, skilled in performing trepanations of the skull. Fifty separate consultations were held, for the stricken boy was heir to the crown, and while the doctors were trying to decide what to do, help came from two unexpected quarters. From Valencia a quack arrived, a Moor bearing two jars of ointment. 'The black one,' he explained, 'has a repercussive action, but the white one is a strong unguent to attenuate it. Black, white. Black, white. It is the warring of the ointments that saves the life.' At the same time a strange troupe appeared from a nearby community, a group of peasants attending several Franciscan friars who bore the cadaver of one Diego (1400–1463), a Franciscan who had died a century before but whose body had not been contaminated by the grave. Standing before the doctors, they pulled back a cloth and displayed Fray Diego's face, and the sunken eyes seemed to be alive. The peasants explained that the cadaver had already worked miracles in their community and they believed it could save Don Carlos.

So three alternatives were laid before the doctors and the king's representatives: Dr. Vesalius could trepan the skull and thus let out the diseased blood that was pressing on the brain and causing the damage; or the Moor could apply his alternating unguents; or the cadaver of Fray Diego could be placed in bed with the unconscious prince in hopes that it might work one more miracle.

What happened that day has since been the subject of much speculation. Don Carlos' two principal physicians each left behind his own report; they agree in the main but are contradictory on important points; foreign ambassadors then resident in Spain collected rumors, which they sent home; and other participants left diaries. From certain reports it seems clear that Dr. Vesalius and his team prepared to do a trepanation and laid back the scalp so that the white skull was well exposed, but when they had done this they satisfied themselves that the blood oozing through the bone of the skull was normal and that a complete trepanation was not called for, so they sewed the scalp back together; other reports indicate that the trepanation was completed and that it saved the boy's life.

We know that the Moor was allowed to apply his unguents, first black, then white, but they seem to have been so powerful, especially the black or repercussive one, that the dying youth grew noticeably worse. The doctors grew frightened and packed the Moor out of Alcalá; he went to Madrid with his jars and there offered to cure the knight Hernando de Vega, but after a few applications of the powerful stuff Hernando died.

We also know that when hope was almost gone, the century-old cadaver of Fray Diego was placed in bed with Don Carlos while the Franciscans prayed, and in the morning Don Carlos awakened, with clear mind, and said that in the night he had seen a vision of a friar in Franciscan habit lying beside him, and this had cured him. At any rate, both he and his father petitioned Rome to declare Fray Diego a saint, for this was but the latest of the miracles this obscure friar had worked; three separate popes delayed action on the matter, but King Felipe was so insistent that a fourth pope, Sixtus V, speeded up the investigation and took pleasure in announcing in 1588 the entry of San Diego into the saintly brotherhood. His day was identified as November 13, and in honor of his having saved the intended King of Spain, a pueblo in the colony of California was some years later named after him.

The saving of Carlos' life was a mixed blessing. In the six years that followed, the young man degenerated pathetically; crippled, hunchbacked, of wandering mind and evil habits, he became a kind of incubus, and it was even rumored that he might have been toying with the idea of becoming a Protestant. What seems more likely is that he had initiated or had been caught up in some kind of intrigue against his father, King Felipe. At any rate, there can be no question about the fact that Felipe believed his son was plotting treason and that the pathetic and even repulsive young man was a danger to Spain. Therefore, at midnight on January 18, 1568, Felipe, accompanied by advisors, marched into the room of Don Carlos, who looked at his father and asked, 'Are you planning to kill me?' Felipe told him to calm himself and in this manner placed him under arrest, without ever giving Carlos or the world any substantive reason for having done so. 'I have reasons,' Felipe said.

Almost immediately the young prisoner, twenty-three years old, began to decline, and this time there was no Dr. Vesalius, no Moor with repercussive unguent and certainly no cadaver of a saint to cure him. What was his malady? No one knew. Was there any specific or even probable cause? No one could say. It was a general illness without a seeming focus and on the evening of July 24 he died. King Felipe refused to give an explanation even to the Pope, and when rumors of the most evil sort circulated, he did not dignify them with notice, let alone an explanation. He spoke of the matter only once, eighteen years after the event, when a book appeared in France claiming that Don Carlos had been killed because he was a secret Protestant. Then Felipe said to the ambassador who reported this, 'You are right in becoming indignant over the false testimony that he was not a good Catholic. It is not wise to allow such a great lie to run current.' Ten years after the death of Don Carlos, Felipe had a second son, by his fourth wife, Ana of Austria, and it was this boy who grew up to be Felipe III, never a great king, never approaching the quality of his father Felipe II or his grandfather Carlos V, but certainly not a degenerate like Don Carlos, who would have inherited the throne had he not died so mysteriously.

In July, 1966, events occurred which were to make the city of Cuenca an almost obligatory excursion from Madrid, and I had the good fortune to make mine in the company of a talented Filipino who had been centrally involved in those events, Don Enrique Francisco Fernando Zóbel de Ayala y Montojo Torrontegui Zambrano, Harvard 1949, sometime bibliographical expert in rare books at the Houghton Library in Cambridge, etcher extraordinary and one of Spain's major abstract artists.

Don Fernando drove me ninety miles east and a little south of Madrid through virtually empty land; a few white-walled villages appeared here and there, clean and inviting in their harsh simplicity, and I was once more impressed with how swiftly in Spain one passes from the heart of a major metropolis like Madrid into empty countryside. On this street a fourteen-story apartment building; fifty yards farther on, open land. In Spain prudent people have long learned to live within the safety of city walls. When we did come upon a village I again noted something that I had often reflected on before: that the rural children of Spain all look as if they had been fifty-six years old at birth. How ancient their faces are.

Our route to Cuenca took us through several types of land that could have been a summary of Spanish history. Here the flat lands of Castilla reminded one of how the clever kings of this region had built a nucleus around which to unite the country. Don Fernando suspected that at one point we were close to the upper edge of La Mancha, and when I saw how bleak and empty it was, without a house to be seen in any direction, I appreciated why Cervantes, wishing to poke fun at the pretensions of would-be nobility, had set his knight down in such prosaic terrain. Next we came to the pine forests of Cuenca province, mile after mile of tilted and rocky land, and I could understand how the Muslims, once they had captured such a fastness, were so difficult to dislodge.

'In some ways a most uninteresting drive,' Zóbel said, 'but if you can imagine the ebb and flow of forces, the movement of kings and peasants, one of the best.'

We passed through two tunnels that served somewhat as the gates to Cuenca and in a short time saw the distant hilltop city perched above the gorges of two rivers that meet here for a run down to Valencia on the coast. Don Fernando was eager that I see Cuenca at its best, so we stopped the car for me to look up at the remarkable collection of houses perched along the edges of some very high cliffs; they seemed about to fall into the rivers but were kept aloft by sturdy cantilevers set into place some five hundred years ago. Porches and balconies projected well out into space and even from below induced vertigo.

'Cuenca is like the prow of a ship sailing into space,' Zóbel suggested, and his image was appropriate. 'When they first proposed Cuenca to me I couldn't visualize locating here, but once I spotted these fantastic houses, these cliffs, winding streets and the tremendous views one gets from everywhere, I knew that this was what I'd been seeking.'

As he spoke, we were in the lower town, which dates from relatively modern times, say four hundred years ago, but we left this by a steep and twisting road which carried us upward at a good rate, and in a few minutes we came upon a medieval square and a very old cathedral with a new face. I entered because I had long ago heard of the four remarkable jacent tombs of Church dignitaries dating from the sixteenth century, and these I wanted to see. They were as lovely as I had been told, four high-relief slabs of stone carved with figures of dead prelates, each highlighted by the addition of a few streaks of color which made them seem almost alive. The tombs were delightful and set the stage for what I was about to see.

Don Fernando led me down a side street which ran along one wall of the cathedral, then took me on a cobbled street which ended in a cul-de-sac marked by several medieval doors of handsome design. 'This is it,' he said as he unlocked one of the huge doors and swung it slowly open.

I entered upon a wonderland, something so unanticipated in a remote city like Cuenca that it has become world-famous in less than a year, for it is a museum of Spanish abstract painting set down in three of the cliff houses, so cleverly interrelated with flights of stairs, balconies, strange corners and large exhibition areas that it is a delight to the eye and a challenge to the mind. From the windows one looks off into miles of empty space, with the Río Huécar six hundred feet below in the gorge. Inside, one sees a series of varying rooms filled with handsome paintings by young artists whose reputations have been made not in Spain but in Paris, London and especially New York. One sees the finest work of men whose names are well known in all art circles: Antoni Tápies, whose earthlike canvases speak so strongly of Spain; Antonio Saura, whose works are in most modern museums; José Guerrero, better known in New York than he is in Madrid; Luis Feito, whose work is as modern and colorful as any being done in the world; Eduardo Chillida, whose heavy, powerful sculpture is much appreciated in foreign exhibitions; and Rafael Canogar, whose reputation is the most recent of the Spanish internationalists.

'This is some of the best painting being done today,' Zóbel says enthusiastically as he points to one after another of the fine canvases. 'Only New York excels in concentration of talent. I believe we have more superbly gifted young painters in Spain today than they have in either Paris or London and certainly more than Berlin or Rome. This group of men is going to create the art history of the next quarter-century. Tell your friends who may be interested that these men are as good as Picasso and Miró were when they began.'

As we wandered through what must be one of the world's loveliest museums, Zóbel estimated that there were more than thirty young Spaniards who had a chance to build major international reputations. 'That's what makes this museum so fascinating,' he said. 'The culture of a nation coming into focus in a way it has not done since the early 1600s.' We found chairs from which, if we looked to the right, we saw the spectacular valley or, to the left, a series of brilliant canvases by painters I had not previously heard of. It was a visual feast, but what interested me as much was the conversation.

Zóbel: For the first time in many years Spain is taking its contemporary artists seriously. This is good for the country. Good for the artists.
Michener: But is it not true that at least eighty out of every hundred

canvases these men paint leave the country? In Pittsburgh we Americans appreciate this art. In Sevilla you Spaniards don't.

Zóbel: Up to now that's been true. This museum may change the percentages. Spaniards may begin to buy Spanish art, other than Sorolla-like scenes in which colorful fisherwomen sell baskets of clams.

Michener: The other day I had lunch with José Ramón Alonso, the editor, and he said the typical Spanish attitude toward art was that of a friend of his who asked, 'Pictures? We have three pictures. Why would we want more?' Alonso asked him what three he had, and he replied, 'One Velázquez, one El Greco, one Goya.'

Zóbel: He was right on both counts. Families like that won't buy paintings. And you'd be amazed at how many El Grecos and Goyas remain in private hands. Spain has always liked paintings, but only the ones they liked, if you understand the contradiction.

Michener: I see less evidence of connoisseurship in Spanish private homes than I would in similar homes in Israel, Japan or Germany.

Zóbel: The basic fact you must accept is the joyous provincialism of Spanish thought. Have you discovered that the Prado is really the most provincial great museum in the world? Only Spanish painting.

Michener: Wait a minute! What about those great Flemish and Italian paintings?

Zóbel: That's what I mean. As long as Flanders and Italy were Spanish colonies we accepted their painting. That's why we have Bosch and Titian. Because we thought of them as Spaniards. Once the colonies broke away, to hell with them and their painting.

Michener: You believe then that this group of artists will be able to make a living by painting in Spain? And selling to Spaniards?

Zóbel: They already are. Every painter you see on these walls makes a good living right now. And they don't have to teach in art schools or colleges the way your painters have to do in the States.

Michener: They make a good living, but doesn't it come from sales abroad? Do Spaniards buy?

Zóbel: Yes, they do. In the old days all you could sell was the kind of romantic subject matter done by Zuloaga and Sorolla. You're right that Picasso and Miró never sold in Spain. And Spanish families would have found it inconceivable to buy something like a Cézanne or a Paul Klee, because those men were not Spanish. Even today no one would buy a Francis Bacon or a Willem De Kooning or even a Morando. But they are beginning to buy Spanish works. And I am proud that this museum has had something to do with that change!

Zóbel had a right to be proud. That morning the Spanish government had convened a gathering of notables at which he was made a member of the Order of Isabel la Católica in gratitude for what he had accomplished in Cuenca, for not only had he personally paid for the heavy expense of converting the cliff houses into a museum, with splendid marblelike floors and much clean and freshly painted wall space, but all the canvases in the museum were also from his private collection. 'Fifteen years ago I did a simple thing,' he said as we finished our conversation. 'I looked about me and saw that Spanish painting was good . . . very good. So I began to collect it. And now the world confirms my judgment.'

The paintings which I had been admiring, by artists I did not know, seemed to support his argument. There was a fine, swinging op art construction by Eusebio Sempere, only forty-three years old; a clean and hard collage by Gustavo Torner, forty-two; a most imaginative portrait of a group of men by the Equipo Crónica (Chronicle Team), a pair of twenty-five-year-old Valencians who collaborate on such excellent work that they must become internationally popular; and what pleased me most, a wonderfully poetic white canvas by Manuel Mompó, forty and also from Valencia. It was so good that I asked to see more of his work, and each thing I saw showed a lyrical quality that was enchanting. Mompó paints somewhat in the style of Miró, but with his own fairyland interpretation, and I suppose he will become well known throughout the world.

Part of the museum structure is leased out to an excellent restaurant, and as we finished our dessert of coffee ice cream garnished with roasted and delicately flavored walnuts, a friend said of Zóbel, 'He and his group are the avowed enemies of corsi.'

I thought, from the way the word was used, that Corsi must have been a competing painter. 'No,' my informant explained, 'it's the most in-word in Spanish society today. You can kill a man with it by saying at a cocktail party, "Cayetano tries hard but he's painfully corsi." ' It means cheap but pretentious, kitsch but heavily pompous. Cuenca is the battleground of the Spanish mind in its war against everything that is corsi.

Some dozen major painters have taken up residence in the cliff houses of Cuenca. Travelers come from all over Spain to the museum. In summer students flock to the exquisite valleys that surround the town, camp out and work during the daytime in the fine museum library. In autumn artists and townspeople alike climb down from their cliff to work in the fields, gathering, by means of delicate brushes, the golden pollen of a lavender flower on which the economy of Cuenca partially depends, for this is the saffron capital of the world. And each day the message of this unusual museum reverberates through Spain.

The pleasure of my visits to Madrid was enhanced when I met one day in the Ritz Hotel my hunting companion from Las Marismas, Don Luis Morenés y Areces. If he had been instructive in the marshes, he was more so in Madrid, for this was his city and he delighted in showing me aspects of it that I would otherwise have missed. I was surprised some time later, as we were walking down the Avenida José Antonio, when a gentleman

Don Luis Morenés,
Marqués de Bassecourt.

stopped us and addressed Don Luis as 'Marqués de Bassecourt.' When he had gone I asked Don Luis about this and he invited me to join him at one of the sidewalk cafés. What he said, often under insistent questioning by me, was a surprise.

'Yes, my father happens to be a grandee of Spain. My family goes back in one straight line to the early eighth century when Pedro Duque de Cantabria fought the Muslims, but to make the line straight a few kinks have to be kicked out here and there. My father's titles happen to be fifteenth Conde de Villada, eighteenth Marqués de Argüeso. In 1491 los Reyes Católicos confirmed our family titles as those of grandees immemorial. Duque de Infantado, Marqués de Argüeso and Marqués de Campoo. The present Infantado and the Campoo are uncles of mine. But I work in government offices, as you see. I'm a clerk who hopes one day to become a chief clerk.'

I asked him to what other families of Spanish history he was related, and he said, 'My own title is eighth Marqués de Bassecourt. It sounds French and this is why. The Bassecourts were knights of the Artois and in the Peace of the Pyrenees in 1659 Felipe IV ceded to Louis XIV the territories in which my ancestors lived, but they refused to take up French citizenship and remained faithful to Spain; so in 1736 Carlos III made Don Francisco de Bassecourt a general of his army and then, because of his heroism in the Two Sicilies, created him a marqués. Alvaro de Luna, whose mobile statue you saw in Toledo, married into our family, which has always been associated with the Medinacelis, the Medina Sidonias and the Osunas. But like most young men from such families I have to work.'

I knew the nobles Don Luis was speaking about, for they passed like golden threads through the history of Spain, people of enormous power whose deficiencies had perturbed me in Sevilla. I asked Don Luis about this and he thought I was wrong. He believed that it had been the permanence of these families that had given Spain its solidity in duress. 'Anyway,' he said, 'the old charge of doing nothing no longer applies. Look at the leaders in government now being provided by these families.'

One of the recurring jokes in Madrid concerned just this matter. There was this management consultant who was explaining to a group of businessmen how he operated in selecting candidates for top jobs in Spain. 'This morning, for example, three contestants for a major job. All equally well groomed, equally educated. So I asked each one privately how much is two and two. The first said instantly, "Four." Solid man, quick, stable, conventional. Second man thought a moment, saw a trap and said "Twenty-two." Imaginative, willing to take a chance, best type of man to head a project entering new fields. Third man thought a long time, looked at me suspiciously and asked, "What do you want to know for?" Finest type of scientific mind, probing, not easily satisfied with snap decisions, can be trusted to get at the heart of things. And that's how we judge men in this business.'

'But which one did you hire?'

'Oh, the Duque de Plaza Toro, of course. We've got to have a title.'

I myself had been vaguely involved when a major American automotive company sought Spanish management for its Iberian branch. They had settled upon a most promising young man with training in London's equivalent of the Harvard Business School and several years' experience with a German motor company in France. To me he seemed an inevitable choice, but Spanish advisors warned the Americans, 'We think you'd do better with the Duque de Plaza Toro.' So the Detroit experts had an interview with Plaza Toro, who arrived in a chauffeur-driven Mercedes, dressed flawlessly, ten pounds underweight and with manners that could have charmed Artaxerxes. When questioned about his qualifications for the job, the duque said, 'I'd want a hundred and twenty thousand dollars a year. And for this I'd let you use my apartment.'

'But what exactly would you do?'

'Do? I'd represent you . . . introduce your people to the right circles.'

'Have you had any business experience?'

'Me! Of course not.'

Understandably, the Detroit people chose the trained young man, and their business went promptly to hell. He had been great in an interview, but he couldn't seem to get anything done. The leases that Detroit needed were not forthcoming; import agreements were stalled and remained so. In despair the Americans sought private counsel as to what had gone wrong, and were told, 'Nothing. Everything's about the way it ought to be at this stage, and the young man is doing a fine job . . . inside. But what you need now is somebody like the Duque de Plaza Toro . . . outside.'

Against their better judgment, the American firm hired the duque for $52,000, and within a few weeks everything was moving smoothly and continues to do so. The duque appears now and then in his Mercedes, hands over his apartment for business negotiations with men of equal breeding who represent other firms, and everyone is happy, especially the young expert who is left free to run the business.

The Marqués de Bassecourt was no figurehead. He worked long hours at his ministry, specializing in tourism, and through watching him I learned something of the new spirit that animates Spain. 'We literally work seven days a week to ensure that you tourists get an even break,' Don Luis said. 'Inspectors, loans to small businesses, new hotels, new roads. For example, how many minutes did it take you this time to get through customs at the airport?'

'I noticed that. From the time the plane landed till I was free to go, nine minutes.'

'It's one of the shortest waiting periods in Europe and we'd like to make it even shorter.'

'How many tourists last year?'

In his methodical way he took a piece of paper, ruled it into columns and wrote down these startling figures:

Number of Tourists Entering España

Year	World	United States
1951	1,263,197	44,677
1954	1,952,266	203,029
1965	14,251,428	687,106
1966	17,251,796	733,109

I told him that my dismal experiences in Toledo had more than instructed me about the sudden flood, and he said, 'All problems like that we're going to clean up. We're going to build a first-class hotel there. We're very excited about the future.'

I asked him if he thought Spain could continue to give the foreign tourist good value, quoting a recent study which gave the following index figures for tourist costs: New York 100, London 94, Paris 90, Rome 79, Madrid 39. 'We're aware of the problem,' he said. 'We can't control all prices. Wouldn't want to if we could. But we can police services, and that we'll do, because tourism is too valuable to us to be abused.'

'How about taxis in Madrid?'

He threw up his hands. 'What city is handling its taxi problem sensibly? Is Madrid as bad as New York, where you simply cannot get a taxi in the evening?'

'I think it's worse,' I said. He shrugged his shoulders, as if he were the mayor of New York, and asked, 'Who can tell taxis what to do?'

Through Don Luis I met a series of minor government officials who introduced me to other Spaniards, and slowly I began to overhear a type of discussion which earlier I had rarely heard: 'What is going to happen to Spain when Franco goes?' In what follows I will not attribute opinions to specific persons, for to do so might cause embarrassment, but they do not come from Don Luis unless I so specify. It was a man from Badajoz who established the theme.

'You must start, Michener, with the fact that Spaniards are utter bastards to govern. We are Texans cubed.'

Once the marqués said, 'In the hundred years prior to the generalísimo we had one hundred and nine changes of government, twenty-six revolutions and three major civil wars. Would you agree that an attitude toward government which produces such results needs overhauling?'

'We lie awake at night wondering what's going to happen when Franco goes. We say little in the newspapers, but that doesn't mean we don't discuss it among ourselves. It is topic one.'

'Forget the trappings about monarchy this or monarchy that. The fundamental fact is this. We will never go back to the United States pattern of a two-party system. It works for you. It doesn't work for us. Through some miracle you are able to divide your country into two parts from September to November, then unite it again the morning after election. Believe me, this is a bigger miracle than you imagine. In Spain we also used to divide into various parties and in the campaign we'd say such dreadful things about each other . . . well, the matter of pundonor comes in. Anyway, on the morning after the election the only thing an honorable man could do was shoot the son-of-a-whore who won. I think that if you were to ask a hundred average Spaniards, a good eighty would say, "Let's have no more party fighting."

'What will take its place? Here we get to the second fundamental. You must view Spain as a nation resting on a three-legged stool. Church, army, landed families. If any one of the three topples they all go down. We have what you might call an ipso facto oligarchy to which the only alternative is anarchy. Therefore, the three legs of the oligarchic stool must support one another. And this they do, not always happily, so that what we will have when Franco goes is something roughly like the present form of government.

'What the Protestant norteamericano sees as the Spanish Church is really two churches, and in his mind he must keep them separated, as they are separated in Spanish life. First there is the hierarchy, meaning the cardinals and bishops. With not more than two or three exceptions these men are the creatures of the regime. They were put in office by the oligarchy, were supported by it and will be loyal to it until death. They oppose all liberalism and have been badly shaken in recent years by the winds of reform that have been sweeping through Rome. At the Vatican councils they voted against every proposed change, and when they lost to the liberal wing of the Church, they returned to Spain more determined than ever to save Spain from the liberal errors of their own Church. Opposed to them are the young Spanish clergy who foresee that if Catholicism does not liberalize, it may be eliminated when Franco goes. So a kind of second Church has grown up consisting of educated Jesuits, priests from worker families, seminarians who take the conclusions of the Vatican councils seriously, and all who vaguely want the Church to sponsor social justice in a tired land. The differences between these two arms of the Church are much greater than the differences between Republicans and Democrats in the United States.'

Another said, 'In your country the Catholic Church argues over matters of liturgy, celibacy of priests, birth control and similar points of procedure. In Spain we are riven apart by fundamental matters like Pope John's two encyclicals, *Mater et Magistra* and *Pacem in Terris,* and especially the Council Schema XIII, with their startling statements on freedom of speech, freedom of belief, freedom of assembly, separation of Church and state, the right of labor and so on. These documents constitute a refutation of everything the Spanish hierarchy stands for, and the young liberal priests know it. If the plan goes through to make Pope John XXIII a saint, his day will not be celebrated in Spain . . . unless the young priests win the current battle.'

On the other hand, a defender of the Church insisted, 'If you look at the three elements of our oligarchy, Church, army, landed families, it has got to be the Church which will lead us to liberal revisionism. Watch! In the years ahead you'll see the conservative army called in to discipline the liberal young leaders of the new Church.'

'The army is much more the key to Spain than outsiders imagine. I include the Guardia Civil as part of the army. In the press you can say things against the Church and maybe you'll get away with it, because everyone wants to slow down the Church a little bit. But you are absolutely forbidden to say anything against the army. They rule. You asked me the other day why individual issues of newspapers are sometimes confiscated. You wondered if the editor had said something against the Church or Franco. It's almost always because they said something against the army. That cannot be tolerated. You also asked which of the three claimants to the throne will finally be installed as king, supposing we have one. That the army will decide.'

I asked, 'Then why doesn't the army rule outright?'

'Because if it did there would be rebellion, and the army knows it. Like the German army the Spanish army has rarely been sagacious. If it were able to rule, we'd probably have a military dictatorship right now. But, of course, if it were a sagacious dictatorship, it would confirm most of the freedoms we now enjoy, so in the long run things would be about the same.'

Another informant challenged these statements about the army. 'Because the army is conspicuous don't overestimate its importance. Of fifteen recent cases when editions of newspapers were confiscated by the censors, only one involved the army. Fourteen involved the hierarchic Church, which is heavily protected by the regime. Jesuit papers were closed down because they supported young priests against police brutality. Two were shut down for criticizing the reactionary attitudes of the hierarchy. Several were disciplined for publishing articles on the succession. And five saw their editions confiscated because they were too enthusiastic in defense of freedom. One suffered because of its editorial, "Protest is not always morally wrong." The censor held that it was.

'The landed families, the third leg to the stool, play a powerful role in Franco's Spain because he can trust them. They're conservative. They're smart. They're self-disciplined. Whether they can drag themselves into the

Spanish soldier waitin,
for the parade to start

twentieth century I sometimes doubt. A fellow like your friend, the Marqués de Bassecourt, knows what the score is. So do hundreds like him, but
they aren't the ruling families, which are at least three hundred paces
farther to the right than chaps like Bassecourt. I see the families continuing as a kind of unelected senate, tough, conservative, determined. A
hundred years from now life in rural Andalucía will be about what it is
right now, if the families have the say. But the Church and the army will
bring pressure on them to liberalize things a bit.'

'The hope of Spain lies in a group you haven't mentioned—the new
industrialists . . . the fellows who are building the apartment houses
along the Mediterranean . . . the big printing plants in Bilbao . . . the
factories in Barcelona. They know. They travel to Germany and Poland.
They have suppliers in Rome and New York. They don't fill any of the
government positions yet, but do something more important. They supply
the taxes and they insist upon modernization of social patterns, education,
military service; I have great hopes for this new class of Spaniards.'

I asked why they didn't exercise more control in government, and my
informant said, 'Because this is Spain and control will always rest in
traditional hands, like that of the Church, the army and the landed
families. If the industrialists made one false move they would be wiped out
overnight and their businesses expropriated.'

I suggested that if this were done, Spain would be bankrupt again.
'That has never bothered a Spaniard. If he feels the industrialists are
modernizing Spain too fast, he'll eliminate them, even though it means
economic chaos for another fifty years. But the question you pose is
academic. The industrialist knows he must move forward slowly with the
rest of us. That's why I place so much hope in his accomplishments.
Within the Spanish pattern he's going to create wonders.'

I asked what technical form the government would take after Franco's departure, but the man to whom I spoke was not interested in so
specific a question. 'The Damoclean question is quite different,' he said.
'What is labor going to do? The other night I watched you in the hotel
lobby when that disgraceful television program came on. The one where
the government reporter asked fifty day laborers what they thought about
Spain's system of controlling labor unions. And each of the fifty came to
the microphone and said, like a parrot, "I think the syndicates are wonderful because they protect the working man." You were embarrassed and
looked at me to see if I was too. I didn't want to express myself in public,
so I kept staring at the television and that preposterous parade. I felt
humiliated. Because you knew and I knew that at the slightest spark those
fifty workmen would ignite and blast that damned-fool government man
right into oblivion. I wouldn't like to guess right now what role labor will
play. If the army, backed up by the Church and the landed families, tries
to imprison all labor in the national syndicate much longer, there's got to
be trouble. But the liberal wing of the Church knows this, and if it attains

power it will press for a freer labor law. When this happens Spain will move to a position similar to Italy's or Germany's.'

In a different part of Spain I asked a group of workmen what they thought on this question. 'You're going to see strikes all over Spain. We've been told for the past twenty-five years that the loss of some of our freedom wasn't too high a price to pay for national solidarity and peace. So we paid it, and all we got was solidarity and peace. The good things went to the rich, and the Church and the army. We got damned little. Now we have to adjust the balance.'

After this discussion of five fields—the controlling trio of Church, army, landed families plus industrial leadership and labor—I returned to my original question: 'What will happen when Franco goes?' and a government official said something that should be remembered: 'You speak as if you thought Generalísimo Franco sat in his office and personally passed all laws. How do you suppose Spain has been governed for the last fifteen years? By a committee, of whom Franco is the most powerful. Much of our government moves forward without involving Franco. He's invaluable as the symbol around which we coalesce. And he can both initiate and veto. But Spain without Franco would still exist. It would have to. So after he's gone I personally suppose that things will continue pretty much as they have in the past. Our great loss will be in a symbol around which to rally. That poses a real problem, but the government per se will go right on.'

'Without trouble?' I asked.

'Without revolution, if that's what you mean.'

A dozen times, a hundred times I heard reassurances like this and always I pressed to the logical consequences, asking, 'Then you think the transition at Franco's death will be peaceful?' Almost without exception the Spaniards replied, 'Once before, we had civil war and we know what that means. Almost any price we might have to pay to avoid rebellion would be worth it.' When I pressed further to identify what 'any price' would include, the typical answer was, 'We don't insist on free elections . . . or the two-party system . . . or this king or that . . . or who actually takes Franco's place in the palace. But a better social justice than we have now . . . that we do insist on.' I asked what would happen if it were denied, and the answer of a man in Pamplona can stand as typical: 'If the army and the Church tried to deny us social justice I suppose we'd have to fight.'

Back in Madrid, I returned to my earlier question: 'What kind of government?'

'It's got to be a continuation of the oligarchy. Once Spain is agreed on that, and I think we are so agreed, then the precise form doesn't matter too much. But to the outside world it's pretty important. The choice is between a dictatorship of some kind or other or a restoration of the monarchy. I believe it will be the monarchy. After all, our constitution states that we are a monarchy and Franco has openly announced that he serves merely as caretaker for that monarchy. There would be an advantage to us in having a king again, because it would make us popular in England and the United States, both of whom love royalty. I suppose nothing we could do would make us more acceptable in the States.'

I asked which of the two claimants, whose conflicting chances I had become acquainted with in the picture gallery at the Coto Donaña, would probably be appointed the next king. 'Ah, but there are three pretenders! We must choose among three.' I said that I knew about Don Juan, the legitimate heir living in exile in Portugal and very unpopular with Franco. And I had met his son Don Juan Carlos, living in Spain and popular with Franco. Who was the third? 'A carry-over from the Carlist Wars of the last century. The Carlist pretender . . . Don Hugo Carlos, who married that pretty Dutch princess who changed from Lutheran to Catholic. I think they live in Paris, and sometimes you see his name as Carlos Hugo, because he only added the name Carlos for effect and we aren't sure whether it goes in front or back. He's a poor third in the running but he does claim the throne and many support him.' When I asked which of the three would win, my informant bit his lip for some moments and said, 'Some time ago Franco authorized Vice-President Muñoz Grandes to conduct a secret poll among the military leaders and to everyone's surprise they favored bringing back Don Juan from Portugal . . . even though Franco had said he didn't want him. I understand the generalísimo was irritated by the vote, but in my judgment it was right. I know young Juan Carlos quite well and he's a weak sort. Maybe when he's fifty he'll be strong enough to govern. So I say give the throne to his father now and give the boy time to grow up. I was in Sevilla when he was presented to the aristocracy of Andalucía and he cut a poor figure.' (Since the taking of this poll Muñoz Grandes has been succeeded in the vice-presidency by Admiral Luis Carrero Blanco, a sixty-four-year-old conservative.)

However, an American businessman who had participated in an extended series of negotiations in which Juan Carlos took part gave this report: 'A most attractive young man with everything he needs in order to reign. By that I mean good looks, a beautiful wife and fine children. He has the manners required for public functions and more than enough intelligence to discharge the duties of a constitutional monarch. Spain will be lucky if he's the one chosen.'

I asked if having a king once more would mean much to Spaniards. 'The fact that the extreme right is so strongly in favor of it makes me have doubts. But Spain is a very difficult country to govern, and I think that having a continuing symbol which remains above politics might give us help. You read our papers. You see how we play up the successes of nations with royalty. Denmark, Greece, Norway, especially England. We are told year after year, "Countries with kings are happy. Those without are miserable." Believe me, since the Estados Unidos installed Jacqueline Kennedy as a kind of queen, your popularity in Spain has risen considerably.'

To the outsider it is perplexing that so many elements in Spain should remain so loyal to an institution that has served her so poorly. For a monarchy to produce a superior form of government, it must discharge certain technical functions, and the British and Danish monarchies, which Spaniards so often cite in defense of the system, have done so, but not the Spanish. Monarchy should provide an unbroken sequence of leadership; but twice in Spain the royal family died out, subjecting the country to the perils of a contested inheritance in which foreign powers became involved. It should provide for an orderly transfer of power at the death of a ruler; but in Spain numerous wars of succession have resulted when the inheritance was questionable, as in 1475, 1520, 1700, 1835 and 1875, to name only a few. It should unite the population behind a symbol; but in Spain it has had the opposite effect, as in the savage divisions of the Carlist period. And it should provide competent if not brilliant leadership; but in Spain it has thrice propelled mental defectives to the throne, as in the case of Juana la Loca, Don Carlos, son of Felipe II, and Carlos the Bewitched, and on numerous occasions it has installed protracted regencies, as in the case of Isabel II and Alfonso XIII. In spite of such a delinquent record, Spain today looks sanguinely to the reestablishment of her monarchy, even though the new trial will begin with three different men contending for the throne. To prophesy success for such a shaky venture requires hope rather than logic.

One Spaniard spoke for the many who had doubts: 'It's one thing to keep a royal family installed in a country like Denmark, which already has it. Quite another to introduce a king into a nation which doesn't. If Spain brings back a nonentity like Juan Carlos he'll rule for about twelve years. He'll side with the landed families, meddle in government and be disciplined by the army, which will then establish a dictatorship in the Primo de Rivera mold. I see no merit whatever in reviving the monarchy.' I asked him what alternative he saw, and he said, 'A one-party state, with liberal safeguards. Power in the hands of a cabinet, pretty much as we have now. More and more, the leaders are coming from the new industrialists. What I'm saying is, a continuation of what we have now with logical improvements.'

Another man explained the prevalence of articles favorable to the monarchy: 'A whole lot of Spaniards visualize the return of the monarchy as a chance for them to shine in an archaic court life. They see the peasants kowtowing to them, carriages drawing up with footmen, titles and prerogatives, castles and sweeping gowns, as if that was what Spain needed today. So they support the concept with articles and books in hopes that when the restoration comes they'll have a part in the court life, no matter how trivial.'

Three different men in three scattered parts of Spain pointed out something I had not formulated for myself. To lead into the generalization they reiterated a truth which I already knew. 'It's a sad fact that during the nineteenth century no Spanish-speaking country on earth learned how to govern itself effectively by a system of ballots. We're a people of such mercurial temperament that the two-party system is quite beyond our capacity to handle. Spanish countries require a one-party state, something perhaps like Mexico's, although I deplore her attitude toward religion.' Then came the surprise. 'You norteamericanos haven't liked Franco, but have you noticed how many travelers to South America report that they were told in Argentina or Uruguay or Bolivia, "What we need here is a Generalísimo Franco"? Believe me, when people from South America see how we achieved balance and peace for more than a quarter of a century, they yearn for the kind of stable government we have.' In succeeding months I watched the Spanish newspapers, which carried numerous stories of this type; many were suspect, because Spanish newspapers subservient to the Franco regime had sponsored the reporters who had dug up the quotes, but others appeared to be authentic. A good many South Americans, lost in the political confusion that seems to be the Spanish heritage, hungered for the hard, tight kind of rule Franco had provided the mother country.

In Barcelona I heard a cautionary report. 'This country is a boiling pot with the lid wired down. Coal continues to be thrown on the stove. Heat continues to generate. And the pressure of steam does not diminish. The army and the Church are going to try to keep the lid clamped down, but they're not going to succeed. I do not think we can avoid major trouble when Franco goes.'

Earlier I reported that whenever I asked the question 'What will happen when Franco goes?' almost without exception my Spanish friends replied that the transition would be both uneventful and peaceful; but when I got to know these people better, sometimes at night or after a long ride, it was they who raised the permanent question that hung over Spain: 'Do you suppose there will be some kind of civil war?' Apparently the problem was much discussed in private. I shall specify the types of persons whose answers I summarize:

A top intellectual from Cádiz: 'We've had twenty-five years of peace. It's been a boon only an idiot would destroy. There will be no war.'

A seminary student from Valencia: 'The Church is so advanced in its social thinking that you wouldn't believe what we discuss among ourselves. There is no need for war against the Church and there will be none.'

Spokesman for a group of students in Barcelona: 'I am worried. I see no sign that the government appreciates how determined the young people of Spain are to have more freedom. If we are refused it, there can be only one result. War is a possibility, but I pray that the government will see reason and take the simple steps necessary to avert it.'

A rancher in Extremadura: 'Let the Communists try. We learned how to handle them last time.'

Guardia Civil.

A strong anti-Communist in Córdoba: 'I am frankly afraid. If there were serious trouble, or even war, I wouldn't be surprised. Our government hasn't done enough to win the working people over to our side. I see many signs that worry me.'

A government official in Madrid: 'War would be impossible . . . impossible. Can you imagine what the last one was like? No one would plunge this country into a repetition of that.'

A literary man in Madrid: 'Spanish history has an aggravating way of repeating itself. In 1833 when King Fernando VII lay dying without a successor who had been agreed upon by the nation, he could foresee the Carlist wars that would follow. He said, "Spain is a bottle of beer and I am the cork. When the cork pops out, all the liquid inside will escape, God knows in what direction." Does the idea seem familiar?'

A housewife in Jerez de la Fontera: 'I come from an educated, liberal family who opposed General Franco in 1936. Today I would kiss his hands, for he has brought us twenty-five years of peace. When I hear students who can't even add two and two trying to tell me what Franco should do, I want to spank them. What can they know of how Spain was during the war? There will be no repetition of that, I can assure you.'

An industrialist in Sevilla: 'I fear there's got to be trouble. When I walk through our plant I can feel the workmen staring at me with hatred, ticking off the days. It will not be pleasant here in southern Spain if trouble breaks out. We can always pray that the transition will be placid, and I must say that the closer we get to it, the more moves we are making to avoid trouble. They're not dumb in Madrid. Slow, but not dumb.'

A diplomat: 'You forget how stable we are economically. There's no cause for war simply over this king or that, this form or that. Now, if the United States hadn't poured in money to help us out ten years ago, and if our tourism hadn't brought us in billions of pesetas in the last five years, there would be cause for upheaval. But now? No.'

In 1967 I found the mood of my informants a little less sanguine. Student riots in Madrid, widespread strikes in the north and the arrest of more young priests in Barcelona were disturbing signs that all could read. There was still no fear of open trouble, for all believed that the oligarchy was strong enough to maintain control and, indeed, there was no desire on anyone's part to have trouble. 'We must keep our heads,' a Madrid businessman said, 'because to do otherwise would be insanity. Let the college students blow off a little steam. The police know how to handle them. Let the young priests agitate. The cardinals know how to bring them back into line. Labor? We may have to give a little here and there, but the future is reasonably secure.'

A leading intellectual from Andalucía startled me by saying, 'The forces we've been discussing—Church, army, labor—don't touch upon the problem which looms largest to me. And to a lot of men like me. What should I do about Opus Dei?' I had first come upon this mysterious organization of Catholic laymen in Mexico in 1959, when some feared that it was destined to take over that country, and I had long been interested in it, having read everything I could about its manner of operation. Those favorable to the movement maintained that it was a beneficial, voluntary organization of Catholics who were dedicated to the job of building better men and women and hence a better society. Those opposed said that it was either the agency for clerical fascism or Catholicism's answer to Free Masonry, but all agreed that it represented a canny preparation for taking over Spain when Franco departed. 'My problem is more difficult than you might imagine,' my Andalusian friend explained. 'On the one hand I am opposed to secret societies of any kind, and when they are led by priests I am terrified. Four times I've been approached to join Opus Dei and the invitations have been subtle. "We are the force of the future. We are the men who will count. Join us and help make the vital decisions." I have never wanted to be a political leader and that sort of reasoning repels me. But now I begin to see that not only are three of the most powerful cabinet ministers Opus Dei, and some of the strongest generals and businessmen, but also the editors of the journals in which I want to publish and the intellectuals with whom I want to associate. And I also see that unless I join Opus Dei, I am going to be slowly excluded from the really important things I want to do.' He was perplexed and I asked him about the politics of the society, which had been launched in 1928 by a devout Spanish priest who saw it as a means to regenerate the world. It had spread to most Catholic countries, and I pointed out that whereas in 1959 it had seemed destined to control Mexico it had subsequently lost its power. 'In Spain it will grow,' he insisted. 'The men in Opus Dei are dedicated. Have you ever met an Opus Dei face to face? He'd surprise you. The typical one is a layman not a priest, but he's taken vows of celibacy and poverty. He lives in a communal hall and gives his salary to the movement. He dresses in an ordinary dark business suit and works in one of the economics branches of the government. Most of Spain's finest economists are Opus Dei. And they're dedicated to public service. Tough-minded, well-behaved, moderate, attractive. Such men enable the Opus Dei to prove its claim . . . that it's the best force in Spain. In the decades to come you may hear a great deal more about Opus Dei.' When I left him I had the feeling that he had about decided to become a member, and that when decisions were reached as to what direction the new Spain should take, he and his fellow members of Opus Dei would do much of the deciding.

But it was a businessman from Barcelona who came closest to my own guess as to what would happen: 'I think that when news of Franco's death flashes through the countryside . . . As a matter of fact, if they're smart they'll not announce his death for two or three days while they move troops into position . . . Well, hotheads in the cities will think, "Now's the time!" and for six or seven days there'll be sporadic trouble, which the army will suppress. Then a dictatorship from the military until things are stabilized . . . six months, maybe . . . then a general relaxation to the same thing we've had for the past fifteen years. I suppose they'll choose young Juan Carlos to be king and throw him out about ten years later. Ultimately a gradual relaxation until we're something like Italy.'

An American expert on Spanish affairs spoke for many foreign observers: 'At the change-over no visible trouble. But six months to two years later a substantial redistribution of power, probably without fighting . . . possibly with.'

Don Luis Morenés: 'The men I watch above me in the government are smart enough to make the adjustments necessary to keep this country stable. We have everything on our side and I can think of no one who would profit by a civil war. I think the transition can be made quite peacefully.'

Index